CCSP Self-Study:
Cisco Secure Virtual Private Networks (CSVPN)
Second Edition

Andrew G. Mason, CCIE No. 7144

Cisco Press

800 East 96th Street
Indianapolis, IN 46240 USA

CCSP Self-Study:
Cisco Secure Virtual Private Networks (CSVPN),
Second Edition

Andrew G. Mason

Copyright © 2004 Cisco Systems, Inc.

Published by:

Cisco Press

800 East 96th Street

Indianapolis, IN 46240 USA

Printed in the United States of America 1 2 3 4 5 6 7 8 9 0

First Printing May 2004

Library of Congress Cataloging-in-Publication Number: 2003105044

ISBN: 1-58705-145-1

Warning and Disclaimer

This book is designed to provide information about the topics that are required for the CSVPN 642-511 exam. Every effort has been made to make this book as complete and accurate as possible, but no warranty or fitness is implied.

The information is provided on an "as is" basis. The authors, Cisco Press, and Cisco Systems, Inc. shall have neither liability nor responsibility to any person or entity with respect to any loss or damages arising from the information contained in this book or from the use of the discs or programs that may accompany it.

The opinions expressed in this book belong to the author and are not necessarily those of Cisco Systems, Inc.

The Cisco Press self-study book series is as described, intended for self-study. It has not been designed for use in a classroom environment. Only Cisco Learning Partners displaying the following logos are authorized providers of Cisco curriculum. If you are using this book within the classroom of a training company that does not carry one of these logos, then you are not preparing with a Cisco trained and authorized provider. For information on Cisco Learning Partners please visit:www.cisco.com/go/authorizedtraining. To provide Cisco with any information about what you may believe is unauthorized use of Cisco trademarks or copyrighted training material, please visit: http://www.cisco.com/logo/infringement.html.

Corporate and Government Sales

Cisco Press offers excellent discounts on this book when ordered in quantity for bulk purchases or special sales. For more information, please contact:

U.S. Corporate and Government Sales 1-800-382-3419 corpsales@pearsontechgroup.com

For sales outside of the U.S. please contact: **International Sales** international@pearsontechgroup.com

Trademark Acknowledgments

All terms mentioned in this book that are known to be trademarks or service marks have been appropriately capitalized. Cisco Press or Cisco Systems, Inc. cannot attest to the accuracy of this information. Use of a term in this book should not be regarded as affecting the validity of any trademark or service mark.

Feedback Information

At Cisco Press, our goal is to create in-depth technical books of the highest quality and value. Each book is crafted with care and precision, undergoing rigorous development that involves the unique expertise of members of the professional technical community.

Reader feedback is a natural continuation of this process. If you have any comments about how we could improve the quality of this book, or otherwise alter it to better suit your needs, you can contact us through e-mail at feedback@ciscopress.com. Please be sure to include the book title and ISBN in your message.

We greatly appreciate your assistance.

Publisher	John Wait
Editor-in-Chief	John Kane
Executive Editor	Brett Bartow
Cisco Representative	Anthony Wolfenden
Cisco Press Program Manager	Nannette M. Noble
Acquisitions Editor	Michelle Grandin
Production Manager	Patrick Kanouse
Development Editor	Allison Beaumont Johnson
Project Editor	Marc Fowler
Copy Editor	Gayle Johnson
Technical Editors	Bob Eckhoff, Muhammad Afaq Khan, Umer Khan, Tim Sammut
Team Coordinator	Tammi Barnett
Cover Designer	Louisa Adair
Compositor	Mark Shirar
Indexer	Tim Wright

CISCO SYSTEMS

Corporate Headquarters
Cisco Systems, Inc.
170 West Tasman Drive
San Jose, CA 95134-1706
USA
www.cisco.com
Tel: 408 526-4000
　　800 553-NETS (6387)
Fax: 408 526-4100

European Headquarters
Cisco Systems International BV
Haarlerbergpark
Haarlerbergweg 13-19
1101 CH Amsterdam
The Netherlands
www-europe.cisco.com
Tel: 31 0 20 357 1000
Fax: 31 0 20 357 1100

Americas Headquarters
Cisco Systems, Inc.
170 West Tasman Drive
San Jose, CA 95134-1706
USA
www.cisco.com
Tel: 408 526-7660
Fax: 408 527-0883

Asia Pacific Headquarters
Cisco Systems, Inc.
Capital Tower
168 Robinson Road
#22-01 to #29-01
Singapore 068912
www.cisco.com
Tel: +65 6317 7777
Fax: +65 6317 7799

Cisco Systems has more than 200 offices in the following countries and regions. Addresses, phone numbers, and fax numbers are listed on the
Cisco.com Web site at www.cisco.com/go/offices.

Argentina • Australia • Austria • Belgium • Brazil • Bulgaria • Canada • Chile • China PRC • Colombia • Costa Rica • Croatia • Czech Republic Denmark • Dubai, UAE • Finland • France • Germany • Greece • Hong Kong SAR • Hungary • India • Indonesia • Ireland • Israel • Italy Japan • Korea • Luxembourg • Malaysia • Mexico • The Netherlands • New Zealand • Norway • Peru • Philippines • Poland • Portugal Puerto Rico • Romania • Russia • Saudi Arabia • Scotland • Singapore • Slovakia • Slovenia • South Africa • Spain • Sweden Switzerland • Taiwan • Thailand • Turkey • Ukraine • United Kingdom • United States • Venezuela • Vietnam • Zimbabwe

About the Author

Andrew G. Mason, CCIE No. 7144, CCDP, CSS1, CCNP Security, CCSP, is the technical director of Boxing Orange (www.boxingorange.com), a UK-based Cisco VPN/Security partner specializing in the design and implementation of Cisco security solutions. He has 13 years of experience in the networking industry and has provided services for many large organizations worldwide.

About the Technical Reviewers

Bob Eckhoff, CCNA, CCSP, is an education specialist at Cisco Systems, Inc., where he designs and develops training on Cisco network security products. He has more than 20 years of experience in the education field, having been a technical instructor and a course developer for Codex, Motorola, Altiga, and Cisco Systems. He graduated from the State University of New York at Buffalo with bachelor's and master's degrees in education.

Muhammad Afaq Khan is a customer support engineer at the Technical Assistance Center (TAC) at Cisco Systems, Inc. He specializes in VPN involving VPN 3000, IOS, PIX Firewall, and third-party products. He has represented Cisco in many virtual security/VPN seminars. He is a CCIE (No. 9070) in Routing and Switching and Security. He holds a bachelor's of engineering degree in computer systems from NEDUET, Pakistan.

Umer Khan, CCIE No. 7410, MCSE, SCSA, SCNA, CCA, SCF, CNX, is the manager of Networking, Security, and Wintel Infrastructure at Broadcom Corporation, where he enjoys the challenging and fast-paced IT environment. His network team is responsible for the design, implementation, and management of highly available global LAN/MAN/WAN/wireless architectures. Among other technologies, Broadcom's network consists of Cisco switching gear end-to-end, dark fiber, SONET, 802.11g wireless, multivendor VPNs, content load balancing, and VoIP. The information security team is in charge of all aspects of information security at Broadcom, dealing with policy creation, intellectual property protection, intrusion detection, incident response/investigation, strong authentication, log analysis, firewalls, and much more. Khan has contributed to several other books on various topics, including Sun Solaris, Sniffer Pro, and PIX Firewalls. He completed his bachelor's in computer engineering at Illinois Institute of Technology. His personal website is located at http://www.umer-khan.net.

Tim Sammut, CCIE No. 6642, is a senior network consultant for Northrop Grumman Information Technology. He has served in key project roles involving technologies from LAN switching to security to SNA integration. He has helped many organizations make the most of their network investment. He holds the CISSP, CCIE Security, and CCIE Service Provider certifications.

Dedications

Behind every great man, there is a greater woman.

I would like to dedicate this book to my family. Helen, my beautiful wife, has yet again endured the late nights and busy weekends with nothing but support and belief in me. My two wonderful children, Rosie and Jack, keep me going and constantly remind me just what a lucky guy I am.

Acknowledgments

In writing this book, I had help from quite a few people. I would like to thank Michelle Grandin, Allison Johnson, and Tammi Barnett of Cisco Press for all their help and guidance. They add so much value to the whole process and ease the burden on the author. Teresa Winget from the Advanced Technologies team at Cisco offered a great deal of help in providing me with up-to-date information on the finer points of the VPN Concentrator. Thanks go out to Avra Gibbs Lamey, Tina Walsh, Brian O'Grady, Renee Martens, and Colin Smillie from Certicom for helping ensure that the sections on movianVPN were technically accurate. The technical reviewers—Karl Solie, Bob Eckhoff, Umer Khan, and Tim Sammut—all helped shape the book and provided an excellent service. Richard Jones provided some great help on the technical side of the book; this is appreciated. Thanks also go out to Matt Cooling, Paul Grey, David Long, Max Leitch, and all the staff at Boxing Orange for their support and help along the way.

Contents at a Glance

Contents

Icons Used in This Book

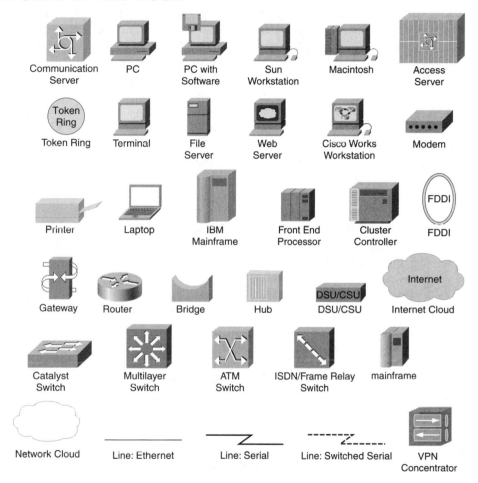

Command Syntax Conventions

The conventions used to present command syntax in this book are the same conventions used in the IOS Command Reference. The Command Reference describes these conventions as follows:

- **Bold** indicates commands and keywords that are entered literally as shown. In actual configuration examples and output (not general command syntax), bold indicates commands that are manually input by the user (such as a **show** command).

- *Italic* indicates arguments for which you supply actual values.

- Vertical bars (|) separate alternative, mutually exclusive elements.

- Square brackets ([ ]) indicate an optional element.

- Braces ({ }) indicate a required choice.

- Braces within brackets ([{ }]) indicate a required choice within an optional element.

Foreword

CCSP Self-Study: Cisco Secure Virtual Private Networks (CSVPN), Second Edition, is a Cisco authorized self-paced learning tool that helps you understand foundation concepts covered on the CSVPN exam. This book was developed in cooperation with the Cisco Internet Learning Solutions group, the team within Cisco responsible for the development of the CSVPN exam. As an early-stage exam-preparation product, this book teaches you the knowledge and skills you need to describe, configure, verify, and manage the Cisco VPN 3000 Concentrator, Cisco VPN Software Client, and Cisco VPN 3002 Hardware Client feature set. Whether you are studying to become CCSP certified or are simply seeking to gain a better understanding of the products, services, and policies that enable you to apply VPN solutions to your network, you will benefit from the information presented in this book.

Cisco Systems and Cisco Press present this material in text-based format to provide another learning vehicle for our customers and the broader user community in general. Although a publication does not duplicate the instructor-led or e-learning environment, we acknowledge that not everyone responds in the same way to the same delivery mechanism. It is our intent that presenting this material via a Cisco Press publication will enhance the transfer of knowledge to a broad audience of networking professionals.

Cisco Press will present other books in the certification self-study series on existing and future exams to help achieve the Cisco Internet Learning Solutions Group's principal objectives: to educate the Cisco community of networking professionals and to enable that community to build and maintain reliable, scalable networks. The Cisco Career Certifications and classes that support these certifications are directed at meeting these objectives through a disciplined approach to progressive learning.

To succeed with Cisco Career Certifications and in your daily job as a Cisco-certified professional, we recommend a blended learning solution that combines instructor-led training with hands-on experience, e-learning, and self-study training. Cisco Systems has authorized Cisco Learning Partners worldwide that can provide you with the most highly qualified instruction and invaluable hands-on experience in lab and simulation environments. To learn more about Cisco Learning Partner programs available in your area, go to www.cisco.com/go/authorizedtraining.

The books Cisco Press creates in partnership with Cisco Systems meet the same standards for content quality demanded of our courses and certifications. It is our intent that you will find this and subsequent Cisco Press certification self-study publications of value as you build your networking knowledge base.

Thomas M. Kelly
Vice President, Internet Learning Solutions Group
Cisco Systems, Inc.
February 2004

Introduction

This book helps professionals and students sort out Virtual Private Networks (VPNs) options and applications by clearly presenting the information covered in the CSVPN course, coupled with real-world examples. It will initially serve as a valuable study aid and will continue to be an invaluable lab-based theory and configuration guide for years to come.

This book covers the topic of establishing VPNs using IP Security (IPSec) protocols in conjunction with long-established encryption, authentication, and hashing protocols. It concentrates on the configuration of the VPN 3000 series of products, including Concentrators, Hardware Clients, and Software Clients.

Goals and Methods

This is a comprehensive, results-oriented book, designed to give you knowledge to plan, administer, and maintain a VPN based on the Cisco VPN 3000 Concentrator. This book closely follows the topics that are required for the CSVPN 642-511 exam. (The previous edition covered the 2.0 CSVPN exam [9EO-570].) New in this edition is full, detailed coverage of the VPN 3000 Concentrator, which is a scalable remote-access platform that offers encryption, high availability, and performance far superior to similar products.

This book helps you accomplish specific tasks:

- Understanding the concepts behind a VPN

- Understanding the two main types of VPNs

- Identifying the features, functions, and benefits of the Cisco VPN 3000 series Concentrator

- Identifying the procedure, steps, and commands required to configure and test a remote-access VPN using preshared keys on the Cisco VPN 3000 Concentrator

- Identifying the procedure, steps, and commands required to configure and test a remote-access VPN using digital certificates on the Cisco VPN 3000 Concentrator

- Identifying the procedure, steps, and commands required to configure and test a remote-access VPN using the Cisco 3002 Hardware Client

- Understanding and being able to implement advanced VPN client features, such as load balancing, reverse route injection, and the use of backup servers

- Providing a sound level of support and administration skills for day-to-day management of a VPN 3000 Concentrator-based VPN using the tools available on the Concentrator

Overall, you will not only understand the theory behind VPNs (and their obvious benefits), but you will also learn actual configurations through detailed steps. This will give you immediate functionality within your environment.

Each chapter begins with objectives. Whether theory or implementation, you will be able to gain the knowledge provided in each chapter in a clear and concise manner most effective in adult learning. This book also provides figures for visual accompaniment to the text.

Who Should Read This Book?

The target audience for this book is intermediate readers who have firsthand knowledge of system administration. Care is taken to include beginners who understand the need for secure VPNs within their infrastructure and who are reading with the objective of achieving a greater understanding of VPN technologies. The most common reader will be system administrators who intend to implement a VPN solution using equipment already in place or soon to be purchased. It is also likely that people studying for the CSVPN exam will be reading this book as a study guide on the road to certification.

How This Book Is Organized

This book is split into 14 chapters and two appendixes. The book presents the background theory behind VPNs and the VPN Concentrator 3000 in the opening chapters before building on this knowledge in the later chapters. Each technology is fully explained with concise examples. Therefore, it is advisable to read the chapters in the order in which they are presented. (The later chapters are useful as an on-the-job reference.)

Chapter 1, "Network Security and Virtual Private Network Technologies"—This opening chapter defines VPNs and introduces the two main types of VPNs. It then goes on to describe the technologies that make up today's IPSec-based VPNs.

Chapter 2, "Cisco VPN 3000 Concentrator Series Hardware Overview"—This chapter introduces the Cisco VPN Concentrator. The Concentrator's basic functions and product placement are covered, and the product features for each model of the VPN Concentrator are discussed.

Chapter 3, "Routing on the VPN 3000"—This chapter looks at the initial routing configuration on the VPN 3000 Concentrator. It covers both static and dynamic routing and provides working examples of how to configure the Routing Information Protocol (RIP) and Open Shortest Path First (OSPF) dynamic routing protocols.

Chapter 4, "Configuring the Cisco VPN 3000 for Remote Access Using Preshared Keys"—Now that the book has covered the basics of VPNs, the Concentrator, and initial routing, this chapter looks at how to configure a VPN 3000 with a remote-access VPN using preshared keys.

Chapter 5, "Configuring the Cisco VPN 3000 for Remote Access Using Digital Certificates"—Moving on from configuring a remote-access VPN with preshared keys, this chapter looks at configuring a remote-access VPN using digital certificates. The chapter starts by providing an overview of the digital certificate process before identifying the configuration steps required on the VPN Concentrator.

Chapter 6, "The Cisco VPN Client Firewall Feature"—This chapter covers the VPN Client Firewall. It starts by providing an overview of the firewall functionality before moving on to looking at the different configuration options available with the VPN Concentrator.

Chapter 7, "Configuring the Cisco 3002 Hardware Client for Remote Access"—This chapter looks at the 3002 Hardware Client. At this point, the book has already covered remote-access VPN configuration with the Software Client. This chapter builds on previous knowledge by introducing the VPN 3002 Hardware Client.

Chapter 8, "Configuring the Cisco 3002 Hardware Client for User and Unit Authentication"—This chapter looks at configuring user and unit authentication for the 3002 Hardware Client. The 3002 Hardware Client brings with it new challenges and also functionality that can be leveraged to provide more-granular user-level security.

Chapter 9, "Configuring Cisco VPN Clients for Backup Server, Load Balancing, and Reverse Route Injection"—This chapter looks at the more-advanced configuration options available with the remote-access VPN Clients, such as backup servers, load balancing, and reverse route injection. All these technologies are explained, and sample configurations are provided for you to follow.

Chapter 10, "Configuring the Cisco 3000 Concentrator for IPSec over TCP and UDP"—This chapter looks at real-world implementations of remote-access VPNs and the most common issue, VPN through NAT. IPSec over TCP and UDP, including NAT Traversal (NAT-T), are covered in this chapter.

Chapter 11, "Configuring LAN-to-LAN VPNs on the Cisco 3000"—As well as remote-access VPNs, there are also LAN-to-LAN VPNs. This chapter looks at the configuration of a LAN-to-LAN VPN on the VPN Concentrator and explains the differences between the LAN-to-LAN VPN and the remote-access VPN. A step-by-step scenario is provided in which a VPN Concentrator-to-VPN Concentrator LAN-to-LAN VPN is configured.

Chapter 12, "Network Monitoring and Administration"—This chapter provides an overview of network monitoring and administration on the VPN Concentrator. The tools presented in this chapter are very useful for day-to-day administration of a VPN Concentrator-implemented network.

Chapter 13, "Troubleshooting"—This chapter looks at the two main types of VPN failures, initial and ongoing. Both types of failures are explained, and information is provided on how to troubleshoot each type.

Chapter 14, "Case Study"—The case study presents a fictitious company that wants to implement a remote-access VPN. The Concentrator is configured as if it were straight from the factory. You are taken through a step-by-step process to configure the VPN Concentrator to enable the remote-access VPN connection.

Appendix A, "Answers to Review Questions"—This appendix provides answers to the chapter-ending review questions.

Appendix B, "Configuring movianVPN"—This appendix introduces movianVPN by Certicom and explains how to configure it for use with the Cisco VPN 3000 series Concentrator.

After completing this chapter, you will be able to perform the following tasks:

- Understand network security
- Understand VPN technologies
- Use the Cisco Security Wheel
- Understand the basics of the IPSec protocol framework

Network Security and Virtual Private Network Technologies

This opening chapter provides an overview of network security and looks at the Cisco Architecture for Voice, Video, and Integrated Data (AVVID) and the SAFE blueprint. It also covers the IP Security (IPSec) framework and identifies the main encryption and algorithm protocols. Then it looks at how IPSec works before finishing with the five steps of IPSec operation. These five steps are very important to remember and also are very useful for implementing and troubleshooting any IPSec-based virtual private network (VPN), whether firewall-, router-, or VPN Concentrator-based.

Network Security Overview

Network security is essential because the Internet is a network of interconnected networks without a boundary. Because of this fact, the organizational network becomes accessible from and vulnerable to any other computer in the world. As companies become Internet businesses, new threats arise because people no longer require physical access to a company's computer assets: They can access everything over the public network.

In a recent survey conducted by the Computer Security Institute (CSI, www.gocsi.com), 70 percent of the organizations polled stated that their network security defenses had been breached and that 60 percent of the incidents came from within the organizations themselves.

Network security faces four primary threats:

- Unstructured threats
- Structured threats
- External threats
- Internal threats

Unstructured Threats

Unstructured threats consist of mostly inexperienced individuals using easily available hacking tools from the Internet. Some of the people in this category are motivated by malicious intent, but most are motivated by the intellectual challenge and are commonly called *script kiddies*. They are not the most talented or experienced hackers, but they have the motivation, which is all that matters.

Structured Threats

Structured threats come from hackers who are more highly motivated and technically competent. They usually understand network system designs and vulnerabilities, and they can understand as well as create hacking scripts to penetrate those network systems.

External Threats

External threats are individuals or organizations working outside your company who do not have authorized access to your computer systems or network. They work their way into a network mainly from the Internet or dialup access servers.

Internal Threats

Internal threats occur when someone has authorized access to the network with either an account on a server or physical access to the wire. They are typically disgruntled former or current employees or contractors.

The three types of network attacks are

- Reconnaissance attacks
- Access attacks
- Denial of service (DoS) attacks

Reconnaissance Attacks

Reconnaissance is the unauthorized discovery and mapping of systems, services, or vulnerabilities. It is also called information gathering. In most cases, it precedes an actual access or DoS attack. The malicious intruder typically ping-sweeps the target network first to determine what IP addresses are alive. After this is accomplished, the intruder determines what services or ports are active on the live IP addresses. From this information, the intruder queries the ports to determine the application type and version as well as the type and version of the operating system running on the target host.

Reconnaissance is somewhat analogous to a thief scoping out a neighborhood for vulnerable homes he can break into, such as an unoccupied residence, an easy-to-open door or window, and so on. In many cases, an intruder goes as far as "rattling the door handle" — not to go in immediately if it is open, but to discover vulnerable services he can exploit later when there is less likelihood that anyone is looking.

Access Attacks

Access is an all-encompassing term that refers to unauthorized data manipulation, system access, or privilege escalation. Unauthorized data retrieval is simply reading, writing, copying, or moving files that are not intended to be accessible to the intruder. Sometimes this is as easy as finding shared folders in Windows 9x or NT, or NFS exported directories in UNIX systems with read or read-write access to everyone. The intruder has no problem getting to the files. More often than not, the easily accessible information is highly confidential and completely unprotected from prying eyes, especially if the attacker is already an internal user.

System access is an intruder's ability to gain access to a machine that he is not allowed access to (such as when the intruder does not have an account or password). Entering or accessing systems that you don't have access to usually involves running a hack, script, or tool that exploits a known vulnerability of the system or application being attacked.

Another form of access attacks involves privilege escalation. This is done by legitimate users who have a lower level of access privileges or intruders who have gained lower-privileged access. The intent is to get information or execute procedures that are unauthorized at the user's current level of access. In many cases this involves gaining root access in a UNIX system to install a sniffer to record network traffic, such as usernames and passwords, that can be used to access another target.

In some cases, intruders only want to gain access, not steal information—especially when the motive is intellectual challenge, curiosity, or ignorance.

DoS Attacks

DoS is when an attacker disables or corrupts networks, systems, or services with the intent to deny the service to intended users. It usually involves either crashing the system or slowing it down to the point where it is unusable. But DoS can also be as simple as wiping out or corrupting information necessary for business. In most cases, performing the attack simply involves running a hack, script, or tool. The attacker does not need prior access to the target, because usually all that is required is a way to get to it. For these reasons and because of the great damaging potential, DoS attacks are the most feared—especially by e-commerce website operators.

Network Security as a Continuous Process

Network security should be a continuous process built around a security policy. A continuous security policy is most effective, because it promotes retesting and reapplying updated security measures on a continuous basis. The Security Wheel, shown in Figure 1-1, represents this continuous security process.

Figure 1-1 *Security Wheel*

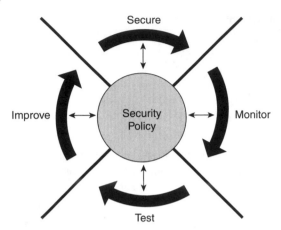

To begin this continuous process known as the Security Wheel, you need to create a security policy that enables the application of security measures. A security policy needs to accomplish the following tasks:

- Identify the organization's security objectives
- Document the resources to be protected
- Identify the network infrastructure with current maps and inventories

To create or implement an effective security policy, you need to determine what it is you want to protect and in what manner you will protect it. You should know and understand your network's weak points and how they can be exploited. You should also understand how your system normally functions so that you know what to expect and are familiar with how the devices are normally used. Finally, consider your network's physical security and how to protect it. Physical access to a computer, router, or firewall can give a user total control over that device.

After the security policy is developed, it becomes the hub on which the next four steps of the Security Wheel are based:

Step 1 Secure the system. This involves implementing security devices—firewalls, identification authentication systems, encryption, and so on—with the intent to prevent unauthorized access to network systems. This is where the Cisco PIX Firewall is effective.

Step 2 Monitor the network for violations and attacks against the corporate security policy. These attacks can occur within the network's secured perimeter—from a disgruntled employee or contractor—or from a source outside your trusted network. You should monitor the network with a real-time intrusion detection device such as the Cisco Intrusion

Detection System (IDS). This helps you discover unauthorized entries. It also serves as a system of checks and balances to ensure that devices implemented in Step 1 of the Security Wheel have been configured and are working properly.

Step 3 Test the effectiveness of the security safeguards that are in place. Use the Cisco Secure Scanner to identify the network's security posture with respect to the security procedures that form the hub of the Security Wheel. Validation is a must. You can have the most sophisticated network security system, but if it is not working, your network can be compromised. This is why you need to test the devices you implemented in Steps 1 and 2 to make sure they are functioning properly. The Cisco Secure Scanner is designed to validate your network security.

Step 4 Improve corporate security. The improvement phase of the Security Wheel involves analyzing the data collected during the monitoring and testing phases and developing and implementing improvement mechanisms that feed into your security policy and the securing phase in Step 1. If you want to keep your network as secure as possible, you must keep repeating the cycle of the Security Wheel, because new network vulnerabilities and risks are created every day.

All four steps—secure, monitor, test, and improve—should be repeated on a continuous basis and should be incorporated into updated versions of the corporate security policy.

Cisco AVVID

The Internet is creating tremendous business opportunities for Cisco and Cisco customers. Internet business solutions such as e-commerce, supply chain management, e-learning, and customer care are dramatically increasing productivity and efficiency.

Cisco AVVID is the one enterprise architecture that provides the intelligent network infrastructure for today's Internet business solutions. As the industry's only enterprise-wide, standards-based network architecture, Cisco AVVID provides the road map for combining customers' business and technology strategies into one cohesive model.

With Cisco AVVID, customers have a comprehensive road map for enabling Internet business solutions and creating a competitive advantage. Cisco AVVID has four benefits:

- **Integration**—By leveraging the Cisco AVVID architecture and applying the network intelligence that is inherent in IP, companies can develop comprehensive tools to improve productivity.

- **Intelligence**—Traffic prioritization and intelligent networking services maximize network efficiency for optimized application performance.

- **Innovation**—Customers can adapt quickly in a changing business environment.

- **Interoperability**—Standards-based application programming interfaces (APIs) enable open integration with third-party developers, providing customers with choice and flexibility.

Combining the network infrastructure and services with new-world applications, Cisco AVVID accelerates the integration of technology strategy with business vision.

The following sections discuss the different parts of the Cisco AVVID architecture. They are shown in Figure 1-2.

Figure 1-2   *Cisco AVVID Architecture*

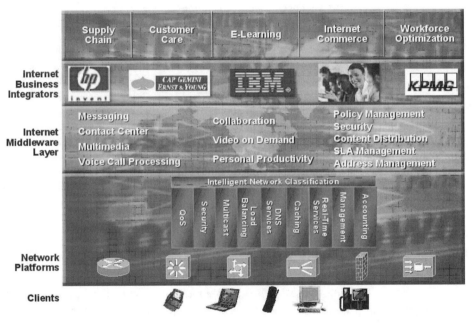

Clients

Clients are the wide variety of devices that can be used to access the Internet business solutions through the network. These can include phones, PCs, personal digital assistants (PDAs), and any other mobile Internet device. One key difference from traditional proprietary architectures is that the Cisco AVVID standards-based solution lets a wide variety of devices be connected—even some not yet in broad use. Unlike traditional telephony and video solutions, proprietary access devices are unnecessary. Instead, functionality is added through the intelligent network services provided in the infrastructure.

Network Platforms

The network infrastructure provides the physical and logical connection for devices, bringing them into the network. Network platforms are the LAN switches, routers, gateways, and other equipment that interconnect users and servers. Cisco network platforms are competitive as far as features, performance, and price, but their key capabilities are the integration and interaction with other elements of the Cisco AVVID framework. This layer of Cisco AVVID is the foundation for all applications that are integrated to solve business problems.

Intelligent Network Services

The intelligent network services, provided through software that operates on network platforms, are a major benefit of an end-to-end architecture for deploying Internet business solutions. From quality of service (QoS) (prioritization) through security, accounting, and management, intelligent network services reflect the enterprise's business rules and policies in network performance. A consistent set of the services end-to-end through the network is vital if the infrastructure is to be relied on as a network utility. These consistent services allow new Internet business applications and e-business initiatives to roll out very quickly without a major reengineering of the network each time. In contrast, networks built on best-of-breed strategies might promise higher performance in a specific device, but they cannot be counted on to deliver these sophisticated features end-to-end in a multivendor environment. Cisco AVVID supports standards to provide for migration and the incorporation of Internet business integrators, but the added intelligent network services offered by an end-to-end Cisco AVVID solution go far beyond what can be achieved in a best-of-breed environment.

Internet Middleware Layer

The next section, including service control and communication services, is a key part of any networking architecture, providing the software and tools to break down the barriers of complexity arising from new technology. These combined layers provide the tools for integrators and customers to tailor their network infrastructure and customize intelligent network services to meet application needs. These layers manage access, call setup and teardown, perimeter security, prioritization and bandwidth allocation, and user privileges. Software, such as distributed customer contact suites, messaging solutions, and multimedia and collaboration provide capabilities and a communication foundation that enable interaction between users and a variety of application platforms. In a best-of-breed strategy, many of these capabilities must be individually configured or managed. In traditional proprietary schemes, vendors dictated these layers, limiting innovation and responsiveness.

Rapid deployment of Internet business solutions depends on consistent service control and communication services capabilities throughout the network. These capabilities are often delivered by Cisco from servers distributed throughout the network. The service control and communication services layers are the glue that joins the Internet technology layers of the Cisco AVVID framework with the Internet business solutions. In effect, this tunes the network infrastructure and intelligent network services to the needs of the Internet business solutions. In turn, the Internet business solutions are adapted for the best performance and availability on the network infrastructure by exploiting the end-to-end services available through the Cisco AVVID framework.

Internet Business Integrators

As part of the open ecosystem, it is imperative to enable partners with Cisco AVVID. Cisco realizes the crucial requirement to team with integrators, strategic partners, and customers to deliver complete Internet business. Cisco AVVID offers a guide for these interactions by describing a consistent set of services and capabilities that form the basis of many types of partner relationships.

Internet Business Solutions

Enterprise customers are deploying Internet business solutions to reengineer their organizations. The applications associated with Internet business solutions are not provided by Cisco, but they are enabled, accelerated, and delivered through Cisco AVVID. Being able to move their traditional business models to Internet business models and to deploy Internet business solutions is key to companies' survival. Cisco AVVID is the architecture on which e-businesses build Internet business solutions that can be easily deployed and managed. Ultimately, the more Internet business solutions that are delivered, the more efficiently and effectively companies will increase productivity and added value.

Cisco SAFE Blueprint

SAFE is a flexible, dynamic security blueprint for networks that is based on Cisco AVVID. SAFE lets businesses securely and successfully take advantage of e-business economies and compete in the Internet economy.

As the leader in networking for the Internet, Cisco is ideally positioned to help companies secure their networks. The SAFE blueprint, in conjunction with an ecosystem of best-of-breed, complementary products, partners, and services, ensures that businesses can deploy robust, secure networks in the Internet age.

Implementing the SAFE blueprint for secure e-business has several major benefits:

- It provides the foundation for migrating to secure, affordable, converged networks.
- It lets companies cost-effectively deploy a modular, scalable security framework in stages.

- It delivers integrated network protection via high-level security products and services.

The SAFE blueprint provides a robust security blueprint that builds on Cisco AVVID. SAFE layers are incorporated throughout the Cisco AVVID infrastructure:

- **Infrastructure layer**—Intelligent, scalable security services in Cisco platforms, such as routers, switches, firewalls, IDSs, and other devices

- **Appliances layer**—Incorporates key security functionality in mobile handheld devices and remote PC clients

- **Service control layer**—Critical security protocols and APIs that let security solutions work together cohesively

- **Applications layer**—Host and application-based security elements that ensure the integrity of critical e-business applications

To facilitate rapidly deployable, consistent security throughout the enterprise, SAFE consists of modules that address the distinct requirements of each network area. By adopting a SAFE blueprint, security managers do not need to redesign the entire security architecture each time a new service is added to the network. With modular templates, it is easier and more cost-effective to secure each new service as it is needed and to integrate it with the overall security architecture. Figure 1-3 shows an example of the module approach.

Figure 1-3   *Cisco SAFE Modular Blueprint*

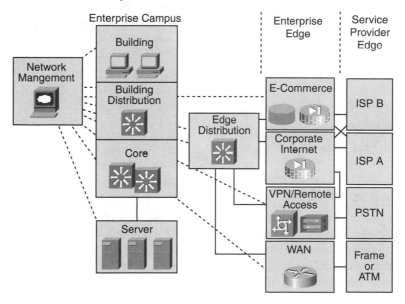

One of the unique characteristics of the SAFE blueprint is that it is the first industry blueprint that recommends exactly which security solutions should be included in which sections of the network, and why they should be deployed. Each module in the SAFE blueprint is designed specifically to provide maximum performance for e-business while allowing enterprises to maintain security and integrity.

Cisco has opened its Cisco AVVID architecture and SAFE blueprint to key third-party vendors to create a security solutions ecosystem to spur development of best-in-class multi-service applications and products. The Cisco AVVID architecture and SAFE blueprint provide interoperability for third-party hardware and software using standards-based media interfaces, APIs, and protocols. This ecosystem is offered through the Security and Virtual Private Network Associate Program, an interoperability solutions program that provides Cisco customers with complimentary tested and certified products for securing their businesses. The ecosystem lets businesses design and roll out secure networks that best fit their business model and enable maximum agility.

Overview of VPNs and IPSec Technologies

A VPN is a service offering secure, reliable connectivity over a shared public network infra-structure, such as the Internet. Cisco products support the latest in VPN technology.

Cisco defines a VPN as an encrypted connection between private networks over a public network, such as the Internet. The V and N stand for virtual network. The information from a private network is transported over a public network, an internet, to form a virtual network. The P stands for private. To remain private, the traffic is encrypted to keep the data confidential. Therefore, a VPN is a private virtual network.

The three types of implementation scenarios for VPNs are

- Remote-access
- Site-to-site
- Firewall-based

Remote-Access VPNs

The first VPN solution is remote access. Remote access is targeted at mobile users and home telecommuters. In the past, corporations supported remote users via dial-in networks. This typically necessitated a toll or toll-free call to access the corporation. With the advent of VPNs, a mobile user can make a local call to his ISP to access the corporation via the Internet wherever he is. This is an evolution of dial networks. Remote-access VPNs can support the needs of telecommuters, mobile users, extranet consumer-to-business, and so on. Figure 1-4 shows a remote-access VPN. The black dotted line shows VPN traffic across the Internet.

Figure 1-4   *Remote-Access VPN*

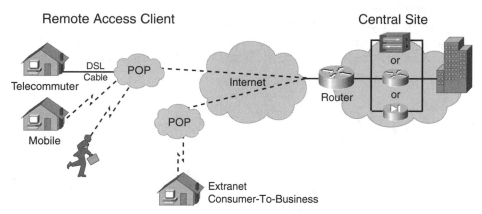

Remote Access VPN—Extension/Evolution of Dial

Site-to-Site VPNs

The next VPN solution is site-to-site (see Figure 1-5). A site-to-site VPN can be used to connect corporate sites. In the past, a leased line or Frame Relay connection was required to connect sites, but now most corporations have Internet access. With Internet access, you can replace leased lines and Frame Relay lines by implementing a site-to-site VPN. Site-to-site VPNs can be used to provide the network connection between the corporation's sites. Site-to-site VPNs can support company intranets and business partner extranets. A site-to-site VPN is an extension of the classic WAN network.

Figure 1-5   *Site-to-Site VPN*

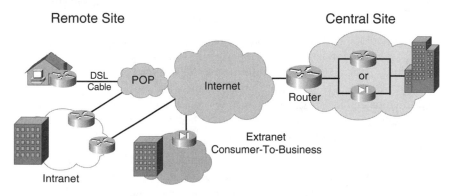

Site-to-Site VPN—Extension of Classic WAN

Firewall-Based VPNs

The last solution is firewall-based VPNs. A firewall-based VPN is inherently a site-to-site solution. Firewall-based VPN solutions are not a technical issue but a security issue. The question is who manages the VPN. If corporate security manages the VPN, a firewall-based VPN might be the VPN solution of choice. Corporations can enhance their existing firewall systems to support VPN services.

The Need for VPNs

The introduction of a VPN into your corporate network infrastructure can provide many benefits:

- **Reduced costs**—Businesses vastly reduce their costs by using the Internet to provide the site-to-site and remote-access infrastructure. Before VPNs, businesses connected using expensive leased lines and telephone systems.

- **Improved communications**—With a VPN, remote-access and home-based users can connect to the central office network from anywhere at any time.

- **Flexibility and scalability**—The introduction of a VPN simplifies and centralizes network administration. The VPN infrastructure can be easily adapted to the company's changing needs, both now and in the future.

- **Security and reliability**—Security is inherent within a VPN, provided through tunneling protocols and encryption software. The reduced number of entry points and the inherent resilience of the Internet mean that the solution is considerably more reliable.

- **Wireless networking**—VPN technology is increasingly combined with wireless connectivity to ensure complete privacy of the data transmitted in environments where data privacy is mandated, such as financial institutions. This ensures that an organization is not vulnerable to inherently weak standard wireless security features.

It is important to note that VPNs can also bring you increased business benefits. They let you develop trust relationships with your suppliers and partners and give your employees round-the-clock access to vital information. Any intranets and extranets that are developed can promote knowledge sharing among partners and employees, and the ease with which information can be accessed and communicated can boost employee morale. These types of benefits cannot be easily measured but can add real value to how you do business and ultimately have a positive impact on turnover and profit.

Implementing a VPN can bring you the benefits outlined here and are a cost-effective, flexible, secure method of managing your digital communications. However, it is important that you work with a partner who ensures that the technology is implemented effectively and forms part of a competent security infrastructure. Many organizations undermine their technical investments, because a lack of detailed knowledge during implementation can leave gaps in security infrastructures that can be exploited and give open access to business-critical information.

IPSec

IPSec acts at the network layer, protecting and authenticating IP packets between participating IPSec devices (peers), such as PIX Firewalls, Cisco routers, Cisco VPN 3000 Concentrators, Cisco VPN Clients, and other IPSec-compliant products. IPSec is not bound to any specific encryption or authentication algorithms, keying technology, or security algorithms. IPSec is a framework of open standards. Because it isn't bound to specific algorithms, IPSec allows newer and better algorithms to be implemented without patching the existing IPSec standards. IPSec provides data confidentiality, data integrity, and data origin authentication between participating peers at the IP layer. IPSec is used to secure a path between a pair of gateways, a pair of hosts, or a gateway and a host.

IPSec spells out the rules for secure communications. IPSec, in turn, relies on existing algorithms to implement the encryption, authentication, and key exchange.

Some of the standard algorithms are as follows:

- **Data Encryption Standard (DES) algorithm**—Used to encrypt and decrypt packet data.
- **3DES algorithm**—Effectively doubles encryption strength over 56-bit DES.
- **Advanced Encryption Standard (AES)**—A newer cipher algorithm designed to replace DES. Has a variable key length between 128 and 256 bits. Cisco is the first industry vendor to implement AES on all its VPN-capable platforms.
- **Message Digest 5 (MD5) algorithm**—Used to authenticate packet data.
- **Secure Hash Algorithm 1 (SHA-1)**—Used to authenticate packet data.
- **Diffie-Hellman (DH)**—A public-key cryptography protocol that allows two parties to establish a shared secret key used by encryption and hash algorithms (for example, DES and MD5) over an insecure communications channel.

Figure 1-6 shows four IPSec framework squares to be filled. When configuring security services to be provided by an IPSec gateway, you first must choose an IPSec protocol. The choices are ESP or ESP with AH. The second square is an encryption algorithm. Choose the encryption algorithm appropriate for the level of security desired: DES or 3DES. The third square is authentication. Choose an authentication algorithm to provide data integrity: MD5 or SHA. The last square is the DH algorithm group. Choose which group to use: DH1, DH2, or DH5. IPSec provides the framework, and the administrator chooses the algorithms used to implement the security services within that framework.

Figure 1-6 *IPSec Protocol Framework*

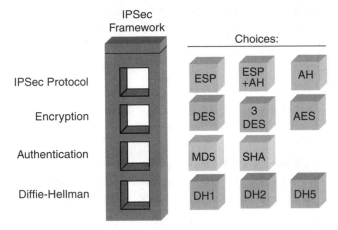

IPSec security services provide four critical functions:

- **Confidentiality (encryption)**—The sender can encrypt the packets before transmitting them across a network. By doing so, no one can eavesdrop on the communication. If intercepted, the communications cannot be read.

- **Data integrity**—The receiver can verify that the data was transmitted through the Internet without being changed or altered in any way.

- **Origin authentication**—The receiver can authenticate the packet's source, guaranteeing and certifying the source of the information.

- **Anti-replay protection**—Anti-replay protection verifies that each packet is unique, not duplicated. IPSec packets are protected by comparing the sequence number of the received packets and a sliding window on the destination host, or security gateway. A packet whose sequence number is before the sliding window is considered late, or a duplicate. Late and duplicate packets are dropped.

Confidentiality

The good news is that the Internet is a public network. The bad news is that the Internet is a public network. Clear-text data transported over the public Internet can be intercepted and read. To keep the data private, it can be encrypted. Through digital scrambling, the data is rendered unreadable.

For encryption to work, both the sender and receiver need to know the rules used to transform the original message into its coded form. Rules are based on an algorithm and a key. An algorithm is a mathematical function that combines a message, text, characters, or all three with a string of characters called a key. The output is an unreadable cipher string. Decryption is extremely difficult or impossible without the correct key.

In Figure 1-7, someone wants to send a financial document across the Internet. At the local end, the document is combined with a key and is run through an encryption algorithm. The output is cipher text. The cipher text is then sent through the Internet. At the remote end, the message is recombined with a key and is sent back through the encryption algorithm. The output is the original financial document.

Figure 1-7   *Encryption*

Two types of encryption keys exist: symmetric and asymmetric. With symmetric key encryption, each peer uses the same key to encrypt and decrypt the data. With asymmetric key encryption, the local end uses one key to encrypt the traffic, and the remote end uses another key to decrypt it. Both are discussed in further detail later in this chapter.

Encryption Algorithms

The degree of security depends on the key's length. If someone tries to hack the key through a brute-force attack, guessing every possible combination, the number of possibilities is a function of the key's length. The time to process all the possibilities is a function of the computer's computing power. Therefore, the shorter the key, the easier it is to break. A 64-bit key with a relatively sophisticated computer can take approximately 1 year to break. A 128-bit key with the same machine can take roughly 10^{19} years to decrypt.

Some of the encryption algorithms are as follows:

- **DES**—DES was developed by IBM. It uses a 56-bit key, ensuring high-performance encryption. DES is a symmetric key algorithm.

- **3DES**—The 3DES algorithm is a variant of the 56-bit DES. 3DES operates similarly to DES, in that data is broken into 64-bit blocks. 3DES then processes each block three times, each time with an independent 56-bit key. 3DES effectively doubles encryption strength over 56-bit DES. 3DES is a symmetric key algorithm.

- **AES**—The National Institute of Standards and Technology (NIST) recently adopted AES to replace the existing DES encryption in cryptographic devices. AES provides stronger security than DES and is computationally more efficient than 3DES. AES offers three different key strengths: 128-, 192-, and 256-bit keys. Cisco now supports VPN encryption from version 4.0 of the VPN Concentrator software and the addition of a SEP-E module. The older SEP modules do not perform hardware encryption on AES, only on DES and 3DES.

- **RSA**—Rivest, Shamir, and Adelman (RSA) encryption, shown in Figure 1-8, uses asymmetric keys for encryption and decryption. Each end, local and remote, generates two encryption keys: a private key and a public key. It keeps its private key and exchanges its public key with people with whom it wants to communicate. To send an encrypted message to the remote end, the local end encrypts the message using the remote's public key and the RSA encryption algorithm. The result is an unreadable cipher text. This message is sent through the insecure network. The remote end uses its private key and the RSA algorithm to decrypt the cipher text. The result is the original message. The only one who can decrypt the message is the destination that owns the private key. With RSA encryption, the opposite also holds true. The remote end can encrypt a message using its own private key. The receiver can decrypt the message using the sender's public key. This RSA encryption technique is used for digital signatures.

Figure 1-8 *RSA Encryption*

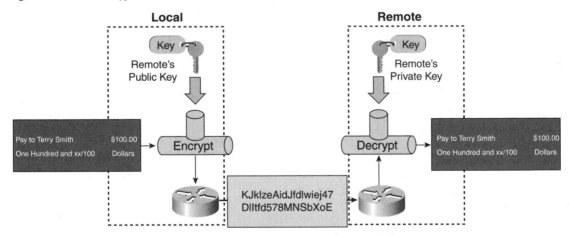

Key Exchange

DES, 3DES, AES, and also the two authentication algorithms, MD5 and SHA-1, all require a symmetric shared secret key to perform encryption and decryption. The question is, how do the encrypting and decrypting devices get the shared secret key?

The keys can be sent by e-mail, courier, overnight express, or public key exchange. The easiest method is DH public key exchange. The DH key agreement is a public key exchange method that provides a way for two peers to establish a shared secret key that only they know, although they are communicating over an insecure channel.

Public key cryptosystems rely on a two-key system: a public key, which is exchanged between end users, and a private key, which is kept secret by the original owners. The DH public key algorithm states that if user A and user B exchange public keys, and a calculation is performed on their individual private key and one another's public key, the end result of the process is an identical shared key. The shared key is used to derive encryption and authentication keys.

Variations of the DH key exchange algorithm are known as DH groups 1 through 7. DH groups 1, 2, and 5 support exponentiation over a prime modulus with a key size of 768 bits, 1024 bits, and 1536 bits, respectively. Cisco 3000 Clients support DH groups 1, 2, and 5. DES and 3DES encryption support DH groups 1 and 2. AES encryption supports DH groups 2 and 5. In addition to these, the Certicom movianVPN Client supports group 7. Group 7 supports Elliptical Curve Cryptography (ECC), which reduces the time needed to generate keys. During tunnel setup, VPN peers negotiate which DH group to use.

Security is not an issue with DH key exchange. Although someone might know a user's public key, the shared secret cannot be generated, because the private key never becomes public.

DH Key Exchange

DH key exchange is a public key exchange method that provides a way for two IPScc peers to establish a shared secret key that only they know, although they arc communicating over an insecure channel.

With DH, each peer generates a public/private key pair. The private key generated by each peer is kept secret and never shared. The public key is calculated from the private key by each peer and is exchanged over the insecure channel. Each peer combines the other's public key with its own private key and computes the same shared secret number. The shared secret number is then converted into a shared secret key. The shared secret key is never exchanged over the insecure channel.

The following steps are used to implement the DH process (see Figure 1-9):

1 Each peer generates a large prime integer, p and q. Each peer sends the other its prime integer over the insecure channel. For example, peer A sends p to peer B. Each peer then uses the p and q values to generate g, a primitive root of p.

2 Each peer generates a private DH key (peer A: X_a, peer B: X_b).

3 Each peer generates a public DH key. The local private key is combined with the prime number p and the primitive root g in each peer to generate a public key, Y_a for peer A and Y_b for peer B. The formula for peer A is $Y_a = g^\wedge X_a \bmod p$. The formula for peer B is $Y_b = g^\wedge X_b \bmod p$. The exponentiation is computationally expensive. The $\wedge$ character denotes exponentiation (g to the X_a power); mod denotes modulus.

4 The public keys Y_a and Y_b are exchanged in public.

5 Each peer generates a shared secret number (ZZ) by combining the public key received from the opposite peer with its own private key. The formula for peer A is $ZZ = (Y_b X_a) \bmod p$. The formula for peer B is $ZZ = (Y_a X_b) \bmod p$. The ZZ values are identical in each peer. Anyone who knows p or g, or the DH public keys, cannot guess or easily calculate the shared secret value—largely because of the difficulty in factoring large prime numbers.

6 Shared secret number ZZ is used to derive the encryption and authentication symmetric keys.

Figure 1-9 *DH Key Exchange*

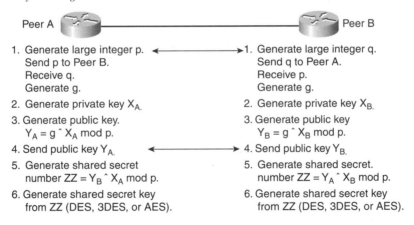

Data Integrity

The next VPN-critical function is data integrity. VPN data is transported over some form of insecure network, such as the Internet. Potentially, this data could be intercepted and modified. To guard against this, each message has a hash attached to it. This is called a Hash-based Message Authentication Code (HMAC). A hash guarantees the integrity of the original message. If the transmitted hash matches the received hash, the message has not been tampered with. However, if there is no match, the message was altered.

In Figure 1-10, someone is trying to send Terry Smith a check for $100. At the remote end, Alex Jones is trying to cash the check for $1000. As the check progressed through the

Internet, it was altered. Both the recipient and the dollar amount were changed. In this case, the hashes do not match, so the transaction is no longer valid.

Figure 1-10   *Data Integrity*

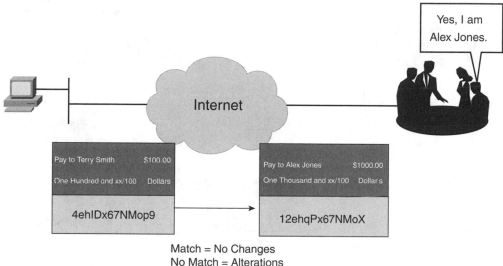

Data integrity is commonly known and talked about as authentication. The packets are authenticated using the hash that is attached to each packet. Two main algorithms facilitate data integrity within the IPSec framework—MD5 and SHA-1.

HMAC guarantees the message's integrity. At the local end, the message and a shared secret key are sent through a hash algorithm, which produces a hash value. Basically, a hash algorithm is a formula used to convert a variable-length message into a single string of digits of a fixed length. It is a one-way algorithm. A message can produce a hash, but a hash cannot produce the original message. It is analogous to dropping a plate on the floor. The plate can produce a multitude of pieces, but the pieces cannot be recombined to reproduce the plate in its original form. The message and hash are sent over the network.

At the remote end, a two-step process occurs, as shown in Figure 1-11. First, the received message and shared secret key are sent through the hash algorithm, resulting in a recalculated hash value. Second, the receiver compares the recalculated hash with the hash that was attached to the message. If the original hash and recalculated hash match, the message's integrity is guaranteed. If any of the original message is changed while in transit, the hash values are different.

Figure 1-11 *HMAC*

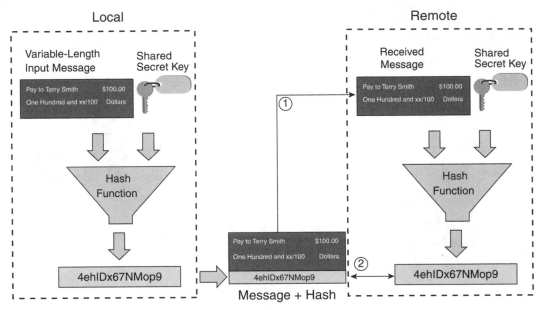

The two common HMAC algorithms are as follows:

- **HMAC-MD5**—HMAC-MD5 uses a 128-bit shared secret key. The variable-length message and the 128-bit shared secret key are combined and run through the HMAC-MD5 hash algorithm. The output is a 128-bit hash. The hash is appended to the original message and forwarded to the remote end.

- **HMAC-SHA-1**—HMAC-SHA-1 uses a 160-bit secret key. The variable-length message and the 160-bit shared secret key are combined and run through the HMAC-SHA-1 hash algorithm. The output is a 160-bit hash. The hash is appended to the original message and forwarded to the remote end.

  HMAC-SHA-1 is considered cryptographically stronger than HMAC-MD5. HMAC-SHA-1 is recommended when its slightly superior security is important.

Origin Authentication

In the middle ages, a seal guaranteed the authenticity of an edict. In modern times, a signed document is notarized with a seal and a signature. In the electronic era, a document is signed using the sender's private encryption key—a digital signature. A signature is authenticated by decrypting the signature with the sender's public key.

In Figure 1-12, the local device derives a hash and encrypts it with its private key. The encrypted hash (digital signature) is attached to the message and is forwarded to the remote end. At the remote end, the encrypted hash is decrypted using the local end's public key. If the decrypted hash matches the recomputed hash, the signature is genuine. A digital signature ties a message to a sender. The sender is authenticated. It is used during the initial establishment of a VPN tunnel to authenticate both ends to the tunnel.

Figure 1-12   *Digital Signature*

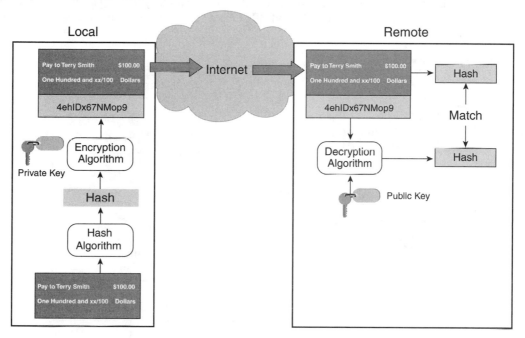

The two common digital signature algorithms are RSA and Directory System Agent (DSA). RSA is used commercially and is the most common. DSA is used by U.S. Government agencies and is not as common.

When conducting business long distance, it is necessary to know who is on the other end of the phone, e-mail, or fax. The same is true of VPNs. The device on the other end of the VPN tunnel must be authenticated before the communication path is considered secure.

The three peer authentication methods are as follows:

- **Preshared keys**—A secret key value entered into each peer manually that is used to authenticate the peer.
- **RSA signatures**—Uses the exchange of digital certificates to authenticate the peers.
- **RSA encrypted nonces**—Nonces (random numbers generated by each peer) are encrypted and then exchanged between peers. The two nonces are used during the peer authentication process.

Preshared Keys

With preshared keys, the same preshared key is configured on each IPSec peer. At each end, the preshared key is combined with other information to form the authentication key. Starting at the local end, the authentication key and the identity information (device-specific information) are sent through a hash algorithm to form hash_I. The local Internet Key Exchange (IKE) peer provides one-way authentication by sending hash_I to the remote peer. If the remote peer can independently create the same hash, the local peer is authenticated, as shown in Figure 1-13.

Figure 1-13 *Preshared Keys*

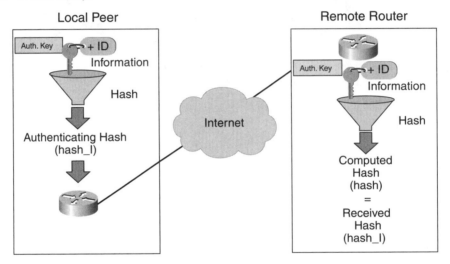

The authentication process continues in the opposite direction. The remote peer combines its identity information with the preshared-based authentication key and sends them through a hash algorithm to form hash_R. hash_R is sent to the local peer. If the local peer can independently create the same hash from its stored information and preshared-based authentication key, the remote peer is authenticated. Each peer must authenticate its opposite peer before the tunnel is considered secure. Preshared keys are easy to configure manually but do not scale well. Each IPSec peer must be configured with the preshared key of every other peer with which it communicates.

RSA Signatures

With RSA signatures (see Figure 1-14), hash_I and hash_R not only are authenticated but also are digitally signed. Starting at the local end, the authentication key and identity information (device-specific information) are sent through a hash algorithm to form hash_I. hash_I is then encrypted using the local peer's private encryption key. The result is a digital signature. The digital signature and a digital certificate are forwarded to the remote peer.

(The public encryption key for decrypting the signature is included in the digital certificate exchanged between peers.)

Figure 1-14 *RSA Signatures*

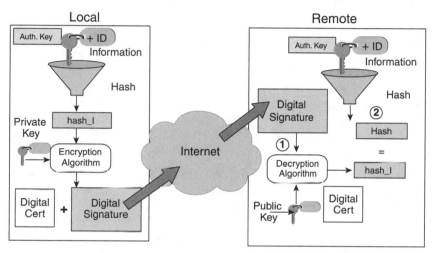

At the remote peer, local peer authentication is a two-step process. First, the remote peer verifies the digital signature by decrypting it using the public encryption key enclosed in the digital certificate. The result is hash_I. Next, the remote peer independently creates hash_I from stored information. If the calculated hash_I equals the decrypted hash_I, the local peer is authenticated (as shown in the figure). Digital signatures and certificates are discussed in more detail in Chapter 5, "Configuring the Cisco VPN 3000 for Remote Access Using Digital Certificates."

After the remote peer authenticates the local peer, the authentication process begins in the opposite direction. The remote peer combines its identity information with the authentication key and sends them through a hash algorithm to form hash_R. hash_R is encrypted using the remote peer's private encryption key—a digital signature. The digital signature and certificate are sent to the local peer. The local peer performs two tasks: It creates hash_R from stored information, and it decrypts the digital signature. If the calculated hash_R and the decrypted hash_R match, the remote peer is authenticated. Each peer must authenticate its opposite peer before the tunnel is considered secure.

RSA Encrypted Nonces

RSA encrypted nonces require that each party generate a nonce—a pseudorandom number. The nonces are then encrypted and exchanged. Upon receipt of the nonce, each end formulates an authentication key made up of the initiator and responder nonces, the DH key, and the initiator and responder cookies. The nonce-based authentication key is combined with device-specific information and run through a hash algorithm, where the output becomes hash_I. The local IKE peer provides one-way authentication by sending hash_I to the remote peer. If the remote peer can independently create the same hash from stored information and its nonce-based authentication key, the local peer is authenticated.

After the remote end authenticates the local peer, the authentication process begins in the opposite direction. The remote peer combines its identity information with the nonce-based authentication key and sends them through a hash algorithm to form hash_R. Hash_R is sent to the local peer. If the local peer can independently create the same hash from stored information and the nonce-based key, the remote peer is authenticated. Each peer must authenticate its opposite peer before the tunnel is considered secure.

Anti-Replay Protection

IPSec uses anti-replay mechanisms to ensure that IP packets cannot be intercepted by a third party or man in the middle and then be changed and reinserted into the data stream. This is implemented in IPSec by the Authentication Header (AH) protocol and the Encapsulating Security Payload (ESP) protocol. The anti-replay mechanism works by keeping track of the sequence number allocated to each packet as it arrives at the VPN endpoint. When a security association is established between two VPN endpoints, the sequence counter is set to 0. The packets that are encrypted and transmitted over the VPN are sequenced starting from 1. Each time a packet is sent, the receiver of the packet verifies that the sequence number is not that of a previously sent packet. If the receiver receives a packet with a duplicate sequence number, the packet is discarded, and an error message is sent back to the transmitting VPN endpoint to log this event.

NOTE AH implements anti-replay by default, although ESP does it only when data authentication is turned on (for example, MD5 or SHA-1) in the IPSec transform-set.

IPSec Protocol Framework

The preceding section discussed encryption, authentication, and integrity. This section explains how encryption, integrity, and authentication are applied to the IPSec protocol suite.

As mentioned, IPSec is a framework of open standards. IPSec spells out the messaging to secure the communications but relies on existing algorithms, such as DES and 3DES, to implement the encryption and authentication. The two main IPSec framework protocols are as follows:

- **AH**—AH, shown in Figure 1-15, is the appropriate protocol when confidentiality is not required or permitted. It provides data authentication and integrity for IP packets passed between two systems. It is a means of verifying that any message passed from

Router A to Router B was not modified during transit. It verifies that the data's origin was either Router A or Router B. AH does not provide data confidentiality (encryption) of packets. It does the following:

— Ensures data integrity

— Provides origin authentication (ensures that packets definitely came from the peer router)

— Uses a keyed-hash mechanism

— Does not provide confidentiality (no encryption)

— Provides anti-replay protection

All text is transported in the clear.

Figure 1-15 *AH*

Router A   Router B

All data in clear text

• Ensures data integrity.
• Provides origin authentication (ensures
  packets definitely came from peer router).
• Uses keyed-hash mechanism.
• Does not provide confidentiality (no encryption).
• Provides anti-replay protection.

• **ESP**—A security protocol may be used to provide confidentiality (encryption) and authentication. ESP, shown in Figure 1-16, provides confidentiality by performing encryption at the IP packet layer. IP packet encryption conceals the data payload and the identities of the ultimate source and destination. ESP provides authentication for the inner IP packet and ESP header. Authentication provides data origin authentication and data integrity. Although both encryption and authentication are optional in ESP, at a minimum, one of them must be selected. ESP provides

— Data confidentiality (encryption)

— Data integrity

— Data origin authentication

— Anti-replay protection

Figure 1-16   *ESP*

• Data confidentiality (encryption).
• Data integrity.
• Data origin authentication.
• Anti-replay protection.

AH

Authentication is achieved by applying a keyed one-way hash function to the packet to create a hash or message digest. The hash is combined with the text and is transmitted. Changes in any part of the packet that occur during transit are detected by the receiver when it performs the same one-way hash function on the received packet and compares the value of the message digest the sender has supplied. The fact that the one-way hash also involves the use of a symmetric key between the two systems means that authenticity is guaranteed.

The AH function is applied to the entire datagram, except for any mutable IP header fields that change in transit (such as Time To Live [TTL] fields that are modified by the routers along the transmission path). AH works as follows:

   1 The IP header and data payload are hashed.

   2 The hash is used to build an AH header, which is inserted into the original packet.

   3 The new packet is transmitted to the IPSec peer router.

   4 The peer router hashes the IP header and data payload.

   5 The peer router extracts the transmitted hash from the AH header.

   6 The peer router compares the two hashes. The hashes must exactly match. Even if one bit is changed in the transmitted packet, the hash output on the received packet changes, and the AH header does not match.

AH supports the HMAC-MD5 and HMAC-SHA-1 algorithms. AH authentication and integrity are shown in Figure 1-17.

Figure 1-17 *AH Authentication and Integrity*

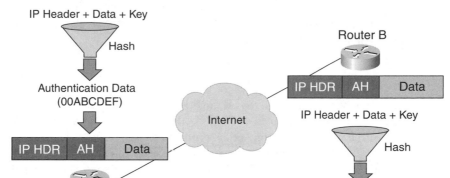

NOTE AH is IP protocol 51. If you are using IPSec, ensure that any perimeter routers will pass IP protocol 51 as well as Internet Security Association and Key Management Protocol (ISAKMP)—that is, UDP port 500.

ESP

ESP, shown in Figure 1-18, provides confidentiality by encrypting the payload. It supports a variety of symmetric encryption algorithms. The default algorithm for IPSec is 56-bit DES. Cisco products also support the use of 3DES and AES for stronger encryption.

Figure 1-18 *ESP Protocol*

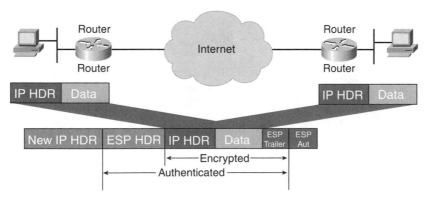

ESP can be used alone or in combination with AH. ESP with AH also provides integrity and authentication of datagrams. First, the payload is encrypted. Next, the encrypted payload is sent through a hash algorithm—HMAC-MD5 or HMAC-SHA-1. The hash provides origin authentication and data integrity for the data payload.

Alternatively, ESP may also enforce anti-replay protection by requiring that a receiving host set the replay bit in the header to indicate that the packet has been seen.

Between two security gateways, the original payload is well protected, because the entire original IP datagram is encrypted. An ESP header and trailer are added to the encrypted payload. With ESP authentication, the encrypted IP datagram and the ESP header or trailer are included in the hashing process. Last, a new IP header is appended to the front of the authenticated payload. The new IP address is used to route the packet through the Internet.

When both ESP authentication and encryption are selected, encryption is performed before authentication. One reason for this order of processing is that it facilitates rapid detection and rejection of replayed or bogus packets by the receiving node. Before decrypting the packet, the receiver can authenticate inbound packets. By doing this, it can detect the problems and potentially reduce the impact of DoS attacks.

NOTE   ESP is IP protocol 50. If you are using IPSec, ensure that any perimeter routers pass IP protocol 50 as well as ISAKMP—that is, UDP port 500.

Modes of Operation

ESP and AH can be applied to IP packets in two different ways, or modes:

- Transport mode
- Tunnel mode

Transport Mode

Transport mode, shown in Figure 1-19, protects the packet's payload, higher-layer protocols, but leaves the original IP address in the clear. The original IP address is used to route the packet through the Internet. ESP transport mode is used between two hosts. Transport mode provides security to the higher-layer protocols only.

Figure 1-19 *Transport Mode*

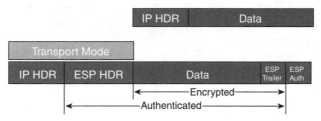

Tunnel Mode

ESP tunnel mode, shown in Figure 1-20, is used when either end of the tunnel is a security gateway, a Concentrator, a VPN optimized router, or a PIX Firewall. Tunnel mode is used when the final destination is not a host, but a VPN gateway. The security gateway encrypts and authenticates the original IP packet. Next, a new IP header is appended to the front of the encrypted packet. The new outside IP address is used to route the packet through the Internet to the remote end security gateway. Tunnel mode provides security for the whole original IP packet.

Figure 1-20 *Tunnel Mode*

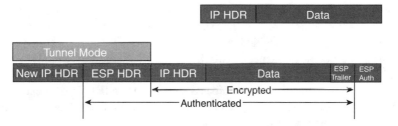

How IPSec Works

The goal of IPSec is to protect the desired data with the needed security services. IPSec's operation can be broken into five primary steps:

Step 1   **Define interesting traffic**—Traffic is deemed interesting when the VPN device recognizes that the traffic you want to send needs to be protected.

Step 2   **IKE Phase 1**—Between peers, a basic set of security services is negotiated and agreed on. This basic set of security services protects all subsequent communications between the peers. IKE Phase 1 sets up a secure communications channel between peers.

Step 3   **IKE Phase 2**—IKE negotiates IPSec security association (SA) parameters and sets up matching IPSec SAs in the peers. These security
parameters are used to protect data and messages exchanged between
endpoints.

Step 4   **Data transfer**—Data is transferred between IPSec peers based on the
IPSec parameters and keys stored in the SA database.

Step 5   **IPSec tunnel termination**—IPSec SAs terminate through deletion or by
timing out.

Step 1: Define Interesting Traffic

Determining what traffic needs to be protected is done as part of formulating a security
policy for use of a VPN. The policy is used to determine what traffic needs to be protected
and what traffic can be sent in the clear. For every inbound and outbound packet, you have
three choices:

- Apply IPSec
- Bypass IPSec
- Discard the packet

For every packet protected by IPSec, the system administrator must specify the security
services applied to the packet. The security policy database specifies the IPSec protocols,
modes, and algorithms applied to the traffic. The services are then applied to traffic destined
for each particular IPSec peer. With the VPN Client, you use menu windows to select
connections you want secured by IPSec. When interesting traffic transits the IPSec client, the
client initiates the next step in the process: negotiating an IKE Phase 1 exchange. Figure 1-21
shows two routers with Host A and Host B at either end. You have to decide whether to
encrypt, not encrypt, or drop the packets.

Figure 1-21   *Step 1: Define Interesting Traffic*

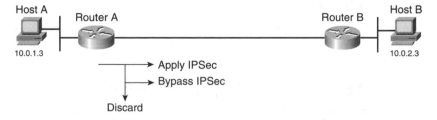

Step 2: IKE Phase 1

The basic purpose of IKE Phase 1, shown in Figure 1-22, is to negotiate IKE policy sets, authenticate the peers, and set up a secure channel between the peers. IKE Phase 1 occurs in two modes: main mode and aggressive mode.

Figure 1-22 *Step 2: IKE Phase 1*

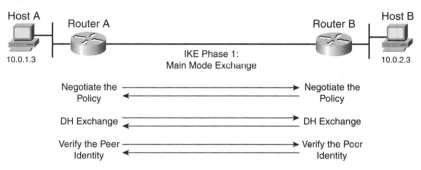

Main mode has three two-way exchanges between the initiator and receiver:

- **First exchange**—The algorithms and hashes used to secure the IKE communications are negotiated and agreed on between peers.

- **Second exchange**—Uses a DH exchange to generate shared secret keys and to pass nonces, which are random numbers sent to the other party, signed, and returned to prove their identity. The shared secret key is used to generate all the other encryption and authentication keys.

- **Third exchange**—Verifies the other side's identity. It is used to authenticate the remote peer. The main outcome of main mode is a secure communication path for subsequent exchanges between the peers. Without proper authentication, it is possible to establish a secure communication channel with a hacker who is now stealing all your sensitive material.

In aggressive mode, fewer exchanges are done and with fewer packets. On the first exchange, almost everything is squeezed in: the IKE policy set negotiation; the DH public key generation; a nonce, which the other party signs; and an identity packet, which can be used to verify the identity via a third party. The receiver sends everything back that is needed to complete the exchange. The only thing left is for the initiator to confirm the exchange.

When trying to make a secure connection between Host A and B through the Internet, IKE security proposals are exchanged between Routers A and B. The proposals identify the IPSec protocol being negotiated (for example, ESP). Under each proposal, the originator must delineate which algorithms are employed in the proposal (for example, DES with MD5). Rather than negotiate each algorithm individually, the algorithms are grouped into IKE transform sets. A transform set delineates which encryption algorithm, authentication algorithm, mode, and key length are proposed. These IKE proposals and transform sets are exchanged during the IKE main mode first exchange phase. If a transform set match is found between peers, the main mode continues. If no match is found, the tunnel is torn down.

In Figure 1-23, Router A sends IKE transform sets 10 and 20 to Router B. Router B compares its set, transform set 15, with those received from Router A. In this instance, a match occurs: Router A's transform set 10 matches Router B's transform set 15.

Figure 1-23 *Step 2: IKE Transform Sets*

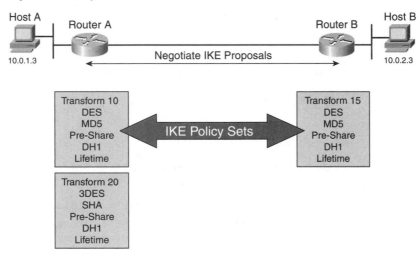

• Negotiates matching IKE transform sets to protect IKE exchange

In a point-to-point application, each end might need only a single IKE policy set defined. However, in a hub-and-spoke environment, the central site might require multiple IKE policy sets to satisfy all the remote peers.

Step 3: IKE Phase 2

The purpose of IKE Phase 2 is to negotiate the IPSec security parameters that are applied to the interesting traffic traversing the tunnel negotiated during Phase 1. IKE Phase 2 performs the following functions:

- Negotiates IPSec security parameters and IPSec transform sets

- Establishes IPSec SAs

- Periodically renegotiates IPSec SAs to ensure security

- Optionally performs an additional DH exchange

IKE Phase 2 has one mode—quick mode. Quick mode occurs after IKE has established the secure tunnel in Phase 1. It negotiates a shared IPSec transform, derives shared secret keying material used for the IPSec security algorithms, and establishes IPSec SAs. Quick mode exchanges nonces that are used to generate new shared secret key material and to prevent replay attacks from generating bogus SAs.

Quick mode is used to renegotiate a new IPSec SA when the IPSec SA lifetime expires. It's also used to refresh the keying material used to create the shared secret key based on the keying material derived from the DH exchange in Phase 1. Figure 1-24 shows the negotiation of IPSec parameters between Router A and Router B.

Figure 1-24   *Step 3: IKE Phase 2*

The ultimate goal of IKE Phase 2 is to establish a secure IPSec session between endpoints. Before that can happen, each pair of endpoints negotiates the level of security required (for example, encryption and authentication algorithms for the session). Rather than negotiate each protocol individually, the protocols are grouped into IPSec transform sets. IPSec transform sets are exchanged between peers during quick mode. If a match is found between sets, IPSec session establishment continues. If no match is found, the session is torn down.

In Figure 1-25, Router A sends IPSec transform sets 30 and 40 to Router B. Router B compares its set, transform set 55, with those received from Router A. In this instance, a match occurs. Router A's transform set 30 matches Router B's transform set 55. These encryption and authentication algorithms form an SA.

When the peers agree on the security services, each VPN peer device enters the information in a security policy database (SPD). The information includes the encryption and authentication algorithm, destination IP address, transport mode, key lifetime, and so on. This information is the SA—a one-way logical connection that provides security to all traffic traversing the connection. Because most traffic is bidirectional, two SAs are required: one for inbound traffic, and one for outbound traffic. The VPN device indexes the SA with a number, a Security Parameter Index (SPI). Rather than send the SA's individual parameters across the tunnel, the source gateway, or host, inserts the SPI into the ESP header. When the IPSec peer receives the packet, it looks up the destination IP address, IPSec protocol, and SPI in its SA database (SAD) and then processes the packet according to the algorithms listed under the SPD.

Figure 1-25 *Step 3: IPSec Transform Sets*

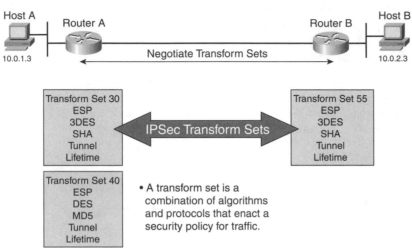

The IPSec SA is a compilation of the SAD and SPD. The SAD identifies the SA destination IP address, IPSec protocol, and SPI number. The SPD defines the security services applied to the SA, encryption and authentication algorithms, and mode and key lifetime. For example, in the corporate-to-bank connection shown in Figure 1-26, the security policy provides a very secure tunnel using 3DES, SHA, tunnel mode, and a key lifetime of 28,800. The SAD value is 192.168.2.1, ESP, and SPI-12. For the remote user accessing e-mails, a less secure policy is negotiated using DES, MD5, tunnel mode, and a key lifetime of 28,800. The SAD values are a destination IP address of 192.169.12.1, ESP, and SPI-39.

With a password on your company PC, the longer you keep it, the more vulnerable it becomes. The same thing is true of keys and SAs. For good security, the SA and keys should be changed periodically. There are two parameters: lifetime type and duration. How is the lifetime measured? Is it measured by the number of bytes transmitted or the amount of time transpired? The second parameter is the unit of measure: kilobytes of data or seconds of time. An example is a lifetime based on 10,000 KB of data transmitted or 28,800 seconds of time expired. The keys and SAs remain active until their lifetime expires or until an external event—such as the client dropping the tunnel—causes them to be deleted.

Figure 1-26   *Step 3: SA*

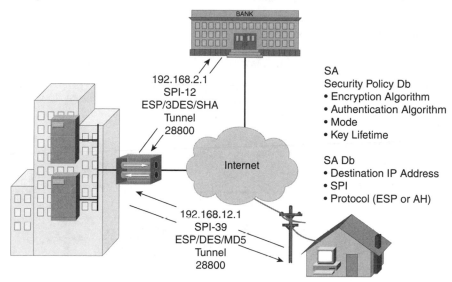

Step 4: Data Transfer

After IKE Phase 2 is complete and quick mode has established IPSec SAs, traffic is exchanged between Hosts A and B via a secure tunnel, as shown in Figure 1-27. Interesting traffic is encrypted and decrypted according to the security services specified in the IPSec SA.

Figure 1-27   *Step 4: IPSec Data Transfer*

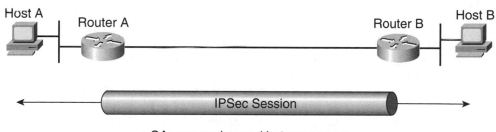

Step 5: IPSec Tunnel Termination

IPSec SAs terminate through deletion or by timing out. An SA can time out when a specified number of seconds has elapsed or when a specified number of bytes has passed through the tunnel. When the SAs terminate, the keys are also discarded. When subsequent IPSec SAs are needed for a flow, IKE performs a new Phase 2 (and, if necessary, a new Phase 1) negotiation. A successful negotiation results in new SAs and new keys. New SAs are usually established before the existing SAs expire so that a given flow can continue uninterrupted. This final step is shown in Figure 1-28.

Figure 1-28 *Step 5: IPSec Tunnel Termination*

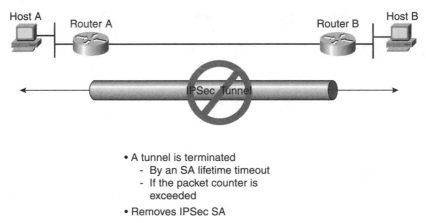

- A tunnel is terminated
  - By an SA lifetime timeout
  - If the packet counter is exceeded
- Removes IPSec SA

Summary

This chapter provided a technology overview that is the foundation of the rest of this book. It started by looking at network security before providing a brief overview of the AVVID program and the Cisco SAFE security blueprint. It then looked at IPSec and the components that make up this framework. There is quite a lot to IPSec, and quite a few permutations can be used, such as encryption and authentication algorithms. This chapter covered each of these options and finished by looking at the five important steps in how IPSec is implemented in all Cisco devices. The next chapters build on this information and delve more into the configuration aspects of VPNs for the Cisco VPN 3000 Concentrator range of products.

Review Questions

The following questions test your retention of the material presented in this chapter. The answers appear in Appendix A, "Answers to Chapter Review Questions."

1 What two main protocols make up the IPSec framework?

2 What IP protocol does ESP use?

3 What are the two modes of IKE Phase 1?

4 What three key lengths can AES currently use?

5 What type of VPN would you be using if you are a user based at home connecting to the central site over a VPN by using a VPN Software Client installed on your laptop computer?

6 What are the four steps of the Security Wheel?

7 What is the normal method of key exchange for the encryption algorithms used in IPSec, such as DES, 3DES, and AES?

8 What is the main issue with firewall-based VPNs?

9 What are the two modes of IPSec operation?

10 What three authentication methods are used in the IPSec protocol's origin identification feature?

After completing this chapter, you will be able to perform the following tasks:

- Identify the model series that makes up the VPN Concentrator range
- Understand the differences between the various models of the VPN 3000 Concentrator
- Understand the differing VPN Clients that operate with the VPN 3000 Concentrator
- Identify the placement options within your network for the VPN 3000 Concentrator

CHAPTER 2

Cisco VPN 3000 Concentrator Series Hardware Overview

The first chapter provided a technical overview of virtual private networks (VPNs) and focused on IPSec as a VPN technology. This chapter provides an overview of the Cisco VPN Concentrator family of products. In January 2000, Cisco bought Altiga Networks. With this acquisition came the new VPN Concentrator product range. The VPN Concentrator is a relatively new product from Cisco Systems. This chapter covers the Cisco VPN 3000 Concentrator Series. It describes the Cisco VPN 3000 Concentrator Series models and details the major features and functions of the hardware.

Cisco VPN 3000 Concentrator Series Models

The Cisco VPN 3000 Concentrator Series provides products that cover the entire spectrum of customer VPN applications. The following models are available:

- 3005
- 3015
- 3020
- 3030
- 3060
- 3080

Table 2-1 compares the features of all the models in the VPN 3000 range. You can use it to determine which model is best for your environment. The top row lists the five models in the Concentrator family. The left column lists some of the Concentrator's features.

NOTE   The following details are based on the 4.1 release of the Concentrator OS. Before 4.1, the simultaneous users on VPNs 3005 and 3015 was only 100.

Table 2-1   *Concentrator Product Comparison*

Feature	3005	3015	3020	3030	3060	3080
Height	1U	2U	2U	2U	2U	2U
Performance	4 Mbps	4 Mbps	50 Mbps	50 Mbps	100 Mbps	100 Mbps
Simultaneous users	200	200	750	1500	5000	10,000
Site-to-site tunnels	100	100	500	500	1000	1000
Encryption	Software	Software	Hardware	Hardware	Hardware	Hardware
Memory	32 MB	64 MB	128 MB	128 MB	256 MB	256 MB
Power supplies	1	Up to 2	1	Up to 2	2	2
SEP/SEP-E modules	0	0	1	1	2	4
Upgradable	No	Yes	No	Yes	Yes	Yes

NOTE   For planning purposes, a simultaneous user is considered to be a remote-access VPN user connected in all tunneling modes. A session includes one Internet Key Exchange (IKE) security association (SA) and two unidirectional IP Security (IPSec) SAs. For environments with rekeying or split tunneling, using a VPN remote-access load-balancing environment with spare capacity is recommended, because these particular sessions use additional system resources that otherwise would be used to support additional users. In mixed environments where a Concentrator must support both remote-access and site-to-site tunnels, the site-to-site tunnel count is subtracted from the overall simultaneous user capability. For example, a 3060, which has 50 site-to-site tunnels, cannot exceed 4950 remote-access sessions.

As you can see from Table 2-1, the main difference between the various models, apart from the initial chassis differences between the 3005 and 3015, is the use of software- or hardware-based encryption. The 3005 supports only software encryption, because the chassis does not have any capability for hardware encryption modules.

Hardware encryption is performed by the Scalable Encryption Processor (SEP). Its hardware-based encryption module lets you offload processor-intensive Data Encryption Standard (DES) and Triple DES (3DES) encryption tasks to hardware.

A newer SEP called SEP-E is now available. SEP-E is supported in version 4.0 of the 3000 Concentrator code and performs Advanced Encryption Standard (AES) hardware encryption.

The following features are supported:

- Digital Signal Processor (DSP)-based hardware encryption
  - SEP is based on Analog Devices' DSP encryption engine
  - Encryption or decryption is offloaded to DSP-based hardware
  - DSP can be reprogrammed as existing standards change and new standards emerge
  - DES and 3DES encryption and AES encryption with the SEP-E
- Performance—Can support up to 100 Mbps of encrypted throughput at wire speed

Concentrator models 3015 and above can contain up to four SEP modules for maximum system throughput and redundancy. Two SEP modules are online, and the other two SEP modules are hot-running spares. These additional modules provide redundancy in case of module failure.

SEP redundancy requires no configuration. It is always enabled and completely automatic; no operator intervention is required.

Redundancy is from top to bottom, which is called a column. If the top SEP fails, the bottom SEP takes over. The Concentrator automatically switches all the active sessions to the redundant SEP. No sessions are lost.

If both SEPs in a column fail, the sessions are handled by the SEPs in the other column. In this scenario, sessions are lost, and the users need to reestablish their sessions.

The following sections look at each model in the VPN 3000 Concentrator range and identify the features of each.

VPN 3005 Concentrator

The following hardware features are supported on the Cisco VPN 3005 Concentrator:

- Height—1U
- Memory—32 MB SRAM, which is standard
- Encryption—Software-based: DES, 3DES, and AES encryption
- Scalability—Up to 100 simultaneous sessions
- Network interface
  - Two auto-sensing, full-duplex 10/100BASE-T Ethernet interfaces
  - The public interface connects to the Internet
  - The private interface connects to the private corporate network
- Power supply—AC operates at 100–240 V and 50/60 Hz with universal power factor correction

- Hardware—Not upgradable
- Software—Upgradable

Figure 2-1 shows a VPN 3005 Concentrator rear panel with the public and private interfaces marked.

Figure 2-1   *Cisco VPN 3005 Concentrator*

VPN 3015 Concentrator

The following hardware features are supported on the Cisco VPN 3015 Concentrator:

- Memory—64 MB SRAM, which is the standard
- Encryption—Software-based: DES, 3DES, and AES encryption
- Scalability—Up to 100 simultaneous remote connections
- Network interface
    - Three auto-sensing, full-duplex 10/100BASE-T Ethernet interfaces
    - The public interface connects to the Internet
    - The private interface connects to the private corporate network
    - The external interface connects to the DMZ
- Power supply
    - AC operates at 100–240 V and 50/60 Hz with universal power factor correction
    - Replaceable power supply
- Upgradable

Figure 2-2 shows the VPN 3015 Concentrator rear panel with the three interfaces marked.

Figure 2-2   *Cisco VPN 3015 Concentrator*

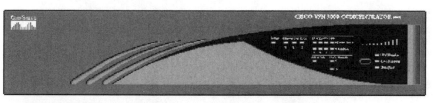

SEP Modules

T1/E1 Modules

10/100 Ethernet

100–240 V Power Supplies
Load Sharing

Private Public External

VPN 3020 Concentrator

The following hardware features are supported on the Cisco VPN 3020 Concentrator:

- Memory—128 MB SRAM, which is the standard
- Encryption—Hardware-based: DES, 3DES, and AES encryption
- Scalability—Up to 750 simultaneous remote connections
- Network interface
  - Three auto-sensing, full duplex 10/100BaseT Ethernet interfaces
  - The public interface connects to the Internet
  - The private interface connects to the private corporate network
  - The external interface connects to the DMZ
- Power supply
  - AC operates at 100–240 V and 50/60 Hz with universal power factor correction
  - Replaceable power supply
- Hardware—Not Upgradable

Figure 2-3 shows the VPN 3020 Concentrator rear panel with the three interfaces marked.

Figure 2-3   *Cisco VPN 3020 Concentrator*

SEP Modules

T1/E1 Modules

10/100 Ethernet

100–240 V Power Supplies   Private Public External
Load Sharing

VPN 3030 Concentrator

The following hardware features are supported on the Cisco VPN 3030 Concentrator:

- Memory—128 MB SRAM, which is the standard
- Encryption—Hardware-based encryption
  - SEP2 encryption module
  - Programmable DSP-based security accelerator
  - DES and 3DES encryption
- Encryption—Software-based AES 128, AES 192, and AES 256 encryption
- Scalability
  - Equipped with one SEP2 module
  - Up to 1500 simultaneous remote connections
  - Up to 500 site-to-site tunnels
- Network interface
  - Three auto-sensing, full-duplex 10/100BASE-T Ethernet interfaces
  - The public interface connects to the Internet
  - The private interface connects to the private corporate network
  - The external interface connects to the DMZ

- Power supply
  - AC operates at 100–240 V and 50/60 Hz with universal power factor correction
  - Replaceable power supply
  - Hot-swappable with optional redundant power supply
- Upgradable

Figure 2-4 shows the VPN 3030 Concentrator rear panel with the three interfaces marked. You can see that one SEP module is inserted into the first SEP slot on a 3030.

Figure 2-4   *Cisco VPN 3030 Concentrator*

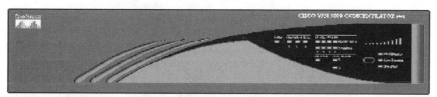

SEP Modules

T1/E1 Modules

10/100 Ethernet

100–240 V Power Supplies
Load Sharing

Private Public External

VPN 3060 Concentrator

The following hardware features are supported on the Cisco VPN 3060 Concentrator:

- Memory—256 MB SRAM, which is the standard
- Encryption—Hardware-based encryption
  - SEP2 encryption module
  - Programmable, DSP-based security accelerator
  - DES and 3DES encryption
- Encryption—Software-based AES 128, AES 192, and AES 256 encryption
- Scalability
  - Equipped with a total of two SEP2 modules
  - Up to 5000 simultaneous remote connections
  - Up to 1000 site-to-site tunnels

- Network interface
  - Three auto-sensing, full-duplex 10/100BASE-T Ethernet interfaces
  - The public interface connects to the Internet
  - The private interface connects to the private corporate network
  - The external interface connects to the DMZ
- Power supply
  - AC operates at 100–240 V and 50/60 Hz with universal power factor correction
  - Standard hot-swappable, redundant power supply
- Upgradable

Figure 2-5 shows a VPN 3060 Concentrator rear panel with the three interfaces marked. You can see that two SEP modules are inserted into the first and second SEP slot on a 3060.

Figure 2-5 *Cisco VPN 3060 Concentrator*

SEP Modules

T1/E1 Modules

10/100 Ethernet

100–240 V Power Supplies
Load Sharing

Private Public External

VPN 3080 Concentrator

The following hardware features are supported on the Cisco VPN 3080 Concentrator:

- Memory—256 MB SRAM, which is the standard
- Encryption—Hardware-based
  - SEP2 encryption module
  - Programmable, DSP-based security accelerator
  - DES and 3DES encryption
- Encryption—Software-based AES 128, AES 192, and AES 256 encryption

- Scalability
  - — Equipped with two active and two inactive SEP2 modules
  - — Up to 10,000 simultaneous remote connections
  - — Up to 1000 site-to-site tunnels
- Network interface
  - — Three auto-sensing, full-duplex 10/100BASE-T Ethernet interfaces
  - — The public interface connects to the Internet
  - — The private interface connects to the private corporate network
  - — The external interface connects to the DMZ
- Power supply
  - — AC operates at 100–240 V and 50/60 Hz with universal power factor correction
  - — Standard hot-swappable, redundant power supply

Figure 2-6 shows a VPN 3080 Concentrator rear panel with the three interfaces marked. You can see that four SEP modules are inserted on a 3080.

Figure 2-6 *Cisco VPN 3080 Concentrator*

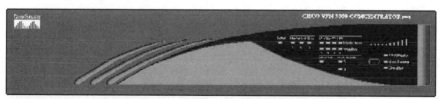

SEP Modules

T1/E1 Modules

10/100 Ethernet

100–240 V Power Supplies
Load Sharing

Private Public External

VPN Clients

Remote-access VPNs rely on a VPN Client to establish and maintain the VPN connection to the VPN Concentrator. VPN Clients can be separated into two main areas—VPN Software Clients and VPN Hardware Clients.

Software Clients

The Cisco VPN Software Client is shipped with every VPN Concentrator with an unlimited license. The Software Client is also called the Cisco Unity Client. The latest release of the Software Client is version 4. Version 4 has a totally new GUI from version 3.5 and includes additional features:

- Virtual adapter
- Common graphical interface for Windows and Macintosh VPN Clients
- Disconnect (with reason information/notification)
- Single IPSec-SA
- Personal firewall enhancements
- Coexistence with third-party VPN vendors
- Improved RADIUS SDI XAuth request handling
- New, ISO-standard format for log filenames

The Software Client is available for the following operating systems and platforms:

- Microsoft Windows (95/98/Me/2000/XP)
- Linux
- Solaris
- Mac OS X

Windows Client

The following are system requirements for the Microsoft Windows Cisco VPN Client:

- Operating system
  - Windows 98 (second edition)
  - Microsoft Windows NT 4.0 running Service Pack 6 or higher
  - Microsoft Windows Me
  - Microsoft Windows 2000
  - Microsoft Windows XP (Cisco VPN Client Release 3.1 or higher)
- Cisco VPN sytem requirements
  - Cisco VPN 3000 Series Concentrator (Release 3.0)
  - PIX Firewall (Release 6.0)
  - IOS 12.2(8)T
- Hard disk space—50 MB

- RAM
    - 32 MB for Microsoft Windows 98
    - 64 MB for Microsoft Windows NT
    - 64 MB for Microsoft Windows Me
    - 64 MB for Microsoft Windows 2000 (128 MB recommended)
    - 128 MB for Microsoft Windows XP (256 MB recommended)

The Cisco VPN Windows Client offers support for a firewall feature. The firewall feature is designed to enhance security for Microsoft Windows-based PCs running the Release 3.5 Cisco IPSec client or later. This feature is applied in one of three modes—Are You There (AYT), stateful firewall (always on), or central policy protection (CPP):

- **AYT**—For security reasons, a network administrator might require remote PCs to be running a firewall application before allowing VPN tunnels to be built. The Are You There feature verifies the presence of a firewall and reports that information back to the Concentrator. Depending on the PC's response, the Concentrator can permit or deny the PC's IPSec tunnel.

- **Stateful firewall (always on)**—The stateful firewall module can be enabled or disabled only by the remote client. With this mode, a default policy is loaded on the firewall. The default firewall filter blocks all inbound traffic (to the client) that is unrelated to an outbound session (from the client). As soon as the user enables the stateful firewall, it is always on, even when there are no established VPN tunnels.

- **CPP**—Lets network administrators define a set of rules (policies) to allow or drop traffic on connected VPN Clients. These policies are pushed from the Concentrator to the Cisco VPN Windows Client at connection time. The VPN Client passes this policy to the firewall module on the client PC. The Concentrator can push policy to the Cisco integrated client firewall and the Zonelabs, Zone Alarm, and Zone Alarm Pro firewall applications. CPP is enforced only while the VPN Client is connected.

Figure 2-7 shows the connection screen from the latest version of the Windows VPN Client.

Figure 2-7 *Windows Cisco VPN Client*

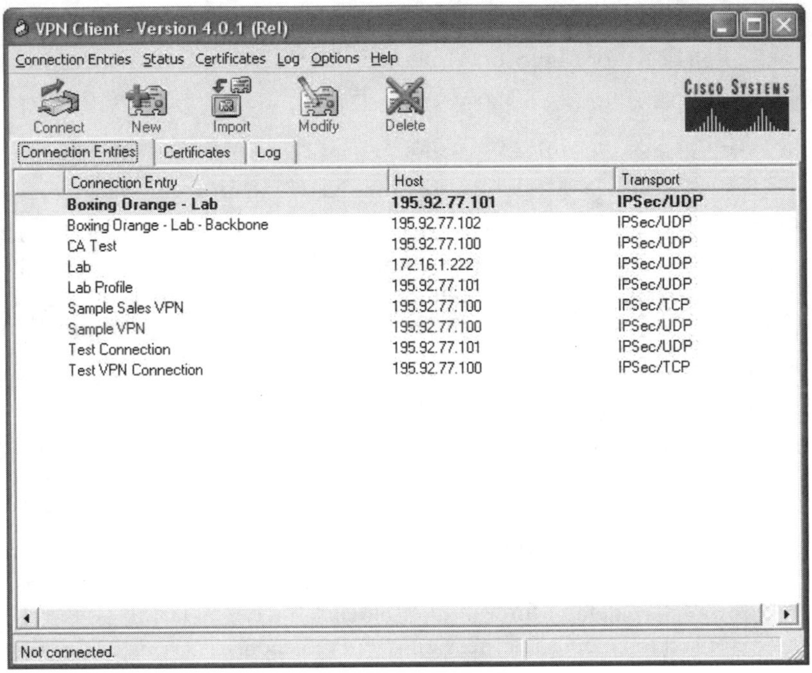

Linux and Solaris Clients

The Cisco VPN Software Client was expanded to include the Linux, Solaris, and Macintosh operating systems. The system requirements for Linux and Solaris client types are as follows:

- Linux
- Red Hat version 6.2 Linux (Intel) or a compatible distribution using kernel version 2.2.12 or later
  - Connection type—PPP and Ethernet
  - Tunneling protocol—IPSec
  - User authentication—RADIUS, RSA SecurID, NT Domain, VPN internal user list, and Public Key Infrastructure (PKI) digital certificates
  - VPN client administration—Command line only
  - 32 MB RAM
  - 50 MB hard disk space

NOTE	The VPN Client does not support Linux kernel version 2.5.

- Solaris UltraSPARC
- Cisco VPN Client Release 4.0 for Solaris: 32-bit or 64-bit kernel OS version 2.6 or later
- Connection type—PPP and Ethernet
- Tunneling protocol—IPSec
- User authentication—RADIUS, RSA SecurID, NT Domain, VPN internal user list, and PKI digital certificates
- VPN client administration—Command line only
- 32 MB RAM
- 50 MB hard disk space

Figure 2-8 shows the connection screen from the Linux/Solaris VPN Client.

Figure 2-8   *Linux/Solaris Cisco VPN Client*

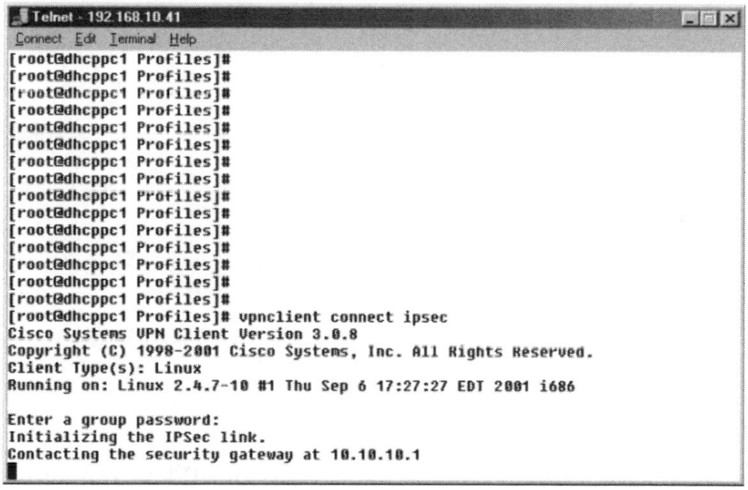

Mac OS Client

In Release 4.0, the Cisco VPN Mac OS X Client supports both a command-line interface (CLI) and a graphical user interface (GUI). The system requirements for the Mac OS X client are as follows:

- Mac OS X version 10.1.0 or later
- Connection type—Ethernet only

- Tunneling protocol—IPSec
- User authentication—RADIUS, RSA SecurID, NT Domain, VPN internal user list, and PKI digital certificates
- VPN client administration—GUI and CLI
- 50 MB hard disk space

The GUI lets the user manage the VPN connections quickly and easily. The management functionality available from the GUI includes the following:

- Certificate management
- Profile management
- Connection management
- Log management

Figure 2-9 shows the connection screen from the Mac OS VPN Client.

Figure 2-9 *Mac OS Cisco VPN Client*

NOTE   As well as the Cisco VPN Client, which supports only IPSec, you can also use any PPTP or L2TP client against a VPN Concentrator.

As well as the Cisco Software Client, you can also obtain a software client from Certicom.

Certicom offers technology through the original equipment manufacturer (OEM) model, embedding security solutions in a wide variety of third-party products. It has implemented an IPSec client called movianVPN to run on cell phones, personal digital assistants (PDAs), and so on. When the devices perform standard IPSec, it is very CPU-intensive. Diffie-Hellman (DH) groups 1 and 2 take minutes to generate a key. Because of this, Certicom developed DH Group 7, Elliptic Curve Cryptography (ECC) support, to provide a key that can be generated in a short time (less than 5 seconds).

You must have the following to use Certicom VPN Client support:

- Certicom VPN Client software
- ECC (DH Group 7) protocol
- Concentrator to terminate an IPSec remote-access tunnel

However, the Certicom client does not support load balancing. Whereas load balancing requires the client to accept and interpret IKE redirect messages, the Certicom client does not support this functionality.

The Certicom client is covered in more detail in Appendix B, "Configuring movianVPN."

Hardware Clients

As well as the Cisco and Certicom software clients, you can also use a hardware client to connect a remote-access VPN to a Cisco VPN Concentrator.

The Cisco VPN 3002 Hardware Client has the Unity Client software built into it, allowing the Hardware Client to emulate the Cisco VPN 3000 Software Client. With the Hardware Client, you can plug remote-site PCs into the Hardware Client instead of having to load the Cisco VPN Client or additional applications on remote-site PCs.

There are two versions of the Hardware Client:

- 3002—One private interface and one public interface
- 3002—8E
    - One public interface, the private interface is a built-in eight-port 10/100BASE-T Ethernet switch that is locked in and cannot be configured.
    - Auto MDIX, which eliminates crossover cables

The Hardware Client has two modes of operation: client mode and network extension. These modes can be configured via the CLI or GUI. They can be remotely managed via IPSec tunnel or secure shell (SSH).

The Hardware Client is powered by an external power supply. It auto-senses the voltage, either 110 V or 220 V.

Figure 2-10 shows a Cisco VPN 3002 hardware client.

Figure 2-10 *Cisco 3002 Hardware Client*

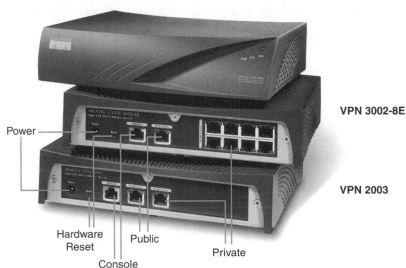

Software Clients Versus Hardware Clients

You can see that both software and hardware clients can be used to establish a remote-access VPN. So how do you know when to use which sort of VPN client? The important thing to remember is that both software and hardware clients use remote-access technologies to connect and establish the VPN. Looking at the connection in VPN Manager on a VPN Concentrator, you will see that the connections are shown as a remote-access VPN.

The main decision comes down to numbers. If you have a remote site with more than three users, it probably would be better to use a hardware client. Remember that the user must initiate the software client when he or she wants to connect to the VPN. The software client also has to be installed and maintained on the user's computer. Any updates have to be managed, and generally a cost is associated with this operation. A hardware client, on the other hand, would cost more initially, because the software client is free. But you have to remember that the VPN connection would then be totally transparent to the user on the remote site. This, coupled with the benefit of not having to maintain and support client software on the user's computer, can make a hardware client much more attractive than a software client.

VPN Concentrator Configuration

The Concentrator supports two configuration options: CLI through a terminal application and GUI through a web browser. For you to use these options, they have to be configured correctly.

For the CLI configuration option, you have to use a straight-through console cable, not a rollover cable as used in other Cisco devices. Connect to the terminal, and set the following:

- Data bits—8
- Parity—N
- Stop bits—1
- Speed—9600

The web interface supports both HTTP and HTTP over Secure Socket Layer (SSL). Operators can use either Internet Explorer or Netscape Navigator. With Internet Explorer and Netscape Navigator, the software revisions must be 4.0 or higher, with both cookies and Java scripts enabled. Use either browser to configure the Concentrator—with one exception: Internet Explorer must be used when programming digital certificates.

Figure 2-11 shows the CLI configuration, and Figure 2-12 shows an example of configuring a VPN 3002 Hardware Client through the GUI.

Figure 2-11 *CLI-Based Administration*

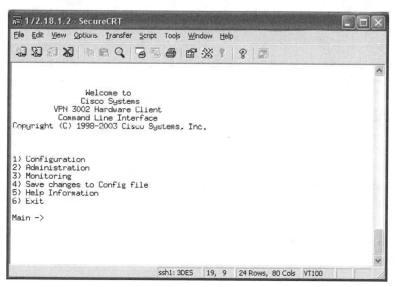

Figure 2-12 *GUI-Based Administration*

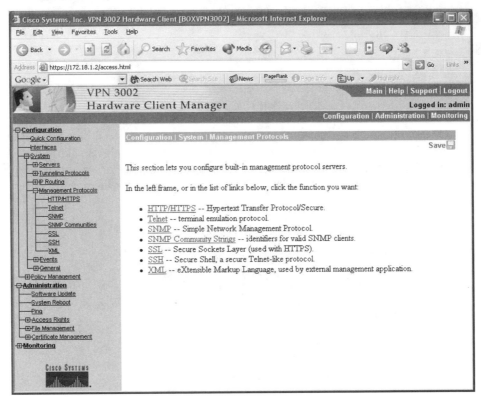

Note that this connection was made using SSH. The VPN 3002 supports SSH- and Telnet-based administration. Only SSH is supported on the public interface for security reasons.

NOTE   The 3002 GUI and the 3005 through 3080 GUI look pretty much the same. Each model just has different configuration options.

VPN Concentrator Placement

The VPN Concentrator is a device that can be placed in numerous locations within a network. The primary purpose of a VPN Concentrator is to provide access to remote users by providing a remote-access VPN. The secondary function of a VPN Concentrator is to provide LAN-to-LAN connectivity by using a LAN-to-LAN VPN tunnel.

The VPN Concentrator has four common placement positions:

- In front of or without a firewall
- Behind a firewall
- In parallel with a firewall
- On a DMZ

In Front of or Without a Firewall

Placing a VPN Concentrator in front of a firewall provides an extra layer of security. The VPN Concentrator itself can be classed as a firewall device because of the rules that can be created and applied to filters on the Concentrator's interfaces. This is a useful scenario when you're configuring a remote-access VPN over the Internet, where the local site does not require external Internet access. It is important to remember that in this option, the Concentrator is in the data path, and all outbound traffic traverses the Concentrator.

This design option is shown in Figure 2-13.

Figure 2-13   *In Front of or Without a Firewall*

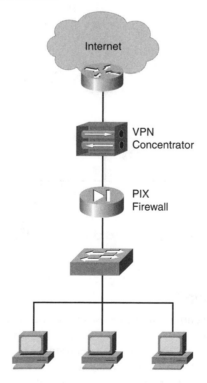

Behind a Firewall

By placing the Concentrator behind a firewall, you are using the Internet-facing firewall as the first line of defense. All traffic getting though the firewall still has to traverse the VPN Concentrator, because the VPN Concentrator is in the data path. In this instance, for remote-access VPN connections to work, you would have to allow IKE and ESP/AH traffic through the external firewall from any source address. This is because you do not know the source IP address that the remote-access clients will use when they initiate their remote-access VPN connections.

This design option is shown in Figure 2-14.

Figure 2-14   *Behind a Firewall*

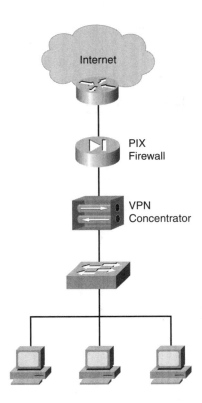

In Parallel with a Firewall

Placing a VPN Concentrator in parallel with a firewall is the preferred configuration option. It's also the option of choice in the Cisco SAFE whitepaper for the enterprise and also the SAFE VPN whitepaper. Placing the Concentrator in parallel with the external firewall has a few advantages. Both the Concentrator and firewall are public-facing, so both must be publicly addressed and routable. In this scenario, the Concentrator is not in the data path.

The remote-access VPN clients use the Concentrator's public address and connect directly to it without having to go through a firewall or another access-limiting device.

After the VPN users are connected, they are still presented as an external entity to the firewall. This means that you can limit the resources that the users can and cannot see based on a single security policy implemented in the firewall.

This design option is shown in Figure 2-15.

Figure 2-15 *In Parallel with a Firewall*

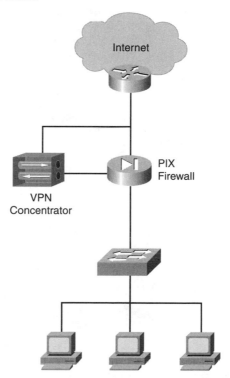

On a DMZ

Placing a VPN Concentrator on a DMZ is the last placement option.

In this instance, for remote-access VPN connections to work, you would have to allow IKE and ESP/AH traffic through the external firewall from any source address. This is because you do not know the source IP address that the remote-access clients will use when they initiate their remote-access VPN connections.

The advantage of this type of design is that the Concentrator is not in the data path. Only VPN connections are permitted to the Concentrator. The downside of this placement is that the private interface of the Concentrator connects directly to the inside network. Therefore, security has to be implemented in the Concentrator to restrict access. This creates two devices on which the access-limiting configuration has to be carried out.

This design option is shown in Figure 2-16.

Figure 2-16 *On a DMZ*

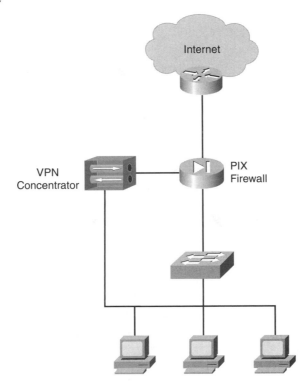

Network Management Solutions

Various Cisco network management options are available to the administrator, including Simple Network Management Protocol (SNMP) monitoring, Syslog monitoring, and Cisco VPN 3000 Concentrator Series configuration. The solutions range from small to large networks and from general network to security-specific management platforms. The following Cisco platforms can monitor and manage the Concentrator:

- **Cisco Info Center (CIC)**—A service-level alarm monitoring and diagnostics tool that provides network fault and performance monitoring, network trouble isolation, and real-time service-level management for large networks. CIC is designed to help operators focus on important network events, offering a combination of alarm processing rules, filtering, customizable alarm viewing, and partitioning. CIC can support administrative VPNs among several Network Operations Centers (NOCs). In some networks, provincial or regional NOCs require a partial view of the network as a local network segment to facilitate local problem detection and resolution. Regional NOCs also might require a localized topological view of the local network portion. Global NOCs support regional NOCs from a central location and provide a view of the entire network and global fault monitoring. CIC focuses on fault monitoring.

- **Cisco View**—A universal graphic device management application that provides real-time display and monitoring of Cisco routers, switches, hubs, concentrators, and access servers. Cisco View plugs into third-party SNMP management platforms such as HP OpenView, NetView, Whats Up Gold, and Snmpc. The Cisco View application supports graphical views of the chassis, device performance information, top ten lists, system summary, session summary (Active, Max, Total), and routing table of Cisco devices. Cisco View runs on Windows NT and Solaris. Cisco View is a general management application.

- **Cisco Works**—Comprised of multiple software applications. Two of these applications are the Cisco VPN Monitor and the Cisco Resource Manager Essentials:

  - **Cisco Resource Manager Essentials**—A suite of web-based applications offering network management solutions for Cisco switches, access servers, routers, and Concentrators (NT- and Solaris-based). It supports the ability to collect detailed inventory, collect and report on syslog messages, generate inventory reports (hardware, software, system info), and distribute software to all Concentrators in the network.

  - **Cisco VPN Monitor**—A web-based management tool that allows network administrators to collect, store, and view information on IPSec VPN connections for remote-access or site-to-site VPN terminations. Cisco VPN Monitor manages VPNs that are configured on Cisco VPN 3000 series Concentrators; VPN series routers; and Cisco 7100, 1700, 2600, 3600, and 7200 series routers. Operational status, performance, and security information can be viewed at a glance, providing status information on IPSec VPN implementations.

- **Cisco IP Solution Center Security Management (IPSCSM)**—Offers IPSec and Multiprotocol Label Switching (MPLS) IP VPN service providers a customizable service and network layer FCAPS (fault, configuration management, accounting, performance, security) management solution to facilitate rapid IP VPN service deployment and to reduce ongoing operational costs.

  - Provisioning IPSec tunnels between Cisco devices—Cisco IOS software devices, Cisco VPN Concentrators, and Cisco PIX Firewalls

  - Provisioning IPSec remote-access services by configuring Cisco IOS software devices and VPN Concentrators

  - This might not be supported by all Cisco IOS software releases

Summary

This chapter provided details about the Cisco VPN Concentrator range of products. It started by looking at the Cisco VPN Concentrator and the differences between the capabilities of the various models. It then moved on to the two main types of VPN Clients, software and hardware, giving breakdowns of each type and the products available. This chapter concluded with a look at the available methods of configuration and network management for the VPN Concentrator range of products.

Review Questions

The following questions test your retention of the material presented in this chapter. The answers appear in Appendix A, "Answers to the Review Questions."

1 Which model of the VPN Concentrator is not hardware-upgradable to use hardware-based encryption?

2 Which encryption protocols can the older SEP encrypt in hardware?

3 Which software VPN client would you use to connect a PDA such as an HP Ipaq to your VPN?

4 Which three modes can the Windows VPN Client Firewall operate in?

5 If you had a small branch office that wanted an upgradable VPN solution for up to 100 users at any one time, which model of the VPN Concentrator 3000 series would you choose?

6 How many site-to-site tunnels are supported on a Cisco VPN 3030 Concentrator?

7 If you required a VPN Concentrator that could terminate 7500 IPSec tunnels, which model(s) could you use?

8 What is the difference between the two models of the 3002 Hardware VPN Client?

9 What is the highest specification model in the VPN 3000 Concentrator series?

10 What operating systems does the current Cisco VPN Unity Client support?

After completing this chapter, you will be able to perform the following tasks:

- Understand the routing options on the Cisco VPN Concentrator
- Configure static routing on a VPN Concentrator
- Enable a static route
- Enable a static default route
- Configure dynamic routing on a VPN Concentrator
- Understand the differences between RIP and OSPF on a VPN Concentrator

CHAPTER 3

Routing on the VPN 3000

This chapter covers the routing functionality of the Virtual Private Network (VPN) Concentrator. Unless your network is very small, you probably will be involved in configuring routing of some sort on the Concentrator. The Concentrator supports both static and dynamic routing. For dynamic routing, the Concentrator supports Routing Information Protocol (RIP) and Open Shortest Path First (OSPF). We will start by providing an overview of routing on the Concentrator. We will look at static routing and how to configure static routes and also the default route on the Concentrator. We will then move on to dynamic routing and cover the basics of RIP and OSPF and show how they are configured on the Concentrator. We will be using a sample VPN network throughout this chapter and refer to it in all sections. We will show you how to add a route to make a remote network visible to remote-access VPN users.

Routing Capabilities of the VPN Concentrator

The Cisco VPN 3000 Concentrator operates as an OSI Layer 3 routing device and therefore must learn routing information to route packets to other destination networks. All the interfaces on a Concentrator must have an IP address that exists on a Layer 3 that is separate from the other interfaces. Most deployments of a VPN Concentrator at a minimum provide remote-access VPN connectivity to remote users who connect over the public Internet. This instantly brings about a requirement for routing, because you do not know what source IP address the remote clients will be coming from. So, in its default form, the Concentrator does not have a route back to the remote clients. This means that the connection attempt instantly fails. The Concentrator supports both static and dynamic routing.

Static Routing

Static routing is the simplest form of routing, because the information is manually entered into the Concentrator. You enter information about the destination network and provide a next-hop gateway, where the traffic has to be sent to reach the remote network.

You can enter two types of static routes into the Concentrator—a normal static route and a default static route (also called just the default route). The default route is the destination of last resort, meaning that if no more-specific route exists in the routing table, all packets are forwarded to this address. It is normal to have a default route pointing to the ISP Internet router on a Concentrator's public interface.

Figure 3-1 shows a sample network with a VPN Concentrator.

Figure 3-1   *Sample VPN Network*

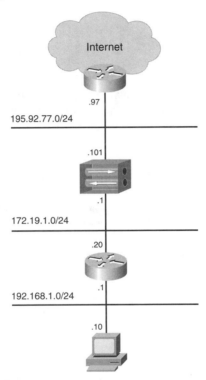

Figure 3-1 shows a VPN Concentrator that is connected to the 172.19.1.0/24 network. The IP address of the Concentrator's private interface is 172.19.1.1. In the default instance, the Concentrator can communicate only with hosts on the 172.19.1.0/24 network, because it has no knowledge of any other networks on the private interface. If communication were required to the host shown in Figure 3-1, with an IP address of 192.168.1.10, you would have to add a static route to the Concentrator.

The IP address of the public Interface on the Concentrator is 195.92.77.101. You can see that the directly connected router that leads to the Internet has an IP address of 195.92.77.97. Therefore, to support VPN Clients with an unknown IP address, you must add a default route to the Concentrator pointing to 195.92.77.97 on the public interface. By adding this default route, you let the Concentrator communicate with the public Internet.

There is a limit to how many static routes can be configured on each platform of the VPN Concentrator. The following shows the number of static routes per device in the VPN 3000 family:

- **3002**—50 routes
- **3005**—200 routes
- **3015**—10,240 routes
- **3020**—10,240 routes
- **3030**—10,240 routes
- **3060**—10,240 routes
- **3080**—10,240 routes

When the routing table is full, the following message appears in the Concentrator's log file:

```
12539 08/30/2001 22:07:55.270 SEV=2 IP/26 RPT=12 Routing Table Full, add new
   route failed.
```

The Concentrator can have only one default route.

NOTE   As well as the default route for the Concentrator, there is also a tunnel default route. This is different from the Concentrator default route, because it applies to only remote-access clients who are connected to the Concentrator.

Configuring a Static Route

Static routes are configured from the Configuration > System > IP Routing > Static Routes screen, as shown in Figure 3-2.

Figure 3-2   *Static Routes Screen*

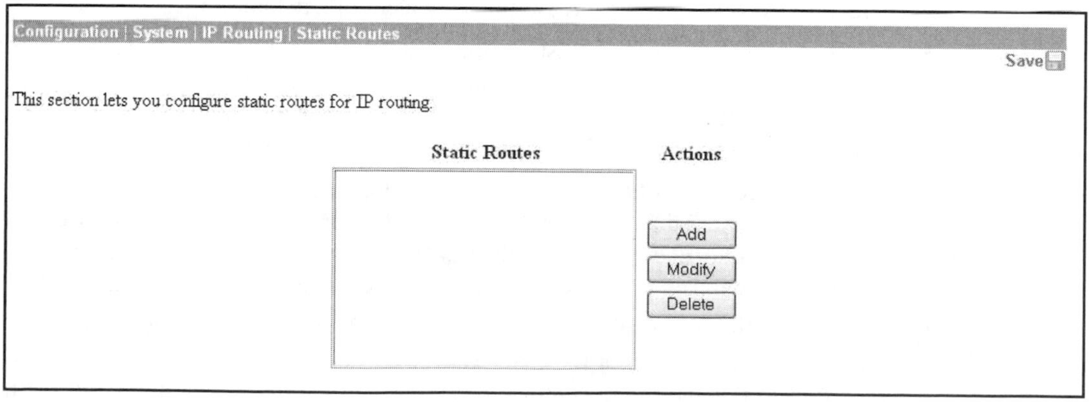

You can see on this screen that no static routes are configured. To configure a static route, click the Add command button. You see a screen asking for the information about the static route, as shown in Figure 3-3.

Figure 3-3   *Configuring a Static Route*

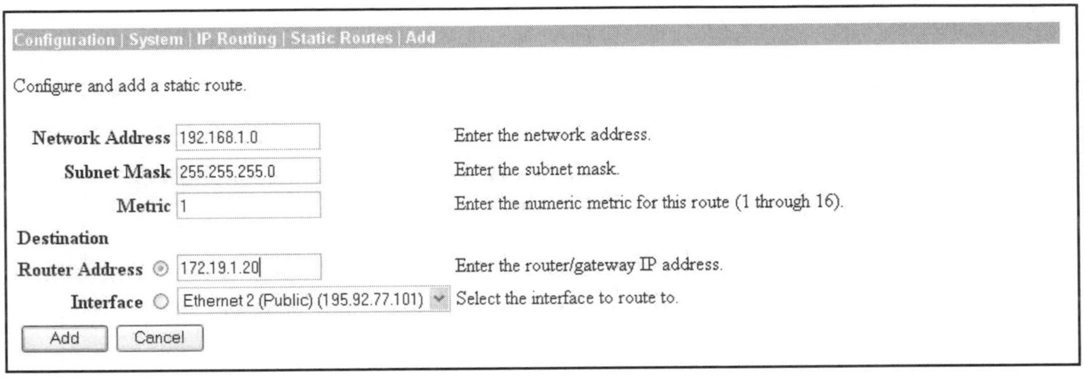

The fields are as follows:

- **Network Address**—Enter the destination network address to which this static route applies. Packets with this destination address are sent to the destination IP address or interface you enter. Using dotted-decimal notation, in this example 192.168.1.0 is added as the network address to enable routing to the remote private network.

- **Subnet Mask**—Enter the subnet mask for the destination network address. Use dotted-decimal notation, such as 255.255.255.0. The subnet mask indicates which part of the IP address represents the network and which part represents hosts. The routing subsystem looks at only the network part. The manager automatically supplies a standard subnet mask appropriate for the IP address you just entered. For example, the IP address 192.168.1.0 is a Class C address, and the standard subnet mask is 255.255.255.0. You can accept this entry or change it. Note that 0.0.0.0 is not allowed here, because that would resolve to the equivalent of a default route.

- **Metric**—Enter the metric, or cost, for this route. Use a number from 1 to 16, where 1 is the lowest cost. The routing subsystem always tries to use the least-costly route. For example, if a route uses a low-speed line, you might assign a high metric so that the system will use it only if all high-speed routes are unavailable.

- **Destination Router Address**—Enter the IP address of the specific router or gateway to which to forward these packets—that is, the IP address of the next hop between the VPN Concentrator and the packet's ultimate destination. Use dotted-decimal notation. In the example linked to Figure 3-1, the destination router address is 172.19.1.20.

- **Destination Interface**—Click the Interface drop-down menu button and choose a configured VPN Concentrator interface as the outbound destination. This menu lists all interfaces that have been configured. The default interface for a static route is the

Ethernet 2 (Public) interface. For example, in a LAN-to-LAN configuration where remote-access clients are assigned IP addresses that are not on the private network, you could configure a static route with those addresses outbound to the Ethernet 1 (Private) interface. The clients could then access the peer VPN Concentrator and its networks.

To add a new static route to the list of configured routes, click Add. This action then includes your entries in the active configuration. The Manager returns to the Configuration > System > IP Routing > Static Routes screen. Any new route appears at the bottom of the Static Routes list.

NOTE   The Manager immediately includes your changes in the active configuration. To save the active configuration and make it the boot configuration, click the Save Needed icon at the top of the Manager window.

Configuring a Default Route

Default routes are configured from the Configuration > System > IP Routing > Default Gateways screen, as shown in Figure 3-4.

Figure 3-4   *Configuring a Default Route*

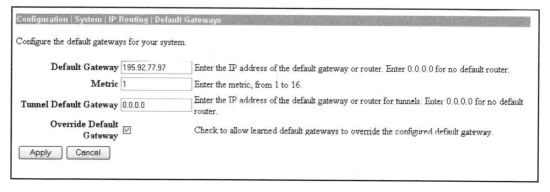

This screen has four configuration fields:

- **Default Gateway**—Enter the IP address of the default gateway or router. Use dotted-decimal notation (in this example, 195.92.77.97). This address must not be the same as the IP address configured on any VPN Concentrator interface. If you do not use a default gateway, enter 0.0.0.0 (the default entry).

  To delete the current configured default gateway, enter 0.0.0.0.

The default gateway must be directly reachable from a VPN Concentrator interface, and it is usually on the public network. The Manager displays a warning screen if you enter an IP address that is not on one of its interface networks. It displays a dialog box if you enter an IP address that is not on the public network.

- **Metric**—Enter the metric, or cost, for the route to the default gateway. Use a number from 1 to 16, where 1 is the lowest cost. The routing subsystem always tries to use the least-costly route. For example, if this route uses a low-speed line, you might assign a high metric so that the system will use it only if all high-speed routes are unavailable.

- **Tunnel Default Gateway**—Enter the IP address of the default gateway for tunneled data. Use dotted-decimal notation, such as 10.10.0.2. If you do not use a tunnel default gateway, enter 0.0.0.0 (the default entry).

  To delete a configured tunnel default gateway, enter 0.0.0.0.

  This gateway is often a firewall in parallel with the VPN Concentrator and between the public and private networks. The tunnel default gateway applies to all tunneled traffic, including IPSec LAN-to-LAN traffic.

- **Override Default Gateway**—To allow default gateways learned via a dynamic routing protocol (RIP or OSPF) to override the configured default gateway, check the Override Default Gateway check box (the default). To always use the configured default gateway, uncheck the box.

To apply the settings for default gateways, and to include your settings in the active configuration, click Apply. The Manager returns to the Configuration > System > IP Routing screen. If you configure a default gateway, it also appears in the Static Routes list on the Configuration > System > IP Routing > Static Routes screen.

NOTE   The Manager immediately includes your changes in the active configuration. To save the active configuration and make it the boot configuration, click the Save Needed icon at the top of the Manager window.

Dynamic Routing

The preceding section covered static routing, looking at normal static routes and the special static route that is called a default route. Static routes are adequate for small networks and networks that do not change very frequently. If you have a large network, or networks with built-in resilience offered via routing, it is a good idea to look at using dynamic routing on your VPN Concentrator. As the name implies, dynamic routing is dynamic in nature and not static. The routes the Concentrator uses are learned from other network devices that participate in dynamic routing based on their own routing information.

Dynamic routing requires a dynamic routing protocol to operate. The two dynamic routing protocols that the VPN Concentrator supports are RIP and OSPF. Both of these routing protocols are based on an open standard, so interoperability is provided between the VPN Concentrator and non-Cisco devices.

Dynamic routing protocols have to be configured on the Concentrator's interfaces. RIP and OSPF can run on the same interface.

RIP

RIP is a distance vector routing protocol. This means that the routing information is based on a simple metric—in the case of RIP, hop count. RIP sends out a routing update by default every 30 seconds that contains the device's full routing table. This makes RIP generate more network traffic than newer dynamic routing protocols such as OSPF. Routing information is based on the best view of the network and secondhand information from other peers. There are two versions of RIP—RIPv1 and RIPv2. RIPv1 is the original implementation of RIP. It supports a maximum of 16 hops and uses broadcasts as its transmission medium. This routing protocol broadcasts on configured interfaces; any other RIP listening devices participate in routing. RIPv2 has a hop count of 15 because the designers felt that even RIPv2 was unsuitable for large network designs and features such as route authentication and a multicast delivery mechanism.

The Cisco VPN Concentrator supports both RIPv1 and RIPv2 for dynamic routing. You can configure the Concentrator to support only RIPv1, only RIPv2, or RIPv1 and RIPv2 combined.

NOTE   This is a very brief overview of RIP. For more information, see *Routing TCP/IP* by Jeff Doyle (Cisco Press, ISBN 1578700418).

Configuring RIP on the VPN Concentrator

Configuring RIP on the VPN Concentrator is very simple and straightforward. RIP has to be enabled on a per-interface basis. When you enable RIP on a per-interface basis, you can configure inbound and outbound routing via RIP. Inbound routing means that RIP is enabled on the interface and that the interface listens for and processes RIP updates sent from other devices on the network that are configured for RIP. These routing updates are processed, and routes are added to the routing table of the VPN Concentrator. Outbound routing means that the VPN Concentrator advertises routes that it knows about internally. These can be static routes and address pools that fall outside the network ranges of the connected interfaces. Outbound routing builds a routing update and sends it out the configured interface every 30 seconds, conforming with RIP standards.

Before you start to configure RIP, look at the routing table of the VPN Concentrator, shown in Figure 3-5.

Figure 3-5   *Concentrator Routing Table*

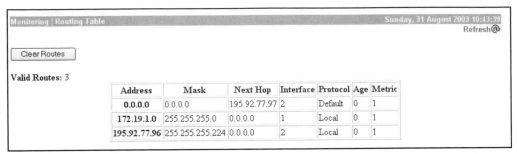

You can see that the only routes contained in the routing table are the default route, indicated by 0.0.0.0 and pointing to 195.92.77.97, and the two connected networks (private and public interfaces).

You will enable RIP on the VPN Concentrator to learn about the 192.168.1.0/24 network from the router, as shown in Figure 3-6.

Figure 3-6   *Sample VPN Network*

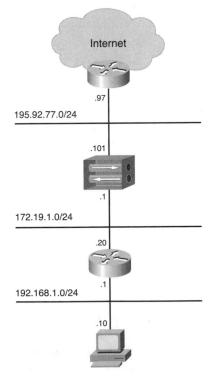

This configuration involves a series of steps:

Step 1   To start the configuration, navigate to the Configuration > Interfaces
screen and click the private interface to be left with the screen, as shown
in Figure 3-7.

Figure 3-7   *Private Interface Configuration*

		Configuration | Interfaces | Ethernet 1	

⚠️ You are modifying the interface you are using to connect to this device. If you make any changes, you will break the connection and you
will have to restart from the login screen.

Configuring Ethernet Interface 1 (Private).

| General | RIP | OSPF | Bandwidth |

		General Parameters	
Sel	**Attribute**	**Value**	**Description**
○	Disabled		Select to disable this interface.
○	DHCP Client		Select to obtain the IP Address, Subnet Mask and Default Gateway via DHCP.
◉	Static IP Addressing		Select to configure the IP Address and Subnet Mask. Enter the IP Address and Subnet Mask for this interface.
	IP Address	172.19.1.1	
	Subnet Mask	255.255.255.0	
	Public Interface	☐	Check to make this interface a "public" interface.
	MAC Address	00.90.A4.00.11.78	The MAC address for this interface.
	Filter	1. Private (Default) ▾	Select the filter for this interface.
	Speed	100 Mbps ▾	Select the speed for this interface.
	Duplex	Full-Duplex ▾	Select the duplex mode for this interface.
	MTU	1500	Enter the Maximum Transmit Unit for this interface (68 - 1500).
	Public Interface IPSec Fragmentation Policy	◉ Do not fragment prior to IPSec encapsulation; fragment prior to interface transmission	
		○ Fragment prior to IPSec encapsulation with Path MTU Discovery (ICMP)	
		○ Fragment prior to IPSec encapsulation without Path MTU Discovery (Clear DF bit)	

[Apply]   [Cancel]

Step 2   Click the RIP tab at the top of the screen to go to the RIP configuration
screen. In this instance, you only want to receive RIP routes, not
advertise them. You also need to configure RIPv2 because that is what the
router is using. Select RIPv2 Only from the Inbound RIP drop-down
menu box, as shown in Figure 3-8.

Figure 3-8 *Configuring Inbound RIP*

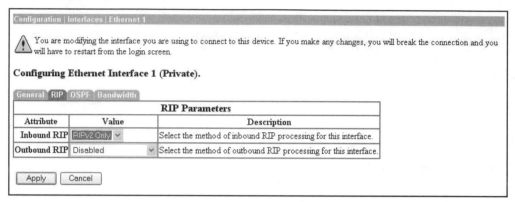

> Step 3   Leave Outbound RIP disabled. This configuration will listen on the
>   private interface for RIPv2 updates but won't send any updates out the
>   interface.
>
> Step 4   Click Apply. View the IP routing table by navigating to the Monitoring >
>   Routing Table screen, as shown in Figure 3-9.

Figure 3-9 *Routing Table*

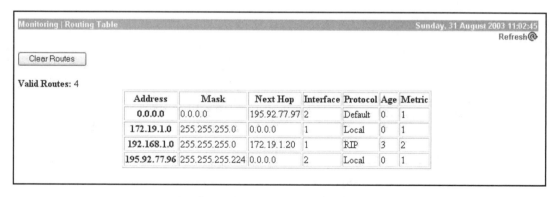

This routing table is identical to the one shown in Figure 3-5, apart from the route to the
192.168.1.0/24 network. This route was learned on interface 1, which is the private
interface. The protocol for this route is advertised as RIP, so you know that this route
was learned by RIP. The route's age is 3. This age equals the number of seconds the router
has learned about the route. This number goes up to 30 and then, under normal circum-
stances, is reset to 0. This is because RIP routing updates are sent every 30 seconds. So,
every 30 seconds the advertising router sends a RIP update, which the Concentrator
receives and processes. Then it resets these counters. If there is a failure in the network, this
age timer increases before eventually going into what is called holddown. Eventually the

route is removed from the Concentrator's routing table. The metric for this route is 2. The metric increments by 1 for every hop generated. A local route is classed as having a metric of 1. If the metric is 2, this means that one routing device sits between the Concentrator and the remote network.

The next hop for this route, as expected, is 172.19.1.20.

With RIP, the interface settings are the only configuration settings that can be changed on the VPN Concentrator.

OSPF

The preceding section covered the configuration of RIP. This section looks at OSPF. OSPF is classed as a much more robust routing protocol than RIP and has distinct scalability and feature improvements. OSPF uses link-state routing algorithms, and it is a newer protocol than RIP. It generates less network traffic and generally provides faster routing updates, but it requires more processing power than RIP. The VPN Concentrator includes IP routing functions that support OSPF version 2 (RFC 2328).

OSPF has to be configured in two places on the interface, as opposed to just one for RIP. OSPF has system-wide parameters and interface-specific parameters that have to be configured.

NOTE   This is a very brief overview of OSPF. For more information, refer to *Routing TCP/IP* by Jeff Doyle (Cisco Press, ISBN 1578700418).

Configuring OSPF on the VPN Concentrator

For this configuration example, you will make the exact same route visible that you used for the RIP example. You will start with a routing table consisting of only the connected interfaces and the default route, as shown in Figure 3-10.

Figure 3-10 *Routing Table*

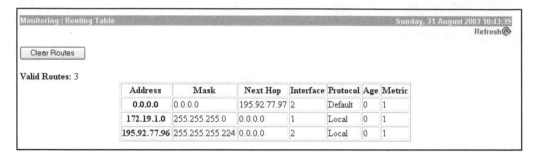

Address	Mask	Next Hop	Interface	Protocol	Age	Metric
0.0.0.0	0.0.0.0	195.92.77.97	2	Default	0	1
172.19.1.0	255.255.255.0	0.0.0.0	1	Local	0	1
195.92.77.96	255.255.255.224	0.0.0.0	2	Local	0	1

You can see from Figure 3-10 that no dynamically learned routes exist in the network table. To recap, you need to make the Concentrator see a route to the 192.168.1.0/24 network, as shown in Figure 3-11.

Figure 3-11 *Sample VPN Network*

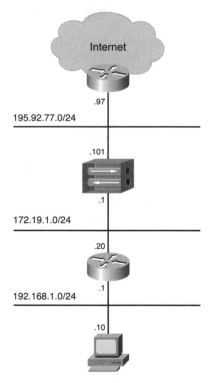

System-Wide OSPF Configuration

Let's start the configuration by looking at the system-wide configuration options. Navigate to the Configuration > System > IP Routing screen. You have two OSPF configuration options—OSPF and OSPF Areas. Click the OSPF menu. It has three options, as shown in Figure 3-12:

- **Enabled**—OSPF is disabled by default. You enable it system-wide by checking this check box.

- **Router ID**—OSPF operates by using a router ID (RID) within its routing updates to uniquely identify itself to other routers participating in OSPF. The router ID uses the same format as an IP address but acts purely as an identifier; it has no function as an IP address. It is normal practice on a VPN Concentrator to use the IP address of the private interface as the router ID. In this example, 172.19.1.1, the IP address of the private interface, is the router ID. The default router ID is 0.0.0.0.

NOTE   After you configure and apply a router ID, you must disable OSPF before you can change it. You cannot change the ID back to 0.0.0.0.

- **Autonomous System**—An OSPF autonomous system (AS) is a collection of OSPF routers that are running under a common administration. An AS boundary router exchanges routing information with routers belonging to other autonomous systems and advertises external AS routing information throughout its own AS. Check the Autonomous System check box to indicate that the VPN Concentrator OSPF router is the boundary router for an autonomous system. If you check this box, the VPN Concentrator also redistributes RIP and static routes into the OSPF areas. By default, this box is unchecked.

Figure 3-12   *IP Routing > OSPF*

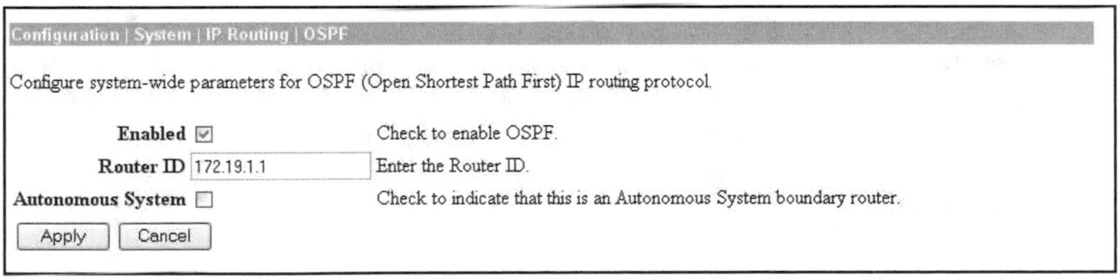

Click Apply to accept these changes and commit them to the active configuration on the VPN Concentrator.

This returns you to the Configuration > System > IP Routing screen. Now click the OSPF Areas menu. OSPF breaks its AS into areas, which provide route summarization and reduce the number of routes propagating throughout the network. The default area is called the backbone area, and it has an ID of 0, or 0.0.0.0. This default configuration is shown in Figure 3-13.

Figure 3-13 *IP Routing > OSPF Areas*

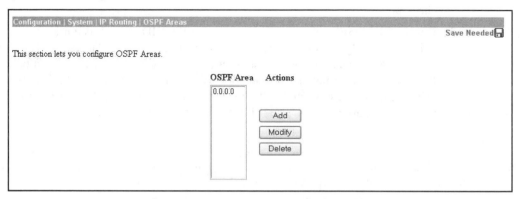

You will use the default area, with an ID of 0.0.0.0. Highlight the 0.0.0.0 area, and then click Modify to look at the settings for the area. Three options are available, as shown in Figure 3-14:

- **Area ID**—Enter the area ID in this field. Use dotted-decimal notation, just as you would for an IP address—for example, 1.0.0.0. The backbone area uses an area ID of 0.0.0.0, as shown in the figure.

- **Area Summary**—Check the Area Summary check box to have the OSPF router generate and propagate summary link-state advertisements (LSAs) into OSPF stub areas. LSAs describe the state of the router's interfaces and routing paths. Stub areas contain only final-destination hosts and do not pass traffic to other areas. By default, this box is unchecked.

- **External LSA Import**—The External LSA Import field has two options—External and No External. If you set External, the Concentrator imports LSA from neighboring autonomous systems. If you set it to No External, the external LSAs are not imported. These two menu options are all that is required for system-wide configuration of OSPF.

Figure 3-14   *OSPF Area 0.0.0.0*

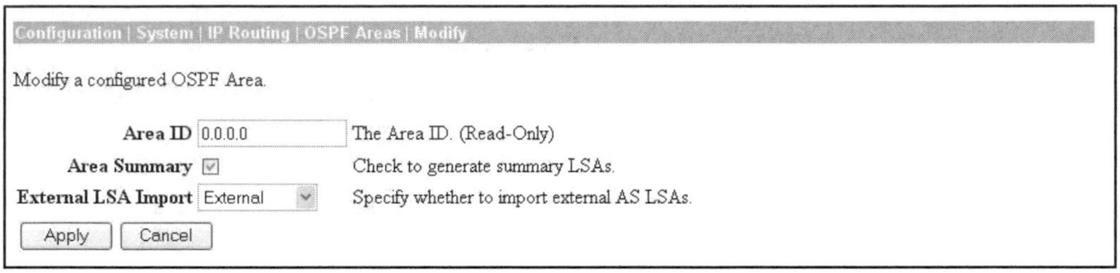

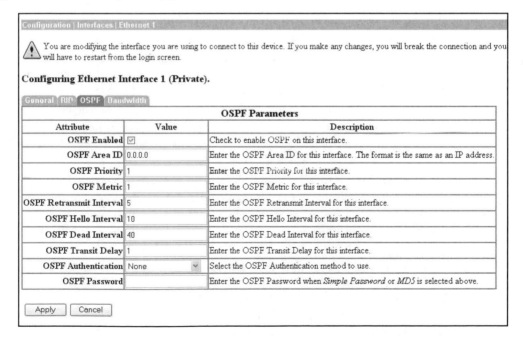

Interface OSPF Configuration

Now that you have enabled OSPF system-wide and have set the default area, you have to configure OSPF on the interface on which you want to use it.

Navigate to the Configuration > Interfaces screen, and click the Private interface. As with the configuration of RIP, an OSPF tab appears at the top of the screen, next to the RIP tab, as shown in Figure 3-7. Click the OSPF tab to see the OSPF interface configuration page, as shown in Figure 3-15.

Figure 3-15   *OSPF Interface Configuration*

There are ten settings on this screen to configure OSPF. OSPF is disabled by default on the interface. You can see in Figure 3-15 that OSPF has been configured. With a standard implementation of OSPF, this is all that you are required to do to start OSPF on the interface.

NOTE	OSPF must be enabled system-wide as well as on the interface to function. Just enabling OSPF on the interface keeps it from operating on the Concentrator.

- **OSPF Enabled**—Check this box to enable OSPF routing on this interface. by default it is unchecked.

- **OSPF Area ID**—Enter the area ID in the field using IP address format in dotted-decimal notation. The default entry is 0.0.0.0, as shown in Figure 3-15. Your entry also appears in the OSPF Area list on the Configuration > System > IP Routing > OSPF Areas screen. It is possible for interfaces on a VPN Concentrator to be in different OSPF areas.

- **OSPF Priority**—This setting assigns a priority to the OSPF router on this interface. OSPF routers on a network elect one neighbor to act as the designated router (DR), which has the master routing database and performs other administrative functions. In case of a tie, the router with the higher priority number wins. An entry of 0 means that this router is ineligible to become the designated router. The priority is entered as a number from 0 to 255. The default is 1.

- **OSPF Metric**—This entry is the metric, or cost, of the OSPF router on this interface. The cost determines preferred routing through the network, with the lowest cost being the most desirable. The metric is entered as a number from 1 to 65535. The default is 1.

- **OSPF Retransmit Interval**—This entry is the number of seconds between OSPF routing updates (LSAs) from this interface, which are messages that the router sends to describe its current state. Enter the interval as a number from 0 to 3600 seconds. The default is 5 seconds, which is a typical value for LANs.

- **OSPF Hello Interval**—This entry is the number of seconds between OSPF Hello packets that the Concentrator sends out OSPF-enabled interfaces to announce its presence, join the OSPF routing area, and maintain neighbor relationships. This interval must be the same for all routers on a common network. The hello interval is entered as a number from 1 to 65535 seconds. The default is 10 seconds.

- **OSPF Dead Interval**—This entry is the number of seconds for the Concentrator to wait before it declares that a neighboring OSPF router is out of service after the router no longer sees the neighbor's Hello packets. This interval should be some multiple of the hello interval, and it must be the same for all routers on a common network. Enter the interval as a number from 0 to 65535 seconds. The default is 40 seconds, which is a typical value for LANs.

- **OSPF Transit Delay**—This entry is the estimated number of seconds it takes to transmit a link-state update packet over this interface. It should include the interface's transmission and propagation delays. This delay must be the same for all routers on a common network. Enter the delay as a number from 0 to 3600 seconds. The default is 1 second, which is a typical value for LANs.

- **OSPF Authentication**—This parameter sets the authentication method for OSPF protocol messages. OSPF messages can be authenticated so that only other trusted neighbors can route messages within the domain. This authentication method must be the same for all routers within the OSPF area.

  Click the OSPF Authentication drop-down menu button and choose the authentication method:

  - **None**—No authentication. OSPF messages are not authenticated (this is the default).

  - **Simple Password**—A simple password uses a clear-text password for authentication. This password must be the same for all routers in the OSPF area. If you choose this method, enter the password in the OSPF Password field that follows.

  - **MD5**—Use the MD5 hashing algorithm with a shared key to generate an encrypted message digest for authentication. This key must be the same for all routers in the OSPF area. If you choose this method, enter the key in the OSPF Password field that follows. This setting is the preferred secure option for authentication.

- **OSPF Password**—If you chose Simple Password or MD5 for OSPF Authentication, enter the appropriate password or key in this field. Otherwise, leave the field blank. For Simple Password authentication, enter the common password. The maximum password length is eight characters. The Manager displays your entry in clear text. For MD5 authentication, enter the shared key. The maximum shared key length is eight characters. The Manager displays your entry in clear text.

You can see from Figure 3-15 that the only setting that has been changed from the default settings is that OSPF has been enabled on this interface.

Apply the changes and take another look at the routing table on the Concentrator. Figure 3-16 shows the routing table on the Concentrator after you have configured OSPF.

Figure 3-16   *Routing Table*

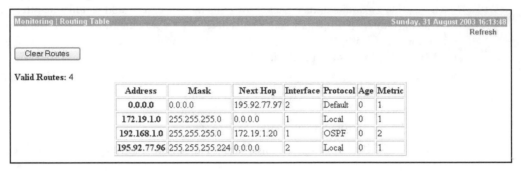

You can see that a route now exists to the 192.168.1.0/24 network via 172.19.1.20 and that it is advertised via OSPF. Notice that the Age field is 0; this is always set to 0. This is because OSPF operates differently than RIP. OSPF sends only incremental updates, not full routing updates, so the routes never age in the same way that RIP routes do.

Summary

This chapter looked at routing on the VPN Concentrator. This chapter used a sample VPN network and covered how to configure the default route to point to the ISP router to facilitate the connections from remote-access VPN Clients. You looked at configuring a static route to make the remote private network reachable to remote-access VPN users. You also looked at the two dynamic routing protocols supported on the Concentrator, RIP and OSPF. A configuration example showed you how to remove the static route and rely on dynamic routing to advertise the remote network to the Concentrator to facilitate communication for remote-access VPN users.

Review Questions

The following questions test your retention of the material presented in this chapter. The answers appear in Appendix A, "Answers to the Review Questions."

1 What versions of RIP are supported on the VPN Concentrator?

2 How many static routes can be configured on a VPN 3005 Concentrator?

3 What is the default time between RIP routing updates?

4 What does OSPF use to uniquely identify the device participating in the OSPF process?

5 What are the three types of OSPF authentication?

6 Of the three OSPF authentication types, which is considered the most secure, and why?

After completing this chapter, you will be able to perform the following tasks:

- Understand remote-access VPNs
- Perform an initial configuration of a VPN 3000 Concentrator
- Configure a VPN 3000 Concentrator to enable a remote-access VPN connection using preshared keys
- Configure advanced settings of the VPN 3000 Concentrator for the remote-access VPN group
- Configure the VPN 3000 Software Client to connect to the VPN 3000 Concentrator

CHAPTER 4

Configuring the Cisco VPN 3000 for Remote Access Using Preshared Keys

The first three chapters provided an overview of virtual private networks (VPNs) and introduced the Cisco VPN 3000 Concentrator. This chapter is the first to delve into the Concentrator's configuration to provide remote-access VPN connectivity. Because this is the first configuration chapter, it starts with the Concentrator as if it is a new unit, just unpacked from the box. This chapter discusses connecting to the Concentrator using the command-line interface (CLI). The main reason for doing this is to assign the Concentrator's private interface an IP address that can then be used to carry out the rest of the configuration through the graphical user interface (GUI), also known as the VPN Manager. All the functionality of the GUI VPN Manager is available at the CLI, but navigation is a lot easier using a standard Internet browser.

As soon as this configuration step is complete, we will look at the quick configuration utility to create a very fast and simple group for remote-access connections. We'll then discuss the more in-depth group configuration options before looking at the Cisco VPN Software Client for the Microsoft Windows operating system.

Overview of Remote Access Using Preshared Keys

This section presents an overview of remote access using preshared keys.

Consider the following scenario. Remote users need to dial into the corporate office and access e-mail, corporate presentations, order entry, and engineering. In addition, Corporate Information Services wants the remote users to access corporate resources fast, inexpensively, and as securely as possible.

Implementing a remote-access VPN with the Cisco VPN 3000 Series Concentrator and the Cisco VPN Software Client is the right choice. It lets the remote users access the corporate resources they require. Corporate Information Services meets their speed, expense, and security requirements. This scenario is shown in Figure 4-1.

Figure 4-1   *Remote-Access VPN*

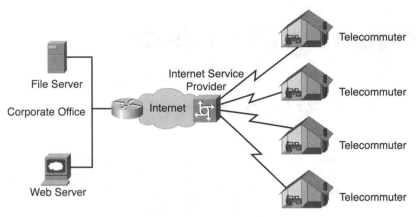

Remote-access VPNs consist of four components: IPSec software client, public network connectivity, IPSec protocol, and, in this case, the Cisco VPN Concentrator.

- **IPSec software client**—The IPSec software client is not native to the Windows operating system and must be loaded on the PC. It is used to encrypt, authenticate, and encapsulate data. It also terminates one end of the tunnel.

- **Public network connectivity**—For a remote-access VPN to be established, there must be some connectivity over the public network. The remote-access client must be able to route traffic to the central site VPN Concentrator.

- **IPSec protocol**—After the ISP authenticates the remote user, the user launches the IPSec client. IPSec establishes a secure tunnel or session through the Internet to the Concentrator.

- **VPN Concentrator**—The VPN Concentrator terminates the opposite end of the tunnel. The Concentrator decrypts, authenticates, and deencapsulates the data.

In Figure 4-2, a telecommuter needs to access information on the corporate server, 10.0.1.10. The source address is the Software Client's virtual IP address, 10.0.1.20. The Concentrator or the Dynamic Host Configuration Protocol (DHCP) server usually supplies it to the Software Client. This gives the Software Client the appearance of residing on the internal network.

Any data flowing from the server to the Software Client must be protected as it traverses the Internet. Therefore, information flowing between the server and the Software Client is encrypted, authenticated, and encapsulated using the Encapsulating Security Payload (ESP) header. This provides confidentiality and data integrity. However, it also presents an issue. If the payload is encapsulated and encrypted, the routers in the Internet are unable to read the packet's source and destination addresses. The routers are unable to route the packet. To solve this problem, an additional IP header is added to the ESP encapsulated data. The outside IP header is used to route the information through the network using a routable address. The source address is the Software Client's network interface card (NIC). The destination address is the Concentrator's public interface. The Software Client-to-server data is sent over the network using an IP-in-IP encapsulation. Upon receipt, the Concentrator strips the outer IP header, decrypts the data, and forwards the packet according to the inside IP address.

Figure 4-2   *IPSec Remote-Access Tunneling*

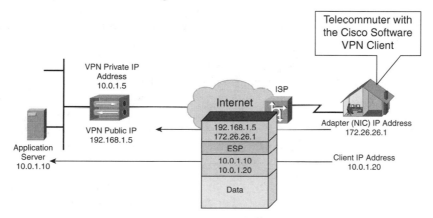

The Software Client works with the Concentrator to create a secure connection, called a tunnel, between your computer and the private network. It uses Internet Key Exchange (IKE) and IPSec tunneling protocols to make and manage the secure connection.

Here are some of the operations the Software Client performs (they are mostly invisible to you):

- Negotiating tunnel parameters—addresses, algorithms, lifetime, and so on
- Establishing tunnels according to the parameters
- Authenticating users by ensuring that users are who they say they are via usernames, group names, passwords, and digital certificates
- Establishing user access rights—hours of access, connection time, allowed destinations, allowed protocols, and so on
- Managing security keys for encryption and decryption
- Establishing the IPSec session
- Authenticating, encrypting, and decrypting data through the tunnel

Initial Configuration of the VPN 3000 for Remote Access

This section explains how to cable the Cisco VPN 3000 series Concentrator and establish a management session between a PC and the Concentrator.

The Concentrator is equipped with universal power factor correction, 100 to 240 volts alternating current (VAC). A power cable with the correct plug is supplied. When the Concentrator arrives from the factory, plug it in and power it up. Connect the corporate LAN to the Concentrator's private interface. Cable the Internet side of the corporate network to the Concentrator's public interface. LAN ports on the Concentrator can be programmed for 10 M or 100 M Ethernet.

IP addresses are not preprogrammed into the Concentrator at the factory. Use the console port to program the correct IP addresses for the VPN private IP address. An application such as HyperTerminal needs to be configured for access to the serial console port. The application needs to be configured for 9600 bps 8 data bits, no parity, and 1 stop bit. When the IP addresses have been added to the Concentrator over the serial port connection and the configuration has been saved, the operator can access the Concentrator via a web browser such as Internet Explorer or Netscape.

After the initial private IP address configuration, the remaining parameters can be configured via a CLI or a browser. For beginners, the menu-driven browser is recommended. The CLI is for those who understand the menu structure. The CLI is accessed by either the direct connect console port or a LAN port Telnet session.

The web interface supports both HTTP and HTTP over Secure Socket Layer (SSL). Operators can use either Internet Explorer or Netscape Navigator. With Internet Explorer and Netscape Navigator, the software revisions must be 4.0 or higher with both cookies and Java Scripts enabled. Use either browser to configure the Concentrator—with one exception: Internet Explorer must be used when programming digital certificates.

Figure 4-3 shows the CLI and browser managers.

Figure 4-3   *CLI and Browser Managers*

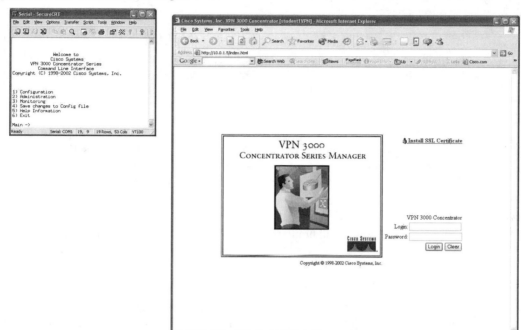

Figure 4-4 shows the main window of the Concentrator after you log in to the device.

Figure 4-4   *GUI VPN Manager*

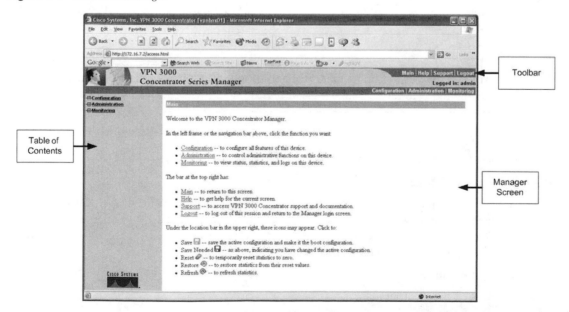

The top frame (the Cisco VPN 3000 Concentrator series Manager toolbar) provides quick access to manager functions.

The left frame (the table of contents [TOC]) provides the TOC to the Manager's windows.

The main frame displays the current Manager's window. From here you can navigate the Manager using either the TOC in the left frame or the Manager toolbar at the top of the frame. To do this, select a title from the left frame. The Concentrator opens the Manager window for that section in the main frame.

When you are finished with the configuration window, click Apply to make the configuration take effect immediately. Click the Save Needed icon to save the changes to memory. If you reboot without saving, your configuration changes are lost.

NOTE   Every time you make a change to the configuration, the Save Needed icon appears. It is *very* important to save your configuration after every major configuration change. If you do not save your configuration, you risk losing the settings if the device loses power or reboots.

There are two ways to configure the Concentrator: Quick Configuration and the main menu. Quick Configuration lets you configure the minimal parameters for operation. It automatically enables remote IPSec client connections via an ISP for a single user group. You use the main menu to add IPSec user groups and configure all features individually. With Quick Configuration, you can program an IPSec remote-access application by accessing six windows. In the main menu, the same application requires the operator to access 12 or more windows. The following sections take you through an IPSec remote-access configuration example.

NOTE   You can run Quick Configuration only once. You must reboot to the factory default configuration to run it again.

Browser Configuration of the Cisco VPN 3000 Concentrator Series

After configuring the Cisco VPN 3000 series Concentrator via the CLI, you can connect and use the browser interface to configure the remaining items. This section explains using the browser interface to configure the Concentrator. You will create access using the Quick Configuration, which has seven configuration parameters:

1 IP interfaces
2 System information

3 Protocols

4 Address assignment

5 Authentication

6 IPSec group

7 Admin password

Step 1: IP Interfaces

Figure 4-5 shows the first Quick Configuration window. It displays the current configuration of the IP interfaces:

Private—Interface toward the internal network

Public—Interface toward the public network (Internet)

Figure 4-5   *Quick Configuration: IP Interfaces*

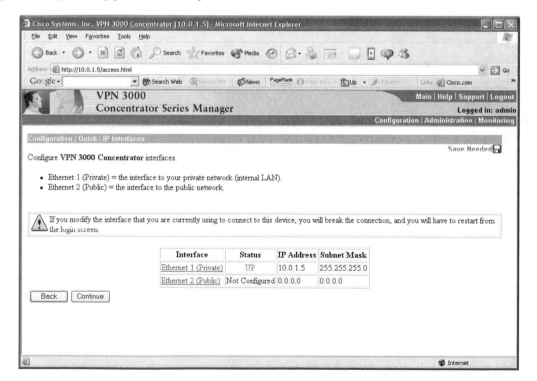

Remember, the private LAN interface was configured via CLI. Configure the public LAN interface (toward the Internet). To do this, click the public interface to access the public interface configuration window.

NOTE   This example uses a 3005 Concentrator. The 3015 Concentrator and above also have an external interface.

The window shown in Figure 4-6 is used to configure the public IP interface in one of three ways: disabled, set as a DHCP client, or configured to use a static IP address.

Figure 4-6   *Public IP Interface*

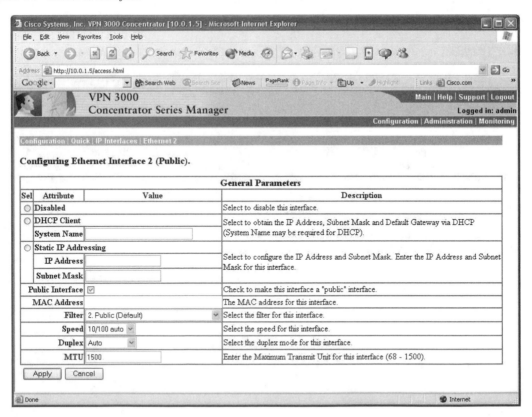

The public IP interface parameters are as follows:

- **Disabled radio button**—The interface is enabled by default. Select the Disabled radio button to disable the interface.

- **DHCP Client radio button**—Select this radio button if you want to enable this interface and use DHCP to obtain an IP address. In the System Name field, enter a name (such as VPN01 for the Concentrator). This name must uniquely identify this device on your network.

- **Static IP Addressing radio button**—Select this radio button if you want to enable this interface and set the static IP address. In the IP Address field, enter the IP address for this interface using dotted-decimal notation (for example, 192.168.1.5). Be sure no other device is using this address on the network. In the Subnet Mask field, enter the subnet mask for this interface using dotted-decimal notation (for example, 255.255.255.0). The Manager automatically supplies a standard subnet mask appropriate for the IP address you just entered. For example, the IP address 192.168.1.5 is a Class C address, and the standard subnet mask is 255.255.255.0. You can accept this entry or change it. Note that 0.0.0.0 is not allowed.

- **Public Interface check box**—Check this check box to make this a public interface.

- **MAC Address field**—The unique hardware Media Access Control (MAC) address for this interface.

- **Filter drop-down menu**—Click the Filter drop-down menu button and choose the Public (Default) filter, which allows only nonsource-routed inbound and outbound tunneling protocols and Internet Control Message Protocol (ICMP). This is the default filter for Ethernet 2.

- **Speed drop-down menu**—Keep the default value.

- **MTU field**—This value specifies the interface's maximum transmission unit (MTU) (that is, packet size) in bytes. Valid values range from 68 through 1500. The default value, 1500, is the MTU for Ethernet.

Step 2: System Information

Use the Configuration > Quick > System Info window, shown in Figure 4-7, to configure basic information about the Cisco VPN 3000 Concentrator.

Figure 4-7 *System Information*

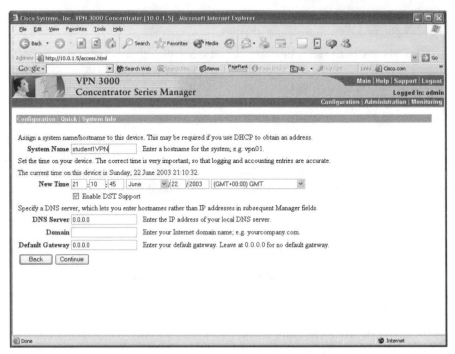

- **System Name field**—Enter a name (such as VPN01) for the Concentrator. This name must uniquely identify this device.

- **Set the time and date on the Concentrator**—The correct time is very important so that logging and accounting entries are accurate. The window shows the current date and time on the device. The values shown in the New Time fields are the time on the browser PC, but any entries you make apply to the Concentrator. Enter the year as a four-digit number. It is very important for the time and date to be correct if you are using digital certificates on your VPN Concentrator.

- **DNS Server field**—Enter the IP address of your local domain name system (DNS) server using dotted-decimal notation (for example, 10.0.1.10). Specifying a DNS server lets you enter Internet host names (for example, vpn.company.com).

- **Domain field**—Enter your Internet domain name (for example, cisco.com is sometimes called the domain name suffix or subdomain).

- **Default Gateway field**—Enter the IP address or host name of the system to which the Concentrator should route packets that are not explicitly routed. In other words, if the Concentrator has no IP routing parameters (Routing Information Protocol [RIP], Open Shortest Path First [OSPF], static routes) that specify where to send a packet, it sends it to this gateway. This address must not be the same as the IP address configured on any Concentrator interface (for example, a default gateway may be to the perimeter router at 192.168.1.1).

Step 3: Protocols

The Configuration > Quick > Protocols window, shown in Figure 4-8, is used to configure the supported remote-access protocols: Point-to-Point Tunneling Protocol (PPTP), Layer 2 Tunneling Protocol (L2TP), and IPSec. The Concentrator can support all three protocols simultaneously. However, for the sake of simplicity, only one application at a time is configured in the lab exercises. Configure IPSec remote access by selecting the IPSec check box. You cannot use Quick Configuration to configure IPSec LAN-to-LAN applications.

Figure 4-8   *Protocols*

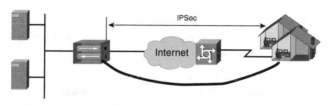

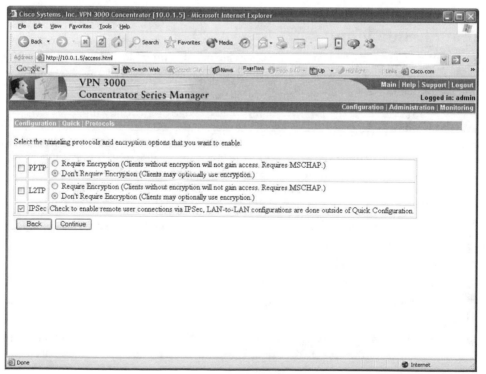

Step 4: Address Assignment

The remote-access PC has two IP addresses: the NIC address and the virtual IP address. With the Concentrator address management window, you define how the remote PC receives the second IP address. You have up to four methods for obtaining the virtual IP address:

- **Client Specified check box**—Check this check box to have the Software Client specify its own IP address. For maximum security, it is recommended that you control IP address assignments and not use the Software Client-specified IP addresses.

- **Per User check box**—Check this check box to assign IP addresses retrieved from an authentication server on a per-user basis. If you are using an authentication server (external or internal) that has IP addresses configured, using this method is recommended.

- **DHCP check box**—Check this check box to use a DHCP server to assign IP addresses.

- **Configured Pool check box**—Select this check box to use the Concentrator to assign IP addresses from an internally configured pool.

The Address Assignment screen is shown in Figure 4-9. Note that DHCP is used to allocate the addresses. It points to a DHCP server with an IP address of 10.0.1.10.

Step 5: Authentication

Before a remote user can gain access to the private corporate network, he or she must be authenticated. Use the Configuration > Quick > Authentication window, shown in Figure 4-10, to define the type of authentication server:

- **Server Type drop-down menu**—Choose one of the following:
  - **RADIUS**—An external RADIUS server.
  - **NT Domain**—An external Windows NT domain server. Use the computer name, not the domain name. If you are unsure of the NT server's computer name, on the PC go to Control Panel > Network > Identification, or ask your network administrator.
  - **Security Dynamics (SDI)**—An external Rivest, Shamir, Adleman (RSA) Security Inc. SecurID server.
  - **Internal server**—The internal Concentrator authentication server (a maximum of 100 groups and users).

- **Authentication Server Address field**—Enter the IP address of the NT domain authentication server (for example, 10.0.1.10).

- **Domain Controller Name field**—Enter the NT Primary Domain Controller host name for this server (for example, Boston). Do not use the domain name.

Figure 4-9   *Address Assignment*

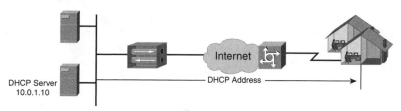

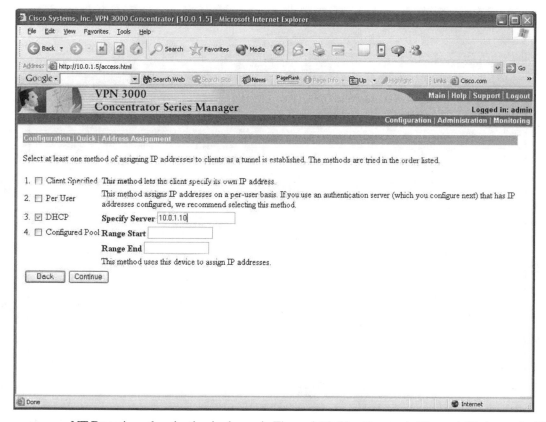

NT Domain authentication is chosen in Figure 4-10. The diagram in Figure 4-10 shows the NT domain server with an IP address of 10.0.1.10. This is reflected in the configuration. You can also see that the Domain Controller name is Boston.

Figure 4-10 *Authentication*

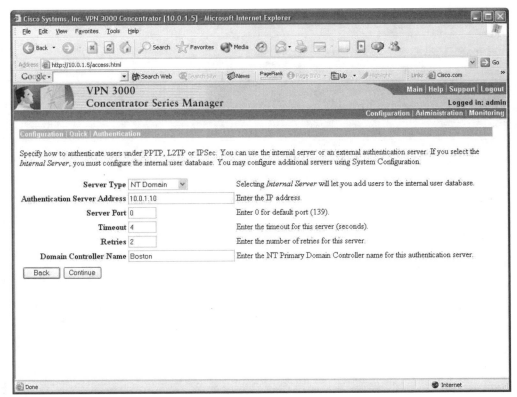

Step 6: IPSec Group

The Configuration > Quick > IPSec Group window, shown in Figure 4-11, lets you enter a group name or username and password. (The figure uses a group name called training.) The Software Client is authenticated by a group to determine its Concentrator access and usage rights. To do this, you must enter information in the following fields:

- **Group Name**—Enter a unique name for this specific group. The maximum is 32 characters.

- **Password**—Enter a unique password for this specific group. The minimum is four characters, and the maximum is 32 characters. The field displays only bullets. The password is the IKE preshared key.

- **Verify**—Reenter the group password to verify it. The field displays only bullets.

Figure 4-11 *IPSec Group*

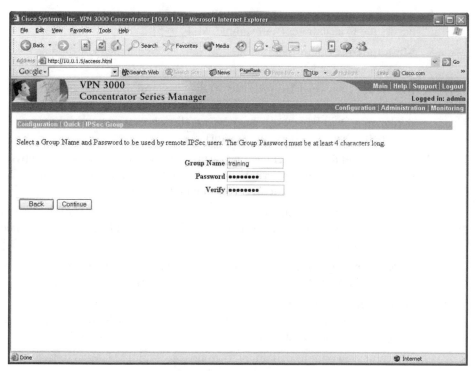

Within a corporation not everyone has the same access requirements. Customer service engineers might require 7-day, 24-hour access; sales entry personnel need 5-day, 8-hour access; and contract help might need 9 a.m. to 5 p.m. with restricted server access. The Concentrator needs to accommodate different access and usage requirements. Different rights and privileges can be defined on a group basis. A customer service engineer, sales entry person, and contractor can be assigned to different groups. Within each group, different access hours, access protocols, idle timeouts, and server restrictions can be configured.

The Concentrator user management configuration tree has three group categories:

- **Base group**—The base group is a default template. The majority of the corporation's access rights and privileges are defined in this group.

- **Groups**—Individual groups inherit the attributes of the base group and then can be customized to meet the group's specific needs.

- **Users**—An individual user might require a unique set of privileges.

By configuring the base group first, specific groups second, and users third, you can quickly manage access and usage rights for large numbers of users.

From the Groups > General window, shown in Figure 4-12, you can configure group attributes on a group-by-group basis:

- **Access Hours drop-down menu**—Choose the named hours when group users can access the Concentrator (for example, M–F, 9–5).

- **Simultaneous Logins field**—Enter the number of simultaneous logins that group users are permitted.

- **Minimum Password Length field**—Enter the minimum number of characters for group user passwords. Allow only alphabetic passwords. Check the Allow Alphabetic-Only Passwords check box to allow base group user passwords with alphabetic characters only (the default).

- **Idle Timeout field**—Enter the time (in minutes). If no communication activity occurs on the connection in this period, the system terminates the connection. Enter **0** to disable the timeout and allow an unlimited idle period.

- **Maximum Connect Time field**—Enter the time in minutes. At the end of this time, the system terminates the connection. Enter **0** (the default) to allow unlimited connection time.

- **Filter drop-down menu**—Define a filter to restrict a group's access to the network based on the Software Client's source address, destination address, or protocol.

- **Inherit check box**—Check this check box if you want the corresponding attribute to apply to the base group configuration. If this check box is not checked, the default group attribute was changed.

More configuration options pertaining to groups are explored later in this chapter.

Figure 4-12 *Groups > General Window*

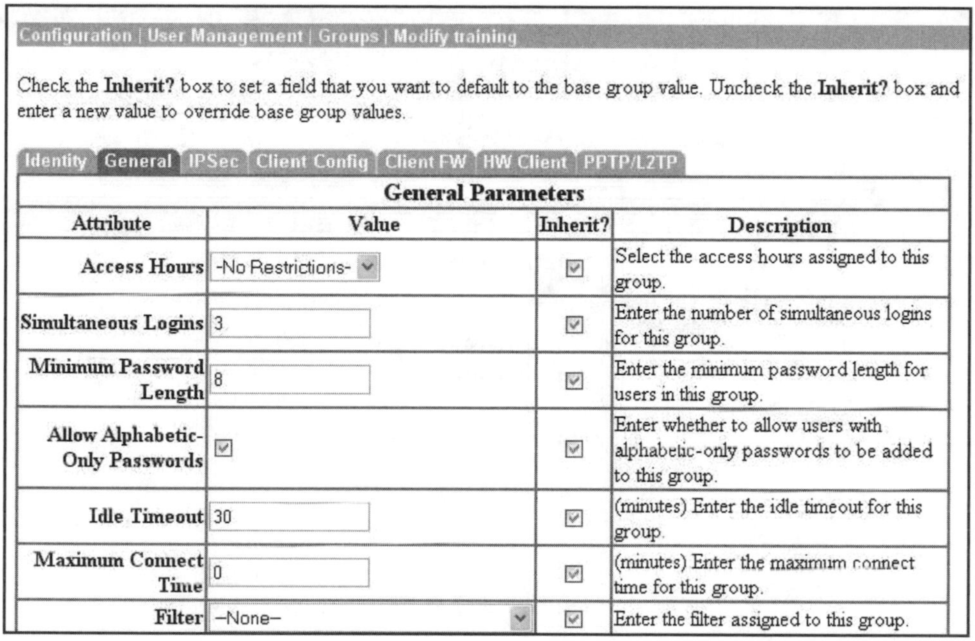

Step 7: Admin Password

The last Quick Configuration window is shown in Figure 4-13. It is used to change the administrative password. Enter information in the following fields to change the administrative password:

- **Password**—Enter or edit the unique password for this administrator. The maximum number of characters is 31. The field displays only bullets.

- **Verify**—Reenter the password to verify it. The field displays only bullets.

NOTE   The default password that Cisco supplies is the same as the username. It is strongly recommended that you change this password in a production environment.

Figure 4-13   *Admin Password*

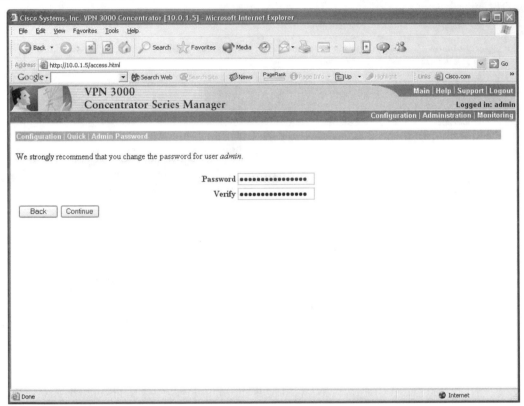

More In-Depth Group Configuration Information

The preceding section explained how to quickly configure a single IPSec tunnel using Quick Configuration. This section explains how to configure or modify IKE, group, and mode configuration parameters.

IKE Proposals

The Concentrator can handle four types of remote clients: the VPN 3 *x*/4 *x* Software Client, the VPN 2.5 Software Client, the Certicom client, and the VPN 3002 Hardware Client. Before the Concentrator can interface with these clients, you must make sure that the appropriate IKE proposal is configured, activated, and prioritized. In remote-access connections, the Software Client sends IKE proposals to the Concentrator. The Concentrator functions only as responder. As the responder, the Concentrator checks the active IKE proposal list, in priority order, to see if it can find a proposal that matches parameters in the Software Client's proposed security association (SA). If a match is found, the tunnel establishment continues. If no match is found, the tunnel is torn down.

The IKE proposals are as follows:

- For the VPN 3.x/4.x Software Client or later clients, use any of the proposals that start with CiscoVPNClient. The default is CiscoVPNClient-3DES-MD5. The VPN 3.0 Software Client or later client proposal must be listed first under the Active Proposals list, or your Unity client will not connect.

- For the VPN 2.5 Software Client, use any of the IKE proposals, except the IKE proposals that end in DH7.

- For the Certicom client, use a proposal that ends in DH7. The Certicom client operates best using a proposal that supports DH group 7 because of the speed increase of DH7 over DH5. The Certicom client does support other DH groups.

Each IKE proposal in the IKE proposals window is a template (see Figure 4-14). The parameters assigned to the template are applied to the individual remote connection. In the next window, the individual parameters can be viewed or modified.

Figure 4-14   *IKE Proposals*

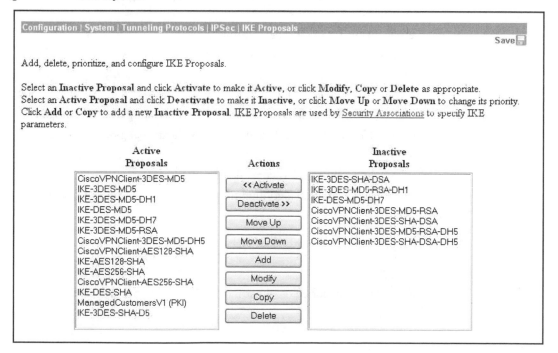

In Figure 4-14, individual IKE templates are displayed in the Active Proposals column. By selecting an IKE proposal and then clicking Modify, the administrator can view or modify the individual parameters of the IKE proposal, or template. Use the Configuration > System > Tunneling Protocols > IPSec > IKE Proposals > Modify window, shown in Figure 4-15, to check the IKE proposals to make sure that you have the correct IKE parameters for a particular Software Client type.

Figure 4-15   *Checking IKE Proposals*

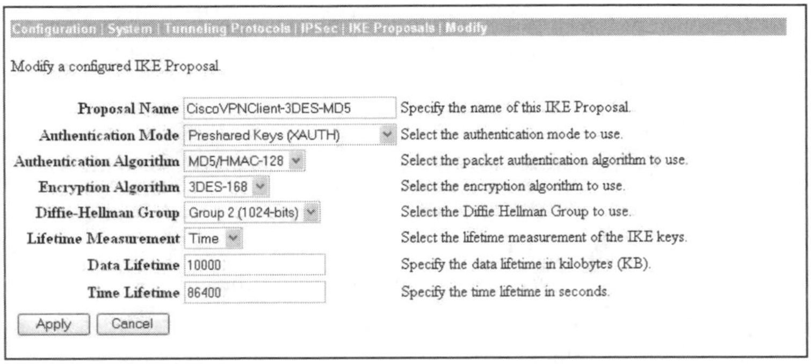

- Choose the proper authentication mode from the Authentication Mode drop-down menu:
  — Preshared Keys (XAUTH) for VPN 3.0 Software Client or later client applications
  — Preshared keys for the VPN 2.5 Software Client
  — Preshared keys with DH7 for Certicom client applications
- Choose the recommended DH group for each Software Client from the Diffie-Hellman Group drop-down menu:
  — Group 1 (768 bits) for Unity and Cisco 2.5 clients using digital certificates
  — Group 2 (1024 bits) for Unity and Cisco 2.5 clients using preshared keys
  — Group 5 (1536 bits) for the Unity client using AES encryption
  — Group 7 (ECC) for the Certicom client.
- Choose the proper encryption algorithm from the Encryption Algorithm drop-down menu:
  — DES-56
  — 3DES-168
  — AES-128
  — AES-192 (not supported on either the VPN Software or Hardware Clients)
  — AES-256

Group Configuration

In the preceding section, you configured a simple remote-access VPN using Quick Configuration. A group called training was created for the remote-access users. You can use the Modify Groups screen to change the parameters of this group.

Seven tabs are located under User Management > Groups > Modify Training: Identity, General, IPSec, Client Config, Client FW, HW Client, and PPTP-L2TP. The following information can be configured:

- **Identity tab**—You can configure the group name, password, and group authentication server type. The group authentication server type specifies whether the group is configured internally, or externally on a security server.
- **General tab**—You can configure access rights, privileges, and protocols.
- **IPSec tab**—You can configure the IPSec tunneling parameters.
- **Client Config tab**—You can configure the Software Client, Microsoft client, and common client parameters.
- **Client FW tab**—You can configure the Software Client firewall parameters.
- **HW Client tab**—You can configure the Hardware Client parameters.
- **PPTP/L2TP tab**—You can configure the PPTP and L2TP tunneling parameters.

Identity Tab

The Identity tab, shown in Figure 4-16, lets you configure the group name, password, and group authentication server location. The Identity parameters can be set as follows:

- **Group Name field**—Enter a unique name for this specific group. The maximum number of characters is 32.
- **Password field**—Enter a unique password for this specific group. The minimum number of characters is four, and the maximum is 32. The field displays only bullets.
- **Verify field**—Reenter the group password to verify it. The field displays only bullets.
- **Type drop-down menu**—Click the drop-down menu button and choose the type of group:
    - **Internal**—Uses the internal Concentrator authentication server to authenticate groups for IPSec tunneling. The internal server is the default selection.
    - **External**—Uses an external authentication server to configure this group (for example, a RADIUS server).

Figure 4-16   *Group Identity Screen*

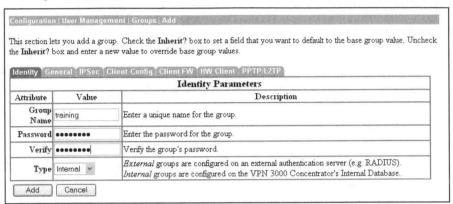

General Tab

The General tab, shown in Figure 4-17, can be broken into three sections. The top section defines access rights and privileges, the center section is used for WINS and DNS information used by the Software Client, and the bottom section defines the tunneling protocols this group supports. The General parameters can be set as follows:

- **Access Hours drop-down menu**—Click the drop-down menu button and choose the hours when group users can access the Concentrator:

    - **No Restrictions**—No restrictions on access hours.

    - **Never**—No access at any time.

    - **Business hours**—Access 9 a.m. to 5 p.m., Monday through Friday.

- **Simultaneous Logins field**—Enter the number of simultaneous logins that group users are permitted. The minimum is 1, and the default is 3. Although there is no maximum limit, allowing several simultaneous logins could compromise security and affect performance.

- **Minimum Password Length field**—Enter the minimum number of characters for group user passwords. The minimum is 1, the default is 8, and the maximum is 32.

- **Allow Alphabetic-Only Passwords check box**—Check this check box to allow user passwords with alphabetic characters only. To protect security, it is strongly recommended that you not allow such passwords.

- **Idle Timeout field**—Enter the group idle timeout period in minutes. If there is no communication activity on the connection in this period, the system terminates the connection.

- **Maximum Connect Time field**—Enter the group maximum connection time in minutes. At the end of this time, the system terminates the connection.

- **Filter drop-down menu**—Filters can be used to restrict a group's access to the network based on source address, destination address, and protocol.

NOTE   The PC overwrites its current values with information from the following fields.

- **Primary DNS field**—Enter the IP address of the DNS server for this group's users.

- **Secondary DNS field**—Enter the IP address of the DNS server for this group's users.

- **Primary WINS field**—Enter the IP address of the WINS server for this group's users.

- **Secondary WINS field**—Enter the IP address of the WINS server for this group's users.

- **SEP Card Assignment check boxes**—These are visible if Scalable Encryption Processors (SEPs) are installed. It is recommended that you leave all four check boxes checked (for redundancy).

- **Tunneling Protocols check boxes**—Select the tunneling protocols that the user Software Clients can use. (Although the Concentrator can support all four protocols simultaneously, for this example deselect PPTP and L2TP. Select IPSec only.)

- **Strip Realm check box**—If you check this check box, authentication is based on the username alone. The realm qualifier at the end of the username is removed (for example, service is stripped from bob@service). If this check box is not checked, authentication is based on a full string (for example, username@realm).

Figure 4-17   *Group General Screen*

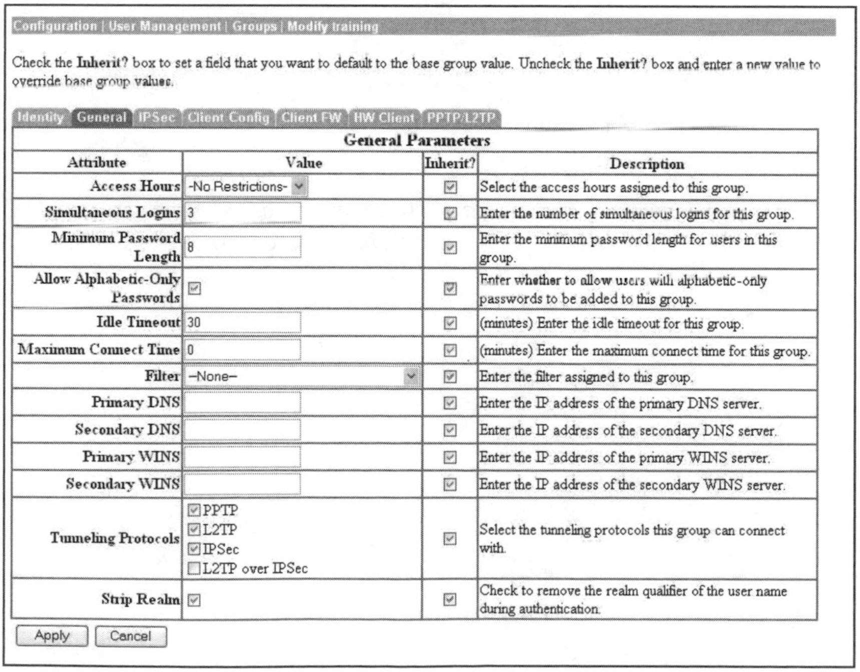

IPSec Tab

The IPSec tab, shown in Figure 4-18, lets you configure IPSec protocol parameters that apply to this group. This window can be divided into two sections: IPSec parameters and remote-access parameters. The IPSec parameters can be set as follows:

- **IPSec SA drop-down menu**—Click the drop-down menu button and choose the IPSec SA assigned to this group's IPSec clients. During tunnel establishment, the IPSec client and server negotiate an SA that governs authentication, encryption, encapsulation, key management, and so on. View or modify IPSec SAs on the Configuration > Policy Management > Traffic Management > Security Associations window.

- **IKE Peer Identity Validation drop-down menu**—This option applies only to tunnel negotiations based on digital certificates.

- **IKE Keepalives check box**—Check this check box to enable this feature. (IKE keepalives are enabled by default.) This feature lets the Concentrator monitor the continued presence of a remote peer and report its own presence to that peer. If the peer becomes unresponsive, the Concentrator initiates removal of the connection. Enabling IKE keepalives prevents hung connections when rebooting either the host or the peer. For this feature to work, both the Concentrator and its remote peer must support IKE keepalives. The following peers support IKE keepalives:

    - Software Client (Release 3.0 and later)

    - Software Client (Release 2.x)

    - Hardware Client

    - Concentrators (with IKE support)

    - Cisco IOS software

    - Cisco PIX Firewall

- **Tunnel Type drop-down menu**—Click the drop-down menu button and choose the remote-access tunnel type. Choose Remote Access for IPSec client-to-LAN applications.

Figure 4-18   *Group IPSec Screen*

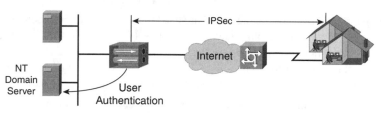

Configuration | User Management | Groups | Modify training

Check the **Inherit?** box to set a field that you want to default to the base group value. Uncheck the **Inherit?** box and enter a new value to override base group values.

Identity   General   IPSec   Client Config   Client FW   HW Client   PPTP/L2TP

IPSec Parameters

Attribute	Value	Inherit?	Description
IPSec SA	ESP-3DES-MD5	☑	Select the group's IPSec Security Association.
IKE Peer Identity Validation	If supported by certificate	☑	Select whether or not to validate the identity of the peer using the peer's certificate.
IKE Keepalives	☑	☑	Check to enable the use of IKE keepalives for members of this group.
Tunnel Type	Remote Access	☑	Select the type of tunnel for this group. Update the Remote Access parameters below as needed.

Remote Access Parameters

Group Lock	☐	☑	Lock users into this group.
Authentication	RADIUS	☑	Select the authentication method for members of this group. This parameter does not apply to **Individual User Authentication**.
IPComp	None	☑	Select the method of IP Compression for members of this group.
Reauthentication on Rekey	☐	☑	Check to reauthenticate the user on an IKE (Phase-1) rekey.
Mode Configuration	☑	☑	Check to initiate the exchange of Mode Configuration parameters with the client. This must be checked if version 2.5 (or earlier) of the Altiga/Cisco client is being used by members of this group.

Apply   Cancel

Dead Peer Detection

Dead peer detection (DPD) messages are used to help VPN devices detect tunnel failure on the devices located at the other end of the tunnels (for example, reboot one device and lose an Internet connection). A worry metric determines how often a DPD message is sent in the absence of data received from the IKE peer. When data is received, the worry timer is reset. If the device's worry timer expires, a DPD message is sent. The worry timers are as follows:

- In the Cisco VPN 3000 Series Concentrator Release 3.0 and later Software Client and Hardware Client, the worry timer is set for 300 seconds. LAN-to-LAN connections set the worry timer to 10 seconds.

- In the Concentrator version 2.5, the worry timer is set for 5 minutes.

If you are configuring a group of mixed peers, and some of those peers support IKE keepalives while others do not, enable IKE keepalives for the entire group. During IKE negotiation, each Software Client identifies whether DPD messages are supported. To be enabled, both ends must support this feature. The feature has no effect on the peers that do not support it.

NOTE To reduce connectivity costs, disable IKE keepalives if this group includes any Software Clients connecting via ISDN lines. ISDN connections normally disconnect if idle, but the IKE keepalive mechanism prevents connections from idling out and, therefore, from disconnecting.

Remote-access parameters include group lock, user authentication IP compression, and mode configuration. These parameters are configured as follows:

- **Group Lock check box**—Locks users into a specific group (for example, RADIUS allows you to lock specific users to a group). You can lock a user to a group based on a certificate's organizational unit (OU) or by using the RADIUS Class attribute OU = groupname. For example, according to the RADIUS server, Joe is a member of the training group. If Joe tries to log in as a member of the IS group, which has different access rights, the connection fails.

- **Authentication drop-down menu**—In the Concentrator, remote users are authenticated twice. This parameter pertains to the private network authentication. It determines how users within the group are authenticated and whether an NT, SDI, or RADIUS server will authenticate them.

- **IPComp drop-down menu**—IP compression runs inside IPSec. Outbound data is compressed and then encrypted. At the remote end, data is decrypted and then decompressed. IP compression uses fewer bytes per transmission. On a low-speed line, fewer bytes to transmit equals faster message transmission. For example, you might put all modem users in a group and enable IP compression. This should speed up the transmissions. However, there is a processing penalty for doing compression. At higher speeds (64 Kbps and above), IP compression tends to slow the transmission because of processing delays, compression, and decompression. Do not enable IP compression for high-speed users. This would slow the performance of the PC and Concentrator.

- **Reauthentication on Rekey check box**—When you check this check box, the Concentrator prompts the user for identification and a password whenever a rekey occurs. The default is unchecked.

- **Mode Configuration check box**—Lets the Concentrator push information to the Software Client.

Client Config Tab

Most of the configuration issues in a remote-access network originate at the remote PC. Many parameters need to be programmed on the remote user's PC. Not everyone can perform the needed changes. IETF IPSec Working Group Internet solved this issue using mode configuration. The end user or IT department loads a minimum IPSec configuration in the end user's PC. During IPSec tunnel establishment, the Concentrator pushes the remaining information to the PC.

The administrator can program this information on the Configuration > User Management > Groups > Client Config tab, as shown in Figure 4-19. The Client Config tab has three sections: one for parameters specific to Cisco clients, one for Microsoft client parameters, and a third for common client parameters.

Cisco Client Parameters

During IPSec tunnel establishment, the Concentrator pushes the Software Client information to the PC, as shown in Figure 4-20. Some of these parameters include a login banner, split tunneling, and IPSec over User Datagram Protocol (UDP).

Figure 4-19 *Group Client Config Screen*

Configuration | User Management | Groups | Modify training			

Check the **Inherit?** box to set a field that you want to default to the base group value. Uncheck the **Inherit?** box and enter a new value to override base group values.

Identity General IPSec **Client Config** Client FW HW Client PPTP/L2TP

Client Configuration Parameters

Cisco Client Parameters

Attribute	Value	Inherit?	Description
Banner		☑	Enter the banner for this group. Only software clients see the banner.
Allow Password Storage on Client	☐	☑	Check to allow the IPSec client to store the password locally.
IPSec over UDP	☐	☑	Check to allow a client to operate through a NAT device using UDP encapsulation of ESP.
IPSec over UDP Port	10000	☑	Enter the UDP port to be used for IPSec through NAT (4001 - 49151, except port 4500, which is reserved for NAT-T).
IPSec Backup Servers	Use Client Configured List	☑	• Select a method to use or disable backup servers. • Enter up to 10 IPSec backup server addresses/names starting from high priority to low. • Enter each IPSec backup server address/name on a single line.

Microsoft Client Parameters

Intercept DHCP Configure Message	☐	☑	Check to use group policy for clients requesting Microsoft DHCP options.
Subnet Mask	255.255.255.255	☑	Enter the subnet mask for clients requesting Microsoft DHCP options.

Common Client Parameters

Split Tunneling Policy	⦿ Tunnel everything ☐ Allow the networks in list to bypass the tunnel ○ Only tunnel networks in the list	☑	Select the method and network list to be used for Split Tunneling. **Tunnel Everything**: Send all traffic through the tunnel. **Allow the networks in the list to bypass the tunnel**: The VPN Client may choose to send traffic to addresses in this list to the client's LAN. Send all other traffic through the tunnel. NOTE: This setting only applies to the Cisco VPN Client.
Split Tunneling Network List	–None–	☑	**Tunnel networks the in list**: Send traffic to addresses in this list through the tunnel. Send all other traffic to the client's LAN.
Default Domain Name		☑	Enter the default domain name given to users of this group.
Split DNS Names		☑	Enter the set of domains, separated by commas without spaces, to be resolved through the Split Tunnel.

Apply Cancel

Figure 4-20   *Group Cisco Client Parameters*

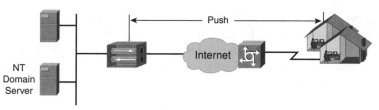

| Configuration | User Management | Groups | Modify training |

Check the **Inherit?** box to set a field that you want to default to the base group value. Uncheck the **Inherit?** box and enter a new value to override base group values.

| Identity | General | IPSec | Client Config | Client FW | HW Client | PPTP/L2TP |

Client Configuration Parameters

Cisco Client Parameters

Attribute	Value	Inherit?	Description
Banner		☑	Enter the banner for this group. Only software clients see the banner.
Allow Password Storage on Client	☐	☑	Check to allow the IPSec client to store the password locally.
IPSec over UDP	☐	☑	Check to allow a client to operate through a NAT device using UDP encapsulation of ESP.
IPSec over UDP Port	10000	☑	Enter the UDP port to be used for IPSec through NAT (4001 - 49151, except port 4500, which is reserved for NAT-T).
IPSec Backup Servers	Use Client Configured List	☑	• Select a method to use or disable backup servers. • Enter up to 10 IPSec backup server addresses/names starting from high priority to low. • Enter each IPSec backup server address/name on a single line.

Cisco VPN Software Client parameters can be set from the Client Config tab as follows:

- **Banner field**—When a Software Client logs into the VPN, the banner that you enter in this field is displayed. It can be up to 510 characters, and it can be multiple lines of text instead of a single line (the text wraps). Enter a period (.) in the CLI to finish the entry and set the banner. If you enter more than 510 characters, the Software Client sees an error during login.

NOTE   Each line break uses two characters. This is because a newline is a carriage return (CR) and a line feed (LF).

- **Allow Password Storage on Client check box**—This is not recommended for security purposes.
- **IPSec over UDP check box**—IPSec packets are wrapped in UDP so that firewalls and routers can perform Network Address Translation (NAT).
- **IPSec over UDP Port field**—For this to be enabled, a UDP port number must be assigned.
- **IPSec Backup Servers**—Lets a Hardware Client connect to the central site when its primary central site Concentrator is unavailable. You configure backup servers for a Hardware Client either on the Hardware Client or on a group basis at the primary central site Concentrator. If you configure backup servers on the central site Concentrator, that Concentrator pushes the backup server policy to the Hardware Client in the group. Chapter 9, "Configuring Cisco VPN Clients for Backup Server, Load Balancing, and Reverse Route Injection," further discusses backup server parameters.

Common Client Parameters

Under the common client parameters you can add settings for the split-tunneling policy, default domain name, and split DNS.

Split Tunneling   Three tunneling options are available to the network administrator, as shown in Figure 4-21: tunnel everything, tunnel everything except local LAN traffic, and split tunneling. The administrator must decide which option is correct for each group of remote Software Clients.

Figure 4-21 *Tunneling Options*

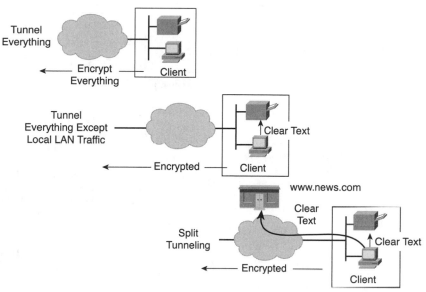

- **Tunnel everything**—After the VPN tunnel is launched, all traffic is directed through the VPN tunnel. The VPN Tunnel Everything option allows only IP traffic to and from the secure gateway, prohibiting any IP traffic to and from resources on a local network (such as printer, fax, and shared files on another system). While the IPSec tunnel is established, all network traffic is forced through the tunnel to the central site.

  Select the Group > Client Config tab to enable the Tunnel everything option. Within this tab, select the Tunnel everything radio button within the Split Tunneling Policy row, as shown in Figure 4-22.

- **Tunnel everything except local LAN traffic**—The local LAN access option provides access to resources on a local LAN while the VPN tunnel is established. The local LAN addresses are pushed to the Software Client. These IP addresses are added to the Software Client driver's access control list (ACL). These bypass addresses route ahead of the VPN tunnel's encryption algorithm. Any data bound for, or received from, the addresses specified in the Mode Configuration message is sent or received in the clear. This allows access to the local LAN while the IPSec tunnel is running. All other traffic is encrypted and forwarded to the central site. For security purposes, the user can disable local LAN access when using an insecure local network (for example, in a hotel).

Figure 4-22 *Tunneling Everything*

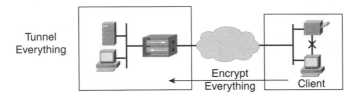

Split Tunneling Policy	● Tunnel everything ☐ Allow the networks in list to bypass the tunnel ○ Only tunnel networks in the list	☑	Select the method and network list to be used for Split Tunneling. **Tunnel Everything:** Send all traffic through the tunnel. **Allow the networks in the list to bypass the tunnel:** The VPN Client may choose to send traffic to addresses in this list to the client's LAN. Send all other traffic through the tunnel. NOTE: This setting only applies to the Cisco VPN Client.
Split Tunneling Network List	–None–	☑	**Tunnel networks in the list:** Send traffic to addresses in this list through the tunnel. Send all other traffic to the client's LAN.
Default Domain Name		☑	Enter the default domain name given to users of this group.
Split DNS Names	cisco.com	☐	Enter the set of domains, separated by commas without spaces, to be resolved through the Split Tunnel. The **Default Domain Name** must be explicitly included in **Split DNS Names** list if it is to be resolved through the tunnel.

Two steps are required to configure this option:

Step 1 Enable the feature. Select the Allow the networks in list to bypass the tunnel radio button within the Split Tunneling Policy row, as shown in Figure 4-23.

Step 2 Supply the referenced IP address list. Choose VPN Client Local LAN (Default) from the Split Tunneling Network List drop-down menu.

Figure 4-23   *Tunneling Everything Except the Local LAN*

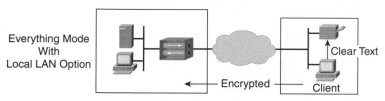

Common Client Parameters			
Split Tunneling Policy	⦿ Tunnel everything ☑ Allow the networks in list to bypass the tunnel ◯ Only tunnel networks in the list	☐	Select the method and network list to be used for Split Tunneling. **Tunnel Everything:** Send all traffic through the tunnel. **Allow the networks in the list to bypass the tunnel:** The VPN Client may choose to send traffic to addresses in this list to the
Split Tunneling Network List	VPN Client Local LAN (Default) ⌄	☐	client's LAN. Send all other traffic through the tunnel. NOTE: This setting only applies to the Cisco VPN Client. **Tunnel networks in the list:** Send traffic to addresses in this list through the tunnel. Send all other traffic to the client's LAN.
Default Domain Name		☑	Enter the default domain name given to users of this group.
Split DNS Names	cisco.com	☐	Enter the set of domains, separated by commas without spaces, to be resolved through the Split Tunnel. The **Default Domain Name** must be explicitly included in **Split DNS Names** list if it is to be resolved through the tunnel.

A local LAN network address list is required for the local LAN option. Go to the Configuration > Policy Management > Traffic Management > Network Lists window, shown in Figure 4-24, to configure the LAN address. The address list pushed down to the Software Client is 0.0.0.0 / 0.0.0.0. This is a special case. It directs the Software Client to interpret the network address or subnet mask of the LAN interface over which the VPN connection is being made as the local LAN address. Route all locally addressed LAN packets in clear text. The 0.0.0.0 / 0.0.0.255 network address list is called the VPN Client Local LAN list.

In Figure 4-24, the Software Client resides on the 192.168.1.0 network. Having received a 0.0.0.0 / 0.0.0.0 network list, the Software Client routes all 192.168.1.0 traffic in clear text. All other traffic is encrypted and sent down the tunnel.

Figure 4-24 *Tunneling Everything Except the Local LAN*

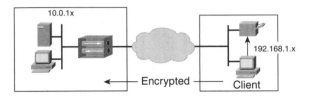

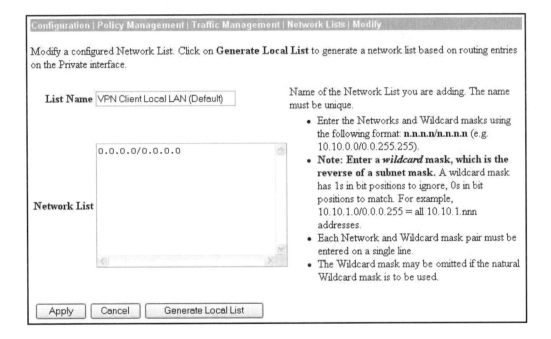

- **Split tunneling**—Split tunneling, shown in Figure 4-25, lets remote users access Internet networks without requiring them to tunnel through the corporate network. Before split tunneling, all traffic originating from the Software Client is encrypted and routed through the secure tunnel. This includes both secure and Internet browsing traffic. The secure traffic is terminated, and Internet traffic is routed back out to the Internet. A large percentage of the corporate backbone bandwidth is used for redirected web browsing traffic from remote users.

  Split tunneling addresses the redirection issue, because split tunneling routes secure, encrypted traffic through the tunnel. Nonsecure traffic (for example, web browsing) is sent in the clear. ISP can route the traffic accordingly (for example, secure traffic to the corporate network and web browsing to the ISP).

Figure 4-25 *Split Tunneling*

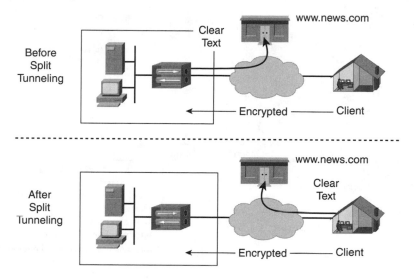

The Concentrator pushes specific IP addresses to the Software Client to implement split tunneling. If the traffic is bound for one of these addresses, it is encrypted and sent to the Concentrator. If the IP address is different from the pushed addresses, the message is sent in the clear, and the ISP can route it.

Configuring split tunneling requires two steps:

Step 1 Enable split tunneling by selecting the Only tunnel networks in list radio button within the Split Tunneling Policy row, as shown in Figure 4-26.

Step 2 Choose the appropriate list from the Split Tunneling Network List drop-down menu. This is a predefined list of secure network addresses.

Figure 4-26 *Split Tunneling Policy*

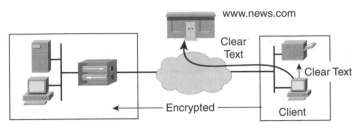

Common Client Parameters			
Split Tunneling Policy	○ Tunnel everything ☐ Allow the networks in list to bypass the tunnel ◉ Only tunnel networks in the list	☐	Select the method and network list to be used for Split Tunneling. **Tunnel Everything**: Send all traffic through the tunnel. **Allow the networks in the list to bypass the tunnel**: The VPN Client may choose to send traffic to addresses in this list to the client's LAN. Send all other traffic through the tunnel. NOTE: This setting only applies to the Cisco VPN Client. **Tunnel networks in the list**: Send traffic to addresses in this list through the tunnel. Send all other traffic to the client's LAN.
Split Tunneling Network List	Pod 1 network list ⌄	☐	
Default Domain Name		☑	Enter the default domain name given to users of this group.
Split DNS Names	cisco.com|	☐	Enter the set of domains, separated by commas without spaces, to be resolved through the Split Tunnel. The **Default Domain Name** must be explicitly included in **Split DNS Names** list if it is to be resolved through the tunnel.

The Concentrator pushes down specific IP addresses to the Cisco VPN Client. If the traffic is bound for one of these addresses, it is encrypted and sent to the Concentrator. These addresses are defined under Configuration > Policy Management > Traffic Management > Network Lists, as shown in Figure 4-27. When you click Add to add a network list, in the List Name field, configure a name for the list. In the Network List field, supply the network and wildcard mask. In Figure 4-27, the administrator wants to send clear text to the Internet and the local printer. The administrator also wants to send encrypted traffic to the headquarters: the 10.0.1.0 network. In the List Name field, a network list name is defined (Pod1 network list), and in the Network List field, the private network IP address and wildcard mask are configured (10.0.1.0/0.0.0.255). As a result of this list, any traffic bound for a host on the 10.0.1.0 network is encrypted and sent down the IPSec tunnel. All other traffic is sent in plain text.

Figure 4-27   *Split-Tunneling Network List*

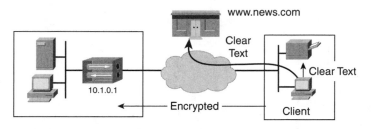

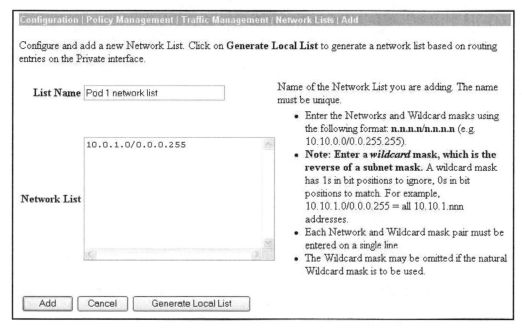

Split DNS   Split DNS, shown in Figure 4-28, is used in split-tunneling connections. The Software Client resolves whether a DNS query packet is sent in clear text or is encrypted and sent down the tunnel. If the packet is encrypted and sent down the tunnel, a corporate DNS server resolves the DNS query. Clear-text DNS requests are resolved by ISP-assigned DNS servers.

Figure 4-28 *Split DNS*

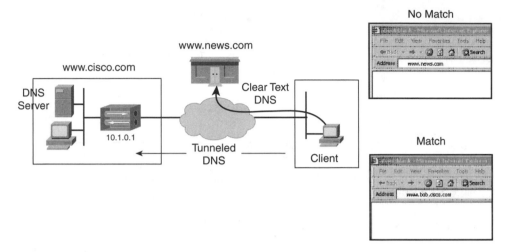

The client receives a comma-delimited list of split DNS names from the Concentrator via mode-config. When the Software Client receives a DNS query packet, the domain name is compared and sequentially checked against the split DNS names. Case-insensitive domain name comparison starts at the end of each domain name string and continues toward the beginning of each string, resulting in a match, or no match. Query packets passing the comparison have their destination IP address rewritten and tunneled using the primary DNS IP address configured on the Concentrator. As an example, the query bob.cisco.com when compared against the split DNS name of cisco.com results in a match. The cisco.com in bob.cisco.com matches the split DNS string of cisco.com. The bob.cisco.com DNS query is encrypted and sent to the primary DNS server. The primary DNS server resolves the IP address of bob.cisco.com. Failover in the case of an unreachable primary split DNS server causes the secondary split DNS server to be used to resolve further queries. Packets not matching the split DNS list pass through the client untouched and are transmitted in clear text. As an example, the query news.com when compared against the split DNS name of cisco.com results in a mismatch. The news.com DNS query is sent in clear text. The ISP-assigned DNS servers resolve the IP address.

In Figure 4-29, the corporate DNS server resolves all cisco.com DNS name requests. The ISP assigned DNS server resolves all clear-text DNS requests. Complete the following five-step process to configure split DNS:

Step 1 Define a list of secure networks. The network list is defined under Configuration > Traffic Management > Policy Management > Network Lists.

Step 2 Configure the Concentrator for split tunneling from the Configuration > User Management > Groups > Client Config tab. Select only tunnel networks in the list to enable split tunneling.

Step 3   From the Configuration > User Management > Groups > Client Config
tab, select the newly defined network list from the Split Tunneling
Network List drop-down menu.

Step 4   From the Configuration > User Management > Groups > Client Config
tab, define the names of the corporate DNS domains in the Split DNS
Names field (for example, cisco.com). Use commas, without spaces, to
separate the names for multiple entries.

Step 5   From the Configuration > User Management > Groups > General tab,
define the primary and secondary DNS server IP addresses. The primary
and secondary DNS servers resolve the encrypted DNS queries.

Figure 4-29   *Configuring Split DNS*

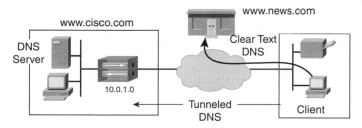

Common Client Parameters			
Split Tunneling Policy	○ Tunnel everything ☐ Allow the networks in list to bypass the tunnel ◉ Only tunnel networks in the list	☐	Select the method and network list to be used for Split Tunneling. **Tunnel Everything:** Send all traffic through the tunnel. **Allow the networks in the list to bypass the tunnel:** The VPN Client may choose to send traffic to addresses in this list to the client's LAN. Send all other traffic through the tunnel. NOTE: This setting only applies to the Cisco VPN Client. **Tunnel networks in the list:** Send traffic to addresses in this list through the tunnel. Send all other traffic to the client's LAN.
Split Tunneling Network List	Pod 1 network list ⌄	☐	
Default Domain Name		☑	Enter the default domain name given to users of this group.
Split DNS Names	cisco.com|	☐	Enter the set of domains, separated by commas without spaces, to be resolved through the Split Tunnel. The **Default Domain Name** must be explicitly included in **Split DNS Names** list if it is to be resolved through the tunnel.

Client FW Tab

The Client FW tab, shown in Figure 4-30, is where the configuration settings are configured for the VPN Software Client firewall. The Client FW tab is covered in more detail in Chapter 6, "The Cisco VPN Client Firewall Feature."

Figure 4-30 *Group Client FW Parameters*

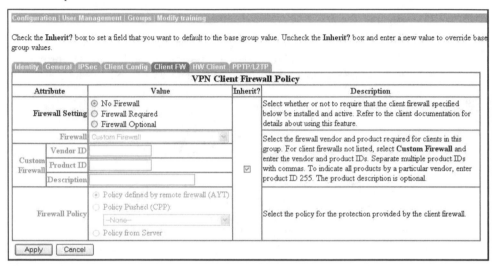

HW Client Tab

The HW Client tab, shown in Figure 4-31, is where the configuration settings are made for the group when it is used by a Cisco VPN 3002 Hardware Client. The HW Client tab is covered in more detail in Chapters 7 through 11, which cover the Cisco VPN 3002 Hardware Client.

PPTP/L2TP Tab

The PPTP/L2TP tab, shown in Figure 4-32, is where configuration settings for the group are applied for PPTP and L2TP connections.

PPTP and L2TP configurations are not covered in this book, because it focuses on IPSec configuration.

Figure 4-31   *Group HW Client Parameters*

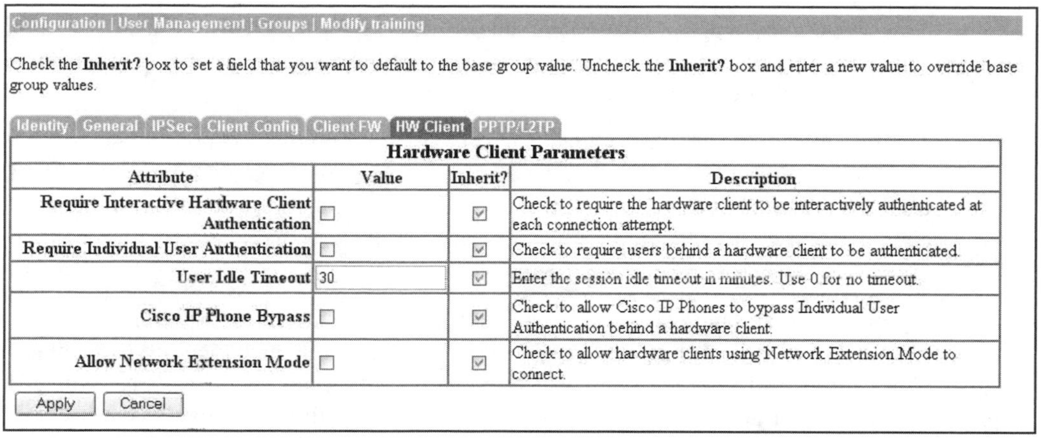

Figure 4-32   *Group PPTP/L2TP Parameters*

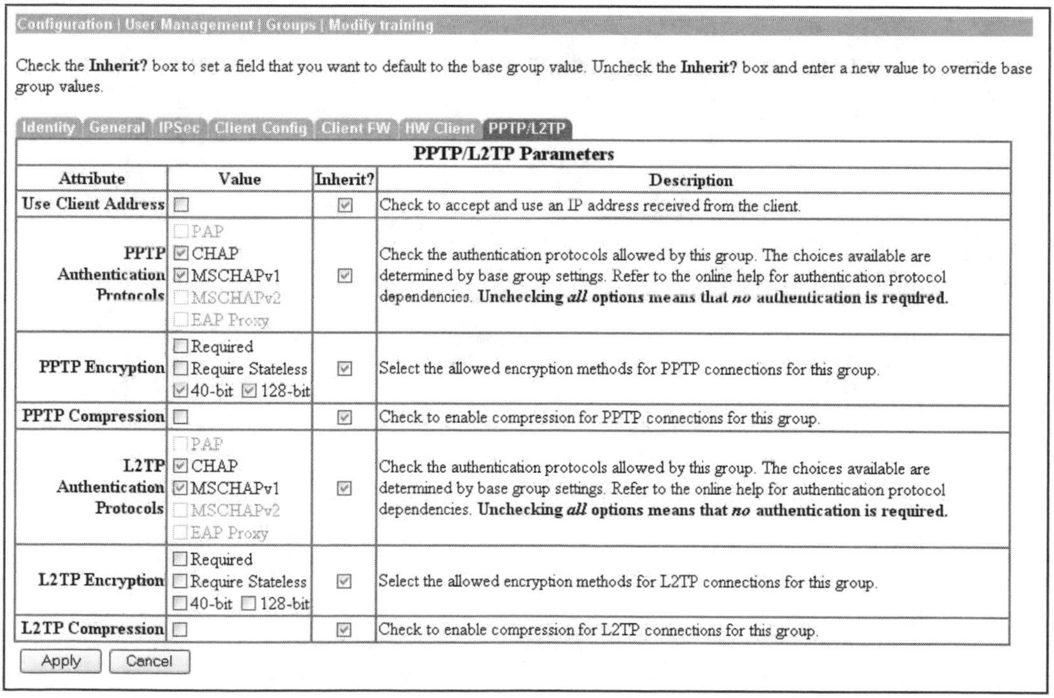

Configuring the Windows VPN Software Client

Now that we have created a sample group for remote access using the quick configuration, and also delved into the available configuration options within a group, we will look at the configuration options for the VPN Software Client.

The Windows VPN Software Client is a software program that runs on Windows 95, 98, Me, 2000, XP, and NT 4.0. The Software Client on a remote PC, communicating with a Concentrator at an enterprise or service provider, creates a secure connection over a public network such as the Internet that lets you access a private network as if you were an on-site user.

Figure 4-33 shows the Software Client window. From this window, you can launch the new connection wizard, change or set optional parameters, and launch the Software Client. The Connection Entry field lets the user provide a unique name for this VPN connection. The address of the Concentrator's public interface is configured in the Host name or IP address of the remote server field.

Figure 4-33 *Windows VPN Software Client*

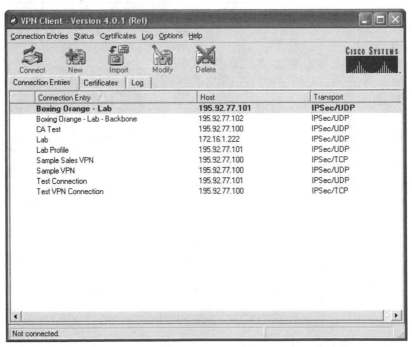

The Connection Entry toolbar menu lets you configure or change optional parameters specific to the selected connection entry. When you click Connection Entries, the following options become available, as shown in Figure 4-34:

- **Connect**—Connects to the VPN entry.

- **Disconnect**—If connected, this disconnects your VPN session.

- **Create Shortcut**—Lets you create a shortcut for your desktop.

- **Modify**—Allows you to modify the settings of the VPN connection.

- **Delete**—Lets you delete a connection entry.

- **Duplicate**—Lets you copy a connection entry with all its properties.

- **Set as Default Connection Entry**—Focus is always given to this entry, and it is highlighted in bold.

- **New**—Adds a new connection entry.

- **Import**—Uses a preconfigured .pcf file that loads the Software Client parameters.

- **Exit VPN Client**—Exits and closes the client application.

Figure 4-34 *Windows VPN Software Client Options*

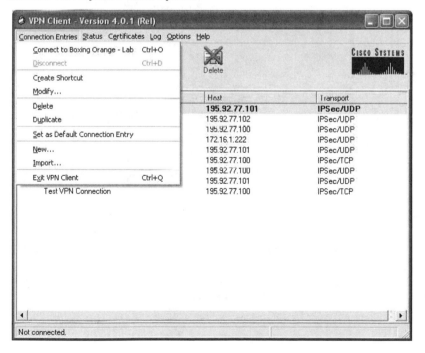

If the system administrator needs to know what Software Client version you have installed on your PC, from the VPN Client window, select Help > About VPN Client to display the version information.

Select Connection Entries > Modify. Under Modify are four tabs, as shown in Figure 4-35:

- **Authentication**—Configures the Software Client's group or digital certificate information.

- **Transport**—Enables IPSec through NAT and displays the status of the local LAN access feature.

- **Backup Servers**—Enables backup connections for the client.

- **Dial-Up**—Links the VPN connection to Dialup Networking phone book entries.

Figure 4-35 *Windows VPN Software Properties Tabs*

The Concentrator and Software Client connection can be authenticated with either the group name and password or digital certificates. The Authentication tab, shown in Figure 4-36, lets you set your authentication information. You need to choose one method, group or certificates, via the radio buttons. Within the Group Authentication information group box, enter the group name and password in the appropriate fields. The group name and password must match what is configured for this group within the Configuration > User Management > Groups > Identity window. Entries are case-sensitive.

Figure 4-36 *Windows VPN Software Authentication Tab*

For certificates to be exchanged, the Certificate Authentication radio button must be selected. The Name drop-down menu lists any personal certificates loaded on your PC. Choose the certificate to be exchanged with the Concentrator during connection establishment. If no personal certificates are loaded in your PC, the drop-down menu is blank.

The next tab is Transport, as shown in Figure 4-37. This setting should mirror what is used on the central site Concentrator, but in most cases it is safe to leave these settings as is. The Allow Local LAN Access check box allows you to access the resources on your local LAN (such as a printer or fax) when you are connected to a central site VPN device. When this parameter is enabled and your central site VPN Concentrator is configured to permit it, you can access local resources while connected. When this parameter is disabled, all traffic from your client system goes through the IPSec connection to the secure gateway.

Figure 4-37 *Windows VPN Software Transport Tab*

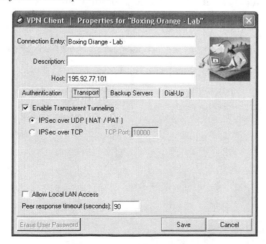

The next tab is Backup Servers, as shown in Figure 4-38. Your system administrator tells you whether to enable a backup Concentrator and gives you its address. If the Software Client cannot reach the primary Concentrator, it tries a backup Concentrator. Check the Enable Backup Servers check box to enable this feature. Then click Add to enter the IP address of the backup Concentrator. Your Software Client attempts to connect to your primary Concentrator first. If that Concentrator cannot be reached, the Software Client accesses the backup list for the addresses of available backup Concentrators.

Figure 4-38   *Windows VPN Software Backup Servers Tab*

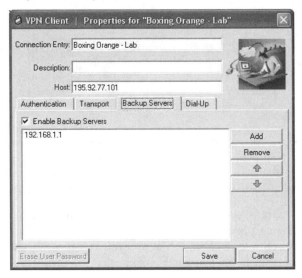

The last tab is Dial-Up, as shown in Figure 4-39. It defines the connection to the Internet via dialup networking.

Connecting to a private network using a dialup connection is typically a two-step process:

Step 1   Use a dialup connection to your Internet service provider (ISP).

Step 2   Use the Software Client to connect to the private network.

Connecting to the Internet via dialup networking (DUN) automatically launches the DUN connection before making the VPN connection. It makes connecting to the ISP and Concentrator an easy, one-step process. To enable this option, check Connect to Internet via dialup.

Figure 4-39 *Windows VPN Software Dial-Up Tab*

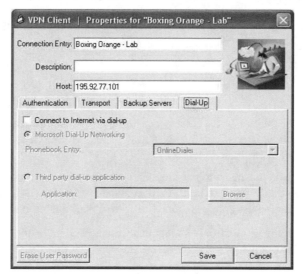

Preconfiguring the Client for Remote Users

An administrator can preconfigure software clients. A folder is placed on the remote user's PC. Inside the folder is a copy of the VPN software plus three additional files:

- **oem.ini**—Installs the Software Client without user intervention. The administrator can create an oem.ini file in Notepad. Under SilentMode, enter **0** or **1**:

  — **1**—Activates silent installation (does not prompt the user).

  — **0**—Prompts the user during installation.

  After the oem.ini file is created, identify the pathname and folder to contain the Software Client software. The default pathname to the VPN software is C:\ProgramFiles\CiscoSystems\VPN Client.

  Last, reboot the system. Under Reboot, enter **0, 1,** or **2**:

  — If Silent Mode is on (1) and Reboot is 0, the system prompts the user for a reboot.

  — If Silent Mode is on (1) and Reboot is 1, the system automatically reboots after installation.

  — If Silent Mode is on (1) and Reboot is 2, the system does not reboot after the installation.

- **vpnclient.ini**—A global profile that you use to set certain standards for all profiles. If this file is bundled with the Software Client software, when it is first installed, it automatically configures the Software Client global parameters during installation.

- **.pcf**—The .pcf file contains all the Software Client configuration parameters. Profiles are created in two ways:

  — The remote user creates connection entries via the New Connection Wizard. The output of the New Connection Wizard is a .pcf file.

  — The administrator creates .pcf files using a text editor and places them in the remote user's local file system: C:\Program Files\Cisco Systems\VPN Client\Profiles directory.

Each connection has its own .pcf file. It can be viewed and edited in Notepad. If this file is bundled with the Software Client software, when the Software Client is first installed, the installer automatically configures the Software Client during installation.

To make a parameter read-only so that the Software Client user cannot change it within the GUI, put an exclamation mark (!) before the parameter name.

The administrator creates these files using a text editor and places them in the remote user's local file system. The files must be located in the same folder as the Software Client's setup.exe file.

Software Client Programs Menu

After the Software Client is installed, access the Software Client Programs menu by choosing Start > Programs > Cisco Systems VPN Client, as shown in Figure 4-40. Under the VPN Client menu, a number of options are available:

- **Help**—Accesses Software Client help text. You also can obtain help by doing the following:

  — Press F1 in any window while using the Cisco VPN Client.

  — Click the Help button on windows that display it.

  — Click the logo in the title bar.

- **Set MTU**—The Software Client automatically sets the MTU size to approximately 1300 bytes. For unique applications, Set MTU can change the MTU size to fit a specific scenario.

- **Uninstall VPN Client**—Only one Software Client can be loaded at a time. When upgrading, the old Software Client must be uninstalled before the new Software Client is installed. Choose Uninstall VPN Client to remove the old Software Client.

- **VPN Client**—This option launches the Cisco VPN Client.

Figure 4-40 *Software Client Programs Menu*

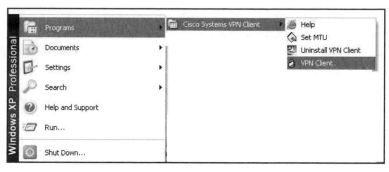

SetMTU Application

The Software Client automatically sets the MTU size to approximately 1300 bytes. For unique applications in which fragmentation is still an issue, SetMTU, shown in Figure 4-41, can change the MTU size to fit the specific scenario. In the Network Adapters (IPSec only) field, select the network adapter. In the MTU Options group box, set the MTU option size by selecting the appropriate radio button. You must reboot for MTU changes to take effect.

Figure 4-41 *SetMTU Application*

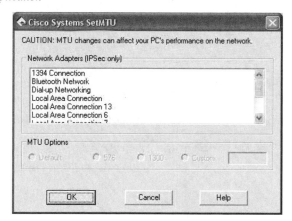

Summary

This chapter started by providing an overview of remote-access VPNs. It looked at the initial configuration of a VPN Concentrator that was factory-shipped. Then it covered creating a group to be used for a remote-access connection by using the Quick Configuration tool, which can be initiated after a factory reset on a VPN Concentrator. This chapter also covered the configuration settings available to the group. The chapter ended by looking at the VPN Client, its configuration, and the tools available when it is installed.

Review Questions

The following questions test your retention of the material presented in this chapter. The answers appear in Appendix A, "Answers to the Review Questions."

1 What two methods can you use to configure the VPN Concentrator?

2 What are the default username and password when you initially connect to a VPN Concentrator?

3 Which interface on a VPN Concentrator would you use to connect to a public network such as the Internet?

4 What is split DNS?

5 Which split-tunneling method should you use if you want to tunnel everything but still access your local LAN?

6 IKE keepalives are enabled by default. When is it advisable to disable them for a remote-access VPN?

7 What three files can an administrator edit to customize the installation of the Software Client on a Windows system?

8 What troubleshooting application comes installed with the VPN Software Client?

9 What default MTU does the VPN Client set?

10 Which interface on a VPN Concentrator would you use to connect to your private LAN?

After completing this chapter, you will be able to perform the following tasks:

- Understand the basics of a CA
- Install a root CA certificate
- Install identity certificates
- Implement a CA-based remote-access VPN
- Configure a Cisco VPN Concentrator for CA support
- Configure the Cisco VPN Client for CA support

CHAPTER 5

Configuring the Cisco VPN 3000 for Remote Access Using Digital Certificates

So far this book has covered the creation of a remote-access virtual private network (VPN) using preshared keys. Public Key Cryptography implemented as a Public Key Infrastructure (PKI) is a way to implement a scalable authentication solution that provides more security than using preshared keys. This chapter provides an overview of certification authority (CA) and digital certificate and signature terminology. It then looks at the steps required to configure the Cisco VPN 3000 to support authentication via digital certificates. A CA is required to perform these steps. The examples use a Microsoft CA server that is part of the Windows 2000 Server operating system. This chapter also covers the steps required on the VPN Client to support digital certificates before tying it all together to create a VPN connection entry on the VPN Client that uses digital certificates for authentication rather than the user preshared key. On a VPN solution using a VPN Concentrator, a preshared key is implemented as a group name and password.

CA Overview

When using certificates, each person has his own certificate that he exchanges between peers. If you were communicating with five people, you would send your own certificate and receive four certificates back, which equals five certificates. When communicating with ten people, you would send your certificate to everyone and receive nine certificates back, which equals ten. Certificates are a linear progression. When adding a person to a certificate-based network, you only need to request a certificate for the new person. The new person is required to send his certificate to everyone with whom he communicates. Certificates are much easier to scale. Figure 5-1 shows how you individually enroll each participating peer with the CA and request a certificate.

Figure 5-1   *CA Server Fulfilling Requests from IPSec Peers*

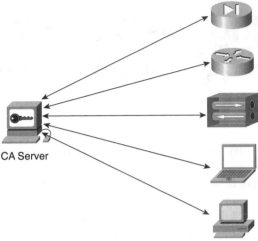

CA Server

Each IPSec peer individually enrolls with the CA Server.

Digital Signature

A key pair has no intrinsic ties to any person or entity. A solution is necessary to reliably tie a person or entity to a key pair. The solution is digital signatures and digital certificates, which provide a way to guarantee the message's source:

- **Digital signature**—Ties a message to a sender's private key. The hash can be decrypted only by the sender's public key.

- **Digital certificate**—Binds a person or entity to a private key. This is analogous to buying an item with a credit card. Typically, the cashier asks for two items: a credit card and some form of signature identification. The credit card is swiped through the register to confirm that the account is valid, that it has not expired, and that it was not revoked. You are then asked to sign the credit slip to authenticate you against the signature on the card. Similarly, a digital certificate is used to bind a person or entity to a digital signature.

The digital signature provides a form of digital credentials that authenticate the identity of the sending party. Digital signatures are used to link data with the holder of a specific private key and consist of the following:

- At the local end, a private key is used to encrypt the hash.

- At the remote end:
    - Running the original message through a hash algorithm produces the hash.

— The hash that was appended to the original message is decrypted using the sender's public key.

- If the hashes match, the message was signed with the sender's private key.
- Only a specific private key can produce the digital signature.

Certificate-Based Authentication

Digital certificates are used to authenticate users. They can be used to identify a person, company, or server. They are the equivalent of a passport or driver's license. The following example based on Figure 5-2 illustrates how this works:

Step 1   Users A and B register separately with the CA:

— Each user generates a public key and a private key.

— Certificate requests are completed by both users and are forwarded to the CA.

— The CA issues separate certificates and digitally signs them with its private key, thereby certifying the user's authenticity.

— Certificates are loaded and verified on both users' PCs.

Step 2   User A sends the certificate to user B.

Step 3   User B checks the authenticity of the CA signature on the certificate:

— The CA public key is used to verify the CA signature on the certificate.

If it passes validation, it is safe to assume that you are who you say you are; therefore, the message is valid.

Step 4   User B sends the certificate to user A:

— The CA public key is used to verify the CA signature on the certificate.

— When it is verified, all subsequent communications can be accepted.

Figure 5-2 *Certificate-Based Authentication*

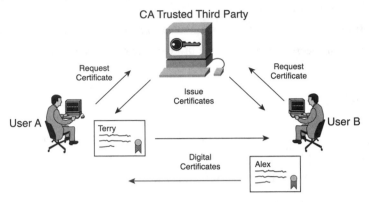

NOTE   Certificates are exchanged during the IPSec or IKE negotiations.

CAs

CAs hold the key to the PKI. A CA is a trusted third party whose job is to certify the authenticity of users to ensure that you are who you say you are.

The CA digital signature, created with the CA private key, guarantees authenticity. You can verify a digital signature using the CA public key. Only the CA public key can decrypt the digital certificate. The CA creates, administers, and revokes invalid certificates.

The CA can be a corporate network administrator or a recognized third party. Trusted sources supported by the Cisco VPN 3000 series Concentrator include the following:

- Entrust
- Rivest, Shamir, Adleman (RSA) Security
- Network Associates PGP
- Baltimore
- Microsoft
- Verisign

PKI

PKI is the set of hardware, software, people, policies, and procedures needed to create, manage, store, distribute, and revoke digital certificates. PKI makes it possible to generate and distribute keys within a secure domain and lets CAs issue keys, associated certificates, and certificate revocation lists (CRLs) in a secure manner. The two PKI models are the central authority and the hierarchical authority, as shown in Figure 5-3:

- **Central**—A flat network design. A single authority, the root CA, signs all certificates. Each employee who needs a certificate sends a request to the root CA. Small companies with several hundred employees may use a central CA.

- **Hierarchical authority**—A tiered approach. The ability to sign a certificate is delegated through a hierarchy. The top of the hierarchy is the root CA. It signs certificates for subordinate authorities. Subordinate CAs sign certificates for lower-level CAs or employees. Large geographically dispersed corporations (such as Cisco Systems) use hierarchical CAs. The root CA is located in San Jose, the company headquarters. Rather than having more than 30,000 employees making certificate requests back to San Jose, subordinate CAs are placed strategically around the world. Local employees request a CA from the local subordinate CA.

Figure 5-3 *PKI Models*

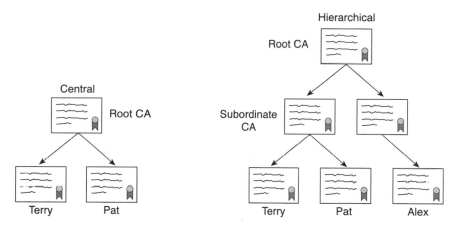

Certificate Generation

Now that you have seen a brief overview of CAs, we will look at how certificates are generated and transferred between a CA and the Cisco VPN 3000 series Concentrator.

An end user (or end entity) must obtain a digital certificate from the CA to participate in a certificate exchange. This is called the enrollment process. It requires three steps (see Figure 5-4):

Step 1   Each user generates a private/public key pair. The requestor generates a certificate request and sends it to the CA.

Step 2   The CA transforms the certificate request into a digital certificate and returns both a root and identity digital certificate to the requestor.

Step 3 The requestor installs the root certificate into the Concentrator. While installing the identity certificate, the Concentrator uses the public key from the root certificate to validate the identity certificate's signature.

Figure 5-4 *Certificate Generation Process*

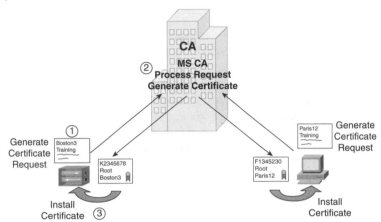

Generating a Certificate Request

In the certificate generation process, first you generate a certificate request called a Public-Key Cryptography Standards (PKCS) #10. User information such as a common name, organizational unit, organization, locality, state, country, and public key is requested. After the information is supplied, the Concentrator generates a certificate request: a PKCS#10. The request is formatted as an Abstract Syntax Notation 1 (ASN.1) message and is sent to the CA. This process is shown in Figure 5-5.

Figure 5-5 *Generating a Certificate Request*

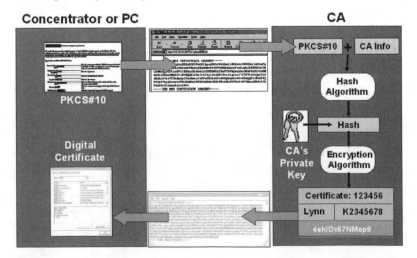

Figure 5-6 shows a sample certificate request form on the Concentrator. The information for a certificate request is as follows:

- **Common Name (CN) field**—A unique name for the Concentrator.

- **Organizational Unit (OU) field**—The Concentrator uses the organizational unit as the group name. By default, the certificate's OU field must match the group attribute data based in the Concentrator.

- **Organization (O) field**—The company name.

- **Locality (L) field**—The city or town where the company resides.

- **State/Province (SP) field**—The state or province where the company resides.

- **Country field**—The country where the company resides.

- **Subject Alternative Name (FQDN) field**—The Concentrator's fully qualified domain name (FQDN) to be used in this PKI.

- **Subject Alternative Name (E-mail Address) field**—The Concentrators e-mail address that is used by the PKI is entered here.

- **Key Size drop-down menu**—The following options are available:

  - **RSA 512 bits**—This key size provides sufficient security and is the default selection. It is the most common and requires the least processing.

  - **RSA 768 bits**—This key size provides normal security. It requires approximately two to four times more processing than the 512-bit key.

  - **RSA 1024 bits**—This key size provides high security. It requires approximately four to eight times more processing than the 512-bit key.

Figure 5-6 *PKCS#10*

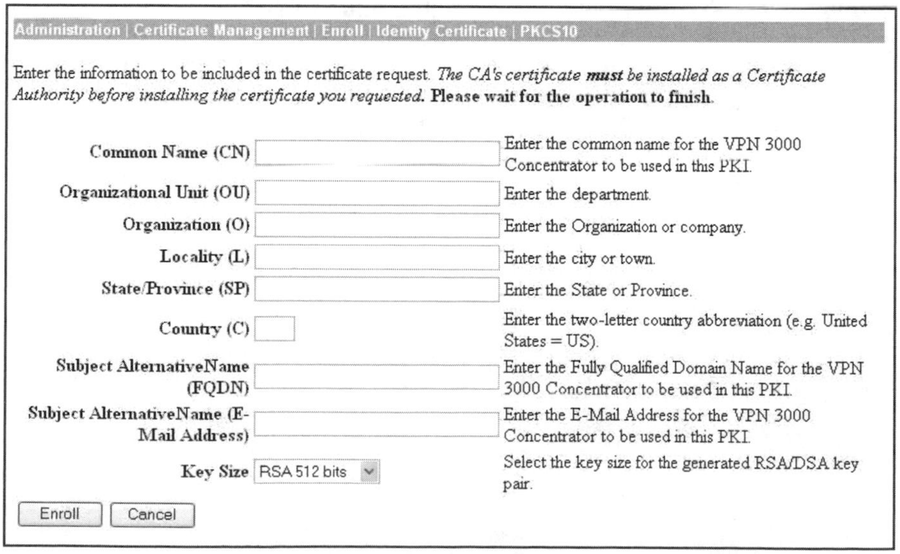

After you enter the information, the Concentrator generates a certificate request. The output is a new certificate request, a PKCS#10, in the ASN.1 message format, as shown in Figure 5-7.

Figure 5-7   *Certificate Request in ASN.1 format*

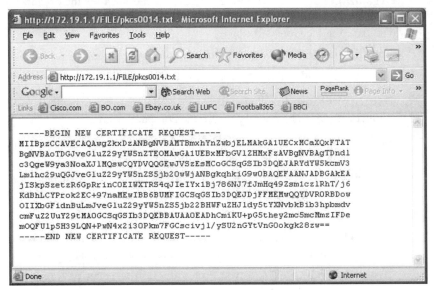

After receiving the PKCS#10, the CA verifies its authenticity. The CA decrypts the digital signature with the requestor's public key to validate it. If valid, PKCS#10 is transformed into an identity certificate. The identity certificate is a composite of information supplied from the PKCS#10 and the CA. For security, a hash algorithm is performed on the combined attributes. The hash value is encrypted using the CA's private key and is attached to the certificate. The identity certificate is then sent to the Concentrator as an ASN.1 formatted message. This process is shown in Figure 5-8.

Figure 5-8 *Generating an Identity Certificate*

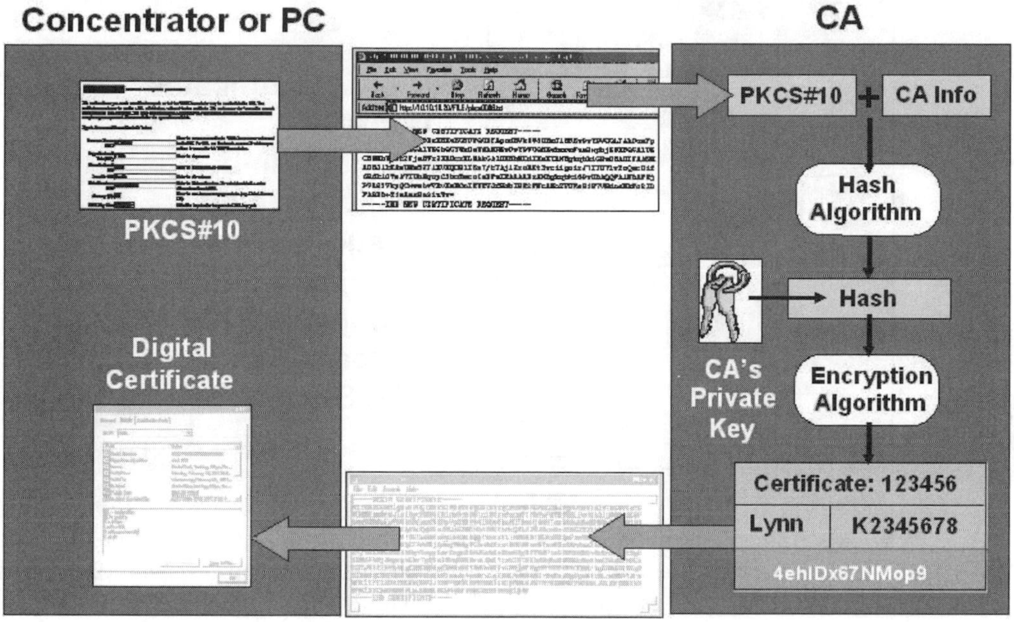

Digital Certificates

The X.509 certificate consists of specific fields and values. Figure 5-9 shows an example of a Microsoft CA certificate. It displays the following information:

- **Certificate format version**—Currently, it is X.509 version 1, 2, or 3.

- **Certificate serial number**—A unique certificate numeric identifier in the CA domain. When a certificate is revoked, the certificate number is listed on the CRL.

- **Signature algorithm**—Identifies the CA's public key and hashing algorithm.

- **Issuer**—The CA's distinguished name.

- **Validity period**—Specifies the certificate's start and expiration dates.

- **Subject X.500 name**—The distinguished name of the entity holding the private key.

- **Subject public key information**—Specifies the subject's public key and hashing algorithm.

- **Extensions**—Extends the certificate to allow additional information.

- **CRL-DPs (distribution points)**—The location of the CRL for this certificate.

- **CA signature**—The CA performs a hash function on the certificate contents. The hash is then signed with the CA's private key to ensure authenticity.

Figure 5-9 *Microsoft Digital Certificate*

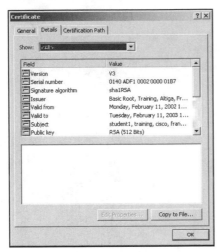

Digital Certificates Contain:
- **Serial Number**
- **Validity Dates**
- **Issuer's Name**
- **Subject's Name**
- **Subject's Public Key Information**
- **CA Signature**

When a certificate is sent between a CA and a Concentrator or PC, the ASN.1 formatted message is encoded. The digital certificate encoding can be one of two types: Distinguished Encoding Rules (DER) data (raw binary format) or Privacy Enhanced Mail (PEM) format (binary converted to base 64 format). Typically when you request a certificate, the CA prompts you for the encoding type: DER or base 64 encoding. This might be an issue if the sender or receiver can support only one encoding type. The Concentrator can support both types.

The CA can send certificates individually using identity and root certificates. You can also request an all-inclusive CA certificate path, PKCS#7. PKCS#7 is a message syntax that allows multiple certificates to be enveloped within one message (the same concept as PKZIP storing multiple files in a .zip file).

Installing the Certificate

Before an identity certificate is installed, the Concentrator checks the following to validate it:

- Is the identity certificate verified with the CA's public key?
- Has the identity certificate expired?
- Has the identity certificate been revoked?

When validated, the certificate is installed on the Concentrator. The identity certificate can now be exchanged with a peer during IPSec tunnel establishment.

Validating Certificates

Digital certificate validation is based on trust relationships within the PKI. If you trust A, and A says that B is valid, you should trust B. This is the underlying premise when validating certificates. When enrolling into a PKI, you must first obtain and install the CA certificates on the Concentrator. In doing so, you implicitly establish a trust relationship in which any documents signed by those CAs are considered valid.

During Internet Key Exchange (IKE) negotiations, when an identity certificate is received from an IKE peer, the Concentrator validates the certificate by determining that the certificate

- Has been signed by a CA that is trusted (checks the signature).
- Has not expired.
- Has not been revoked.

Signature Validation

The first step in validating a digital certificate is to validate the signature. Signature validation consists of the following steps (see Figure 5-10):

Step 1   At the CA, the original identity certificate is put through a hash algorithm, the output hash is encrypted by the CA's private key, and the hash is appended to the end of the certificate.

Step 2   At the remote end, a two-step process occurs:

— The receiver uses the CA's public key to decrypt the hash appended to the certificate. The result is the original hash value.

— The received message is sent through the hash algorithm to produce a second hash.

Step 3   The CA-generated hash and Concentrator-generated hash are compared:

— If they match, the identity certificate is genuine.

— If they do not match, the certificate is invalid; there is an invalid signature or identity certificate.

Figure 5-10 *Signature Validation*

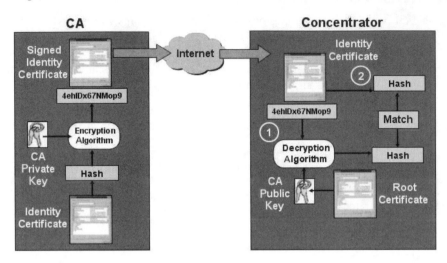

Certification Chain

It was mentioned that the Concentrator needs a copy of the CA's public key to decrypt the hash. The question is, where does the Concentrator find a copy of that key? It depends on the CA environment, central or hierarchical. In a central, or flat, CA, the root CA signs the identity certificate. The root certificate must be installed before trying to install the identity certificate so the Concentrator has access to the root's public key. One of the root CA fields is a copy of the CA's public key. In Figure 5-11, using the public key of the root certificate checks the signature of Terry's certificate.

Figure 5-11 *Signature Validation*

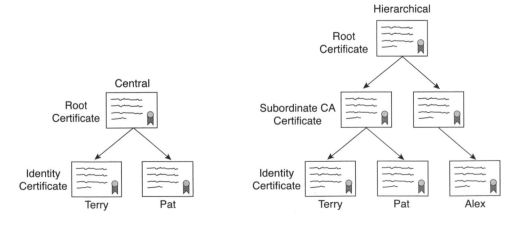

In a hierarchical environment, the ability to sign is delegated through the hierarchy. The top is the root CA; it signs certificates for subordinate CAs. The subordinate CA signs certificates for lower-level CAs. Ultimately, a subordinate CA signs the user's identity certificate. The certificate must be validated up the chain of authority. In Figure 5-11, Alex's certificate is validated with the public key of the subordinate CA. The subordinate CA is validated with the public key of the root CA.

Validity Period

The next step is to check the validity period. A certificate is valid for a specific period of time. The validity period (range) is set by the CA and consists of valid from and valid to fields. On the Concentrator, when you try to add a certificate, the validity range is compared against the system clock. If the system clock is not within the validity range—either too early or too late—you receive an error message.

CRL

Checking the CRL is the last validation step. A CRL is a list issued by the CA that contains certificates that are no longer valid. CRLs are signed by the CA and are released periodically or on demand. CRLs are valid for a specific amount of time, depending on the CA vendor used. Here are some reasons a certificate might be invalidated:

- User data changes (for example, the username).
- A key is compromised.
- An employee leaves the organization.

The CRL must be consulted by anyone using a certificate to ensure that it is still valid. There is no requirement on devices to ensure that the CRL is current.

A CRL has two tabs: General and Revocation List. The General tab, shown in Figure 5-12, includes information about the CRL itself, such as the name of the CA that issued the list, the date the list was issued, and the date of the next publication. The date of the next publication could be hourly, daily, weekly, and so on, as defined by the revocation list, which includes all the revoked certificates. The certificates are listed by certificate serial number and revocation date. The Revocation List tab, shown in Figure 5-13, shows the certificate's serial number and revocation date and time.

Figure 5-12   *CRL: General Tab*

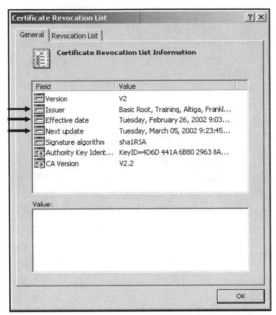

A number of CRL-DPs are accessible from the web. Because the web is a large place, it is difficult for the Concentrator to check a particular certificate to see if it is valid or revoked. As part of the X.509 certificate, the CRL extension includes the CRL-DP. The CRL-DP information is included in the X.509 extension fields. If you double-click the CRL-DPs icon in the certificate, the CRL-DP's URL is included. In Figure 5-14, the CRL is located at http://domain_remote.training.altiga.com.

Figure 5-13   *CRL: Revocation List Tab*

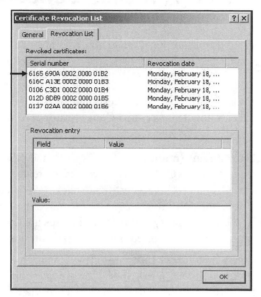

Figure 5-14   *CRL: Distribution Point Location (CRL-DP)*

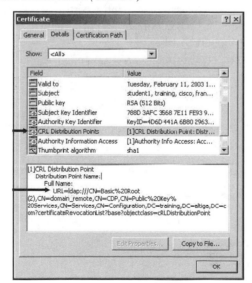

Configuring the Cisco VPN 3000 Concentrator for CA Support

We have now covered the basics of a CA and how digital signatures and certificates operate, so we will move on to discuss how to install digital certificates on Cisco VPN 3000 Concentrators.

For the Concentrator to participate in the certificate exchange, a certificate needs to be loaded on the Concentrator. This is called Concentrator certificate enrollment, and it has two types:

- **File-based enrollment (manual)**—This is a manual process. You can enroll by creating a request file, PKCS#10. When you have created a request file, you can either e-mail it to the CA and receive a certificate back, or you can access the CA's website and cut and paste the enrollment request in the area that the CA provides. When generated by the CA, identity and root certificates are downloaded to the PC. The certificates must then be imported onto the Concentrator.

- **Network-based enrollment (automated)**—This is an automated process that lets you connect directly to a CA via Simple Certificate Enrollment Protocol (SCEP). Complete the enrollment form to connect to a CA via SCEP. The Concentrator contacts the CA via SCEP, and the CA returns a CA certificate. When the CA certificate is verified, the Concentrator uses SCEP to send the enrollment request to the CA, where the CA issues an identity certificate. The CA then returns the identity to the Concentrator. For network-based enrollment to work, both the Concentrator and the CA must support SCEP.

Figure 5-15 shows the two types of enrollment.

Figure 5-15 *Concentrator Enrollment Support*

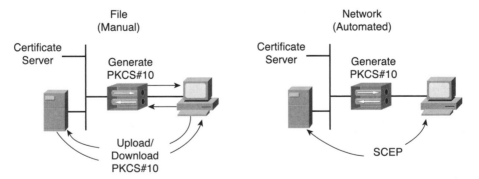

File-Based Enrollment (Manual)

The Concentrator certificate manual loading process consists of the following steps, as shown in Figure 5-16:

- Generate the certificate request, and upload it to a CA.
- The CA generates the identity and root certificates. Each is downloaded to a PC.
- The certificates are loaded onto the Concentrator.

Figure 5-16   *Concentrator Certificate Manual Loading Process*

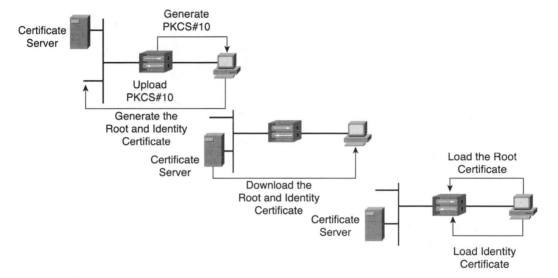

The first step in the Concentrator certificate manual loading process is to generate a certificate request. Follow these steps to accomplish the task:

Step 1   Choose Administration > Certificate Management > Enroll. The Enroll window opens. Click the Identity certificate link. The choice is between creating an SSL or an identity certificate. Choose identity certificate.

Step 2   Choose Administration > Certificate Management > Enroll > Identity Certificate. The Identity Certificate window opens. Click the Enroll via PKCS10 Request (Manual) link. You can enroll with a CA manually via PKCS#10 or automatically via SCEP. In this instance, you choose the manual process.

Step 3   Choose Administration > Certificate Management > Enroll > Identity Certificate > PKCS10. The PKCS10 window opens, as shown in Figure 5-17. Fill out the PKCS10 form.

Figure 5-17   *Concentrator PKCS10 Screen*

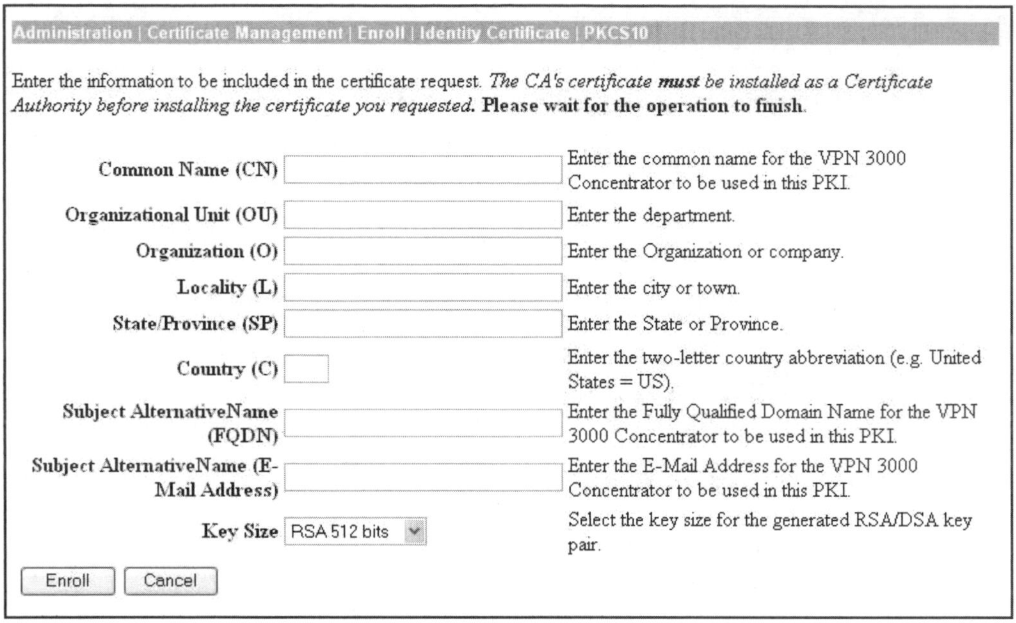

Group Matching

When a certificate arrives at the Concentrator during IKE Phase 1, the Concentrator authenticates the remote peer and extracts the group information from the certificate. The Concentrator attempts to match the extracted information with the Concentrator's group name database. The group name identifies the remote user's Concentrator access privileges. If a match is found, the remote user is afforded the access rights and privileges of the matching group. By default, the Concentrator uses the OU field for group matching. The Configuration > Policy Management > Certificate Group Matching > Policy window, shown in Figure 5-18, lets the administrator configure alternative group matching options. For example, an administrator might choose to use the organization and organizational unit or organizational unit and locality.

Figure 5-18 *Concentrator Group Matching Policy*

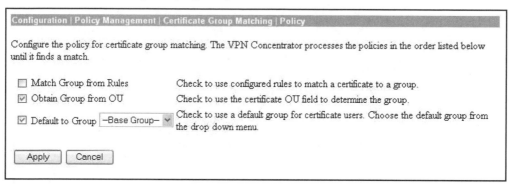

Configuring certificate group matching consists of two steps: configuring the matching policy and configuring the rules. You have three group matching policy options:

- **Match Group from Rules**—Use the rules you have defined for certificate group matching (for example, organizational unit and organization). If the administrator plans to use the match group from rules policy, define the rules before selecting the policy.

- **Obtain Group from OU**—Use the organizational unit in the certificate to specify the group to match. This choice is enabled by default.

- **Default to Group**—Use a default group or the base group for certificate matching. Use the group matching rules set up for this group.

The Concentrator processes the policies in the order they are enabled until it finds a match.

Group Matching Rules

The Configuration > Policy Management > Certificate Group Matching window, shown in Figure 5-19, lets an administrator define rules to match an identity certificate to a permission group based on fields in the identity certificate. You can apply a combination of certificate fields. For a user to be identified as belonging to a certain group, specific fields of the received certificate must match the rules defined for that group. In Figure 5-19, for a user to be recognized as being a member of the training group, the following rules must be met: the received identity certificates OU = training and O = Cisco.

Figure 5-19 *Concentrator Group Matching Rules*

Define the rules, and enable each rule for the selected group to specify a policy for group matching by rules. A group must already exist in the configuration before you can create a rule to apply to it. You can assign multiple rules to the same group. Rules assigned to the same group are combined, and a match results when all rules test true. Also, you must configure a matching policy. You can define rules and matching policies in any order.

Uploading the PKCS#10

Upload the PKCS#10 to the CA after the Concentrator generates it. To do this, follow these two steps:

Step 1 Manually copy the PKCS#10 output, and paste it into the CA. Figure 5-20 displays an example of a Microsoft CA. The process is virtually the same for the other CAs, but the CA windows and commands vary.

Step 2 The CA validates the request. Validation may be automatic or may require CA administrator intervention. With automatic approval, the identity certificate is generated with no delay. With required administrator approval, the identity certificate generation is delayed until approved. The approval process varies by CA and company account.

Figure 5-20   *Downloading the Certificate*

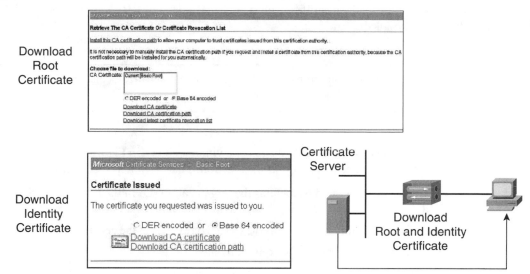

The CA then produces an identity and root certificate. The root and identity certificates then need to be downloaded to the PC. The Microsoft CA provides prompts to guide you through the process.

Installing the Root Certificate

The certificates are transferred from the PC to the Concentrator. They must be loaded in order. The root certificate is loaded first, followed by the identity certificate.

Follow these steps to install the root certificate:

Step 1   Choose Administration > Certificate Management > Install. The Install window opens. Click the Install CA certificate link.

Step 2   Choose Administration > Certificate Management > Install > Install CA Certificate. The CA Certificate window opens. Click Upload File from the Workstation.

Step 3   Choose Administration > Certificate Management > Install > Install CA Certificate > Upload File from the Workstation. Click Browse to browse to the root certificate file on the workstation.

Step 4   Click Install to install the root certificate.

When the root certificate is loaded, it is validated. To be valid, the signature on the certificate must be valid, and the certificate must not have expired. A CRL lookup is optional. By default, it is disabled.

NOTE If you receive an expiration error when loading your root certificate, ensure that the Concentrator's date and time are set correctly.

The Administration > Certificate Management window, shown in Figure 5-21, displays the root certificate in the Certificate Authorities section. This section has five fields:

- **Subject**—The Common Name plus the Organization (O) in the certificate's Subject field.

- **Issuer**—The Common Name plus the Organization (O) in the certificate's Issuer field.

- **Expiration**—The certificate's expiration date.

- **SCEP Issuer**—For an identity certificate to be available for SCEP enrollment, the root must first be installed via SCEP. This field indicates if the certificate is SCEP-enabled. It has two variables:

  - **Yes**—This certificate was installed via SCEP.

  - **No**—This certificate was not installed via SCEP.

- **Actions**—This column allows you to manage particular certificates. The actions available vary with the certificate's type and status:

  - **View**—Shows you details of this certificate.

  - **Configure**—Enables CRL checking for this CA certificate, modifies SCEP parameters, or enables the acceptance of subordinate CA certificates.

  - **Delete**—Deletes this certificate from the Concentrator. Certificates cannot be deleted if they are in use. To remove them from use, first remove the identity certificate from any preexisting security associations (SAs). Then delete the certificate.

Figure 5-21 *Certificate Management Screen*

The Administration > Certificate Management > View window, shown in Figure 5-22, lets the administrator view the installed root certificate. It contains the following information:

- **Subject**—The subject's common name.

- **Issuer**—The CA or other entity (jurisdiction) that issued the certificate.

- **Serial Number**—The certificate's serial number.

- **Signing Algorithm**—The cryptographic algorithm that the CA or other issuer used to sign this certificate.

- **Public Key Type**—The algorithm and size of the certified public key.

- **MD5 Thumbprint**—A 128-bit message digest algorithm 5 (MD5) hash of the complete certificate contents, shown as a 16-byte string. This value is unique for every certificate, and it positively identifies the certificate. If you question a root certificate's authenticity, you can check this value with the issuer.

- **SHA1 Thumbprint**—A 160-bit Secure Hash Algorithm 1 (SHA-1) hash of the complete certificate contents, shown as a 20-byte string. This value is unique for every certificate, and it positively identifies the certificate. If you question a certificate's authenticity, you can check this value with the issuer.

- **Validity**—The time period during which this certificate is valid. The Manager checks the validity against the Concentrator's system clock, and it flags expired certificates by issuing event log entries.

- **Subject Alternative Name (Fully Qualified Domain Name)**—The FQDN for this Concentrator that identifies it in this PKI. The alternative name is an optional additional data field in the certificate. It provides interoperability with many Cisco IOS software and PIX Firewall systems in LAN-to-LAN connections.

- **Subject Alternative Name (E-mail Address)**—The Concentrators email address that is used by the PKI is entered here.

- **CRL Distribution Point**—The DP for CRLs from the issuer of this certificate. If this information is included in the certificate in the proper format, and you enable CRL checking, you do not have to provide it in the Administration > Certificate Management > Configure CA Certificate window.

Figure 5-22 *View Certificate Screen*

Installing the Identity Certificate

Now that you have installed the root certificate, you will install the identity certificate by following these steps (see Figure 5-23):

Step 1   Choose Administration > Certificate Management > Install. The Install window opens. Click the Install certificate obtained via enrollment link.

Step 2   Choose Administration > Certificate Management > Install certificate obtained via enrollment. The Install Certificate Obtained Via Enrollment window opens. In the Enrollment Status section, click the Install link in the Actions column.

Step 3   Choose Administration > Certificate Management > Install > Identity Certificate. The Identity Certificate window opens. Click the Upload File from Workstation link.

Step 4   Choose Administration > Certificate Management > Install > Identity Certificate > Upload File from Workstation and click the Browse button to browse to the identity certificate on the PC. Click Install.

Figure 5-23   *Identity Certificate Process*

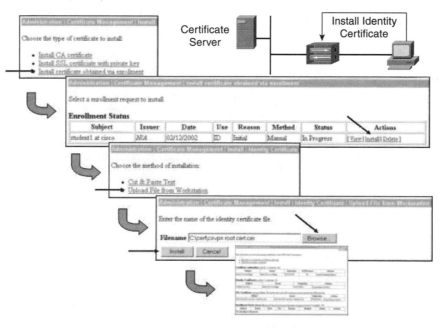

When the identity certificate is loaded, it is validated. To be valid, the signature on the certificate must be valid, and the certificate must not have expired. A CRL lookup is optional. By default, it is disabled.

NOTE   If you receive an expiration error when loading your identity certificate, ensure that the Concentrator's date and time are set correctly.

The Administration > Certificate Management > Certificates window, shown in Figure 5-24, lets the administrator view installed certificates.

Figure 5-24   *Viewing the Certificates*

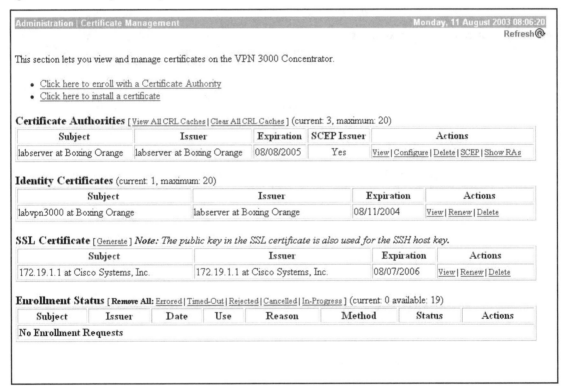

The Identity Certificates section has four fields:

- **Subject**—The Common Name plus the Organization in the certificate's Subject field.
- **Issuer**—The Common Name plus the Organization in the certificate's Issuer field.
- **Expiration**—The certificate's expiration date.
- **Actions**—This column allows you to manage particular certificates. The actions available vary with the certificate's type and status:
    - **View**—Shows you details of this certificate.

— **Renew**—A shortcut that allows you to generate an enrollment request based on the content of an existing certificate.

— **Delete**—Deletes this certificate from the Concentrator.

The number of enrollment requests you can make at any given time is limited to the Concentrator's identity certificate capacity. Most Concentrator models allow a maximum of 20 identity certificates. For example, if you already have five identity certificates installed, you can create only up to 15 enrollment requests. The Cisco VPN 3005 Concentrator is an exception, supporting only two identity certificates. On the Cisco VPN 3005 Concentrator only, you can request a third certificate, even if two certificates are already installed, but the Concentrator does not install this certificate immediately. First you must delete one of the existing certificates. Then, activate the new certificate to replace the one you just deleted. The Concentrator automatically deletes entries that have the status Timed out, Failed, Cancelled, or Error and that are older than one week.

The Administration > Certificate Management > View window, shown in Figure 5-25, lets the administrator view the installed identity certificate. The end-user certificate contains the following information:

- **Subject**—The subject's common name (for example, student1be).

- **Issuer**—The issuer's common name (for example, Basic Root).

- **Serial Number**—The certificate's serial number. This is used when revoking the certificate.

- **Signing Algorithm**—The cryptographic algorithm that the CA or other issuer used to sign this certificate.

- **Public Key Type**—The algorithm and size of the certified public key.

- **MD5 Thumbprint**—A 128-bit MD5 hash of the complete certificate contents, shown as a 16-byte string. This value is unique for every certificate, and it positively identifies the certificate.

- **SHA1 Thumbprint**—A 160-bit SHA-1 hash of the complete certificate contents, shown as a 20-byte string. This value is unique for every certificate, and it positively identifies the certificate.

- **Validity**—The period of time during which the certificate is valid (for example, from 7/23/02 to 7/23/03).

- **Subject Alternative Name (Fully Qualified Domain Name)**—Defines an alternative FQDN for the certificate.

- **Subject Alternative Name (E-Mail Address)**—Defines an alternative e-mail address for the certificate.

- **CRL Distribution Point**—Identifies the location of the CRL. The CRL can be retrieved and put in cache for future reference.

Figure 5-25 *Viewing an Identity Certificate*

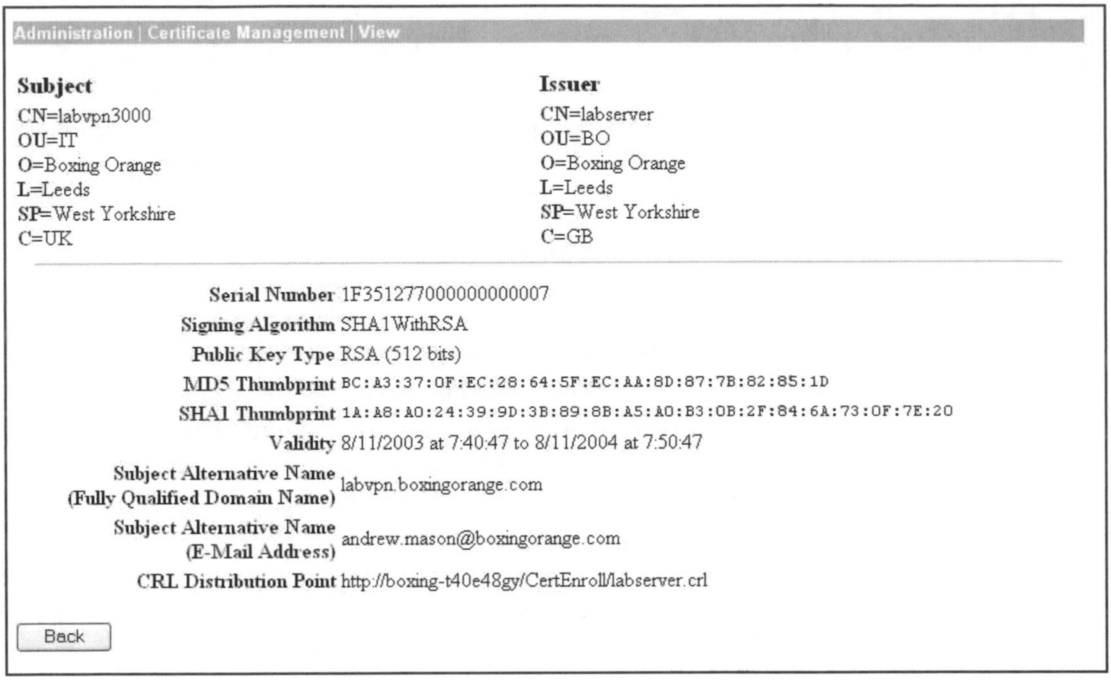

Certificate Renewal

Certificate renewal, shown in Figure 5-26, is a shortcut that allows you to generate an enrollment request based on the content of an existing certificate. Use this screen to reenroll or rekey a certificate. If you reenroll the certificate, the new certificate uses the same key pair as the expiring certificate. If you rekey the certificate, it uses a new key pair.

- **Certificate**—The type of certificate you are reenrolling or rekeying.
- **Renewal Type radio button**—Specifies the type of request:
  - **Re-enrollment**—Uses the same key pair as the expiring certificate.
  - **Re-key**—Uses a new key pair.
- **Enrollment Method drop-down menu**—Specifies an enrollment method:
  - **PKCS10 Request (Manual)**—Enrolls using the manual process.
  - **Certificate Name via SCEP**—Enrolls automatically using this SCEP CA.
- **Challenge Password field**—Your CA might have given you a password as a means of verifying your identity. If you have a password from your CA, enter it here.
- **Verify Challenge Password field**—Reenter the challenge password you just entered.

- **Renew button**—Renews the certificate.
- **Cancel button**—Stops the certificate renewal.

Figure 5-26 *Renewing an Identity Certificate*

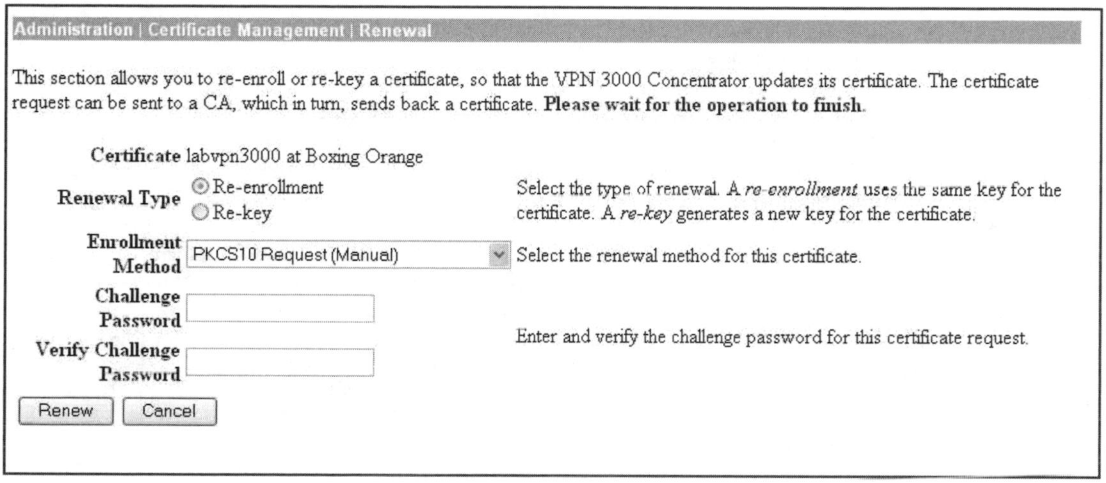

CRLs

CAs issue CRLs to identify revoked certificates. A CRL-DP specifies the location of a CRL on a server from which it can be downloaded. To verify the revocation status, the Concentrator retrieves the CRL from the primary CRL-DP or one of the backup CRL-DPs. The Concentrator checks the peer certificate serial number against the list of serial numbers in the CRL. If none of the serial numbers match, it is assumed that the peer certificate has not been revoked.

Because the system has to fetch and examine the CRL from a network DP, enabling CRL checking might slow system response times. Also, if the network is slow or congested, CRL checking might time out. Enable CRL caching to mitigate these potential problems. This stores the retrieved CRLs in local volatile memory, thus allowing the Concentrator to verify the certificates' revocation status more quickly.

Configuring the CA

This section looks at three sections of the Administration > Certificate Management > Configure CA Certificate window, shown in Figure 5-27: CRL Retrieval Policy, CRL Caching, and CRL Distribution Points Protocols.

Figure 5-27   *Configuring the CA Certificate*

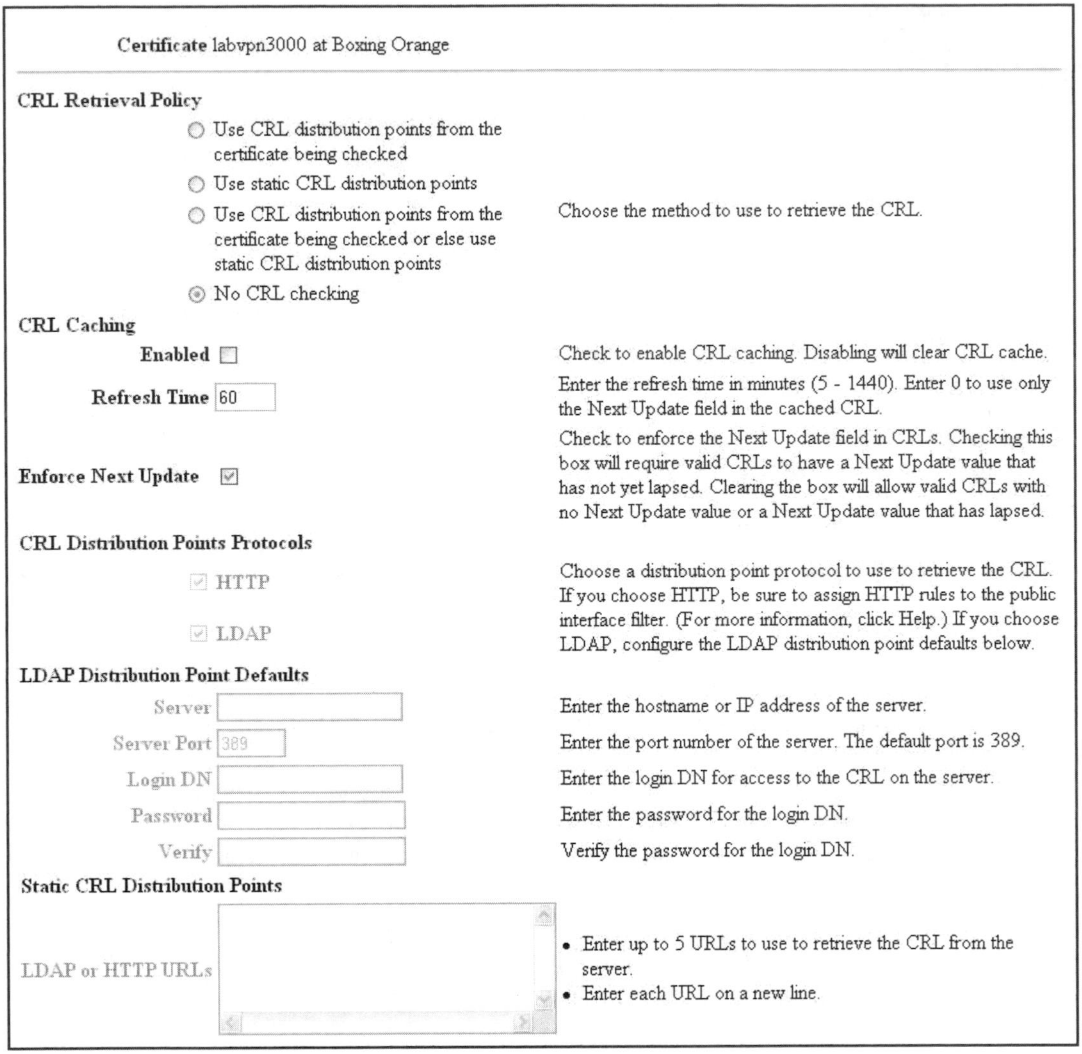

Enabling CRL checking means that every time the Concentrator uses the certificate for authentication, it also checks the latest CRL to ensure that the certificate has not been revoked. The CRL retrieval policy defines where to find the CRL-DP location. The choices are as follows: on a CA certificate, statically defined on the Concentrator, a combination of both, or disable CRL checking.

The next section is CRL caching. Because the Concentrator has to fetch and examine the CRL from a network-based DP, CRL checking might slow system response times or cause the IPSec tunnel to fail because of IKE timeout issues. Enable CRL caching to mitigate these potential problems. CRL caching stores the retrieved CRLs in local volatile memory. This lets the Concentrator verify certificates' revocation status more quickly.

The last section is configuring the location of CRL-DPs. One of a CA's responsibilities is to create a database of all revoked certificates—a CRL. CAs locate CRLs at network-based DPs (CRL-DPs). Many certificates include the location of these CRL-DPs. If the CRL-DP is present in the certificate and is in the proper format, you do not need to configure any CRL-DP fields in this window. If a CRL-DP is not present or you choose to define additional CRL-DPs, define them in the Static CRL-DP window.

Configuring the Concentrator for a Remote-Access VPN with a Digital Certificate

You must do the following before the client-to-LAN with digital certificates tunnel can be configured:

Step 1   Check the active IKE proposal list. For client-to-LAN with digital certificates to work, the Concentrator requires the use of an RSA IKE proposal.

Step 2   Check the IKE proposal.

Step 3   Modify or add an SA.

Step 1: Check the Active IKE Proposal List

Go to Configuration > System > Tunneling Protocols > IPSec > IKE Proposals and activate an RSA proposal. Figure 5-28 shows that an RSA IKE proposal is activated and has been highlighted.

Step 2: Check the IKE Proposal

Check the activated RSA IKE proposal to ensure that it meets the authentication, encryption, Diffie-Hellman (DH), and lifetime requirements. In Figure 5-29, the RSA IKE proposal supports the following:

- **Authentication Mode**—RSA digital certificates
- **Authentication Algorithm**—MD5
- **Encryption Algorithm**—3DES
- **Diffie-Hellman Group**—DH group 2
- **Lifetime Measurement**—Time
- **Data Lifetime**—10,000 seconds
- **Time Lifetime**—86,400 seconds

Figure 5-28 *IKE Proposal Screen*

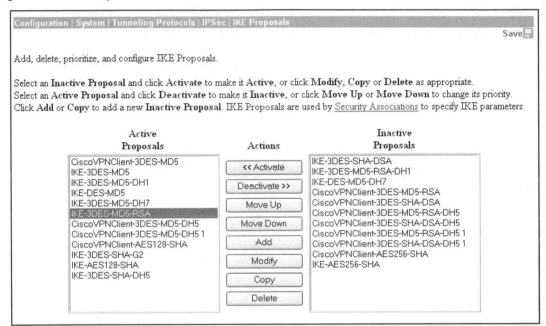

Figure 5-29 *Viewing the IKE Proposal*

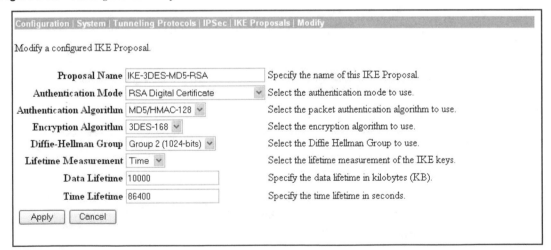

NOTE	For IPSec client-to-LAN applications, the authentication mode that is used is digital certificates.

Step 3: Modify or Add an SA

The SA is a template that defines IPSec and IKE attributes. There are two choices: modify an existing SA, or add a new one. If you modify an existing SA, you change it from preshared keys, which is the default, to RSA signed digital certificates. By changing it, you might enable the client-to-LAN with digital certificates tunnels but disable the use of preshared keys for someone else. The best choice is to add an SA. On the Configuration > Policy Management > Traffic Management > Security Associations screen, shown in Figure 5-30, click Add.

Figure 5-30   *Security Associations Screen*

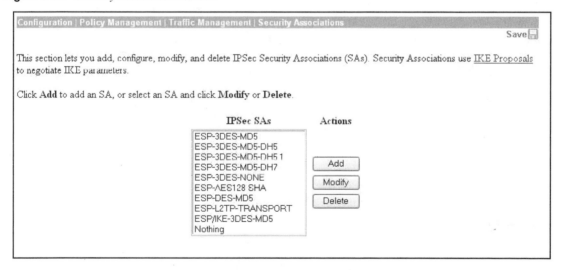

When adding an SA, as shown in Figure 5-31, give it a descriptive name, such as RSA-3DES-MD5. Next, there are two sections to check: IKE and IPSec. In the IPSec parameter section of the window, verify the authentication, encryption, Perfect Forward Secrecy, and lifetime parameters. In Figure 5-31, the IPSec proposal supports the following:

- **Authentication Algorithm**—MD5
- **Encryption Algorithm**—3DES
- **Encapsulation Mode**—Tunnel
- **Perfect Forward Secrecy**—Disabled

- **Lifetime Measurement**—Time
- **Data Lifetime**—10,000 seconds
- **Time Lifetime**—28,800 seconds

Figure 5-31 *Adding an SA*

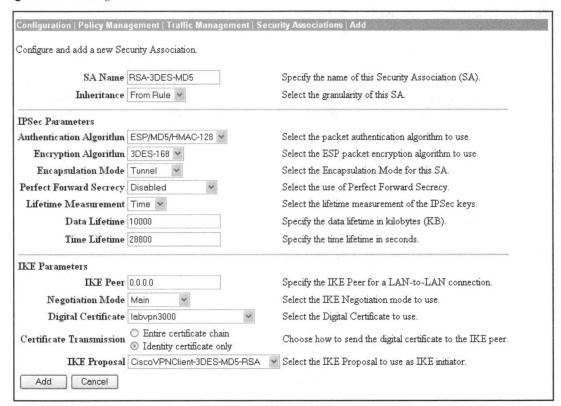

Choose the IKE parameters that will be applied to this SA in the IKE Parameters section. Choose the correct certificate from the Digital Certificate drop-down menu to do this. In the figure, the labvpn3000 certificate is chosen. This certificate is used during the certificate exchange. Next, choose CiscoVPNClient-3DES-MD5-RSA from the IKE Parameters drop-down menu and click Apply.

Cisco Software VPN Client Certificate Support

For the VPN Client to participate in the certificate exchange, a certificate needs to be loaded on the PC. This is called VPN Client enrollment. There are two types of VPN Client enrollment, as shown in Figure 5-32:

- **File-based enrollment**—This is a manual process. You can enroll by creating a request file, PKCS#10. After you have created a request file, you can either e-mail it to the CA and receive a certificate, or you can access the CA's website and cut and paste the enrollment request in the area that the CA provides. When the certificates are generated by the CA, they are downloaded to the PC. The certificates must then be imported into the certificate section of the VPN Client.

- **Network-based enrollment**—This is an automated process that lets you connect directly to a CA via SCEP. Complete the enrollment form to connect to a CA via SCEP. The Certificate Manager uses SCEP to send the request to the CA, where the CA issues an identity certificate. The CA then returns both the identity and CA certificates to the Certificate Manager. For network-based enrollment to work, both the end device and the CA must support SCEP.

Figure 5-32   *Types of VPN Client Enrollment*

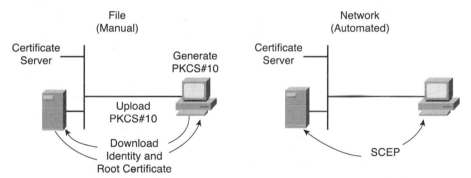

From Release 4.0 of the VPN Software Client, the certificates are handled within the application from the Certificates tab, as shown in Figure 5-33. Before version 4.0 of the client, a separate application called Certificate Manager handled the certificates.

Under the Certificates tab of the 4.0 and later client, you can do the following:

- Import certificates.

- Manage certificates by viewing, verifying, deleting, or exporting them.

- Manage enrollment requests.

You can enroll automatically through the network or manually via a file exchange.

Figure 5-33 *Client Certificates Tab*

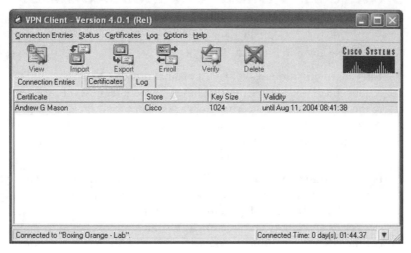

The VPN Client uses the notion of a store to convey a location in your local file system for storing personal certificates. The major store for the VPN Client is the Cisco store, which contains certificates you have enrolled through the Cisco VPN Client. Your system also includes a Microsoft certificate store that contains Microsoft-generated certificates that your organization provides or that you have installed to use with a previous version of the VPN Client software. This means that your old certificates now show up in the Microsoft store. You can manage them just like the certificates in your Cisco store, or you can move them to your Cisco store. When you enroll new certificates, the Certificate Manager places them in the Cisco store.

The Certificate Manager has three tabs:

- **Personal Certificates**—Identity certificates
- **CA Certificates**—Registration authority (RA) certificates and CA certificates
- **Enrollment Requests**—Certificate requests

Software Client Certificate Enrollment

As previously discussed, there are two ways to enroll with a CA to obtain a certificate with the Software Client—file or network. With the 4.0 Client and later, network enrollment is also called online enrollment. The following sections look at these two types of enrollment.

File Enrollment

From the VPN Client, choose Certificates > Enroll to start the enrollment process. You see the screen shown in Figure 5-34. Note that the File radio button is selected and a filename of test and a password of test have been entered (the password is obscured with asterisks).

Figure 5-34   *File-Based Enrollment*

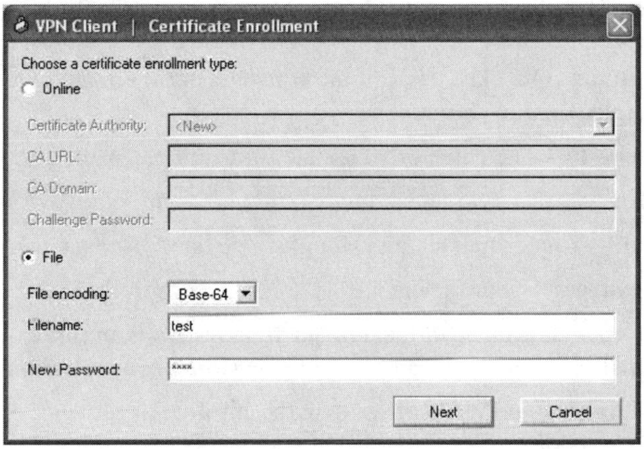

Using a password to protect your certificate provides an additional level of security. By protecting your certificate with a password, any operation that requires access to the certificate's private key requires the specified password to continue.

The password is optional. If you do not want to password-protect your certificate, do not enter any information in the fields, and click Next to continue.

You then see the enrollment form shown in Figure 5-35 (it's similar to the one you completed on the VPN 3000 Concentrator).

Figure 5-35   *File-Based Enrollment Form*

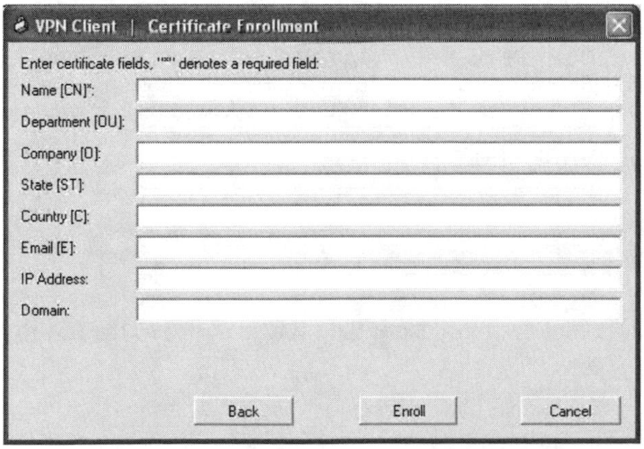

Before the Certificate Manager can build a certificate request, the administrator must supply some enrollment information. The enrollment form has eight fields:

- **Name (CN)**—The unique name used for this certificate. This field is required. It will become the name of the certificate (for example, student1).

- **Department (OU)**—The name of the department to which you belong (for example, training). This field correlates to the OU. For example, the OU is the same as the group name configured in a Concentrator.

- **Company (O)**—The name of the company or organization to which you belong (for example, Boxing Orange).

- **State (ST)**—The name of your state (for example, West Yorkshire).

- **Country** —The two-letter country code for your country (for example, UK).

- **Email**—Your e-mail address (for example, Andrew.mason@boxingorange.com).

- **IP Address**—Your system's IP address (for example, 172.26.26.1).

- **Domain**—The name of the domain your system is in (for example, boxingorange.com). It can be an FQDN (for example, training.boxingorange.com).

When you finish entering information in the enrollment form, click Enroll to complete the operation. A dialog box appears, telling you that the file request has been created. This file request will have been saved to the Cisco VPN Client install directory. This is normally C:\Program Files\Cisco Systems\VPN Client.

The contents of a sample PKCS#10 file are shown in Figure 5-36.

Figure 5-36 *Sample PKCS#10 File Created by File-Based Enrollment*

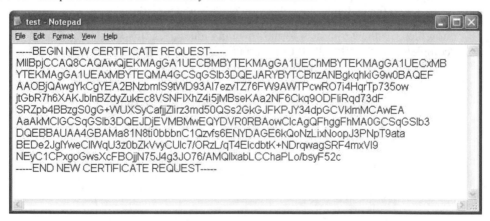

At this point, you have to transmit the PKCS#10 file to the CA to obtain a certificate.

When the VPN Client generates an enrollment request file, the file is on the PC hard drive. You access the file, copy its contents, and paste it into the appropriate window on the Microsoft CA. To do this, follow these steps (see Figure 5-37):

Step 1   Locate the enrollment request file on the PC and double-click it. The file should resemble a Notepad file.

Step 2   Select the file's contents by selecting Edit > Select All. Copy the contents by selecting Edit > Copy.

Step 3   Copy the contents of the enrollment request file into the appropriate window on the CA. Select the CA window, and press Ctrl+V. This pastes the contents of the paste buffer into the area provided by the CA. The CA now creates an identity certificate.

Figure 5-37   *Pasting the Certificate Request*

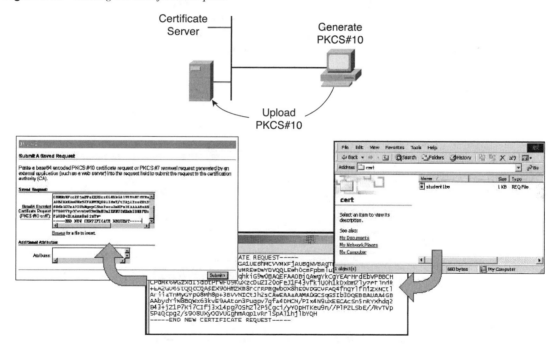

From an enrollment form, the Certificate Manager creates an enrollment request. The contents of the request file are transferred to the CA via cut and paste. The CA issues a new identity certificate. After the CA generates an identity certificate, the identity and root certificates are downloaded to the PC. Follow these steps to download the certificates:

Step 1   Choose an encoding scheme: DER or base 64 encoding. Either will work. The client can handle both schemes.

Step 2   Select the type of download: CA certificate or CA certificate path. The CA certificate downloads the identity certificate only. The root certificate is downloaded next, or the CA certificate path is selected. The CA certificate path downloads both the identity and root certificate, PKCS#7. Selecting the download type starts the download.

Step 3   The Save-in window opens. Choose the destination folder from the Save In drop-down menu. In the File Name window, enter the name of the file; the default filename is certnew. Rename the file something more descriptive, such as PC new_york. Make note of the destination folder and filename; you will need them when the certificates are imported. Click Save.

Step 4   The Download Complete window opens. Click Close. The process is complete. The certificates are on the PC's hard drive.

The last step is to import the identity and root certificates into the certificate store. Choose Certificates > Import within the VPN Client. In the Import Certificate window, shown in Figure 5-38, click Browse. In the Open window, choose All Files from the Files of type drop-down menu.

Figure 5-38   *Importing the Certificate*

The Certificate Manager supports the following four file types:

- **Cisco Export Certificate (.cec)**—Allows the administrator to back up a copy of a certificate resident in the Certificate Manager.

- **Microsoft Personal Exchange Files (.pfx)**—Imports a certificate resident in Internet Explorer.

- **PKCS#7 (.p7b)**—Imports a PKCS#7 certificate.

- **X509 files (.der and .cer)**—Imports an individual identity or root certificate sourced from a PC hard drive.

- **All files**—Displays all the files in the directory—.cec, .pfx, .p7b, .der, and .ccr.

Browse to the certificate file and also enter the password that was saved to the certificate file, as shown in Figure 5-38. This completes the file-based certificate enrollment steps.

The administrator can view the contents of the certificates by selecting Certificates > View, as shown in Figure 5-39. The root certificate fields are as follows:

- **Common Name**—The name of the owner—usually the first and last names.

- **Department**—The name of the owner's department, which is the same as the OU. Note that when connecting to a Concentrator, the OU must match the Group Name configured for the owner in the Concentrator.

- **Company**—The organization where the owner is using the certificate.

- **State**—The state where the owner is using the certificate.

- **Country**—The two-character country code.

- **Email**—The e-mail address of the certificate's owner.

- **MD5 and SHA-1 Thumbprint**—A hash of the certificate's complete contents, which provides a means of validating the certificate's authenticity. For example, you can contact the issuing CA and use this identifier to verify that this certificate is the right one.

- **Key Size**—The size of the encryption key (for example, 512).

- **Subject**—The FQDN of the certificate's owner.

- **Issuer**—The root CA.

- **Serial Number**—A unique identifier used to track the certificate's validity on CRLs.

- **Not valid before**—The beginning date that the certificate is valid.

- **Not valid after**—The end date beyond which the certificate is no longer valid.

Figure 5-39 *Viewing the Certificate*

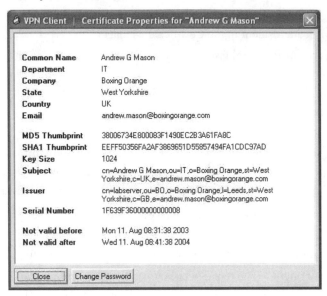

Network (Online) Enrollment

File-based enrollment is a file transfer-intensive process; however, network-based enroll-ment is an automatic process that lets you connect directly to a CA via SCEP. Complete the enrollment form to connect to a CA via SCEP. The Certificate Manager uses SCEP to send the request to the CA, and the CA issues an identity certificate. The CA then returns the CA, RA, and identity certificates to the Certificate Manager. For network-based enrollment to work, both the end device and the CA must support SCEP.

The SCEP operates between the client and the certificate server. The certificate request process is always the same, but the approval process varies, depending on whether the identity certificate is approved automatically or manually. The approval process varies between CAs. In a private network where the corporation owns the CA, the approval process might be set to automatic: The user makes a request, the CA approves the request, and an identity certificate is generated. If the user is making the request of a public CA, the request might be delayed pending a manual approval process. The SCEP process is as follows, as shown in Figure 5-40:

- Send the CA or RA certificate request to the CA.
- The CA returns a CA or RA certificate.
- The VPN Client:
  — Verifies the CA or RA.

- — Generates keys.
- — Generates the certificate request.
- — Sends the certificate request to the CA.

- The CA processes the request, generates an identity certificate, and returns it to the VPN Client.

- Or, the CA places the request in a pending (approval) file and returns the pending message to the VPN Client.

- — The Certificate Manager periodically sends a poll to the CA.
- — If the identity certificate is approved, the CA sends it to the Certificate Manager.

Figure 5-40   *SCEP*

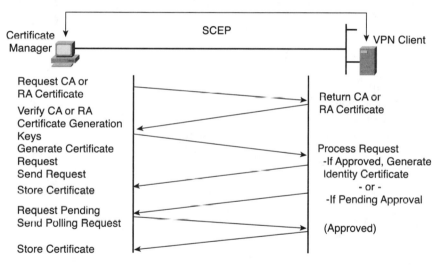

From the VPN Client, choose Certificates > Enroll to start the enrollment process. You see the screen shown in Figure 5-41. Note that the Online radio button is selected and a CA of labserver has been chosen. When this information is entered, the URL is automatically filled in, as is the CA domain. The only information required is the challenge password.

For new CAs, the CA network address or URL is required. Some CAs require the IP address only. Other CAs require the IP address plus an additional string. For instance, with a Microsoft CA you need to add the string certsrv/mscep/mscep.dll to the end of the IP address. If you add only certsrv to the IP address, you access only the file cut-and-paste section of the CA, not the SCEP code. Check with your administrator for the exact phrasing.

Figure 5-41 *Online Certificate Enrollment Screen*

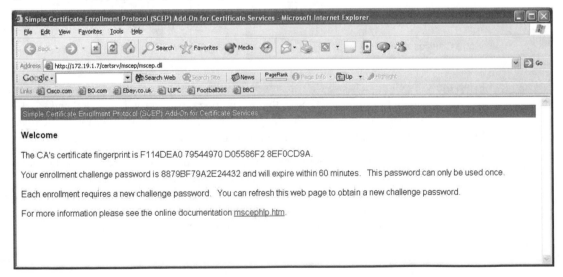

Enter the server's FQDN in the CA Domain field. This information is also available from your CA administrator.

Enter a password in the Challenge Password field. Some CAs require that you enter a password to access the site. Enter the password in the CA Password field. You can get the password from the CA or your network administrator. On a Microsoft CA, you obtain a challenge password by browsing to the IP address or FQDN of the CA /certsrv/mscep/mscep.dll. Figure 5-42 shows a sample challenge screen.

Figure 5-42 *Sample Microsoft CA Challenge Password Screen*

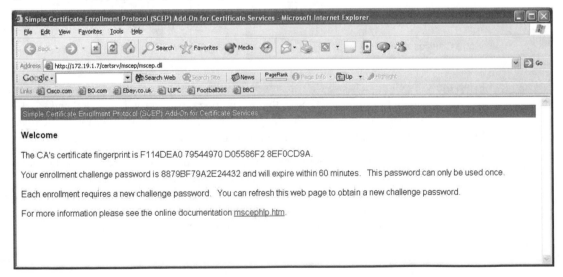

Just like the file-based method, you need to fill out an enrollment form. It has eight fields:

- **Common Name (CN)**—The unique name used for this certificate. This field is required. It becomes the name of the certificate (for example, student1).

- **Department (OU)**—The name of the department to which you belong (for example, training). This field correlates to the OU. For example, the OU is the same as the group name configured in a Concentrator.

- **Company (O)**—The name of the company or organization to which you belong (for example, Boxing Orange).

- **State (ST)**—The name of your state (for example, West Yorkshire).

- **Country** —The two-letter country code for your country (for example, UK).

- **Email**—Your e-mail address (for example, Andrew.mason@boxingorange.com).

- **IP Address**—Your system's IP address (for example, 172.26.26.1).

- **Domain**—The name of the domain your system is in (for example, boxingorange.com). It can be an FQDN (for example, training.boxingorange.com).

When you finish entering the information in the enrollment form, click Enroll to continue.

You then can view the certificate from the Certificates tab of the VPN Client, as shown in Figure 5-43.

Figure 5-43 *Enrolled Identity Certificates*

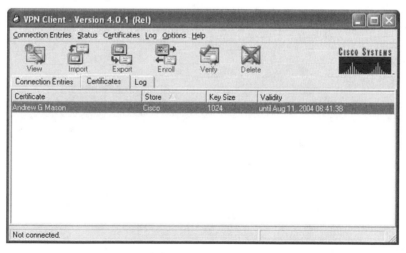

One of the distinct benefits of using SCEP is that the identity and root certificates are automatically loaded into the Certificate Manager. You can view the CA Certificate by selecting Certificates > View CA/RA Certificates. These are then added to the identity certificates in the main Certificates screen, as shown in Figure 5-44.

Figure 5-44   *CA, RA, and Enrolled Identity Certificates*

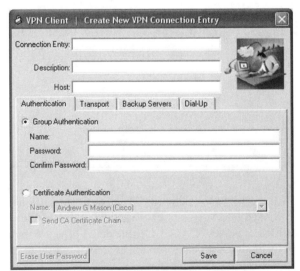

Connecting a Remote-Access VPN Using a Certificate

Now that you have configured both the Concentrator and the VPN Client to support digital certificates, you can take the final step and create a connection entry that lets you establish a remote-access VPN using these certificates.

Start the VPN Client in the usual manner, and select Connection Entries > New. You see the Create New VPN Connection Entry window, as shown in Figure 5-45.

Figure 5-45   *Create New VPN Connection Entry Window*

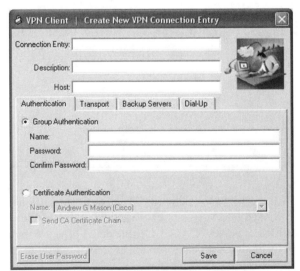

Enter the connection information. Rather than using the default, Group Authentication, select the Certificate Authentication radio button instead. By default, the first installed identity certificate is highlighted. This is Andrew G Mason (Cisco), as shown in Figure 5-46.

Figure 5-46   *Selecting Certificate Authentication*

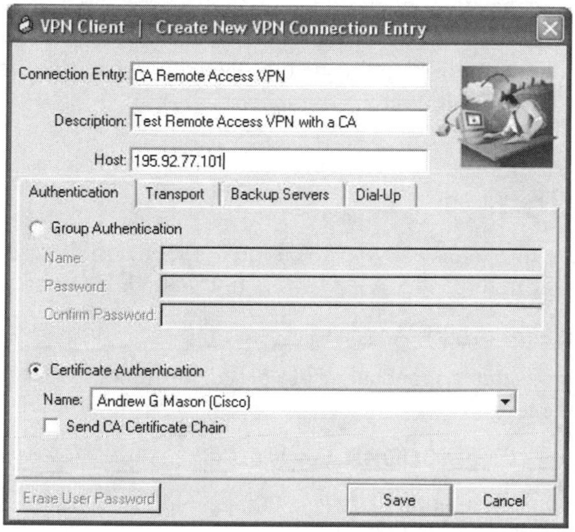

Change any of the required settings on the Transport, Backup Servers, and Dial-Up tabs, and then click Save to save the new connection entry.

Double-click the newly created connection entry. You are prompted for the certificate password, as shown in Figure 5-47.

Figure 5-47   *Entering the Certificate Password*

Enter the certificate password if you configured the identity certificate with one. If the entire configuration is correct, the VPN is established with the central site.

Summary

This chapter covered the basics of a PKI solution. You learned about the CA and the differences between a digital certificate and a digital signature before looking at the steps required to configure the VPN 3000 to support digital certificate authentication. This chapter covered the different enrollment options—manual with a PKCS#10 and automatic using SCEP. Next you saw the steps required to configure the VPN Client to support digital certificate authentication. You finished the chapter by creating a connection entry on the VPN Client to use the configured digital certificate.

Review Questions

The following questions test your retention of the material presented in this chapter. The answers appear in Appendix A, "Answers to the Review Questions."

1 What are the two PKI models?

2 When you start the manual or file-based enrollment, what file is created by the enrollment form?

3 What does CRL stand for, and what is it?

4 From which screen on the VPN 3000 can you view all the CA, identity, and SSL certificates?

5 How many identity certificates are supported on a VPN 3005 Concentrator?

6 File-based enrollment uses a PKCS#10 file. What protocol does automatic (also called network or online) enrollment use?

7 By default, does an MS CA support SCEP?

8 On the VPN Client, how do you use a certificate within a connection entry?

9 What is the major certificate store for the VPN Client?

10 When you create a new IKE proposal to use certificate authentication, what should you set the authentication field to?

After completing this chapter, you will be able to perform the following tasks:

- Understand the firewall feature of the VPN Client
- Configure the Are You There option
- Create a customized firewall policy for the Cisco integrated firewall client

CHAPTER 6

The Cisco VPN Client Firewall Feature

The last two chapters looked at configuring the Cisco VPN Client for remote access. This chapter looks at a very important feature of the VPN Software Client—a client-installed software firewall that protects the device that is connected to the VPN. For example, if you give remote workers VPN access, you cannot control from where they access your network over the VPN. If they connect their laptop to a third-party network, it is at risk from other network users. This risk is compounded when the remote worker initiates a remote-access VPN connection to the corporate network. The firewall feature ensures that the corporate network is protected from any third-party networks by enforcing various rules and policies.

This chapter starts by looking at the different types of firewalls, and then it looks at how each firewall feature is configured. It provides a sample custom firewall feature that allows only remote users to access HTTP resources over the VPN.

Firewall Feature Overview

The Software Client is designed for split tunneling, Internet traffic, and applications. Split tunneling has three types of traffic:

- **Encrypted tunnel**—All traffic bound for the secure network is encrypted and sent down a tunnel, which is relatively safe.

- **Local LAN**—Local LAN traffic is typically between a remote user's PC and a printer under his or her desk, which is also relatively safe.

- **Internet traffic**—Internet traffic is between the remote user and sites on the Internet. Enabling split tunneling (the ability to raise a tunnel and talk to the Internet in clear text) raises security issues. The Software Client firewall feature is designed to address the Internet traffic security issue.

The Cisco VPN 3000 Series Concentrator contains four firewall features designed to enhance system security for Microsoft Windows-based PCs running the VPN Software Client:

- **Are You There (AYT)**—This feature verifies that a specific firewall product is operational on a client PC before any tunnels are allowed.

- **Stateful firewall**—A predefined stateful firewall that is turned on or off at the remote Software Client. If enabled, it is active for both tunneled and nontunneled traffic.

- **Central Policy Protection (CPP)**—Lets network administrators centrally define firewall policies for connected VPN Clients. This policy is pushed down to the Software Client at connection time.

- **Cisco Integrated Client (CIC) firewall**—As of Cisco VPN 3000 Series Concentrator Release 3.5, the Microsoft Windows-based Software Client contains a CIC firewall module. The CIC firewall feature supports the stateful firewall feature and the CPP feature.

Are You There Feature

Often network administrators require remote-access PCs to run a firewall application before allowing virtual private network (VPN) tunnels to be built. The network administrator can configure the Concentrator to require all Software Clients in a group to have a specific firewall operating on the PC.

The Software Client monitors that firewall to ensure that it is running. If the firewall stops running, the Software Client drops the connection to the Concentrator. This firewall policy is also called are you there (AYT) because the Software Client polls the firewall periodically to determine if it is still there. If no reply is received from the firewall, the Software Client knows that the firewall is down and terminates its connection to the Concentrator.

Configuring the Are You There Feature

Go to the Configuration > User Management > Groups > Modify window and select the Client FW tab, as shown in Figure 6-1.

Figure 6-1 *Client FW Tab*

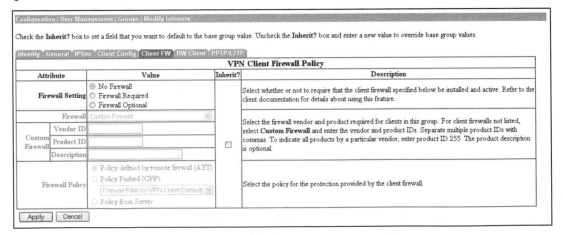

The AYT, CIC, and CPP features can be configured from this window. You will configure each feature individually.

AYT is the first feature you will configure:

Step 1   Select a firewall setting from the Firewall Setting row.

Step 2   Identify a firewall in the Firewall row.

Step 3   (Optional) Configure a custom firewall in the Custom Firewall row.

Step 4   Select the firewall policy from the Firewall Policy row.

Step 1: Select a Firewall Setting

When configuring the AYT feature, you must first select a firewall setting. By default, no firewall is required for remote users in this group, so the No Firewall radio button is already selected. If you, as the administrator, want users in this group to be firewall-protected, select either Firewall Required or Firewall Optional:

- No Firewall is the default. If you leave this radio button selected, no firewall is required for remote users in this group.

- If you select Firewall Required, all remote users in this group must use a firewall. Only users with the designated firewall can connect to the Concentrator. The Concentrator drops any session that attempts to connect without the designated firewall installed and running. If you require a firewall for a group, make sure that the group does not include any Software Clients without the designated firewall or that the group does not include any non-Windows Software Clients, because they will be unable to connect.

- If you select Firewall Optional, all remote users in this group can connect to the Concentrator. Those who have the designated firewall must use it. Those without the required firewall can still connect but receive a notification message. This setting is useful if you have a group that is in gradual transition, in which some members have set up firewall capacity and others have not.

You can see from Figure 6-2 that we have chosen for the Firewall to be optional.

Figure 6-2   *Setting the Firewall Settings*

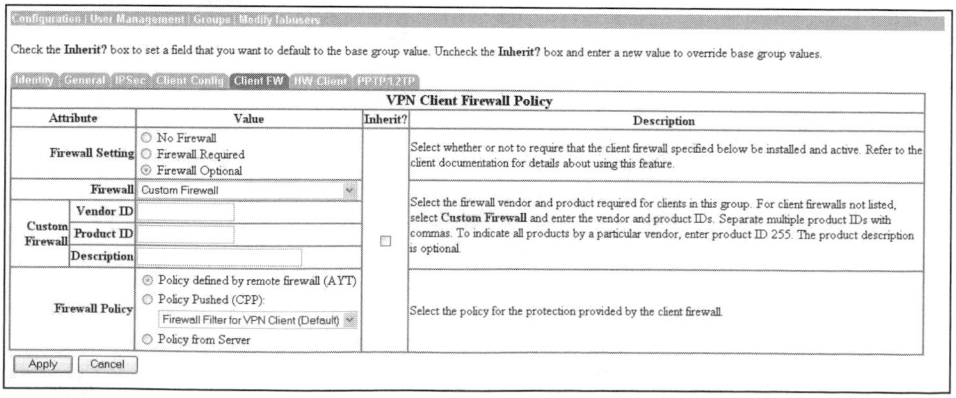

Step 2: Identify a Firewall

After you establish the firewall setting, the second step is to identify a firewall. To do this, choose a firewall from the Firewall drop-down menu, as shown in Figure 6-3:

- **Cisco Integrated Client Firewall**—The firewall built into the Software Client.

- **Network ICE BlackICE Defender**—The Network ICE BlackICE Agent or Defender Firewall.

- **Zone Labs ZoneAlarm**—The Zone Labs ZoneAlarm firewall.

- **Zone Labs ZoneAlarm Pro**—The Zone Labs ZoneAlarm Pro firewall.

- **Zone Labs ZoneAlarm or ZoneAlarm Pro**—Either the Zone Labs ZoneAlarm firewall or the Zone Labs ZoneAlarm Pro firewall.

- **Zone Labs Integrity**—An enterprise security solution from Zone Labs.

- **Sygate Personal Firewall**—The basic version of the personal firewall from Sygate.

- **Sygate Personal Firewall Pro**—The professional personal firewall from Sygate.

- **Sygate Security Agent**—The Security Agent application from Sygate.

- **Cisco Intrusion Prevention Security Agent**—The new Cisco Security Agent, running as Host-based Intrusion Prevention (HIPS) as well as personal firewall mode (formerly Okena).

- **Custom Firewall**—For future use (as discussed next).

Figure 6-3 *Firewall Options*

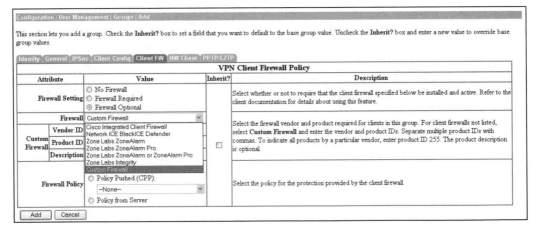

Step 3: Configure a Custom Firewall (Optional)

An optional step when configuring the AYT feature is to configure a custom firewall. Currently, every supported firewall can be selected from the Firewall drop-down menu. In the future, this might not be true. For example, suppose an additional firewall is supported in a future Concentrator software release—firewall brand XYZ. The customer wants to support the new XYZ firewall, but he is not ready to migrate the to the new Concentrator software release. The new firewall can be supported on the older version of the Concentrator software by choosing the Custom Firewall option. To support the new XYZ firewall, the administrator must configure the new vendor code and product code in the Vendor ID and Product ID fields. An optional description of the new firewall can be added in the Description field.

Each vendor has a unique vendor identity and firewall product identity. Table 6-1 lists the currently supported firewall vendors and their products.

Table 6-1   *Custom Firewall Options*

Vendor	Vendor Code	Product	Product Code
Cisco Systems	1	CIC	1
Cisco Systems	1	Cisco Intrusion Prevention Security Agent	2
Zone Labs	2	ZoneAlarm	1
Zone Labs	2	ZoneAlarm Pro	2
Zone Labs	2	Zone Labs Integrity	3
Network ICE	3	BlackICE Defender/Agent	1
Sygate	4	Personal Firewall	1
Sygate	4	Personal Firewall Pro	2
Sygate	4	Sygate Security Agent	3

In Figure 6-4, the administrator defines a custom firewall with a vendor identification of 2, Zone Labs, and a product identity of 2, ZoneAlarm Pro. Future vendor and product identifications will be available in the Cisco VPN 3000 product release notes.

Figure 6-4   *Configuring a Custom Firewall*

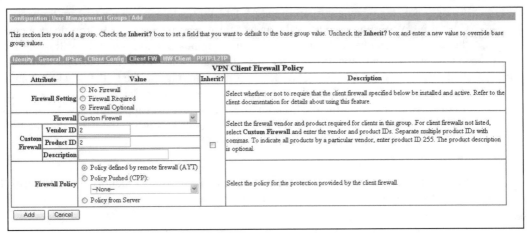

Step 4: Select the Firewall Policy

The last step when configuring the AYT feature is to select the firewall policy. Three policies are available. For the AYT feature, select the Policy defined by remote firewall (AYT) radio button. The AYT policy choice is sent to the Software Client in the mode config messages that are communicated between IKE Phase I and IKE Phase II.

The default setting for all groups is to use AYT. Therefore, for a new group, there is no need to change the radio button. In Figures 6-2 and 6-4, the AYT radio button is selected.

How the Are You There Feature Works

The administrator configures the Concentrator to require a particular firewall to be present on the remote Software Client's PC. At Software Client connection time, the following steps occur:

Step 1   The Software Client polls the firewall.

Step 2   The Software Client reports the presence of a specific firewall to the Concentrator via the mode config messages.

Step 3   The Concentrator checks the reported firewall information against the VPN Client's group firewall settings.

Step 4   Depending on how the firewall parameters are set, the Concentrator's actions are as follows:

— **No Firewall setting**—No firewall is required, so tunnel establishment continues.

— **Firewall Required setting**—If the designated firewall is installed and running, the connection is allowed. When the connection is established, the Software Client polls the firewall every 30 seconds to ensure that it is still running. If the firewall stops running, the Software Client terminates the session.

— **Firewall Optional setting**—VPN Clients that have the designated firewall may connect if the firewall is running. VPN Clients without the designated firewall may still connect, but they receive a notification message warning them that the firewall is not running because the Software Client did not match any of the Concentrator's firewall configurations. The message also defines the expected firewall.

Stateful Firewall Feature

From Software Client Release 3.5, an integrated stateful firewall module licensed from Zone Labs called the CIC firewall is included. Components of this feature include a dynamic link library (DLL) combined with a Zone Labs stateful firewall module driver. The DLL acts as an interface between the traditional Software Client and the firewall driver.

A default stateful firewall policy is loaded on the CIC firewall. The stateful (CIC) firewall blocks all inbound traffic that is not related to an outbound session. The two exceptions to this rule are Dynamic Host Configuration Protocol (DHCP) and Address Resolution Protocol (ARP) traffic, where inbound packets are allowed through specific holes in the stateful firewall. When the user enables the stateful firewall, it is always on. The firewall is active for both tunneled and nontunneled traffic.

The administrator can accept the default policy, or he can customize the firewall policy. To alter the firewall policy, the administrator can use the CPP feature. CPP lets the Concentrator's administrator centrally define a set of rules for the CIC firewall. This policy is pushed to the CIC firewall module. CPP is discussed more later in this chapter.

The remote client controls the stateful firewall feature. By default, the stateful firewall feature is disabled, or unchecked, on the Software Client. There are two ways to enable the stateful firewall feature. From the main Software Client window, remote users can click Options and choose Stateful Firewall (Always On), as shown in Figure 6-5. You can also access the Stateful Firewall option by right-clicking the lock icon on the system tray. When enabled, the Stateful Firewall feature filters both tunneled and nontunneled traffic.

Figure 6-5   *Stateful Firewall Feature*

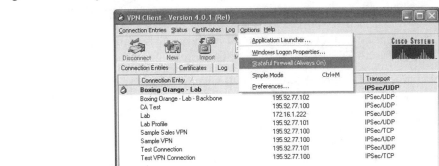

Central Policy Protection Feature

Some administrators prefer to enforce a more centralized firewall policy approach. They do this by first defining a policy (a set of rules to allow or drop traffic) on the Concentrator. When the connection is made, these policies are pushed from the Concentrator to the Software Client using mode config messages. The Software Client, in turn, forwards the policy to the local firewall, which enforces it. See Figure 6-6.

Figure 6-6   *CPP Feature*

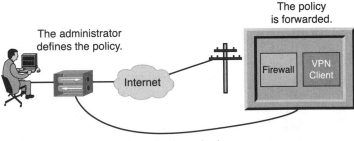

The Software Client can forward the policy to the following firewalls:

- **CIC**—Concentrator and Software Client Release 3.5
- **ZoneLabs**—Minimum version of 2.6.357

Configuring CPP

Configuring CPP is a two-step process:

Step 1   From the Firewall drop-down menu, the administrator chooses a CPP-supported firewall—either CIC or a Zone Labs firewall.

Step 2   From the Firewall Policy row, the administrator selects Policy Pushed (CPP). From the Policy Pushed (CPP) drop-down menu, the administrator chooses a filter to push to the firewall. The default policy is Firewall Filter for VPN Client (Default).

In Figure 6-7, the administrator has selected ZoneAlarm Pro as the required firewall, with the default CPP policy of Firewall Filter for VPN Client (Default). The default policy forwards all inbound and outbound encrypted tunnel traffic. It blocks all Internet inbound traffic that is not related to an outbound session.

Figure 6-7   *Configuring the CPP Feature*

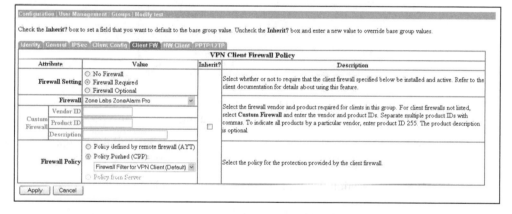

Software Client Firewall Statistics

After a Software Client tunnel is established, the remote user can verify the firewall configuration and filtering information through the Cisco Systems VPN Client Connection Status window. At the bottom of the General tab is firewall information. The available firewall status parameters are as follows:

- Personal Firewall is the name of the firewall in use on the Software Client PC, such as the Cisco Integrated Client, Zone Labs ZoneAlarm, ZoneAlarm Pro, BlackICE Defender, and so on.

- Firewall Policy lists the firewall policy in use. The options are as follows:

  — AYT, which corresponds to the policy defined by the remote firewall (AYT) from a Concentrator's point of view.

  — CPP or policy pushed, as defined on the Concentrator.

- The client or server corresponding to the policy from the server (Zone Labs Integrity) on the Concentrator. Zone Labs Integrity is not covered in this book.

In Figure 6-8, the firewall running on the remote PC is the CIC firewall. The firewall policy is defined via CPP.

Figure 6-8 *Software Client Firewall Statistics: General Tab*

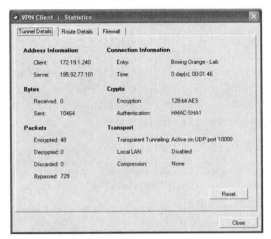

The information on the Firewall tab, shown in Figure 6-9, varies according to the policy—AYT or CPP. For CPP, the Firewall tab is divided into three sections:

- The top section displays the name of the firewall policy and firewall product.

- The middle section displays a list of rules.

- The bottom section displays information about a selected rule.

Figure 6-9 *Software Client Firewall Statistics: Firewall Tab*

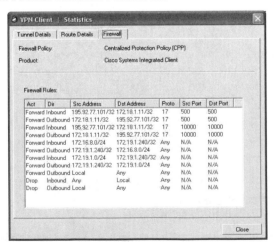

To display rule-specific information, click in the middle section. Use the arrow key to highlight a rule in the list. The bottom section displays information about the highlighted rule. Each firewall rule includes the following fields:

- **Action**—The action taken if the data traffic matches the rule:
  - **Drop**—Discards the session.
  - **Forward**—Allows the session to go through.
- **Direction**—The direction of traffic to be affected by the firewall:
  - **Inbound**—Traffic coming into the PC, also called the local machine, from the public network while the Software Client is connected to a secure gateway through the secure tunnel.
  - **Outbound**—Traffic going out from the PC to all networks while the Software Client is connected to a secure gateway.
- **Source Address**—The address of the traffic that this rule affects:
  - **Any**—All traffic (for example, drop any inbound traffic). This field can also contain a specific IP address and subnet mask.
  - **Local**—The local machine. If the direction is outbound, the source address is local.
- **Destination Address**—The packet's destination address that this rule checks (the recipient's address):
  - **Any**—All traffic (for example, forward any outbound traffic).
  - **Local**—The local machine. If the direction is inbound, the destination address is local.
- **Protocol**—The Internet Assigned Numbers Authority (IANA) number of the protocol that this rule concerns (6 for TCP, 17 for UDP, and so on):
  - **Source Port**—The source port used by TCP or UDP.
  - **Destination Port**—The destination port used by TCP or UDP.

Creating a Customized Firewall Policy

As well as the default VPN Client Firewall Policy, you can also create and apply a custom policy to your client firewall.

Most of the time, the default policy works fine. However, if the administrator needs to restrict the outbound clear-text traffic to a few protocols or a handful of remote locations, the administrator should create a new policy. Building custom CPP policies is a four-step process on the Concentrator:

Step 1   Define rules to restrict traffic.

Step 2   Add a new policy (called a filter on the VPN Concentrator).

Step 3   Associate the new rules with the newly created policy.

Step 4   Assign the new policy to the CPP.

Step 1: Define Rules to Restrict Traffic

A firewall policy is comprised of rules. These rules are used to shape the traffic and define whether the firewall should forward or drop the traffic. In creating a new policy, the administrator first has to create new rules. To create the new rules, do the following:

Step 1   Go to the Configuration > Policy Management > Traffic Management > Rules window, shown in Figure 6-10.

Figure 6-10   *Traffic Management > Rules Window*

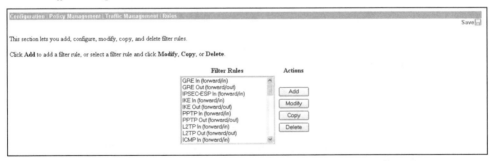

Step 2   From the Actions column, click Add.

Step 3   From the Configuration > Policy Management > Traffic Management > Rules > Add window, define the new rule.

The following is a description of the rule parameters (see Figure 6-11):

- **Rule Name field**—Enter the name of the filter rule.

- **Direction drop-down menu**—Choose the data direction to which this rule applies:

  — **Inbound**—Into the Software Client.

  — **Outbound**—Out of the Software Client.

- **Action drop-down menu**—Choose the action to take if the data traffic (packet) matches all parameters that follow:

  — **Drop**—Discards the packet. This is the default choice.

  — **Forward**—Allows the packet to pass.

- **Protocol drop-down menu**—This parameter refers to the IANA-assigned protocol number in an IP packet. The descriptions include the IANA number, in brackets, for reference. Click the Protocol or Other drop-down menu button and choose the protocol to which this rule applies:
    - **Any**—Any protocol (the default choice).
    - **ICMP**—Internet Control Message Protocol (used by **ping**). If you choose this protocol, you should also configure ICMP Packet Type.
    - **TCP**—Transmission Control Protocol (connection-oriented, such as FTP, HTTP, SMTP, or Telnet). If you choose this protocol, you should configure TCP Connection and TCP/UDP Source Port or Destination Port.
    - **EGP**—Exterior Gateway Protocol (used for routing to exterior networks).
    - **IGP**—Interior Gateway Protocol (used for routing within a domain).
    - **UDP**—User Datagram Protocol (connectionless, such as SNMP). If you choose this protocol, you should also configure TCP/UDP Source Port or Destination Port.
    - **ESP**—Encapsulating Security Payload (applies to IPSec).
    - **AH**—Authentication Header (applies to IPSec).
    - **GRE**—Generic Routing Encapsulation (used by PPTP).
    - **RSVP**—Resource Reservation Protocol (reserves bandwidth on routers).
    - **IGMP**—Internet Group Management Protocol (used in multicasting).
    - **OSPF**—Open Shortest Path First (interior routing protocol).
- **Other**—Another protocol not listed here. If you choose Other here, you must enter the IANA-assigned protocol number in the Other field.
- **TCP Connection drop-down menu**—Do not configure this field if you are using this rule for a client firewall filter.
- **Source Address**—Specify the packet source address that this rule checks:
    - **Network List drop-down menu**   Click the Network List drop-down menu button and choose the configured network list that specifies the source addresses. A network list is a list of network addresses that are treated as a single object.
    - **IP Address field**—Enter the source IP address in dotted-decimal notation. The default is 0.0.0.0.
    - **Wildcard-mask field**—Enter the source address wildcard mask in dotted-decimal notation. The default is 255.255.255.255.

- **Destination Address**—Specify the packet destination address that this rule checks:
  - **Network List drop-down menu**—Click the Network List drop-down menu button and choose the configured network list that specifies the destination addresses. A network list is a list of network addresses that are treated as a single object.
  - **IP Address field**—Enter the destination IP address in dotted-decimal notation. The default is 0.0.0.0.
  - **Wildcard-mask field**—Enter the destination address wildcard mask in dotted-decimal notation. The default is 255.255.255.255.
- **TCP/UDP Source Port**—If you chose TCP or UDP from the Protocol drop-down menu, choose the source port number that this rule checks. To do this, click the Port drop-down menu button and choose the process.
- **TCP/UDP Destination Port**—If you chose TCP or UDP from the Protocol drop-down menu, choose the destination port number that this rule checks. To do this, click the Port drop-down menu button and choose the process.

Figure 6-11 *Sample Rule*

Figure 6-11 shows an example of a rule configuration. The administrator wants to limit the remote user to using outbound HTTP traffic only when accessing the Internet. To accomplish this, the administrator configures the rule parameters as follows:

- **Rule Name**—HTTP Only
- **Direction**—Outbound
- **Action**—Forward
- **Protocol**—TCP
- **Source and Destination Address**—Ignore. The administrator is limiting the end user to a protocol, HTTP, not a specific address. The end user can surf the web if he or she is using only HTTP.
  - **TCP/UDP Source Port**—Ignored.
  - **TCP/UDP Destination Port**—Port 80, HTTP. The administrator is limiting the remote user to HTTP.

NOTE   This configuration does not allow the user to use host names. The firewall will not pass Domain Name System (DNS) information. Another rule allowing DNS is advisable.

Step 2: Add a New Policy

After the rules are defined, a new filter is added. Do the following to create the new filter:

Step 1   Go to the Configuration > Policy Management > Traffic Management > Filters window, shown in Figure 6-12.

Figure 6-12   *Traffic Management > Filters Window*

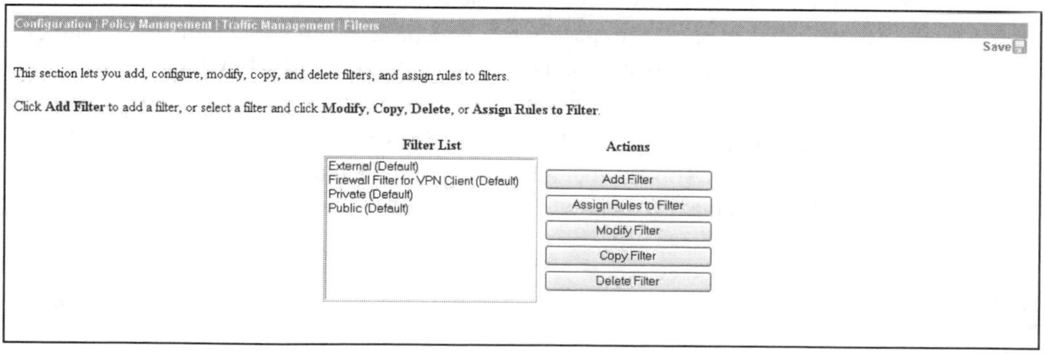

Step 2   Under the Actions column, click Add Filter.

Step 3   In the Configuration > Policy Management > Traffic Management > Filter > Add window, create the new filter.

The following is a description of the new filter parameters (see Figure 6-13):

- **Filter Name field**—Enter a unique name for this filter. The maximum is 48 characters.

- **Default Action drop-down menu**—Click the Default Action drop-down menu button and choose the action that this filter takes if a data packet does not match any of the rules on this filter:

  - **Drop**—Discards the packet (the default choice).

  - **Forward**—Allows the packet to pass.

  - **Drop and Log**—Discards the packet and logs a filter debugging event (FILTERDBG event class). See the following Note.

  - **Forward and Log**—Allows the packet to pass and logs a filter debugging event (FILTERDBG event class). See the following Note.

NOTE   The Log actions are intended for use only while debugging filter activity. Because they generate and log an event for every matched packet, they consume significant system resources and might seriously degrade performance.

- **Source Routing check box**—Ignored. Check the Source Routing check box to allow IP source-routed packets to pass. A source-routed packet specifies its own route through the network and does not rely on the system to control forwarding. This box is unchecked by default.

- **Fragments check box**—Ignored. Check the Fragments check box to allow fragmented IP packets to pass. Large data packets might be fragmented on their journey through networks, and the destination system reassembles them. This box is checked by default.

- **Description field**—Enter a description of this filter. This field is optional. It is a convenience for you or other administrators; use it to describe the purpose or use of the filter. The maximum number of characters is 255.

Figure 6-13 *Filter Example*

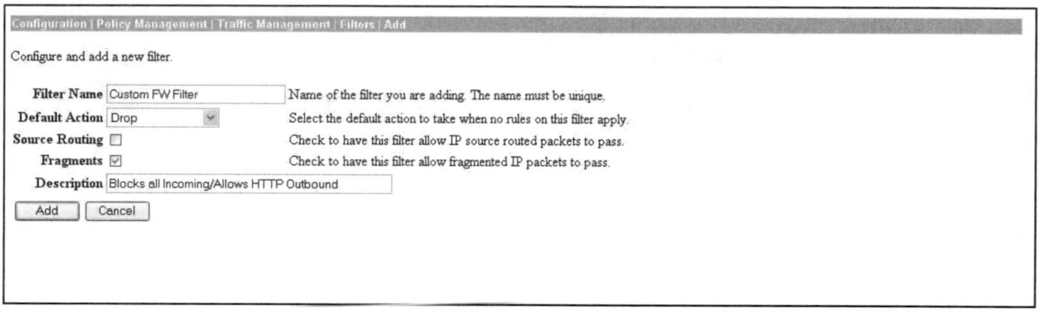

In Figure 6-13, the administrator defines a new filter named Custom FW Filter. The default action is to drop any packets that do not match any firewall rules.

Step 3: Associate the New Rules with the New Policy

The next step is to add the rules created in the first step to the new filter created in the second step:

Step 1 Go to the Configuration > Policy Management > Traffic Management > Filters window.

Step 2 Within the Filter List field, select the new filter.

Step 3 Under the Actions column, click Assign rules to filter. The Configuration > Policy Management > Traffic Management > Assign Rules to Filters window opens, as shown in Figure 6-14.

Figure 6-14 *Adding a Rule to a Filter*

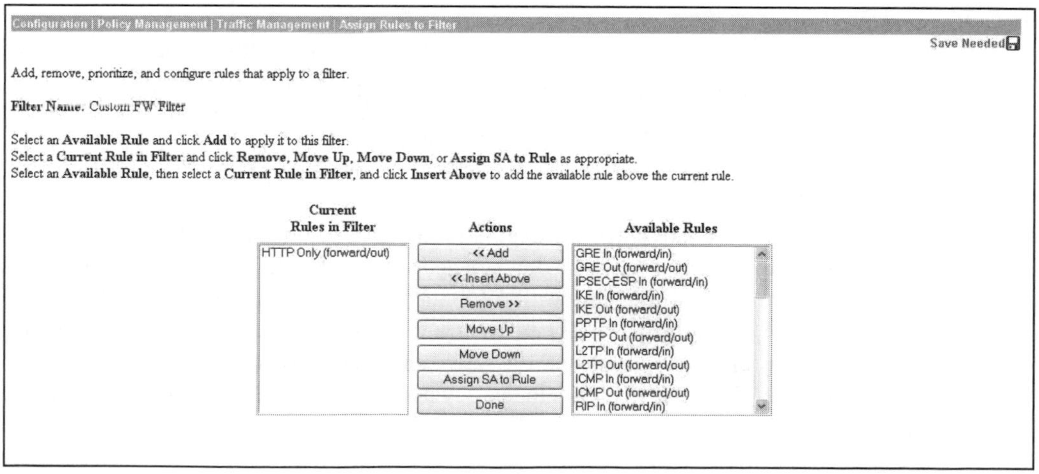

Step 4 Scroll through the Available Rules column, and select the new rules.

Step 5 Click Add under the Actions column. This action assigns the new rules to the new filter.

In Figure 6-14, the administrator adds the HTTP Only (forward/out) rule to the custom firewall filter.

Step 4: Assign the New Policy to the CPP

The last step is to assign the custom firewall policy to a group's firewall policy:

Step 1 Go to the Configuration > User Management > Groups window and select a group.

Step 2 Click Modify, and then click the Client FW tab, shown in Figure 6-15.

Figure 6-15 *Assigning the Policy to the CPP*

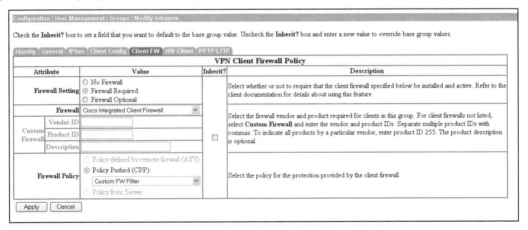

Step 3 From the Firewall Policy row, select Policy Pushed (CPP).

Step 4 From the Policy Pushed (CPP) drop-down menu, choose the new policy.

Step 5 Click Apply.

The next time a Software Client belonging to this group connects to the Concentrator, the new custom firewall filter policy is downloaded to the VPN Client. The Software Client forwards the new policy to the firewall. With the new policy, the remote user has access to the Internet via HTTP. Any HTTP inbound traffic associated with an outbound session is forwarded. Any unsolicited inbound HTTP (or any other protocol) traffic is dropped using the default rule. Figure 6-15 shows the policy assigned via CPP to the Cisco-integrated client firewall.

NOTE	CPP rules/filters are stateful in nature, but rules/filters for the Concentrator itself (such as those applied to an interface or VPN group) are not stateful.

Summary

This chapter started by providing an overview of the need for an integrated firewall within the VPN Software Client. It then covered the four main firewall features and the configuration steps required. It finished by explaining how to create a simple filter that contains a rule to allow only HTTP access over the VPN. This is very important and helps with the overall design of your secure remote-access VPN. Every remote-access VPN has users with differing requirements, and one good way to restrict what they can do is through the client firewall features and the Cisco-integrated client.

Review Questions

The following questions test your retention of the material presented in this chapter. The answers appear in Appendix A, "Answers to the Review Questions."

1 What are the four firewall features of the Cisco VPN 3000 Concentrators?

2 If the Firewall Required option is set, and no firewall is in use by the Software Client, what happens?

3 Where on the menu system do you navigate to to create filters and rules to apply to a firewall?

4 What four vendors of software firewalls are currently configured to work with the VPN Concentrator?

5 What are the two methods of enabling the stateful firewall feature?

6 What is the main feature of the AYT firewall option?

7 What is the name of the default CPP policy?

8 When you create a filter, what is the default action if a rule does not match a rule added to the filter?

9 If the Firewall Optional option is set and no firewall is in use by the Software Client, what happens?

10 With a custom firewall, if you set a vendor code of 2 and a product code of 3, what product would you be using?

After completing this chapter, you will be able to perform the following tasks:

- Understand the Cisco VPN 3002 Hardware Client
- Understand the difference between client and network extension modes
- Configure a VPN 3002 with preshared keys
- Enable the Hardware Client auto-update feature

CHAPTER 7

Configuring the Cisco 3002 Hardware Client for Remote Access

Chapter 2, "Cisco VPN 3000 Concentrator Series Hardware Overview," covered the Software and Hardware VPN Clients that can communicate with the Cisco VPN 3000 range of Concentrators. The Cisco VPN 3002 Hardware Client is a purpose-built hardware device that operates using the Cisco Unity VPN Client to provide a hardware-based VPN solution using remote-access VPN technologies. This has benefits when moderate numbers of VPN Clients exist at a remote site because of the transparency of the VPN connection to the central site and the removal of any software requirement on the end client computers.

This chapter looks at configuring a remote-access VPN using a Cisco 3002 Hardware Client at the remote site and a Cisco 3000 Concentrator at the central site. You will configure the VPN using preshared keys and look at the two main modes of operation for the 3002 Hardware Client. This chapter ends by looking at the auto-update feature of the 3002 Hardware Client.

Cisco VPN 3002 Hardware Client Overview

If a single remote user wants to be able to dial into the corporate network, typically the VPN Software Client is loaded onto the PC, which lets the remote user establish secure communications with the central site. With the client resident on the PC, the user does not have to carry any external hardware. The caveat is that the software client works for only the single PC on which it is installed.

Small office/home office (SOHO) is better positioned to use the Hardware Client. Just plug the SOHO PCs into the Hardware Client. The Hardware Client establishes secure communications for all the SOHO PCs. The Hardware Client supports up to 253 concurrent users. There is no need to add any VPN applications to the SOHO PC. The Hardware Client transparently takes care of all the tunneling requirements.

In Figure 7-1, the Cisco VPN Software Client is ported over to the Hardware Client. The Hardware Client provides the VPN Software Client functionality on a hardware platform. The Hardware Client works with the Cisco VPN 3000 Series Concentrator to create a secure connection, called a tunnel, between the 3002 Hardware Client and the private network. It uses Internet Key Exchange (IKE) and IPSec tunneling protocols to make and manage the secure connection. No applications need to be installed or run on the SOHO PC to perform the tunneling. The 3002 Hardware Client uses a software crypto engine, and no hardware acceleration is performed.

Figure 7-1   *3002 Client for a Remote-Access VPN*

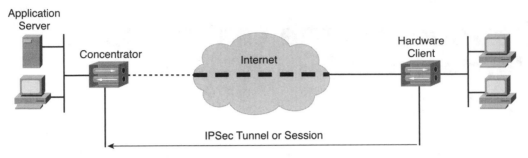

The Hardware Client is equipped with a universal power factor correction, 100-240 VAC, external power supply. A power cord with the correct plug is supplied. When the Hardware Client arrives from the factory, plug it in and power it up. Connect the SOHO PC or local LAN to the Hardware Client's private interface. Cable the Internet side of the network to the public interface of the Hardware Client. Plug a PC into the console port. The serial port needs to be configured for 9600 8 data bits, no parity, and 1 stop bit (also known as 8N1). These connectors are shown in Figure 7-2.

Figure 7-2   *3002 Physical Connections*

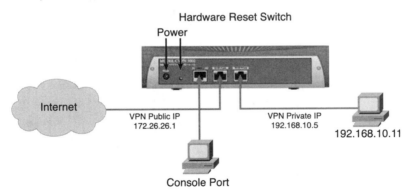

Hardware Client Modes of Operation

The 3002 Hardware Client has two modes of operation: client mode and network extension mode, as shown in Figure 7-3. It is important to remember that the 3002 Hardware Client is always classed as a remote-access user as far as the central site 3000 Concentrator is concerned. This is true even when the 3002 Hardware Client is operating in network extension mode.

Figure 7-3 *3002 Modes of Operation*

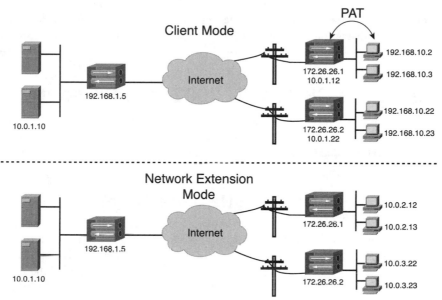

Client Mode

Client mode is for those who want to deploy a VPN quickly and easily in small remote offices. If there is no need to see the devices behind the Hardware Client, and ease of use is the key, client mode should be implemented. In client mode, the Hardware Client uses Port Address Translation (PAT) to hide its private network from the public network. SOHO PCs behind the Hardware Client are invisible to the outside world. PAT causes all traffic from the SOHO PCs to appear on the private network as a single source IP address. In Figure 7-3, the Hardware Client receives a virtual IP address—10.0.1.12 or 10.0.1.22, respectively— from the Concentrator during tunnel establishment. All remote PCs addresses in the client mode section have their IP address translated to either 10.0.1.12 or 10.0.1.22, depending on which network they reside on.

When you configure a tunnel, the default is to use client mode.

Network Extension Mode

In network extension mode, all SOHO PCs on the Hardware Client network are uniquely addressable via the tunnel. This allows direct connection to devices behind the Hardware Client. It lets Management Information Systems (MIS) personnel at the central site directly address devices behind the Hardware Client over the IPSec tunnel. Most companies use the Hardware Client in network extension mode because it enables the benefits of a true site-to-site VPN but uses remote-access technologies.

NOTE   Because the IP addresses at the remote site become part of the network, it is important to design a nonoverlapping IP address scheme to ensure that a unique address range is used at each remote site that is connected using a 3002 Hardware Client in network extension mode.

Configuring the Cisco VPN 3002 with Preshared Keys

This section discusses creating a VPN connection from a VPN 3002 Hardware Client to a VPN 3000 Concentrator. You will connect to a preconfigured group on the VPN 3000 Concentrator called training and will use the preconfigured user account called student1.

Initial Configuration of the 3002 Hardware Client

When the Hardware Client physical hardware is connected, the administrator must gain access to the Hardware Client manager. The Hardware Client comes from the factory with a private interface IP address of 192.168.10.1. Hook up a PC to the private port and configure the PC's TCP/IP address. To gain access to the Hardware Client, point the browser to the IP address of the private interface, http://192.168.10.1. Log in using **admin/admin**. No command-line interface (CLI) intervention is required.

However, if you would rather configure the Hardware Client via the CLI, or if you need to change the default address on the private LAN interface, you can use the CLI. The default serial port setting is 9600 8N1. The CLI is shown in Figure 7-4.

Figure 7-4   *3002 CLI*

The GUI manager is very similar to the GUI manager on a Cisco VPN 3000 Concentrator. Figure 7-5 shows the GUI manager login screen.

Figure 7-5   *3002 GUI Manager*

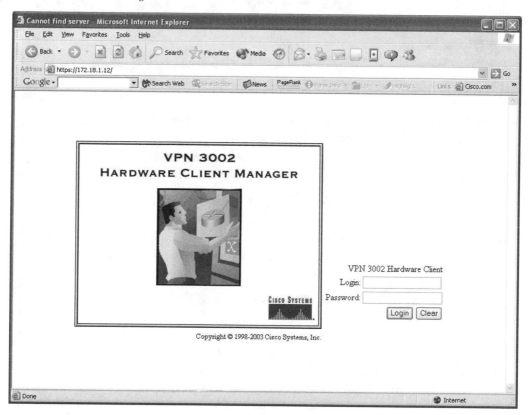

There are two ways to configure the Hardware Client: quick configuration and the main menu. The goal of quick configuration is to provide the minimal parameters needed for operation. Quick configuration guides you through the windows necessary to get a single tunnel up and running. Use the main menu to tune an application or configure features individually. The quick configuration screen is shown in Figure 7-6.

Figure 7-6 *3002 GUI Quick Configuration Screen*

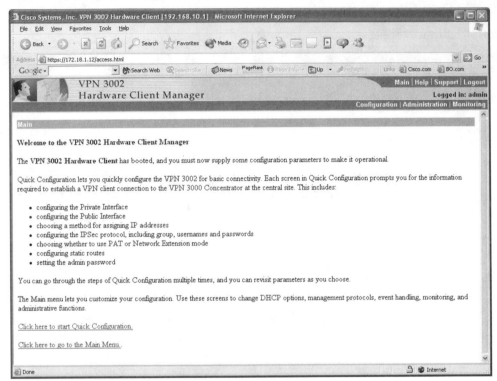

For this example, you will use the main menu to manually configure a VPN 3002 Hardware Client rather than going through quick configuration. You will start by configuring a VPN using client mode and then make the necessary changes to modify to network extension mode.

After you log in using the default username and password of admin/admin, you see the screen shown in Figure 7-7.

Figure 7-7   *3002 GUI Manager Screen*

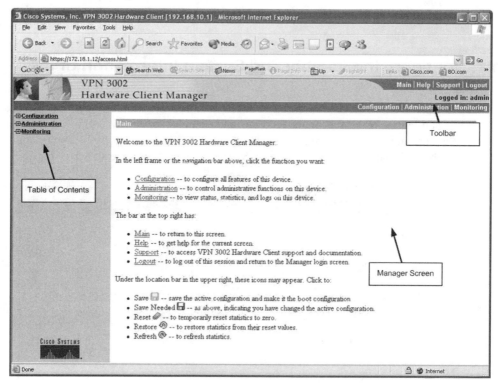

- The top frame (the Hardware Client Manager toolbar) provides quick access to manager functions, configuration, administration, and monitoring.

- The left frame (table of contents) provides the table of contents to the Manager's windows.

- The main frame (Manager) displays the current Hardware Client Manager window. From here you can navigate the Manager using either the table of contents in the left frame or the toolbar at the top of the frame. Select a title on the left frame of the window, and the Hardware Client introduces the manager window for the selected title.

- Under the location bar, the Save Needed icons might appear. When you're finished with a configuration window, click Apply. Apply allows the configuration to take effect immediately. Click Save Needed to save the changes to memory. If you reboot without saving, your configuration changes are lost.

The initial configuration of a VPN 3002 can be broken into four simple steps:

Step 1   Configure the identity and system information of the VPN 3002.

Step 2   Configure network information on the 3002.

Step 3 Configure the VPN 3002 group and user information.

Step 4 Configure the VPN operation mode.

Step 1: Configure the Identity and System Information of the VPN 3002

The first step is to configure the VPN 3002's identity and system information. This consists of naming the 3002, setting the location, and also configuring system information such as the time and date configured on the Hardware Client. Two locations need to be configured. Both are found under Configuration > System > General and are shown in Figure 7-8.

Figure 7-8   *General System Administration*

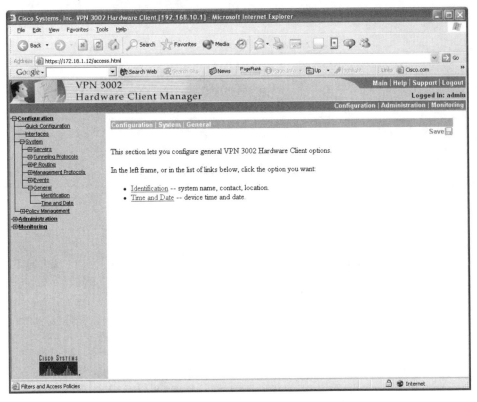

From this menu, select Identification to enter the identification details about the 3002 Hardware Client. Figure 7-9 shows the identification screen with the added information particular to this 3002 Hardware Client.

Figure 7-9   *Configuration > System > General > Identification Screen*

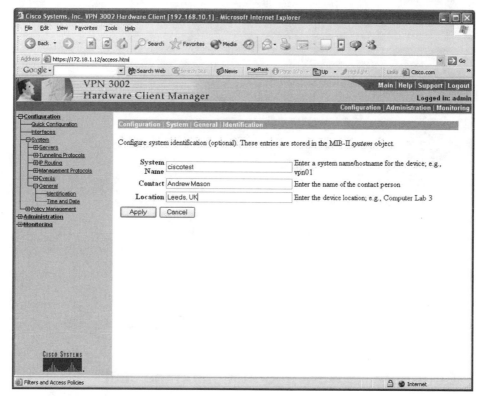

Click Apply and then select Time and Date to configure the time options. Enter the correct time and date, as shown in Figure 7-10, and then click Apply.

Figure 7-10   *Configuration > System > General > Time and Date Screen*

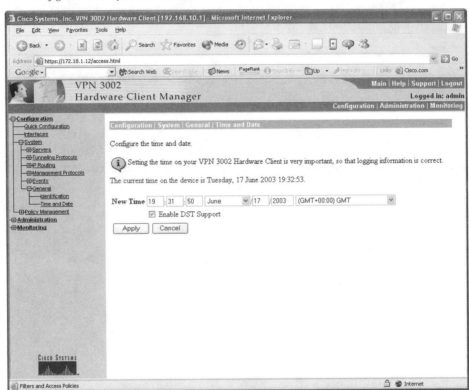

Step 2: Configure Network Information on the 3002

The next step is to configure the network settings on the 3002 Hardware Client. These include the DNS information, IP addressing, routing, and any other additional services, such as DHCP.

You will start by configuring the IP information for the Hardware Client. Select Configuration > Interfaces. You see the screen shown in Figure 7-11.

Figure 7-11 *Configuration > Interfaces Screen*

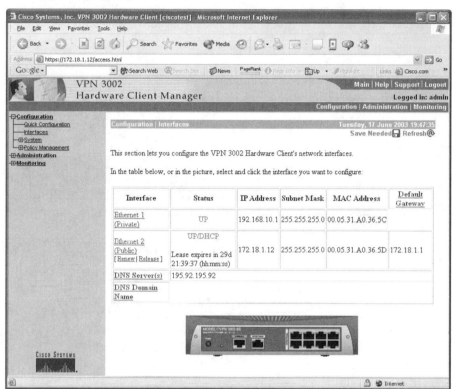

This screen shows you the status of each interface as well as the IP address, subnet mask, and default route for the public interface. Note that the private interface is set to have an IP address of 192.168.10.1/24. This is the default IP address for the private interface. The public interface automatically picked up an IP address on boot via DHCP. Because of this, it also picked up a default gateway. The IP address currently in use is 172.18.1.12/24, with a default gateway of 172.18.1.1. The DNS server information also was received from DHCP, because you have yet to manually enter any network-level configuration information. You therefore can deduce that DHCP is enabled by default on the public interface.

You will change the IP address of the public interface to 172.18.1.3/24 and the IP address of the private interface to 172.18.2.1/24. To achieve this, click Ethernet1 (Private), and enter the required information. Figure 7-12 shows this information set for the private interface.

NOTE When you change the IP address of the interface you are connected to, you are disconnected, and you have to reestablish a management connection.

Figure 7-12 *Configuration > Interfaces > Private Interface Screen*

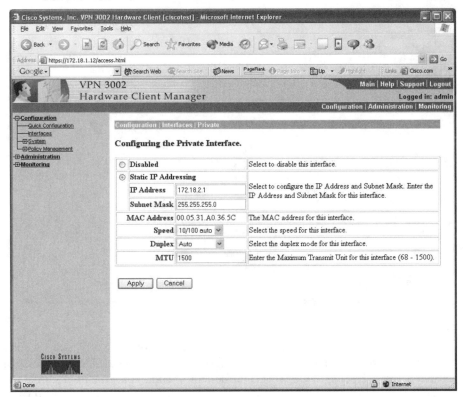

Next, go back to the Interfaces screen, and click Ethernet2 Public to be taken to the public interface configuration screen. Figure 7-13 shows this screen with the correct information entered.

Figure 7-13   *Configuration > Interfaces > Public Interface Screen*

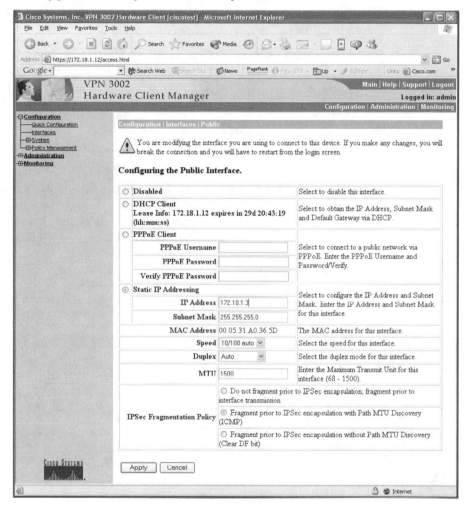

Note that this screen has quite a few more configuration options.

You have three ways to configure the IP address for the public interface: get an address from a DHCP server, use PPP over Ethernet (PPPoE) to connect, or define a static IP address. The configuration options of the public interface IP address are as follows:

- **DHCP Client**—The Hardware Client can act as a DHCP client. Select the DHCP Client radio button to receive an address from a DHCP server. This is the default setting for the public interface.

- **PPPoE Client**—If you want to connect to your Internet provider using PPPoE, select the PPPoE Client radio button, and then enter information in the following fields:

  — **PPPoE User Name**—Enter a valid PPPoE username.

  — **PPPoE Password**—Enter the PPPoE password for the username you just entered.

  — **Verify PPPoE Password**—Enter the PPPoE password again to verify it.

- **Static IP Address**—Select the Static IP Addressing Radio Button to use a static IP address, and enter the information in the following fields:

  — **IP Address**—Enter the IP address for this interface using dotted-decimal notation (for example, 172.18.1.3). Note that 0.0.0.0 is not allowed.

  — **Subnet Mask**—Enter the subnet mask for this interface using dotted-decimal notation (for example, 255.255.255.0). The Manager automatically supplies a standard subnet mask appropriate for the IP address you just entered. You can accept this entry or change it. Note that 0.0.0.0 is not allowed.

Click Apply. You are taken back to the interface configuration screen. You can see in Figure 7-14 that the correct IP addresses have been assigned.

Figure 7-14 *Configuration > Interfaces Screen*

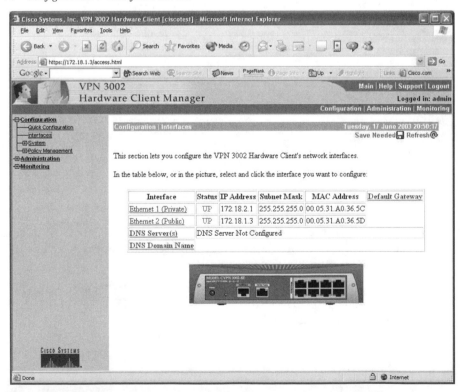

There are three important items to note here. The first is the Save Needed icon in the toolbar. It appears because a change to the configuration has been made. Clicking it saves the configuration.

NOTE   If the 3002 Hardware Client were to reboot at this stage, all configuration changes would be lost. It is good practice to regularly save your configuration after any changes.

The second point to note is that the default gateway for the public interface is now blank. This is because before configuring a static IP address, you used DHCP, and the default gateway was learned via DHCP. This brings us to the third point: DNS is now not configured. This is also because you are no longer using DHCP.

Let's remedy these two problems. You add a default route by navigating to Configuration > System > IP Routing > Default Gateways. You can then add 172.18.1.1. The result is shown in Figure 7-15.

Figure 7-15   *Adding a Default Gateway*

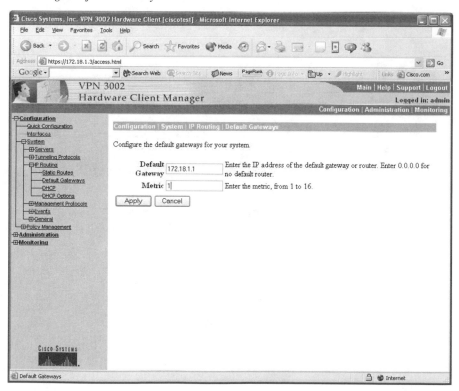

Next, navigate to Configuration > System > Servers > DNS and enter the DNS information, as shown in Figure 7-16.

Figure 7-16 *DNS Configuration*

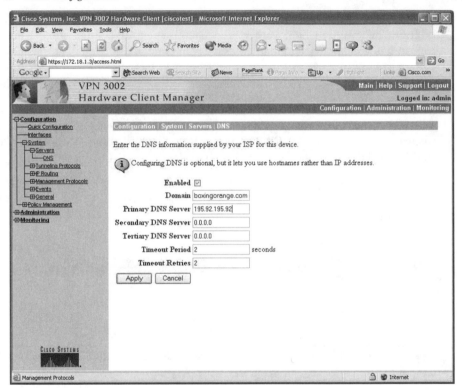

Now navigate back to the interface configuration screen, shown in Figure 7-17, and look at its settings.

You can see that the default gateway is applied to the public interface. You also can see the DNS domain name and DNS server. This concludes the second step—configuring network information on the 3002 Hardware Client.

Figure 7-17   *Configuration > Interfaces Screen*

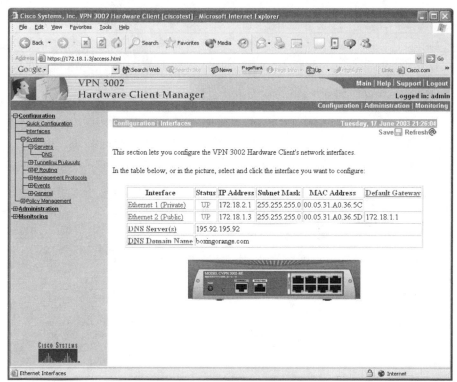

Step 3: Configure the VPN 3002 Group and User Information

Now that you have configured the system, identification, and network information on the 3002, you can move on to configuring the VPN-specific settings. The entire configuration is applied under Configuration > System > Tunneling Protocols > IPSec and is very straightforward.

Figure 7-18 shows the configuration you have entered to connect to a single VPN Concentrator with an IP address of 195.92.77.101 using the preconfigured group training and the preconfigured user student1.

Figure 7-18 *Configuration > System > Tunneling Protocols > IPSec Screen*

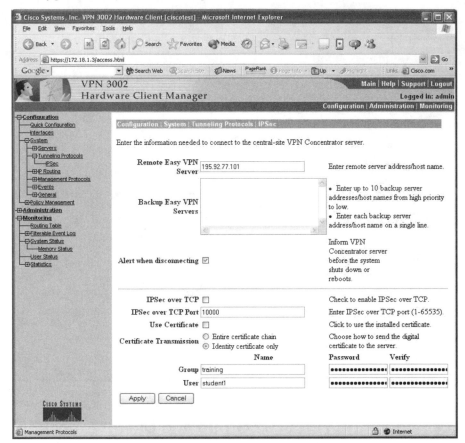

Information is entered in the required fields:

- **Remote Easy VPN Server field**—Enter the IP address of the Concentrator to which this Hardware Client connects (for example, 195.92.77.101).

- **Backup Easy VPN Servers field**—You can enter up to ten additional IP addresses for backup servers that are contacted in chronological order in case the primary VPN server cannot be contacted.

- **Alert when disconnecting check box**—Informs the VPN Concentrator server before the system shuts down or reboots.

- **IPSec over TCP check box**—Encapsulates encrypted data traffic within TCP packets. This feature lets the Hardware Client operate in an environment in which standard Encapsulating Security Protocol (ESP, protocol 50) or IKE (UDP 500) cannot function or can function only with modification to existing firewall rules.

IPSec over TCP encapsulates both the IKE and IPSec protocols within a TCP packet and enables secure tunneling through both Network Address Translation (NAT) and PAT devices and firewalls.

— **IPSec over TCP**—Enables IPSec connections using TCP encapsulation. This feature must also be enabled on the Concentrator to which this Hardware Client connects.

— **IPSec over TCP Port**—Enter the IPSec over TCP port number. You can enter one port. The port you configure on the Hardware Client must also be configured on the Concentrator to which this Hardware Client connects.

- **Use Certificate check box**—Check the Use Certificate check box to use digital certificates for authentication. If you are using digital certificates, there is no need to enter a group name and group password. The Hardware Client checks certificates loaded in the Hardware Client. If no certificate is loaded, an error message appears after you click the Continue button.

- **Certificate Transmission**—If you configured authentication using digital certificates, choose the type of certificate transmission:

— **Entire certificate chain**—Sends the identity certificate and all issuing certificates to the peer. Issuing certificates include the root certificate and any subordinate CA certificates.

— **Identity certificate only**—Sends only the identity certificate to the peer.

- **Group field**—If you are not using digital certificates, in the Group field, enter a unique name and password for this group. This is the same group name and password you configured for this Hardware Client on the central site Concentrator (for example, training). If the Hardware Client group name and password match the entries in the Concentrator database, the user gains entrance to the Concentrator.

- **User field**—In the User Name and Password field, enter a unique name and password for the Hardware Client user. This is the same username and password you configured in the authentication server (for example, student1). If the Hardware Client username and password match the entries in the authentication server database, the user gains entrance to the corporate network.

Click Apply; the VPN settings are applied. At this stage, as long as the corresponding group and user exist on the central site VPN Concentrator, you can establish a VPN in one of two ways. It auto-initiates if any traffic comes into the private interface destined for the remote network over the VPN, or you can manually connect the VPN by selecting Monitoring > System Status.

Figure 7-19 shows this screen when the VPN is *not* connected.

Figure 7-19 *Monitoring > System Status Screen Without a VPN Connection*

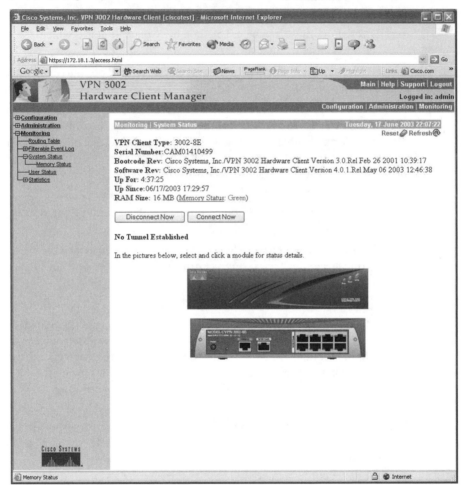

You can see that the screen reports that no tunnel is established. Clicking the Connect Now button connects the VPN, as shown in Figure 7-20.

Figure 7-20 *Monitoring > System Status Screen with a VPN Connection*

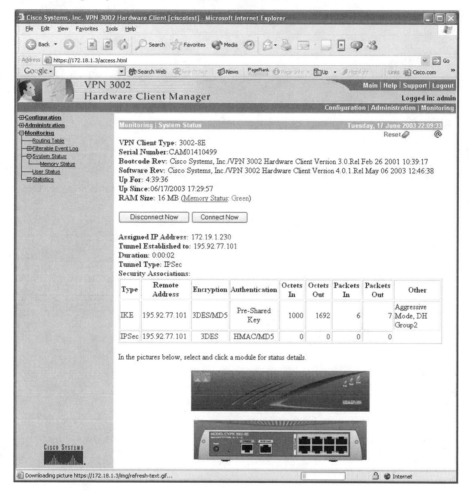

You can see that the VPN connection has been established. Figure 7-20 shows the connection settings that have been pushed down from the central site VPN Concentrator. Remember that this connection is treated the same as a remote-access VPN connection, so you do not configure any authentication and encryption protocols on the remote site device. All the IPSec settings are configured on the central site and are pushed down to the Hardware Client after initial group authentication has successfully completed.

You can confirm this VPN connection by looking at the Monitoring > Sessions screen on the central site VPN Concentrator, as shown in Figure 7-21.

Figure 7-21 *Central Site VPN 3000 Monitoring > Sessions Screen with a VPN Connection*

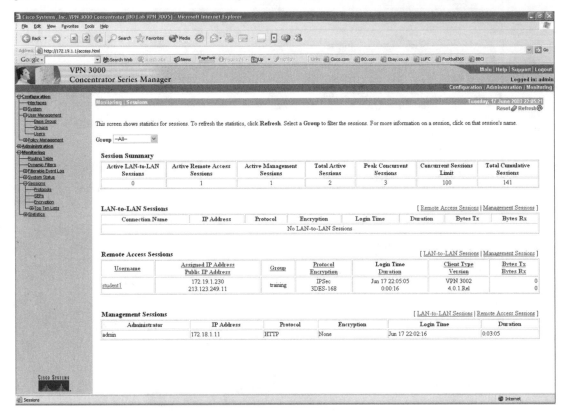

You can see that the remote-access connection shown is for the user student1 using the group training. The client type has been identified as a Cisco 3002 Hardware Client running version 4.0.1 of the OS.

Step 4: Configure the VPN Operation Mode

As mentioned earlier, the VPN 3002 Hardware Client has two modes of operation: client mode and network extension mode. The default setting is client mode, as shown in Figure 7-21. Note the IP address assignment in this figure. The public IP address is 213.123.249.11, and the private IP address that has been assigned to the VPN 3002 Hardware Client is 172.19.1.230. This is the first address out of the pool that has been created and applied to the training group on the central site VPN Concentrator. Therefore, all VPN users on the 172.18.2.0/24 network communicate with the central site VPN hiding behind the 172.19.1.230 host IP address using PAT.

You will now make a slight change to allow the 3002 Hardware Client to operate in network extension mode. Select Configuration > Policy Management > Traffic Management > PAT > Enable, and then disable PAT, as shown in Figure 7-22.

Figure 7-22   *Configuration > Policy Management > Traffic Management > PAT > Enable Screen*

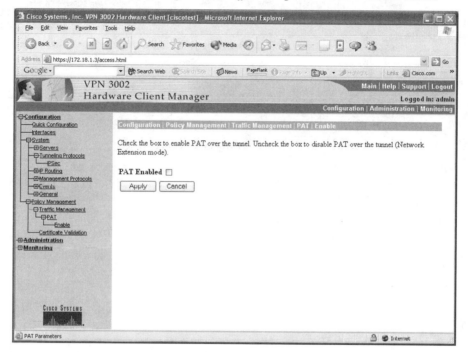

This is all that is required on the VPN 3002 Hardware Client to enable network extension mode. However, this does not work by default. You have to make a change to the group on the central site 3000 Concentrator to allow network extension mode.

Modify the training group and check the Allow Network Extension Mode check box on the HW Client tab, as shown in Figure 7-23.

Figure 7-23 *Central Site VPN 3000 Modifying the Training Group*

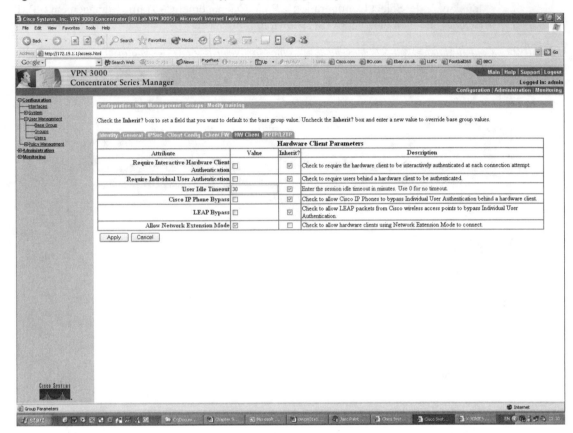

Click Apply and then save all changes. Revert to the VPN 3002 and establish the tunnel. Note the connection visible in Figure 7-24, and compare it to the Client connection shown in Figure 7-20.

Figure 7-24   *Network Extension Mode Session*

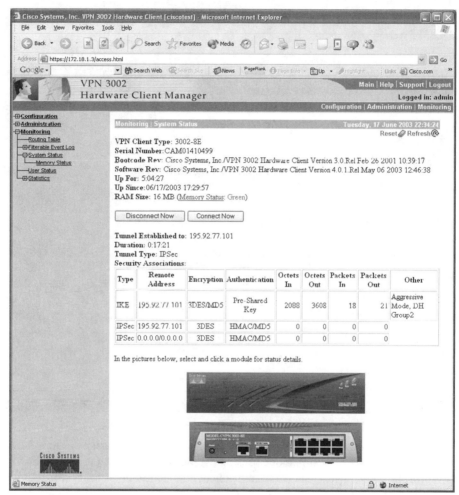

The noticeable difference between Figures 7-20 and 7-24 is that with network extension mode the client is *not* assigned an address, as it is in client mode. You also can see this by looking at the sessions on the central site VPN 3000 Concentrator, as shown in Figure 7-25.

Figure 7-25 *Central Site VPN 3000 Monitoring > Sessions Screen with a Network Extension VPN Connection*

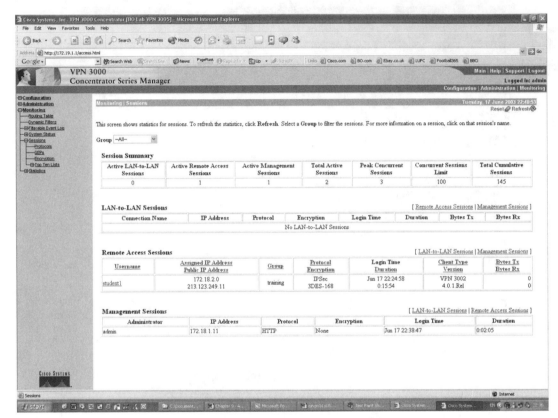

Compare the address assignment screen of Figure 7-25 with that of Figure 7-21. You can see that network extension mode uses the whole IP network of the private interface on the 3002 Hardware Client. In contrast, the client connection hides everything behind a PAT address that is assigned to the 3002 Hardware Client from the central site VPN 3000 Concentrator.

Overview of the Auto-Update Feature

The Cisco VPN 3002 Hardware Client update feature lets administrators at a central location automatically update software for Hardware Clients deployed in diverse locations. When you enable Hardware Client update, upon connection, the central site Cisco VPN Concentrator sends an IKE packet that contains an encrypted message, which notifies the VPN 3002 of acceptable versions of executable system software and their locations. If the Hardware Client is not running an acceptable version, its software is automatically updated via TFTP. During the update process, the Hardware Client logs event messages at the start of the update. When the update completes, the Hardware Client reboots automatically.

If the Hardware Client is already connected to the Concentrator, the administrator has the option of sending an update notification message. The update message notifies the Hardware Client of acceptable versions of software and their locations. If the Hardware Client is not running an acceptable version, its software is automatically updated via TFTP. The administrator may choose to update all the Hardware Client in his network all at once, or he may choose to update VPN 3002s on a group-by-group basis. This chapter discusses both options.

Configuring the Hardware Client software auto-update feature is a three-step process:

Step 1   Enable Hardware Client update functionality (disabled by default) on the Concentrator.

Step 2   Set the group update parameters (such as Hardware Client and Software Client type, URL, and revisions).

Step 3   (Optional) Send an update notice to active clients.

Step 1: Enable Hardware Client Update Functionality

The first step is to enable the VPN Concentrator's client update feature:

Step 1   Choose the Configuration > System > Client Update window, and click the Enable link. The Configuration > System > Client Update > Enable window opens, as shown in Figure 7-26.

Figure 7-26   *Enabling the Client Update*

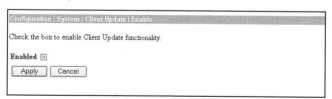

Step 2   Check the Enabled check box.

Step 3   Click Apply.

When this functionality is enabled, the administrator must decide how to update the Cisco VPN clients: globally or by group. With a global update, all clients are updated to a specific software release from a specific server. If a more systematic, group-by-group approach is preferred, different servers can update different groups, at different times, to different releases of software.

Step 2: Set the Group Update Parameters

Now that you have enabled the client update feature, you can go to the groups you use for VPN 3002 access and modify the client update options for the group.

Figure 7-27 shows the group screen with two active groups. Select the 3002 group and then click the Client Update button to configure the group-specific auto-update parameters.

Figure 7-27 *Group Screen*

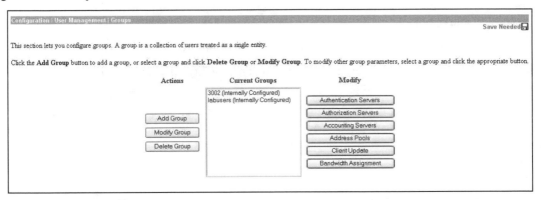

Go to the Configuration > System > Client Update > Entries window to view the Client Update Entries list. Because no updates have been configured, the list displays Empty. Click Add under the Actions column to add a new VPN Client update entry. The Manager opens the window shown in Figure 7-28. The entries are as follows:

- **Client Type**—For the VPN 3002, the entry must be vpn3002 (case- and space-sensitive).

- **URL**—The format is tftp://*server_address/directory/filename*. The server address can be either an IP address or a host name if you have configured a DNS server. An example is tftp://10.0.1.10/vpn3002-3.5.Rel-k9.bin, where 10.0.1.10 is the server address and vpn3002-3.5.Rel-k9.bin is the filename on the TFTP server.

- **Revisions**—Enter a comma-separated list of software images appropriate for the Hardware Client (for example, 3.5.1.Rel). The entries are case-sensitive. The Hardware Client considers 3.5.1.Rel and 3.5.1.rel different versions of software.

Figure 7-28 *Adding a VPN Client Update Entry*

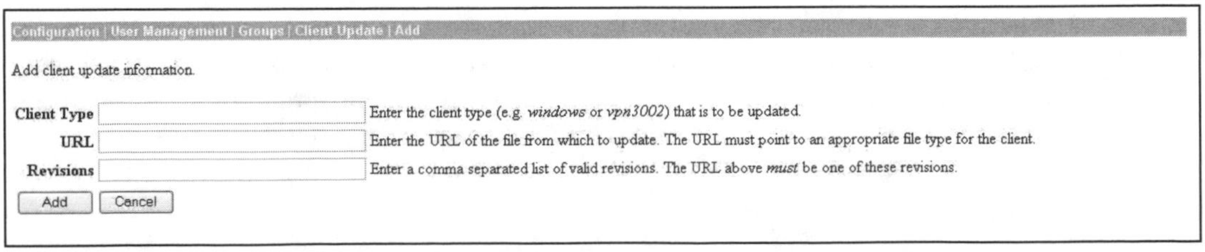

If the VPN Client is already running a software version in the list, it does not need a software update. If the Hardware Client is not running a software version in the list, an update is needed. The Hardware Client software is updated automatically via TFTP.

Figure 7-29 shows the client update information added, with a client type of vpn3002, a URL of tftp://172.18.5.2/vpn3002-4.0.1.Rel-k9.bin, and a revision of 4.01.Rel.

Figure 7-29   *VPN Client Update Entry Values*

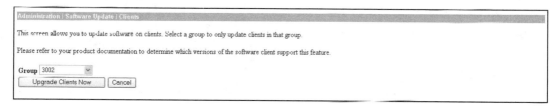

These settings upgrade the VPN 3002 to version 4.01 of the VPN software.

Step 3: Send an Update Notice to Active Clients

The last step is to send an optional update notification to the Hardware Client:

Step 1   Go to the Administration > Software Update window, and click the Clients link. The Administration > Software Update > Clients window opens, as shown in Figure 7-30.

Figure 7-30   *Selecting the Group to Upload*

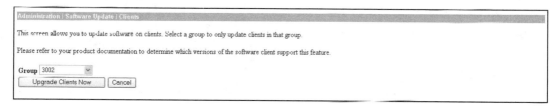

Step 2   Choose the Hardware Client group for this update from the Group drop-down menu. The default is All, which lets you update the software for all groups. The Concentrator updates VPN Clients by group, in batches of ten, at 5-minute intervals.

Step 3   Click Upgrade Clients Now to send the update notification. If it is sent successfully, the Success window opens.

In Figure 7-30, the 3002 group is selected to get an update notification. When you click Upgrade Clients Now, the Success window opens. The connected VPN Clients in the 3002 group receive an update notification message. This is a proactive, forceful attempt to update clients without waiting for the client to drop the IPSec tunnel and reconnect. This might be necessary in cases where an update is immediately required for functionality, for security reasons, or for clients that have "always-on" connections. The disconnected members of the 3002 group receive an update message the next time they connect to the Concentrator.

As well as upgrading a specific group, you can enable a global update.

With global updates, all groups upgrade to the same software from the same TFTP server. Do the following to define global update parameters:

Step 1   Choose Configuration > System > Client Update > Entries, and click Add. The Configuration > System > Client Update > Entries > Add window opens.

Step 2   Configure the global VPN Client type, URL, and revision number by entering the information in the corresponding fields.

Step 3   Click Apply. You can see the final results in the Configuration > System > Client Update > Entries window.

In Figure 7-31, the VPN Client type is VPN 3002. The Hardware Client software file vpn3002-4.0.1.Rel-k9.bin is available for download from the TFTP server 172.18.5.2. The valid revision level is set to 4.01.Rel. This information can be sent to a specific group or to all groups. Go to the Administration > Software Update > Clients window to send the update notification message.

Figure 7-31   *Global Client Update*

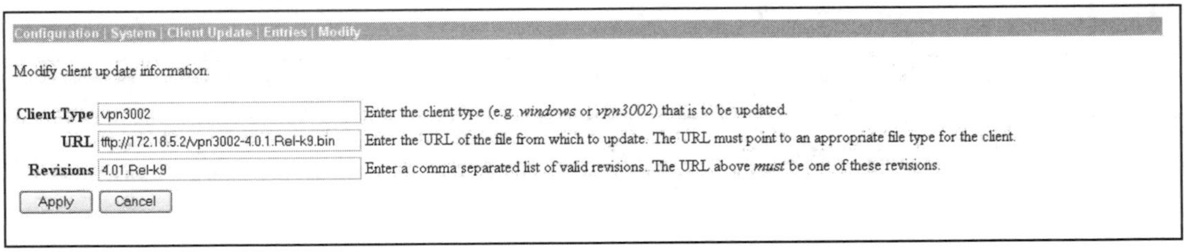

Monitoring the Cisco VPN 3002 Hardware Client Software Auto-Update Feature

When the update notification is sent, the administrator can monitor the status of the upgrade on the Hardware Client.

In the Monitoring > Filterable Event Log window, shown in Figure 7-32, the administrator can view the Hardware Client update information. To view only the update-specific information, scroll down in the Event Class section and select AUTOUPDATE. In Figure 7-32, the Hardware Client receives a notification message. The software version on the Hardware Client is up to date. No upgrade is necessary.

Figure 7-32 *Successful VPN Client Update Status*

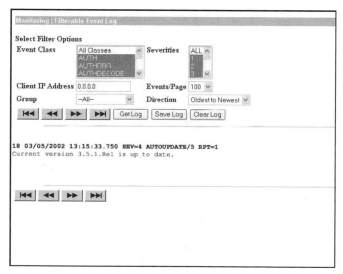

In the event log shown in Figure 7-33, the Hardware Client software version does not match the software version in the notification message. The Hardware Client software is updated from 3.5.1.Rel to 3.5.2.Rel. The software file vpn3002-3_5_2_Rel-k9.bin is downloaded from the TFTP server 10.0.1.10. The image is successfully loaded, and the Hardware Client automatically reboots.

Figure 7-33 *VPN Client Update*

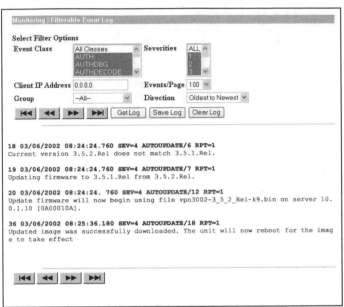

The Hardware Client stores image files in two locations: the active location, which stores the image currently running on the system, and the backup location. Updating the image overwrites the stored image file in the backup location and makes it the active location for the next reboot. The client auto-update process includes a test to validate the updated image. In the unlikely event that a VPN Client auto-update is unsuccessful, the VPN Client does not reboot, and the invalid image does not become active. The auto-update feature retries up to 20 times at 3-minute intervals. If an auto-update is unsuccessful, the log files contain information indicating TFTP failures.

NOTE   The auto-update event log messages are used to troubleshoot the Hardware Client software upgrade. The software version is case- and space-sensitive. Every time a notification message is sent or the Hardware Client reconnects to the Concentrator, an update takes place.

Summary

This chapter provided an overview and initial configuration of the 3002 Hardware Client. As we did with the 3000 Concentrator series, we started with a factory-shipped unit and looked at the initial configuration to get the VPN connected. You opted out of using quick configuration and did the configuration manually using the full menu system. As you can see, this configuration is relatively simple and uses technology similar to the Cisco Unity VPN Software Client. The VPN you configured used group and user information, so this is classed as a VPN using a preshared key. This chapter then covered the simple steps that are necessary to change the connection from client mode to network extension mode. Sample output from both the 3002 Hardware Client and the central site 3000 Concentrator was shown to fully explain the differences. The last section looked at the auto-update functionality that is essential if you have numerous hardware clients installed at remote locations. This feature really reduces the support overhead when major updates of the system code are released.

Review Questions

The following questions test your retention of the material presented in this chapter. The answers appear in Appendix A, "Answers to the Review Questions."

1 What are the two modes of operation for the 3002 Hardware Client?

2 Upon initial configuration of the 3002 Hardware Client, what is the default IP address of the private interface?

3 When initially configuring a 3002 Hardware Client, you notice that the public interface receives an IP address automatically. Why is this?

4 What default username and password are used to connect to the GUI manager for the 3002 Hardware Client?

5 You have made the necessary change on a 3002 Hardware Client to enable network extension mode, but the VPN is not operating in network extension mode. What is the probable cause of this error?

6 What protocol does auto-update use to transfer the new image to the 3002?

7 What is the auto-update client type for a 3002 Hardware Client?

8 Which interface on the 3002 Hardware Client supports PPPoE?

9 What is the default operation mode for a 3002 Hardware Client?

10 What are the two ways to connect the VPN on a 3002 Hardware Client?

After completing this chapter, you will be able to perform the following tasks:

- Understand user and unit authentication for the 3002 Hardware Client
- Configure the Hardware Client Interactive Unit Authentication feature
- Configure the Hardware Client User Authentication feature
- Monitor the Hardware Client user statistics

CHAPTER 8

Configuring the Cisco 3002 Hardware Client for User and Unit Authentication

Chapter 7, "Configuring the Cisco 3002 Hardware Client for Remote Access," provided an initial configuration of a remote-access VPN using the 3002 Hardware Client. This chapter looks at one of the valuable features of the Hardware Client, the user and unit authentication feature. From a design perspective, one reason that the 3002 Hardware Client is chosen over competing hardware-based VPN devices is because of its ability to do individual user authentication.

This chapter starts by looking at the types of authentication, and then it provides a detailed look at the configuration of both unit and user authentication on the 3002 Hardware Client.

User and Unit Authentication Overview

The Cisco 3002 Hardware Client allows up to 253 devices to be logged in behind it. Unlike the Cisco VPN Software Client, the Hardware Client, using the default unit authentication, saves the username and password permanently. During tunnel establishment, the Hardware Client automatically forwards the authentication information to the central site. When the tunnel is established, anyone can gain access to the corporate network. No remote site user intervention is required. Unfortunately, this can be viewed as a security weakness. It prevents administrators from requiring a Hardware Client user to enter a password before gaining access to the central site network. This is the default method used to authenticate the unit.

In Release 3.5 and later of the Hardware Client software, the administrator has three authentication options:

- **Unit authentication**—The Hardware Client stores the username and password and forwards them automatically to the central site when the tunnel is established. This is the default.

- **Interactive unit authentication**—The user password is no longer stored in memory on the Hardware Client. When launching a tunnel, a user behind the Hardware Client must supply the username and password each time a tunnel is established. When the tunnel is established, anyone on the Hardware Client private LAN can gain access to the corporate network.

- **User authentication**—The first time a user attempts to gain access to corporate networks over the tunnels, he is prompted for his authentication credentials. User authentication addresses unauthorized user access. Each individual user must authenticate himself.

Interactive unit authentication and user authentication are shown in Figure 8-1.

Figure 8-1 *Hardware Client Authentication*

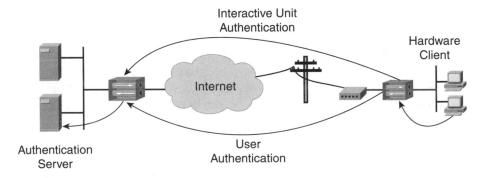

Configuring the Hardware Client Interactive Unit Authentication Feature

The interactive unit authentication feature is enabled and disabled on the central site Cisco VPN Concentrator. You can do this by checking or unchecking the Require Interactive Hardware Client Authentication check box within the Configuration > User Management > Groups > HW Client tab:

- If this box is checked, the Hardware Client does not save the user password. A remote user must supply the username and password before the tunnel is established.

- If this box is unchecked, the Hardware Client supplies the username and password from memory when the tunnel is established. This is the default setting.

This configuration screen is shown in Figure 8-2.

NOTE   There is a check box labeled Allow Password Storage on Client within the Mode Config tab. This check box enables and disables password storage on only the Software Client.

Figure 8-2   *Hardware Client Authentication Configuration on the Central Site VPN Concentrator*

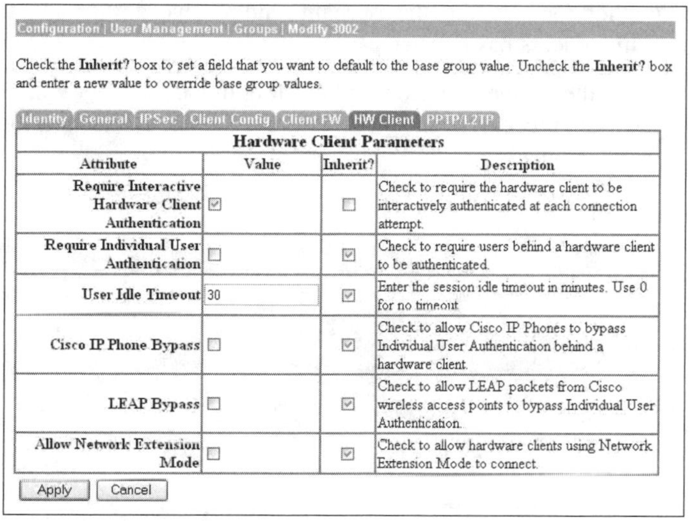

The interactive unit authentication feature is enabled and disabled from the central site Concentrator. This information is communicated to the Hardware Client in mode configuration messages each time the tunnel is established. When the Hardware Client is first turned on without an existing configuration file, the GUI lets the user enter a username and password as part of the quick configuration process. This initial username and password are used the first time a tunnel is established to the central site Concentrator, as shown in Figure 8-2. If the Concentrator enables the interactive unit authentication feature during the tunnel negotiation, the Hardware Client removes the password from local memory and configuration files. Subsequent tunnel establishment requires the user to enter a password manually.

Connection Methods

When the Hardware Client interactive unit authentication feature is enabled on the Concentrator, a username and password must be supplied to the Hardware Client before a tunnel can be established. There are three methods by which you access the username password prompt:

- Connect via the Hardware Client manager
- Connect via the System Status window
- Connect via the redirect message

Connecting Via the Hardware Client Manager

The first method for accessing the username and password is through the Hardware Client manager. This process has three steps:

Step 1   Click the Connection/Login Status link in the manager window to start the login process, as shown in Figure 8-3. The Connection/Login Status window opens.

Figure 8-3   *GUI Manager Window*

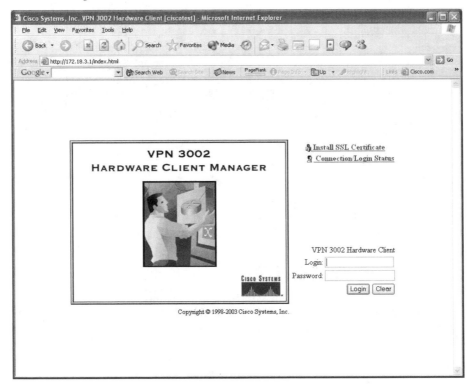

Step 2   The Connection/Login Status window displays the current status of the Hardware Client tunnel. The Hardware Client is disconnected message indicates that the tunnel is currently down, as shown in Figure 8-4. To continue the process, click Connect Now. The Hardware Client Interactive Authentication window opens, as shown in Figure 8-5.

Figure 8-4   *Connection/Login Status Window*

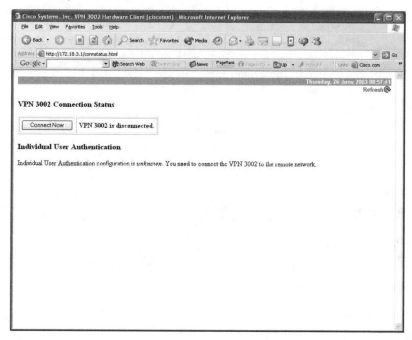

Figure 8-5   *Logging in Through the Hardware Client Interactive Authentication Window*

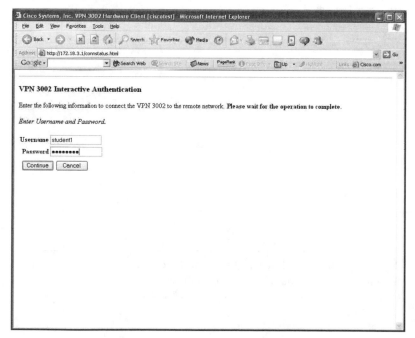

Step 3 In the Hardware Client Interactive Authentication window, enter a username and password in the corresponding fields, and click Connect. Clicking Connect initiates Internet Key Exchange (IKE) tunnel negotiation, and clicking Cancel sends the user back to the Hardware Client interactive authentication. If interactive unit authentication is disabled, clicking Connect immediately establishes a tunnel to the central site network.

If tunnel negotiation is successful, the Hardware Client is connected message is returned. If tunnel negotiations fail, a message is posted, and the user is sent back to the same page to reenter a new username and password combination. A successful connection is shown in Figure 8-6.

Figure 8-6   *Successful Connection*

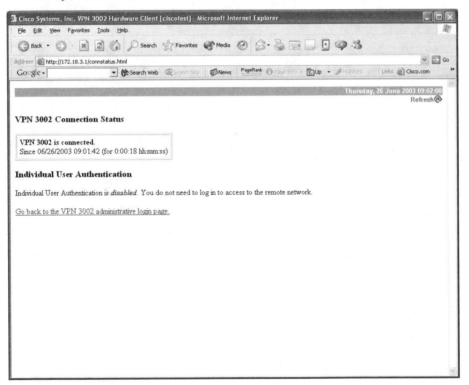

NOTE   If the remote host tears down the tunnel or if the system reboots, the Hardware Client must reauthenticate before the tunnel is reestablished.

Connecting Via the System Status Window

Another way to access the login prompt is from the Hardware Client Manager Monitoring > System Status window, as shown in Figure 8-7:

Step 1 Determine if the tunnel is established.

Step 2 If no tunnel is established, click Connect Now to access the username and password prompts.

Step 3 When a username and password are provided, click Continue to establish the tunnel, as shown in Figure 8-8. Clicking Continue initiates IKE tunnel negotiation.

Figure 8-7 *System Status Window*

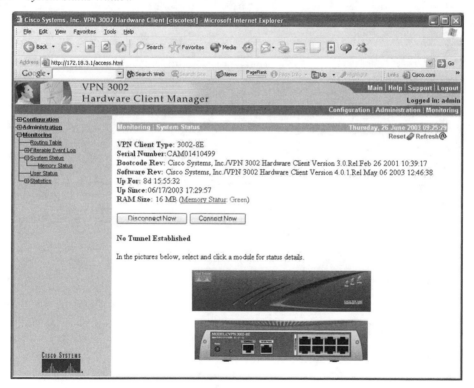

Connecting Via the Redirect Message

The last method for obtaining a login prompt is through message redirection. For example, a remote user powers up the Hardware Client and then attempts to connect to a corporate server via a web browser. Because the interactive unit authentication feature is enabled and the tunnel is not established, the Hardware Client redirects the remote user's web browser to the Hardware Client Connection/Login Status window. If the Hardware Client interactive unit authentication is successful, the remote user's web browser is redirected to the original destination. The Hardware Client unit authentication feature is a four-step process:

Step 1   You, as the remote user, try to make an HTTP connection through the Hardware Client tunnel, but the tunnel is down. With the Hardware Client interactive unit authentication feature enabled, the Hardware Client redirects the user to the Hardware Client Connection/Login Status window, shown previously in Figure 8-4.

Step 2   The window displays the status of the window as being disconnected. Click Connect Now to continue the process.

Figure 8-8   *System Status Username and Password Window*

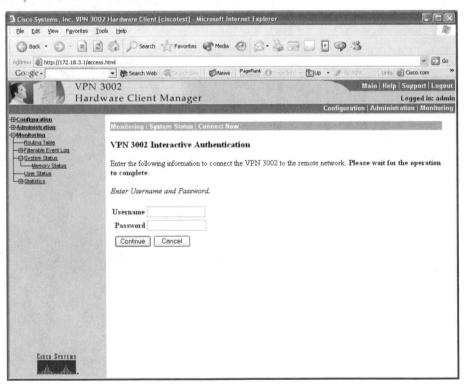

Step 3   Enter the username and password in the corresponding fields within the Hardware Client Interactive Authentication window to connect the Hardware Client to the remote network, as shown previously in Figure 8-5.

Step 4   Click Continue to initiate IKE tunnel negotiation. If this action is successful, the Hardware Client opens the Connection/Login Status window. Here you see that the Hardware Client is connected and individual user authentication is disabled. After about 10 seconds, the original destination window replaces the connection/login status window.

If the central site network enables the interactive unit authentication feature during tunnel negotiation, the Hardware Client removes the password from the local memory and configuration files.

In Figure 8-9, notice the password and verify that the password fields are blank.

Figure 8-9   *IPSec Window*

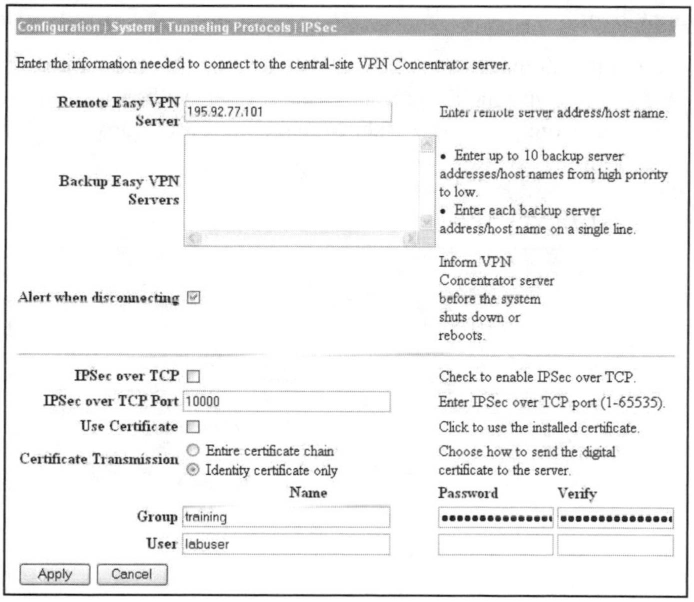

Configuring the Hardware Client User Authentication Feature

Many corporations such as, banks, investment houses, and manufacturers, envision using the Hardware Client to grant employees access to their corporate networks from home. By default, the Hardware Client saves the password and username permanently. This prevents corporations from requiring a user to enter a password before gaining access to the central site network. In addition, it does not allow prompted authentication, such as token cards, so only fixed password authentication can be used (such as RADIUS and NT Domain). Without some level of user authentication, the Hardware Client represents a substantial risk if placed in an unsecured environment, such as an employee's home.

The user authentication feature enables the authentication of users behind each Hardware Client. When a user attempts to gain access to the corporate network over the tunnel, his usernames and IP and MAC addresses are checked. If no record of the user is present on the Hardware Client, he is prompted for authentication credentials. This protects the central site from unauthorized users, such as friends and family members, on the same LAN as the Hardware Client.

The user authentication feature is enabled and disabled on the central site Concentrator. You can do this by checking the Require Individual User Authentication check box on the HW Client tab of the Configuration > User Management > Groups > Modify training window, as shown in Figure 8-10.

Figure 8-10 *HW Client Tab of the Group*

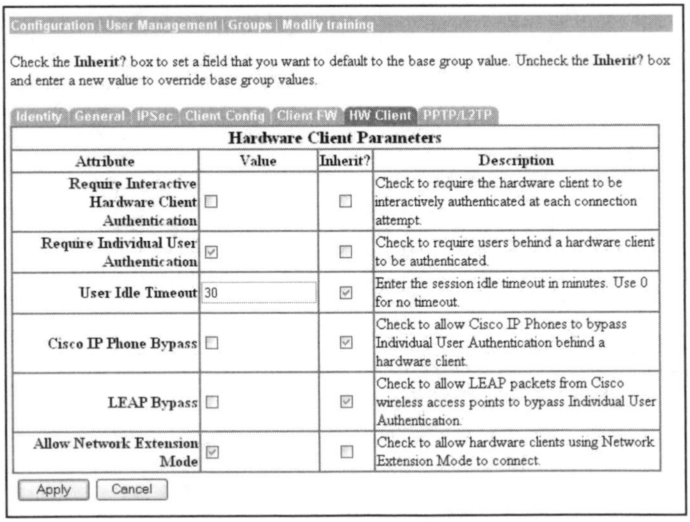

The user authentication feature is enabled and disabled from the central site Concentrator. This information is communicated to the Hardware Client each time the tunnel is established via mode configuration messages. When the Hardware Client is turned on without an existing configuration file, the GUI lets the user enter a username and password for the unit as part of this quick configuration process. This initial username and password are used the first time a tunnel is established to the central site Concentrator. If the central site network enables the user authentication feature during the tunnel negotiation, the Hardware Client removes the password from the local memory and configuration files, as shown in Figure 8-9. Subsequent tunnel establishment and logins require the user to enter a password manually.

Connection Methods

When the Hardware Client individual user authentication feature is enabled on the Concentrator, a username and password must be supplied to the Hardware Client before an individual can access the Hardware Client tunnel. There are three ways an end user can gain access to the individual user authentication process:

- Connect via the Hardware Client manager
- Connect via the System Status window
- Connect via the redirect message

Connecting Via the Hardware Client Manager

The first method of accessing the username and password is through the Hardware Client manager. This process has three steps:

Step 1   Click the Connection/Login Status link in the manager window to start the login process, as shown in Figure 8-11. The Connection/Login Status window opens.

Figure 8-11 *GUI Manager Screen*

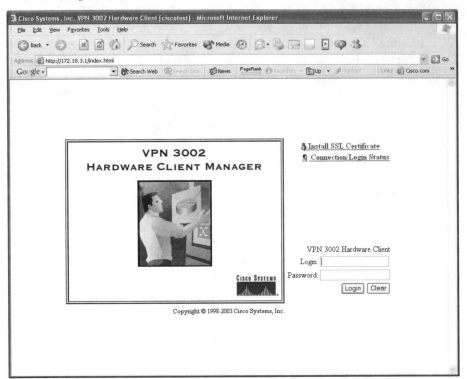

Step 2 The Connection/Login Status window, shown in Figure 8-12, displays the Hardware Client tunnel status and individual user authentication. The VPN 3002 Connection status indicates that the tunnel is connected but the individual user is not logged in. To continue the process, click Log In Now. The Individual User Authentication window opens, as shown in Figure 8-13.

Figure 8-12   *Connection Status/Individual User Authentication*

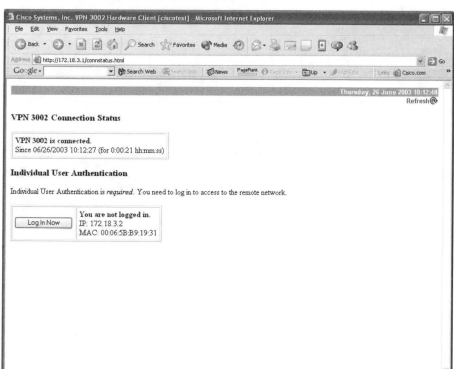

Step 3   In the Individual User Authentication window, enter a username and password in the corresponding fields, and click Continue. Clicking Continue initiates IKE tunnel negotiation, and clicking Cancel sends the user back to the Hardware Client interactive authentication. If tunnel negotiation is successful, a logged-in message is returned, along with the remote user's MAC and IP address. The Hardware Client tracks successfully logged-in remote users by their MAC and IP addresses.

Figure 8-13   *Individual User Authentication Username/Password Screen*

Connecting Via the System Status Window

Another way to access the login prompt is from the Hardware Client Manager System Status window:

Step 1   Click Connect Now in the Monitoring > System Status window, as shown in Figure 8-14.

Figure 8-14 *System Status Window*

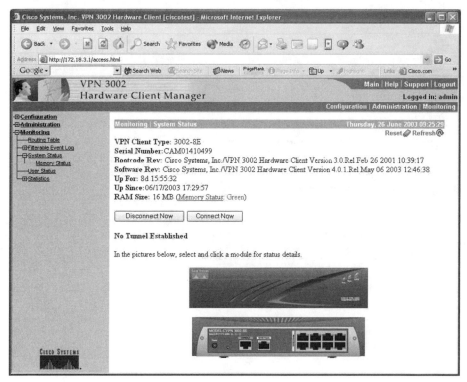

Step 2   As shown in Figure 8-15, enter a username and password in the corresponding fields, and click Continue to establish the tunnel. Clicking Continue initiates IKE tunnel negotiation.

Figure 8-15 *Connect Now Window*

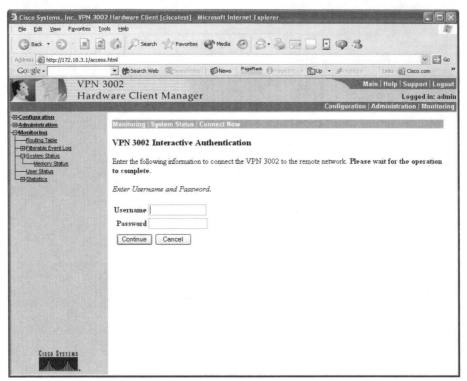

Connecting Via the Redirect Message

If individual user authentication is required, any attempt to access the central site network via HTTP immediately redirects the user's web browser to the user's Connection Login Status window. The "You are not logged in" message appears. To access the original central site website, the user must first log in successfully.

If individual user authentication is enabled and the source IP and MAC addresses associated with the user's browser access are not authenticated, the Connection Login Status window indicates that the user is not logged in. By clicking Log In Now, the user is transferred to the Individual User Authentication window, where he or she must enter a username and password in the corresponding fields and click Login. The Hardware Client initiates an authentication sequence.

During user authentication, the central site Concentrator determines if the username specified in the Individual User Authentication window was used to authenticate another machine. If the current authentication exceeds the simultaneous user login count for this group, the authentication fails, and the user's browser is transferred back to the Connection

Login Status window with an error message. If the user authentication is successful, the Hardware Client returns a Connection/Login Status window with a "You are logged in" message. The source IP and MAC address and username are saved as an authenticated machine.

If individual user authentication is disabled and the IKE tunnel has been established, the user does not need to log in to access the remote network.

Monitoring the Hardware Client User Statistics

Individual user statistics are available in the Hardware Client in the Connection/Login Status and Monitoring > User Status windows. In the Connection/Login Status window, you can view your username, IP and MAC address, and login time and duration.

In the Monitoring > User Status window, a new authenticated user's window is added to the Hardware Client. This window displays the IP address, MAC address, username, login time and duration, and logout function for currently authenticated users. If the individual user authentication feature is disabled, this window is displayed under the Monitoring > User Status window. In place of the user authentication information, this page displays a message indicating that individual user authentication is disabled.

On the Concentrator, individual user information is added to the Administration > Sessions > Detail display window. When multiple authentications execute for a given IKE tunnel, the central site Concentrator displays the username, login duration, and source IP address information. The user's MAC and IP addresses are visible only on the Hardware Client.

Summary

This chapter covered the authentication features of the VPN 3002 Hardware Client. One issue with hardware clients is that the default configuration is to hard-code both the group and the user information into the configuration on the hardware client. This causes problems where other LAN users can access the corporate LAN over the VPN without knowing, and this obviously causes a security concern. You do not really want end users having configuration access to the 3002 because of the support headache this can cause, so the answer is to enforce unit or user authentication. Unit authentication is good for when only a single user is using the VPN or when all users on the LAN can access the VPN but you want to ensure that the authentication is carried out manually. User authentication is for each individual user on the network. This offers true authentication and is ideal when not all LAN users have access to the VPN.

This chapter covered the configuration of both unit and user authentication and provided sample output to show you what to expect.

Review Questions

The following questions test your retention of the material presented in this chapter. The answers appear in Appendix A, "Answers to the Review Questions."

1 What is the main difference between user authentication and unit authentication?

2 You have configured a 3002 for user authentication. A user is not authenticated and tries to establish an HTTP connection over the VPN to the central site. What happens to the user's session?

3 What do you do to enable interactive unit authentication for a group configured on the central site VPN 3000 Concentrator?

4 Which authentication method do you use if you have a 3002 Hardware Client on a network with other users who are not permitted to use the VPN?

5 What do you do to enable user authentication for a group configured on the central site VPN 3000 Concentrator?

6 What is the default authentication method for a VPN 3002 Hardware Client?

After completing this chapter, you will be able to perform the following tasks:

- Understand backup servers
- Understand load balancing
- Understand reverse route injection
- Be able to configure the Concentrator for backup servers, load balancing, and reverse route injection

Configuring Cisco VPN Clients for Backup Server, Load Balancing, and Reverse Route Injection

This chapter provides an overview of three advanced features that arc available when using a VPN based on Cisco VPN 3000 technology: backup servers, load balancing, and reverse route injection. These three features focus on VPN availability and the prospective routing issue that exists when enabling redundant solutions.

The main configuration for these features is carried out on the central site Concentrator. These features arc common for both the VPN Software and Hardware Clients.

Cisco VPN Client Backup Server Feature

IPSec backup servers let a Hardware Client and a VPN Software Client connect to a backup Concentrator when its primary Concentrator is unavailable. You configure backup servers on the Concentrator, either on the Hardware Client and the VPN Software Client or on a group basis. Figure 9-1 shows a simple network with three central site VPN Concentrators. This example has a primary server and a backup server.

Figure 9-1   *Primary and Backup Servers*

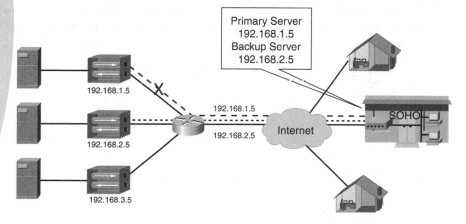

The following is an example of what happens when you configure a backup server:

- The Hardware Client attempts to contact the primary peer.
- If the Hardware Client does not receive an Internet Key Exchange (IKE) reply packet from the primary Concentrator within 8 seconds, the Hardware Client declares the packet lost and logs the event.
- After 4 seconds, the Hardware Client attempts a connection with a backup server. A backup server list is traversed from top to bottom. If the bottom of the list is reached with no connection, the tunnel establishment process is terminated. The Hardware Client does not automatically begin again from the top.

Backup Server: Concentrator Configuration

The IPSec backup server feature lets a Hardware Client and VPN Software Client connect to a backup Concentrator when its primary Concentrator is unavailable. During tunnel negotiation, the VPN Clients ask for a policy from the Concentrator. The Concentrator responds to the request via a Mode Config policy message. The VPN Clients check the policy message and respond appropriately. Three backup server options are available:

- **Use Client Configured List**—Instructs the VPN Clients to use their own backup server list.
- **Disable and Clear Configured List**—Disables and clears the configured list and instructs the VPN Clients to clear their own backup server list and disable the feature.
- **Use List Below**—Instructs the VPN Clients to use the list of backup servers supplied by the Concentrator. The list is pushed down to the VPN Clients in a proprietary Mode Config message, replacing any backup list on the VPN Clients.

In Figure 9-2, from the IPSec Backup Servers drop-down menu, the Use List Below option is chosen for the training group. Beneath the drop-down menu, four backup server addresses are listed. This information is pushed down to the Hardware and Software Client during tunnel setup. The IPSec backup server is configured on a group-by-group basis.

Figure 9-2   *Backup Server: Concentrator Configuration*

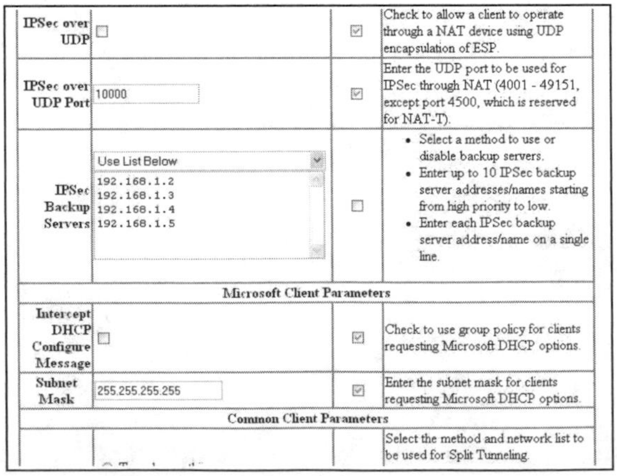

Backup Server: Hardware Client Configuration

If the Concentrator IPSec backup server option is set for Use Client Configured List, the Hardware Client uses the backup server addresses configured in the Hardware Client. To configure backup servers on a Hardware Client, go to the Configuration > System > Tunneling Protocols > IPSec window, as shown in Figure 9-3. In the Backup Easy VPN Servers window, enter up to ten backup servers, listed from high to low priority. If the Concentrator sends a backup server list to the client, the Hardware Client adds the downloaded list, replacing any entries currently on the backup list. Figure 9-3 shows this screen with the address of 195.92.77.100 added as the backup VPN server.

Figure 9-3 *Backup Server: Hardware Client Configuration*

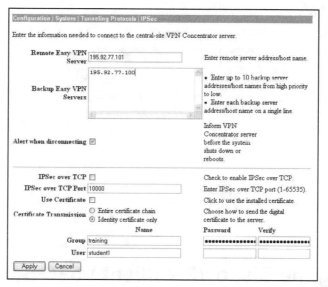

The PC needs accurate Windows Internet Naming Service (WINS) and Domain Name System (DNS) information to navigate through the central site. Typically the WINS and DNS information is sent to the Hardware Client during tunnel establishment. In turn, the Hardware Client passes the WINS and DNS information to the remote PC in Dynamic Host Configuration Protocol (DHCP) offer messages. To update the WINS and DNS information, you might have to release and then renew the PC's IP address. By doing so, the PC contacts the Hardware Client for a new IP address. In the resulting DHCP offer message, the PC receives an IP address and WINS and DNS information. To enable the WINS and DNS update process, the Hardware Client is configured as a DHCP server, and the PC is set to obtain an IP address via DHCP.

Backup Server: Software Client Configuration

If the Concentrator IPSec backup server option is set to Use Client Configured List, the VPN Software Client uses the backup server addresses configured in the VPN Software Client. Go to Start > Programs > Cisco Systems VPN Client > VPN Client to configure backup servers on a VPN Client. The VPN Software Client window opens. Click the Connection Entries > Modify > Backup Servers tab. The Connections tab opens. In the Connections window, enter up to ten backup servers, listed from high priority to low priority. If the Concentrator sends a backup server list to the client, the VPN Software Client adds the downloaded list, replacing any entries currently on the backup list.

Figure 9-4 shows the Software Client with backup servers enabled and three backup servers added to the connection entry.

Figure 9-4 *Backup Server: Software Client Configuration*

Configuring the Cisco VPN Client Load-Balancing Feature

If you have a Cisco VPN Concentrator configuration in which you are using two or more Concentrators connected on the same network to handle remote sessions, you can configure these devices to share their session load. This feature is called load balancing. Load balancing directs session traffic to the least-loaded device, thus distributing the load among all devices. It makes efficient use of system resources and provides increased performance and high availability.

In load balancing, a group of Concentrators work together as a single entity—a cluster—as shown in Figure 9-5. The cluster is known by one IP address—a virtual address—to the outside client space. This virtual IP address is not tied to a specific physical device in the VPN cluster but is serviced by the virtual cluster master. Connections to the load-balancing cluster are based on the load.

Figure 9-5   *Load-Balancing Cluster*

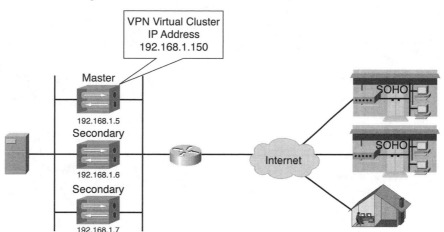

The virtual IP address is a valid, routable address. When remote clients attempt to establish a tunnel, the clients route the IKE messages to the cluster's IP address—the virtual IP address. The virtual cluster master responds to the messages.

The designated virtual cluster master Concentrator maintains load information from all secondary Concentrators in the cluster. Each secondary Concentrator periodically sends load information in a keepalive message exchange to the master Concentrator. Load is calculated as a percentage of current active sessions divided by the configured maximum allowed connections. When a VPN Client makes a connection request, the master Concentrator checks the load list for the least-loaded Concentrator. The master Concentrator directs the VPN Client toward the least-loaded Concentrator in the cluster. The least-loaded Concentrator terminates the new tunnel.

Load balancing is supported on the following VPN Client versions:

- VPN Software Client Release 3 and above
- Hardware Client Release 3.5 and above

Load Balancing Connection Process

When a VPN Client is launched, it attempts to establish an IKE tunnel to the VPN virtual cluster IP address 192.168.1.150, as shown in Figure 9-6. The cluster master responds to the IKE messages by sending a redirect message to the VPN Client.

Figure 9-6   *Load-Balancing Connection Process*

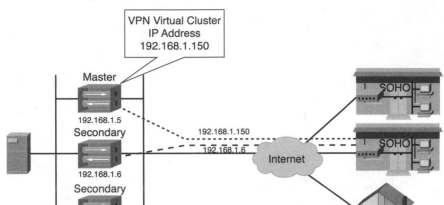

In the redirect message is the physical IP address of the least-loaded Concentrator within the cluster. The cluster master determines the least-loaded Concentrator by consulting its load table. The load table is continuously updated with the secondary Concentrator's current load information. At IKE tunnel connection time, the cluster master consults its load table and picks the least-loaded secondary Concentrator. The cluster master Concentrator forwards the IP address of the least-loaded secondary Concentrator to the remote client. In Figure 9-6, the IP address of the least-loaded Concentrator within the cluster is 192.168.1.6.

The VPN Client in turn attempts to establish a new tunnel to the least-loaded Concentrator: 192.168.1.6. The original tunnel to the cluster master's virtual IP address is torn down. Load balancing is performed only during tunnel establishment.

Virtual Cluster Agent

For load balancing to operate, a new application must be added to the Concentrator—Virtual Cluster Agent (VCA). VCA is the process executing on each Concentrator in the cluster. It is responsible for the following:

- Joining and exiting the virtual cluster
- Establishing IPSec connections between peers in the cluster
- Calculating the load
- Sending periodic load and health check information to the cluster master
- Determining a failed cluster master
- Participating in a virtual master election process

For the VCA messages to flow between cluster Concentrators, a VCA filter must be enabled on each Concentrator's public and private interface. Figure 9-7 shows the flow of VCA between the Concentrators.

Figure 9-7   *VCA*

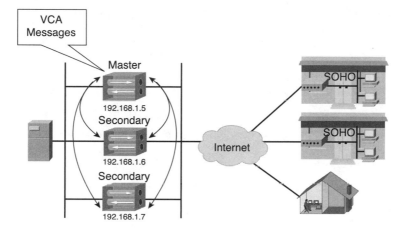

Configuring Load Balancing

Load balancing is a three-step process:

Step 1   Add VCA capability to the Concentrator's public and private interfaces.

Step 2   Configure each Concentrator within the cluster for load balancing.

Step 3   Configure each client with the cluster's virtual address.

Step 1: Add VCA Capability to the Concentrator

The first step of load balancing is to enable VCA message transmissions between Concentrators in the cluster. To do this, you must add a rule to the public and private interface of each Concentrator in the cluster:

Step 1   On each Concentrator in the cluster, go to the Configuration > Policy Management > Traffic Management > Filters window.

Step 2   Choose Public from the Current Rules in Filter list, and click Assign Rules to Filter. The Configuration > Policy Management > Traffic Management > Assign Rules to Filter window opens.

Step 3   In the Available Rules list, choose VCA In, and click Add. VCA In moves to the Current Rules in Filter list.

Step 4   In the Available Rules list, choose VCA Out, and click Add. VCA Out moves to the Current Rules in Filter list.

Step 5   Add VCA in and VCA out filters to both filters applied to the Concentrator's public and private interfaces.

Step 6   The functions of VCA In and VCA Out are as follows:

— **VCA In (forward/in)**—Forwards any inbound (to this VPN 3000) UDP packet with a destination port of 9023 (VCA port).

— **VCA Out (forward/out)**—Forwards any outbound (from this VPN 3000) UDP packet originating from source port 9023 (VCA port).

Figure 9-8 shows the public filter with the VCA In and VCA Out rules added.

Figure 9-8   *Filter with VCA Rules Added*

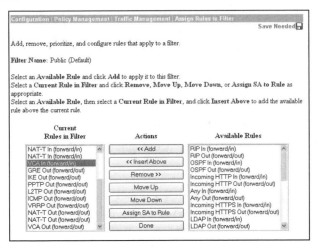

Step 2: Configure the Cluster

The second step in load balancing is to configure each Concentrator in the cluster for load balancing. The configuration consists of cluster and device configuration. Cluster configuration must be the same for all Concentrators in the cluster. Device configuration parameters can vary across the cluster. The device parameters are Concentrator-specific.

To configure load balancing on the Concentrator, go to the Configuration > System > Load Balancing window, and complete the following parameters (as shown in Figure 9-9):

- **VPN Virtual Cluster IP Address field**—Enter the single IP address that represents the entire virtual cluster. Choose an IP address that is within the public subnet address range shared by all the Concentrators in the virtual cluster.

- **VPN Virtual Cluster UDP Port field**—9023 is the default UDP port address. If another application is using this port, enter the UDP destination port number you want to use for load balancing.

- **Encryption check box**—The Concentrators in the virtual cluster communicate via LAN-to-LAN tunnels using IPSec. To ensure that all load-balancing information communicated between the Concentrators is encrypted, select this check box.

- **IPSec Shared Secret field**—This option is available only if you have checked the preceding Encryption check box. Enter the IPSec shared secret for the virtual cluster. The shared secret is a common password that authenticates members of the cluster. IPSec uses the shared secret as a preshared key to establish secure tunnels between virtual cluster peers.

- **Verify Shared Secret field**—Reenter the IPSec shared secret.

- **Load Balancing Enable check box**—Select this check box to include this Concentrator in the virtual cluster.

- **Priority field**—Enter a priority for this VPN Concentrator within the virtual cluster. The priority is a number from 1 to 10 that indicates the likelihood of this device's becoming the cluster master, either at startup or when an existing cluster master fails. The higher you set the priority (for example, 10), the more likely this device is to become the cluster master. If your cluster includes different models of Concentrators, it is recommended that you choose the device with the greatest load capacity to be the cluster master. For this reason, priority defaults are hardware-dependent. If your cluster is made up of identical devices (for example, if all the devices in the virtual cluster are Concentrator 3060s), set the priority of every device to 10. Setting all identical devices to the highest priority shortens the length of time needed to select the virtual cluster master. The default priorities are as follows:
    - Concentrator 3005—1
    - Concentrator 3015—3
    - Concentrator 3030—5
    - Concentrator 3060—7
    - Concentrator 3080—9

- **NAT Assigned IP Address field**—If this Concentrator is behind a firewall using Network Address Translation (NAT), NAT has assigned it a public IP address. Enter the NAT IP address. If this device is not using NAT, enter 0.0.0.0. The default setting is 0.0.0.0.

Figure 9-9 *Load-Balancing Parameters*

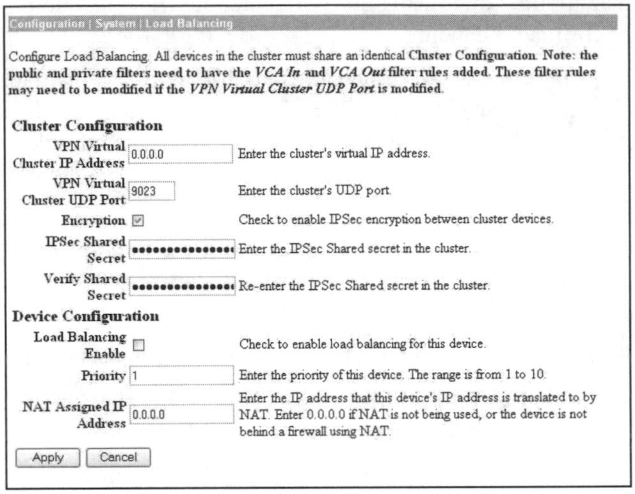

Step 3: Configure the Client

We will now look at the final step in configuring load balancing. We will look at this for both the VPN Hardware and Software Clients.

Hardware Client

This is the final step in configuring load balancing in the Hardware Client. In the Hardware Client, go to the Configuration > System > Tunneling Protocols > IPSec window. In the Remote Easy VPN Server field, verify that the cluster virtual IP address is specified. If it isn't, modify the Remote Server IP address to reflect the virtual, rather than physical, IP address of the Master Concentrator. In Figure 9-10, the cluster virtual IP address is 192.168.1.150.

Figure 9-10 *Hardware Client Load Balancing*

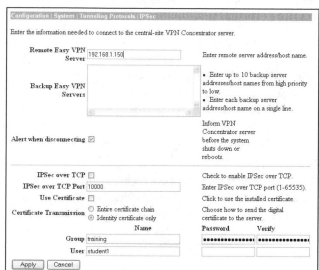

To support the load-balancing feature, the Hardware Client must use Release 3.5 software or later. In prior releases, the Hardware Client does not support redirect messages.

Software Client

This is the final step in configuring load balancing in the Software Client. In the Software Client, go to the Start > Programs > Cisco Systems VPN Client > VPN Client window. Click Connection Entries > Modify, and then add the cluster virtual IP address. In Figure 9-11, the cluster virtual IP address is 192.168.1.150.

Figure 9-11 *Software Client Load Balancing*

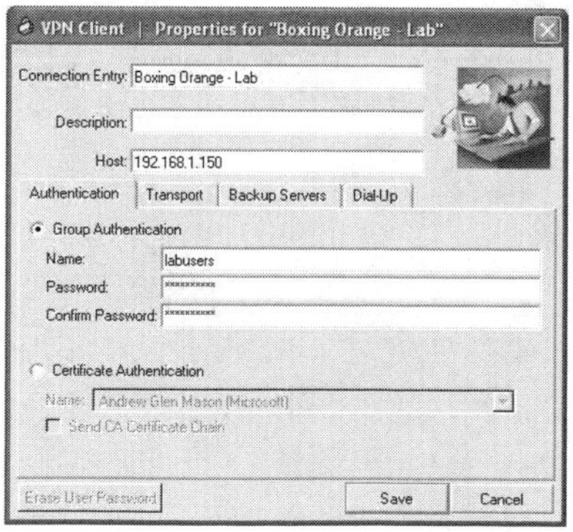

Overview of the Cisco VPN Client Reverse Route Injection Feature

Load balancing lets the VPN Client connect to the least-loaded Concentrator. The good news is the VPN Client load is shared across multiple Concentrators. The bad news is how a headend device connects to the client when it is connected to a different Concentrator each time a tunnel is established. The answer is Reverse Route Injection (RRI). Each time the VPN Client connects to a Concentrator, the Concentrator advertises the IP address of the VPN Client through its private interface. When the tunnel is disconnected, the Concentrator stops advertising the route. RRI lets a central site device connect to the client regardless of which Concentrator the VPN Client is attached to at the time.

After a VPN Client tunnel is established, the Concentrator can add static or host routes to the routing table and announce these routes using OSPF or outbound RIP. RRI has two VPN Client applications: client RRI and network extension RRI.

Client RRI

The VPN Client RRI feature applies to all VPN Software and Hardware Clients using Port Address Translation (PAT) mode. To enable it, go to the Configuration > System > IP Routing > Reverse Route Injection window, shown in Figure 9-12, and check the Client Reverse Route Injection check box from the central site Concentrator.

Figure 9-12 *Client RRI*

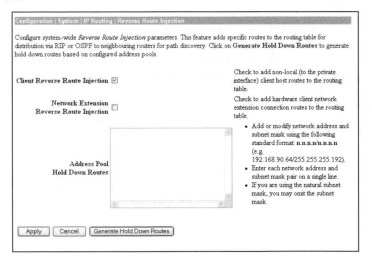

After the client tunnel is established, the Concentrator adds a host route to its routing table. The host route is advertised through the private interface providing OSPF, or outbound RIP is enabled on the private interface. The Concentrator deletes the route when the client disconnects.

In Figure 9-13, client RRI is enabled at the Concentrator, and the Hardware Client is running in PAT mode.

Figure 9-13   *Client RRI: Connected Routing Table*

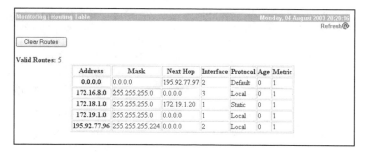

When the tunnel is launched, the Concentrator assigns the Hardware Client a virtual IP address: 172.19.2.224. Notice that in the routing table, 172.19.2.224 is listed and is advertised through the private interface on the Concentrator. When the tunnel is disconnected, the host entry is deleted from the routing table. Notice in Figure 9-14 that the 172.19.2.224 host route was deleted because the tunnel was dropped.

Figure 9-14   *Client RRI: Disconnected Routing Table*

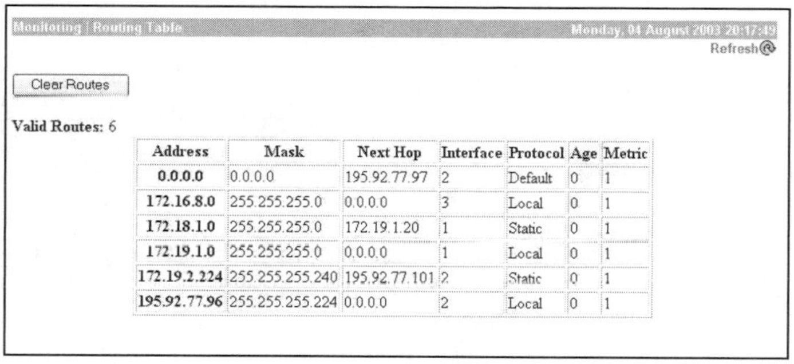

Address	Mask	Next Hop	Interface	Protocol	Age	Metric
0.0.0.0	0.0.0.0	195.92.77.97	2	Default	0	1
172.16.8.0	255.255.255.0	0.0.0.0	3	Local	0	1
172.18.1.0	255.255.255.0	172.19.1.20	1	Static	0	1
172.19.1.0	255.255.255.0	0.0.0.0	1	Local	0	1
195.92.77.96	255.255.255.224	0.0.0.0	2	Local	0	1

Valid Routes: 5

Network Extension RRI

The network extension RRI feature applies only to a Hardware Client using network extension mode. To enable it, go to the Configuration > System > IP Routing > Reverse Route Injection window and check the Network Extension Reverse Route Injection check box, as shown in Figure 9-15.

Figure 9-15   *Network Extension Route Injection*

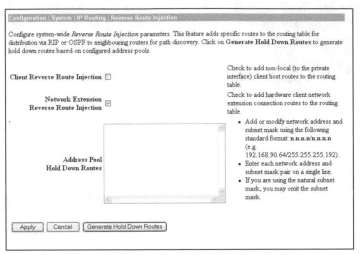

When the tunnel is established, the Concentrator adds routes to the remote subnet to its routing table, as it did with client mode. The host routes are advertised through the private interface providing OSPF, or outbound RIP is enabled on the private interface. The routes are deleted when the client disconnects.

Summary

This chapter covered three features of the VPN 3000 Concentrator: backup servers, load balancing, and reverse route injection. It started by looking at backup servers and how they can benefit your remote-access VPN installation. You saw that a simple configuration entry on the clients can enable this feature. Next, we looked at load balancing. This is the next step from backup servers, where you can actually cluster VPN Concentrators at the headend and have them appear to the clients as a single Concentrator. This chapter covered the necessary configuration steps to support this configuration on the VPN Concentrators.

This chapter finished by looking at the RRI feature, which dynamically injects a route into the Concentrators routing table when a host connects. This then operates with the configured routing protocol on the Concentrator (RIP or OSPF) to propagate this route throughout your network.

Review Questions

The following questions test your retention of the material presented in this chapter. The answers appear in Appendix A, "Answers to the Review Questions."

1 On the 3000 Concentrator, which tab do you use to change the IPSec Backup Servers option?

2 What default protocol and port does the VCA use?

3 Which method of RRI is supported only on a Cisco VPN 3002 Hardware Client?

4 If you have configured the Central Site Cisco VPN 3000 Concentrator to "Use List Below" for the IPScc Backup Servers, what happens to any backup servers that have been manually entered into the Software Client?

5 What is the default value for the IPSec Backup Servers field when you are modifying a group on a Cisco VPN 3000 Concentrator?

6 What two types of RRI can be configured on a Cisco VPN 3000 Concentrator?

After completing this chapter, you will be able to perform the following tasks:

- Understand how IPSec interacts with NAT
- Configure IPSec over UDP
- Configure NAT-Traversal
- Configure IPSec over TCP
- Monitor session statistics

CHAPTER 10

Configuring the Cisco 3000 Concentrator for IPSec over TCP and UDP

Previous chapters looked at configuring remote-access VPNs using the VPN Software Client and the Hardware Client. The one major headache when configuring any type of VPN is Network Address Translation (NAT) and Port Address Translation (PAT). This configuration headache exists for both site-to-site VPNs and remote-access VPNs and is common for every product in the Cisco VPN family. Luckily, the Cisco VPN Concentrator range of products provides tools to ease this burden.

The topics covered in this chapter were industry-leading and eventually led to NAT-Traversal's obtaining standardization so that other vendors could use this technology.

Most Internet service providers (ISPs) allocate each dial-in user a unique dynamically assigned public IP address each time the user connects. Therefore, there is no NAT or PAT device between the user and the central site VPN headend. This makes VPN connections easy, because you do not need to consider NAT/PAT issues. However, more employees are getting broadband connections that come with a router or even a firewall using PPP over Ethernet (PPPoE). In these instances, the user would probably use a private address range (as outlined in RFC 1918) for the private (or inside) address and would perform address translation to the outside world, thus hiding the inside hosts behind the outside address. This will immediately cause a traditional remote-access VPN to break.

This chapter starts by providing a technical overview of NAT and PAT and how they operate to overcome a problem. We then look at the issues caused by NAT and PAT and their inter-action with IPSec VPNs. Finally, this chapter covers the configuration steps necessary to configure your remote-access VPN to work with intermediary NAT and PAT devices.

The IPSec and NAT Problem

Before IPSec over User Datagram Protocol (UDP) or IPSec over TCP is discussed, the issues surrounding IPSec through PAT or NAT devices must be covered.

NAT

The Internet Assigned Numbers Authority (IANA, www.iana.org) created a series of nonroutable private IP address space:

- **Class A** — 10.0.0.0 to 10.255.255.255
- **Class B** — 172.16.0.0 to 172.31.255.255
- **Class C** — 192.168.0.0 to 192.168.255.255

Nonroutable private address space gives companies more addresses to use within their companies. These private addresses can be routed within the company's private network. The issue is how does a company route the information between campuses or companies over the Internet? These addresses are not globally unique; the Internet cannot route them. Only globally unique addresses can be routed through the Internet. NAT allows nonroutable address space to be translated into routable, globally unique addresses. A NAT device translates a nonroutable address into one of the globally unique addresses assigned to the company. The newly addressed packet can be routed through the Internet.

In Figure 10-1, at the remote end, the PC has been assigned a nonroutable, private IP address of 192.168.1.5. The end user wants to communicate with the corporate server at a different location. The packet must travel through the Internet to travel between sites. Unfortunately, with the current private addressing scheme, the packet cannot be routed through the Internet. The issue is solved by first sending the packet to a NAT device. By using a NAT device, the nonroutable source address can be translated into a routable address of 205.151.254.10. The packet is now routable and is sent through the Internet to the destination address of 205.151.255.10. The NAT device receives this packet at the central site, changes the destination address from 205.151.255.10, and redirects it to the corporate server, which has a private address of 10.0.1.5.

Figure 10-1   *NAT*

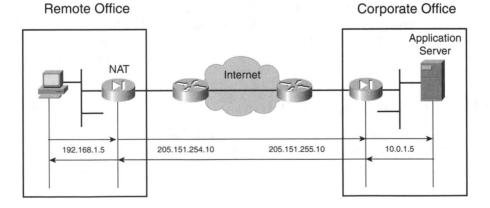

The corporate applications server receives the data within the packet, formulates a response, and returns the response to the destination public IP address 205.151.254.10, the NAT address for the remote PC. The NAT device translates the packet address from 205.151.254.10 back to 192.168.1.5 and forwards it to the PC at the remote end.

NAT works on a one-for-one relationship: one nonroutable address in and one routable address out. A problem develops when the company has a large number of nonroutable source addresses that need to translate into a finite number of routable addresses. The routable address pool might soon dry up.

The challenge comes in when there are multiple devices at the remote end. Figure 10-2 shows two computers with separate nonroutable addresses of 192.168.1.5 and 192.168.1.6. Both devices need to talk to the application server through a NAT device. The issue is that only one available globally unique IP address exists.

Figure 10-2 *NAT with Two Hosts*

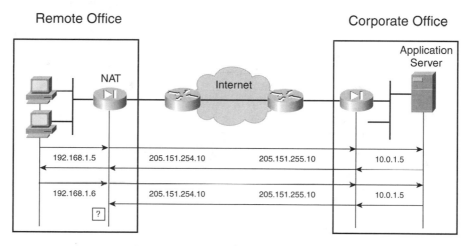

In the first instance, 192.168.1.5 sends a message to the NAT device, which translates the source address from 192.168.1.5 to 205.151.254.10. The message is routed through the Internet to the destination address of 205.151.255.10. The corporate application server receives the message, formulates a response, and sends a reply back to 205.151.254.10, the NAT device. The NAT device in turn translates the routable address back to 192.168.1.5.

When the second of the two PCs tries to send a packet, 192.168.1.6 sends a message to the application server. The PC forwards the packet to the NAT device, which translates the source address from 192.168.1.6 to 205.151.254.10. The message is sent through the Internet. The corporate application server receives the message, formulates a response, and sends a reply via the 205.151.254.10 address. The NAT device is confused. Who is the recipient of the packet, PC 1 or PC 2? The NAT device cannot differentiate between the two remote PCs.

This is where a PAT device fits in.

PAT

PAT works at the TCP and UDP port level. It lets multiple devices be multiplexed over one globally unique IP address. Each time the PAT device receives a connection, it translates that connection into an IP address and port number. A unique port number supports each device. One IP address can support multiple devices using different port numbers for each device.

In Figure 10-3, in the first instance, the first PC, 192.168.1.5, sends a message to the PAT device, which translates the address from 192.168.1.5 port 10000 to 205.151.254.10 port 600. The message is routed through the Internet. The corporate application server receives the message, formulates a response, and sends a reply via 205.151.254.10 port 600. The PAT device receives the message and in turn translates the response address back to 192.168.1.5 port 10000.

Figure 10-3 *PAT*

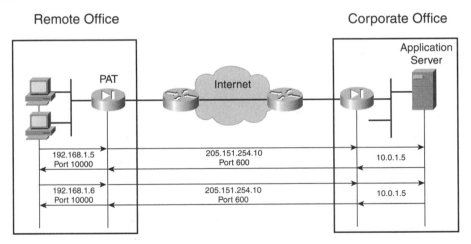

In the next instance, the second PC, 192.168.1.6, sends a message to the PAT device, which translates the address from 192.168.1.6 port 10000 to 205.151.254.10 port 601. The message is sent through the Internet. The corporate application server receives the message, formulates a response, and sends a reply via 205.151.254.10 port 601. The PAT device receives the message and translates the response from 205.151.254.10 port 601 to 192.168.1.6 port 10000. In this case, the information is sent to the second PC. The UDP port numbers, 600 and 601, are used to differentiate between unique remote devices. Within the PAT devices, a translation table is used to translate between nonroutable and routable IP addresses. In Figure 10-4, a remote PC needs to send a message to the corporate office. To do so, the remote office sends the message to the PAT device. In the PAT device is a translation table. The first entry in the table dictates that a nonroutable address and port number of 192.168.1.5 port 10000 should be translated into a routable IP address and port number of 205.151.254.10 port 600. When translated, the PAT device forwards the message to the corporate office.

Figure 10-4 *PAT Table*

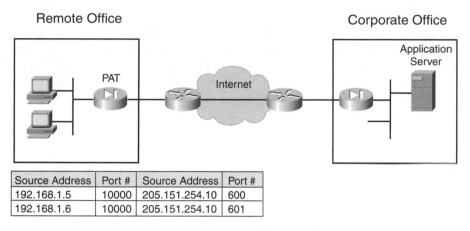

Source Address	Port #	Source Address	Port #
192.168.1.5	10000	205.151.254.10	600
192.168.1.6	10000	205.151.254.10	601

PAT works well, but there is an issue with using PAT when a virtual private network (VPN) is deployed.

The IKE and UDP Issue

Customers often require a Cisco VPN Client to operate in an environment where standard Encapsulating Security Payload (ESP, IP 50) or Internet Key Exchange (IKE, UDP port 500) either doesn't function or doesn't function transparently (without modification to existing firewall rules). VPN uses IKE for tunnel setup and security association (SA) negotiations. IKE uses UDP, so a nonroutable IP address and port number can be translated into a routable public address and port number. PAT can translate IKE packets using its inherent UDP port number. The problem arises when the VPN device tries to get the IPSec session established. IPSec uses ESP as the encapsulation protocol. ESP does not use UDP port numbers, because it is an IP protocol in the same sense that UDP and TCP are IP protocols. The PAT method of translating UDP port numbers does not work with IPSec. The translating device drops the IPSec packet.

Here are some situations in which standard ESP or UDP 500 does not work:

- A small home office router performing PAT, where the router does not support IPSec Pass-Thru.

- A PAT-provided IP address behind a large router. This could exist if a service provider provides nonpublic addresses to clients and then performs PAT. This scenario is identical to that just described.

IPSec over UDP: Cisco-Proprietary

Cisco has created a proprietary fix to solve the IPSec PAT translation issue. By default, in the Cisco VPN 3000 Series Concentrator, a standard IPSec packet is wrapped in ESP and IP with no UDP port number. If the packet must traverse a NAT device, the Concentrator can be programmed to add a UDP header between the outer IP address and the ESP header. After the configuration change, when the packet arrives at the PAT device the packet address can be translated because of the UDP encapsulation, as shown in Figure 10-5.

Figure 10-5   *IPSec over UDP*

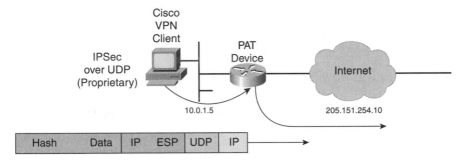

IPSec over UDP is negotiated during tunnel establishment. During tunnel negotiations, if enabled in both the Cisco VPN Client and the Concentrator, IPSec is wrapped in UDP for the duration of the tunnel. This is configured on a group-by-group basis. Groups whose frames traverse a NAT device can be configured to support IPSec over UDP. All other groups can be left at the default, with IPSec over UDP disabled. Some groups might require IPSec over UDP, and others might not.

NAT-Traversal: Standards-Based IPSec over UDP

NAT-Traversal (NAT-T) is an IETF standards-based IPSec-over-UDP solution. NAT-T performs two tasks: It detects if both ends support NAT-T, and it detects intermediate NAT devices along the transmission path. During IKE phase 1, the client and IPSec gateway exchange vendor identification (VID) packets. A NAT-T VID must be sent and received by both ends for the NAT-T negotiations to continue.

Next, NAT-Discovery (NAT-D) payloads are exchanged. NAT-T's second task is to determine if there are any NAT devices along the transmission path. Intervening NAT devices change the data packets' IP address or port numbers. NAT-D payloads are exchanged to determine if there are any IP address or port number changes. Two NAT-D payload packets are sent in each direction. Each NAT-D payload is a hash of the original IP address and port number: one NAT-D packet for the source IP address and port number, and another for the destination IP address and port number. After receiving the NAT-D packets, both ends compare the received address and port number with the hashed NAT-D payloads.

If they match, there are no NAT devices along the transmission path. If they do not match, a NAT device translated either the IP address or port address. NAT-T should be performed. The IPSec packet is wrapped in a UDP packet with a port address of 4500.

In Figure 10-6, the Cisco VPN Client and Concentrator exchange NAT-T VID packets. Both ends support NAT-T, so the NAT-T negotiations continue. In packets 2 and 3, both ends exchange NAT-D payloads. The NAT-D hashed IP address and port number are compared with the IKE packet IP address and port number, and they do not match. The IKE packet address was modified as the packet transited the NAT device. As a result, both ends change the UDP port number to 4500. The remaining IPSec packets are wrapped in a UDP header using port number 4500, NAT-T encapsulation. If both IPSec over UDP and NAT-T are enabled, NAT-T takes precedence.

Figure 10-6 *NAT-T*

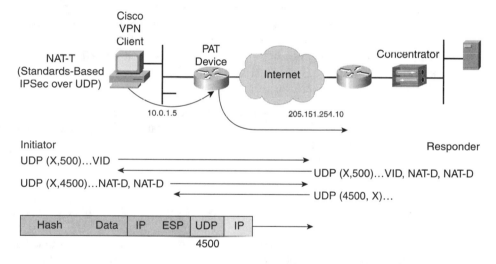

IPSec over TCP: Cisco-Proprietary

A third type of transparent tunneling support is IPSec over TCP (see Figure 10-7). Concentrator devices support IPSec over UDP, NAT-T, or IPSec over TCP. With IPSec over TCP, there is no room for negotiation, as there is in IPSec over UDP. IPSec-over-TCP packets are encapsulated from the start of the tunnel establishment cycle. From the very beginning, all traffic to the Concentrator is encapsulated in TCP. At the point where IKE normally negotiates the use of IPSec over UDP, IPSec over TCP is already active. In the Concentrator and the Cisco VPN Clients, IPSec over TCP takes precedence over both NAT-T and IPSec over UDP.

Figure 10-7 *IPSec over TCP*

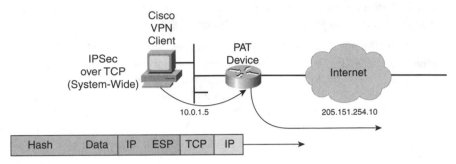

The goal of IPSec over TCP is to allow the Cisco VPN Clients to operate in the environments by using TCP to encapsulate both IKE and ESP. This takes advantage of the known fact that most firewalls allow outgoing TCP traffic and the inbound packets associated with the outbound connection. Using TCP is preferred over UDP through firewalls because state can be maintained for TCP packets, resulting in higher security. The TCP implementation defaults to port 10000 but does not restrict the administrator's ability to configure the Cisco VPN Client to use on different ports.

Although TCP is used to encapsulate IKE and IPSec, this feature is not intended to provide the reliability found in a fully deployed TCP implementation. The application layer (IKE) already provides much of the reliability needed.

IPSec Through PAT Mode

There are three IPSec through NAT applications, as shown in Figure 10-8: IPSec over UDP, NAT-T, and IPSec over TCP. NAT-T is a global attribute. IPSec over UDP (proprietary version) is a group attribute. The use of NAT-T or IPSec over UDP is negotiated during tunnel setup. If IPSec over UDP is enabled at both ends, and NAT-T is disabled, IPSec packets are encapsulated in proprietary UDP packets. If both IPSec over UDP and NAT-T are enabled, and a NAT device is discovered in the transmission path, IPSec packets are encapsulated using NAT-T. If no NAT device is discovered, UDP encapsulation of the IPSec packets is performed.

Figure 10-8   *IPSec Through PAT Mode*

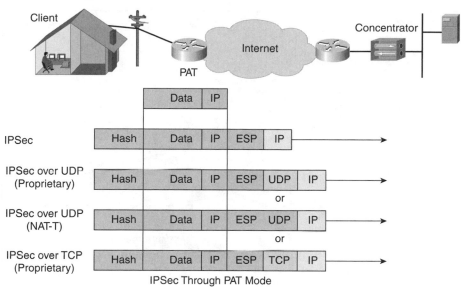

IPSec Through PAT Mode

IPSec over TCP is a system-wide feature. Groups do not negotiate it. If enabled at both ends, it is on from the start of the IKE negotiations. If both NAT-T and IPSec over TCP are enabled, IPSec over TCP takes precedence. It is enabled globally, across all groups.

Configuring IPSec over UDP

Configuring IPSec over UDP is a two-step process. Step 1 is to configure the Concentrator, and step 2 is to configure the VPN Software Client.

Concentrator Configuration

IPSec over UDP must be enabled first. Do the following to configure IPSec over UDP:

Step 1   Choose Configuration > User Management > Groups. The Groups window opens.

Step 2   Select a group.

Step 3   Within the Client Config tab, shown in Figure 10-9, check the IPSec over UDP check box.

Figure 10-9 *Configuring IPSec over UDP: Concentrator*

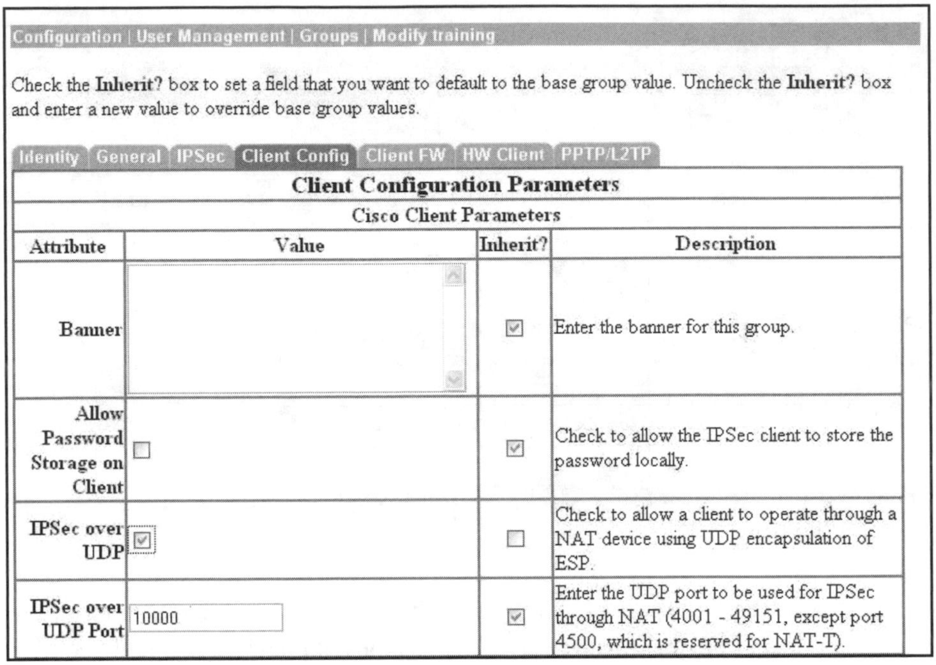

> **Step 4** You must define an IPSec over UDP Port number by entering in the IPSec over UDP field any UDP port number between 4001 and 49151, except for 4500, which is used for NAT-T. The default is 10000.
>
> **Step 5** IPSec over UDP is configured on a group-by-group basis on the Concentrator. When IPSec over UDP is enabled, the defined UDP port number is pushed down to the Cisco VPN Client via Mode configuration.

VPN Software Client Configuration

For IPSec over UDP to work, it must be enabled in both the Cisco VPN Client and the Concentrator. By default, this feature is enabled in the Cisco VPN Client but disabled in the Concentrator. To verify the Cisco VPN Client configuration, select the Cisco VPN Client > Connection Entries > Modify > Transport tab, as shown in Figure 10-10. Ensure that the Enable Transparent Tunneling check box is checked and that the IPSec over UDP (NAT/PAT) radio button is selected. Click OK after you verify that IPSec over UDP is enabled in the Cisco VPN Client.

Figure 10-10 *Configuring IPSec over UDP: Software Client*

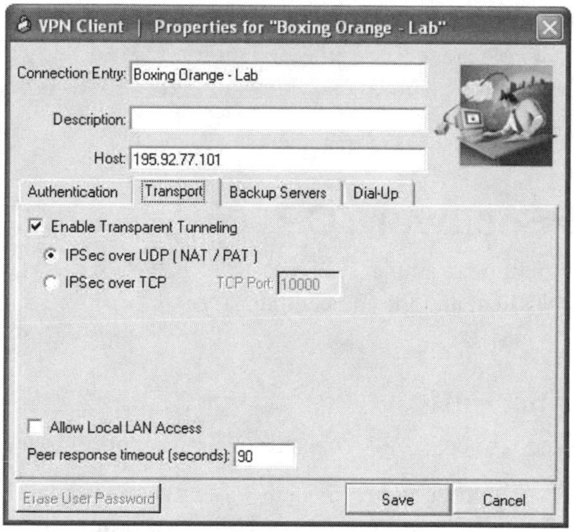

Configuring NAT-T

For NAT-T to work, it must be enabled in both the Cisco VPN Client and the Concentrator.

Concentrator Configuration

Choose Configuration > System > Tunneling Protocols > IPSec. The Tunneling Protocols window opens. Select NAT Transparency to enable NAT-T on the Concentrator. Check IPSec over NAT-T in the NAT Transparency window, as shown in Figure 10-11. NAT-T is enabled on a system-wide basis for all client-to-LAN connections.

Figure 10-11 *Configuring IPSec over NAT-T*

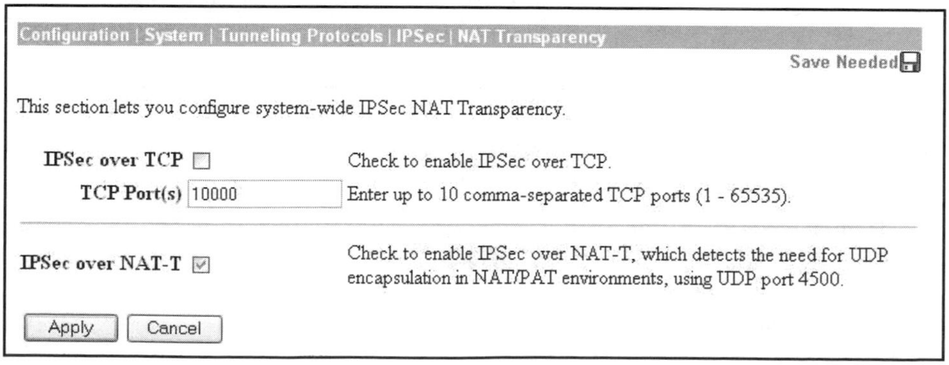

VPN Software Client Configuration

NAT-T functions automatically from the VPN Client because IPSec over UDP is the default setting for the VPN Client. The configuration for this is exactly the same as configuring IPSec over UDP in the preceding section, and Figure 10-10 is the identical screen shot of the client settings.

Configuring IPSec over TCP

The last configuration example is IPSec over TCP. IPSec over TCP must be enabled in both the Cisco VPN Client and the Concentrator for it to work.

Concentrator Configuration

Follow these steps to enable IPSec over TCP in the Concentrator:

Step 1   Choose Configuration > System > Tunneling Protocols > IPSec to verify the Concentrator configuration. The IPSec window opens.

Step 2   Click the NAT Transparency link. The Configuration > System > Tunneling Protocols > IPSec > NAT Transparency window opens, as shown in Figure 10-12.

Figure 10-12   *Configuring IPSec over TCP: Concentrator*

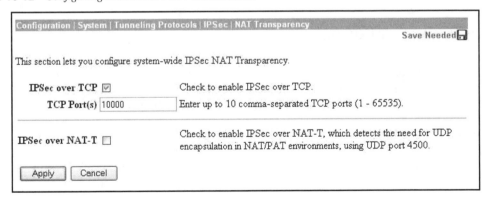

Step 3   From this window, ensure that the IPSec over TCP check box is checked and that the TCP port number is supplied.

Up to ten comma-delimited port addresses can be supplied. Different remote Cisco VPN Clients can use different TCP port numbers. The pool of usable TCP port numbers is defined in the Concentrator. The port number used by each Cisco VPN Client is defined on the individual Cisco VPN Client.

This is a global parameter. If IPSec over TCP is enabled on both the Concentrator and the Cisco VPN Client, all frames are encapsulated in IPSec over TCP regardless of which group the Cisco VPN Client belongs to.

VPN Software Client Configuration

Follow these steps to configure IPSec over TCP in the Software Client:

Step 1   Choose the Connection Entry and then Connection Entries > Modify > Transport Tab. The Transport Properties window opens, as shown in Figure 10-13.

Figure 10-13   *Configuring IPSec over TCP: Software Client*

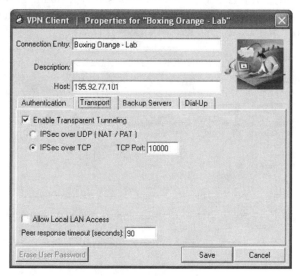

Step 2   Check the Enable Transparent Tunneling check box.

Step 3   Select the IPSec over TCP radio button.

Step 4   Enter the TCP port number in the TCP Port field. You can enter any TCP port number from 1 to 65535, but it must match one of the TCP port numbers programmed into the Concentrator TCP port(s) field on the Concentrator Configuration > System > Tunneling Protocols > IPSec > NAT Transparency screen.

NOTE   To support IPSec over TCP, the VPN Software Client and the central site Concentrator must both be version 3.5 or later. NAT-T support was introduced in version 3.6 of the VPN Software Client and Concentrator.

Monitoring Session Statistics

The administrator can check the session's status in both the Software Client and the Concentrator. When checking the session's status for the Software Client, after the tunnel is established, right-click the IPSec tunnel icon on the toolbar and select Statistics. On the Tunnel Details tab, shown in Figure 10-14, you can check whether transparent tunneling is active or inactive. If it is active, the encapsulation type and port number are available. In Figure 10-14, transparent tunneling is active. IPSec-over-UDP encapsulation is used with a port number of 4500, so you know that this is NAT-T.

Figure 10-14 *Monitoring the Software Session Status*

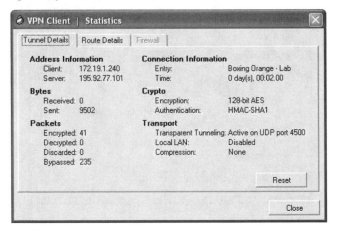

The statistics can also be viewed at the Concentrator. To do this, go to the Monitoring > Sessions window, as shown in Figure 10-15.

Figure 10-15   *Monitoring the Concentrator Session Status*

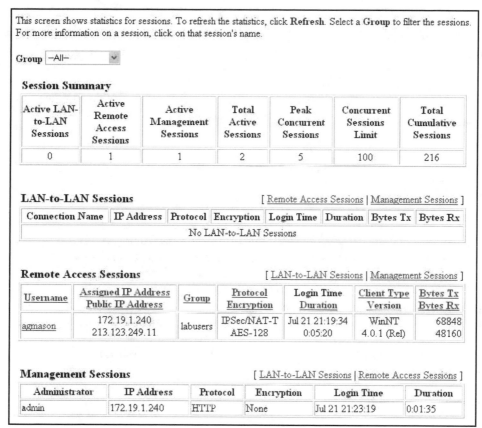

This screen shows statistics for sessions. To refresh the statistics, click **Refresh**. Select a **Group** to filter the sessions. For more information on a session, click on that session's name.

Group –All–

Session Summary

Active LAN-to-LAN Sessions	Active Remote Access Sessions	Active Management Sessions	Total Active Sessions	Peak Concurrent Sessions	Concurrent Sessions Limit	Total Cumulative Sessions
0	1	1	2	5	100	216

LAN-to-LAN Sessions   [Remote Access Sessions | Management Sessions]

Connection Name	IP Address	Protocol	Encryption	Login Time	Duration	Bytes Tx	Bytes Rx
No LAN-to-LAN Sessions							

Remote Access Sessions   [LAN-to-LAN Sessions | Management Sessions]

Username	Assigned IP Address Public IP Address	Group	Protocol Encryption	Login Time Duration	Client Type Version	Bytes Tx Bytes Rx
agmason	172.19.1.240 213.123.249.11	labusers	IPSec/NAT-T AES-128	Jul 21 21:19:34 0:05:20	WinNT 4.0.1 (Rel)	68848 48160

Management Sessions   [LAN-to-LAN Sessions | Remote Access Sessions]

Administrator	IP Address	Protocol	Encryption	Login Time	Duration
admin	172.19.1.240	HTTP	None	Jul 21 21:23:19	0:01:35

The encapsulation type is visible in the Protocol column in the Remote Access Sessions section. In Figure 10-15, UDP NAT-T over IPScc is used. Click the agmason link in the Remote Access Sessions section to get more information on the port number, as shown in Figure 10-16.

Figure 10-16 *Monitoring the Concentrator Session Detail Status*

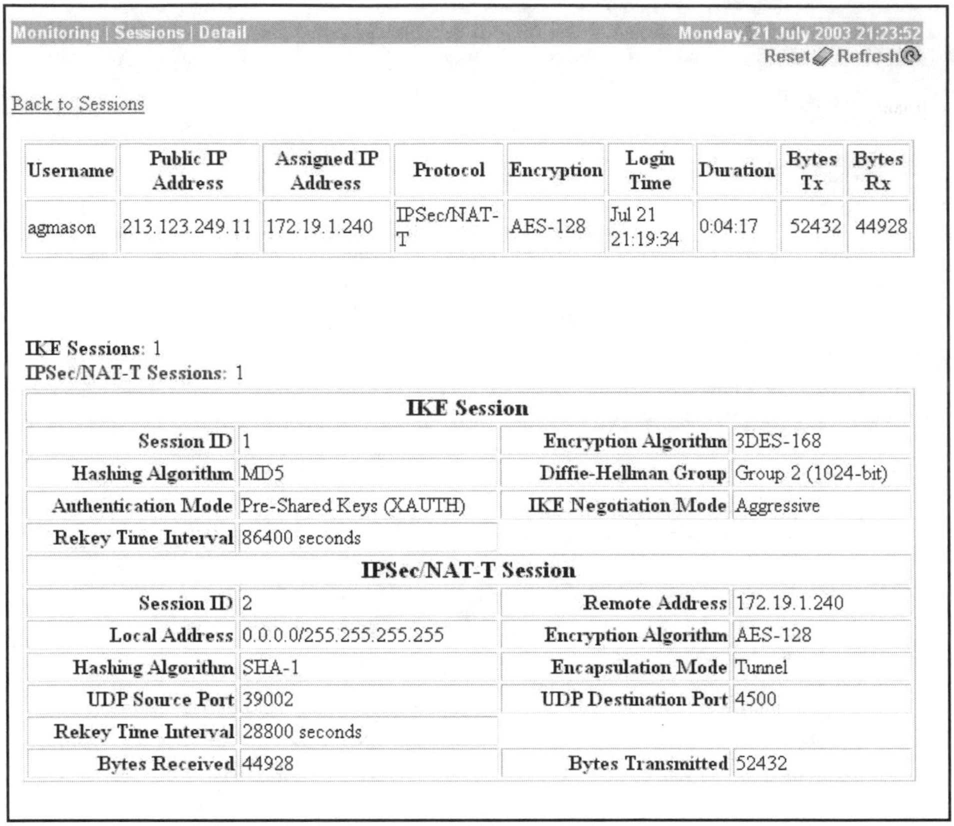
Monitoring | Sessions | Detail
Monday, 21 July 2003 21:23:52
Reset Refresh
Back to Sessions
Username
Public IP Address
Assigned IP Address
Protocol
Encryption
Login Time
Duration
Bytes Tx
Bytes Rx
agmason
213.123.249.11
172.19.1.240
IPSec/NAT-T
AES-128
Jul 21 21:19:34
0:04:17
52432
44928
IKE Sessions: 1
IPSec/NAT-T Sessions: 1
IKE Session
Session ID 1
Encryption Algorithm 3DES-168
Hashing Algorithm MD5
Diffie-Hellman Group Group 2 (1024-bit)
Authentication Mode Pre-Shared Keys (XAUTH)
IKE Negotiation Mode Aggressive
Rekey Time Interval 86400 seconds
IPSec/NAT-T Session
Session ID 2
Remote Address 172.19.1.240
Local Address 0.0.0.0/255.255.255.255
Encryption Algorithm AES-128
Hashing Algorithm SHA-1
Encapsulation Mode Tunnel
UDP Source Port 39002
UDP Destination Port 4500
Rekey Time Interval 28800 seconds
Bytes Received 44928
Bytes Transmitted 52432

In the Monitoring > Sessions > Detail window, two sessions are listed: one IKE session and one IPSec session. Under the IPSec sessions, the encapsulation type and port numbers are available. In Figure 10-16, tunnel encapsulation is used, and the UDP destination port number assigned is port 4500 (this is shown as NAT-T).

Figure 10-17 shows the same screen, but this time you can see that IPSec over UDP port 10000 is used.

Figure 10-17 *Monitoring the Concentrator Session Detail Status: IPSec over UDP*

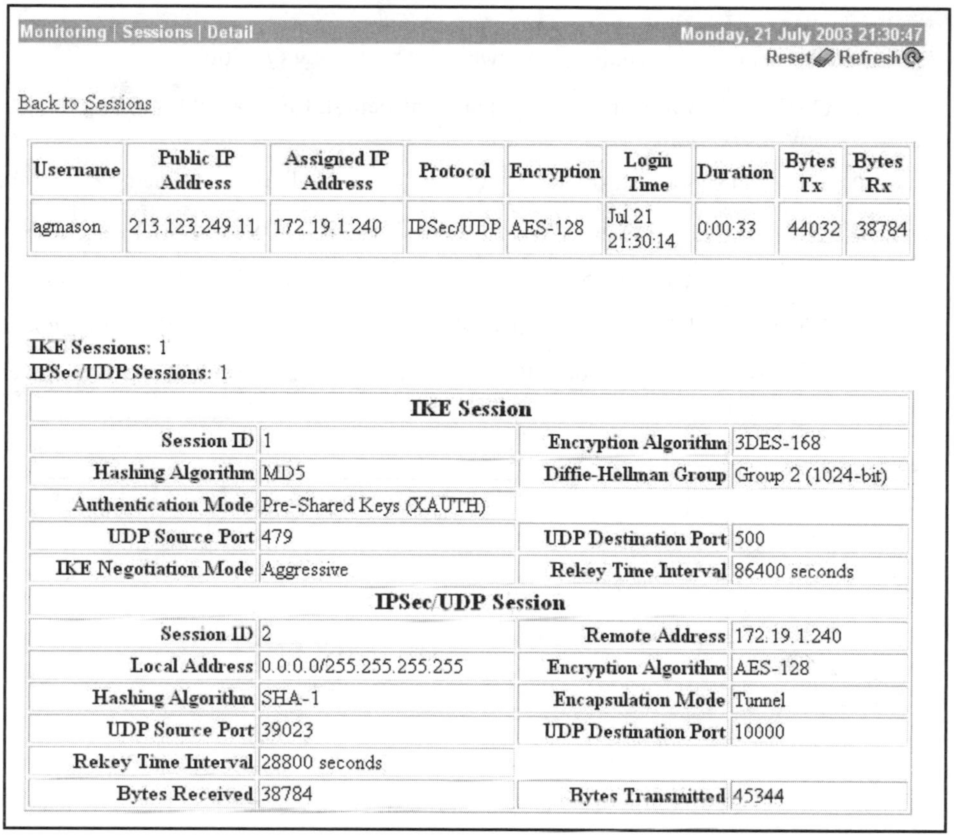
Monitoring | Sessions | Detail
Monday, 21 July 2003 21:30:47
Reset Refresh
Back to Sessions
Username | Public IP Address | Assigned IP Address | Protocol | Encryption | Login Time | Duration | Bytes Tx | Bytes Rx
agmason | 213.123.249.11 | 172.19.1.240 | IPSec/UDP | AES-128 | Jul 21 21:30:14 | 0:00:33 | 44032 | 38784
IKE Sessions: 1
IPSec/UDP Sessions: 1
IKE Session
Session ID 1
Encryption Algorithm 3DES-168
Hashing Algorithm MD5
Diffie-Hellman Group Group 2 (1024-bit)
Authentication Mode Pre-Shared Keys (XAUTH)
UDP Source Port 479
UDP Destination Port 500
IKE Negotiation Mode Aggressive
Rekey Time Interval 86400 seconds
IPSec/UDP Session
Session ID 2
Remote Address 172.19.1.240
Local Address 0.0.0.0/255.255.255.255
Encryption Algorithm AES-128
Hashing Algorithm SHA-1
Encapsulation Mode Tunnel
UDP Source Port 39023
UDP Destination Port 10000
Rekey Time Interval 28800 seconds
Bytes Received 38784
Bytes Transmitted 45344

Summary

This chapter covered the issues facing a network administrator when trying to configure a remote-access VPN to work with PAT and NAT devices. It started by providing an overview of NAT and PAT and how they cause issues with the forming of IPSec remote-access VPNs. Taking this information, we looked at what Cisco has done to remedy this situation with IPSec over UDP and IPSec over TCP support in the VPN 3000 range of concentrators. We also looked at how the standardized NAT-T works and the differences between it and the Cisco-proprietary IPSec over TCP and IPSec over UDP.

Configuration steps were provided for IPSec over UDP, IPSec over TCP, and IPSec using NAT-T for both the VPN Software Client and the Concentrator. This chapter closed by looking at the monitoring that is available when a connection is established on both the VPN Software Client and the Concentrator.

Review Questions

The following questions test your retention of the material presented in this chapter. The answers appear in Appendix A, "Answers to the Review Questions."

1 On the VPN Software Client, what is the default transparent tunneling mode for any new connection?

2 What transport layer protocol and port does NAT-T use as defined by the standard?

3 Where do you configure NAT-T on the Cisco VPN Concentrator?

4 Where do you configure IPSec over UDP on the Cisco VPN Concentrator?

5 What is the default IPSec over UDP port number used for transparent tunneling?

6 What is the configuration difference between IPSec over UDP and IPSec over TCP/NAT-T?

After completing this chapter, you will be able to perform the following tasks:

- Understand the principle of LAN-to-LAN virtual private networks
- Configure a LAN-to-LAN VPN with preshared keys
- Administer LAN-to-LAN tunnels
- Deal with multiple subnets
- Configure a LAN-to-LAN VPN with digital certificates

CHAPTER 11

Configuring LAN-to-LAN VPNs on the Cisco 3000

Up to this point we have looked at remote-access Virtual Private Networks (VPNs). The two types of VPNs are remote-access and LAN-to-LAN. This chapter looks at the configuration of a LAN-to-LAN VPN using preshared keys and digital certificates. If you invest in a Cisco VPN 3000 Concentrator for your remote-access requirements, the VPN 3000 can also be used to terminate LAN-to-LAN tunnels. The configuration of a LAN-to-LAN tunnel is totally different from configuring a remote-access VPN. To configure a LAN-to-LAN VPN, you have to create a LAN-to-LAN connection entry. The connection entry then automatically creates a group, Internet Key Exchange (IKE) proposal, and security association (SA).

Overview of LAN-to-LAN VPNs

In Figure 11-1, a corporation wants to tie together remote sites via a VPN. Each remote site has 500 people. One option is to run a remote VPN where the VPN Client is installed on every PC. This is a logistical and administrative nightmare.

Figure 11-1 *LAN-to-LAN*

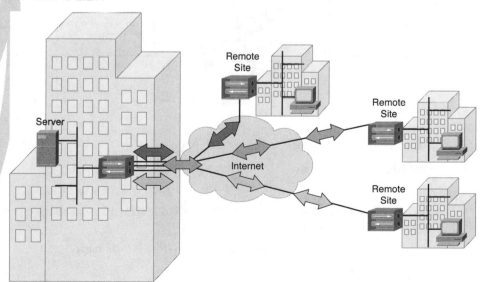

The better option is to use the VPN capabilities of the Concentrator. One Concentrator is installed at each site, and all remote PC traffic is routed to the Concentrators. The Concentrators encrypt and encapsulate the traffic. The Concentrators perform all IPSec functionality and route all interoffice VPN traffic through the Internet. This option requires that no additional software be installed on the PCs. This application is called a LAN-to-LAN VPN.

In Figure 11-2, the user on a remote LAN wants to access an application server at corporate headquarters. An IP packet is built with a source address of 10.0.2.10 and a destination address of 10.0.1.10. The packet is routed to the Concentrator. The Concentrator encrypts and encapsulates the IP packet with an Encapsulating Security Protocol (ESP) header. The packet is secure, but the packet is nonroutable because of the encrypted address. Therefore, an outside address header is added to the IP packet. The Concentrator uses the network interface card (NIC) addresses of the two Concentrators: 192.168.1.5 and 192.168.2.5. The outside address lets the IP packet be routed through the Internet. An IPSec tunnel is established between the Concentrators' public interfaces: 192.168.1.5 and 192.168.2.5. When the tunnel is up, a session is established between the two private networks: 10.0.1.0 and 10.0.2.0.

Figure 11-2 *LAN-to-LAN*

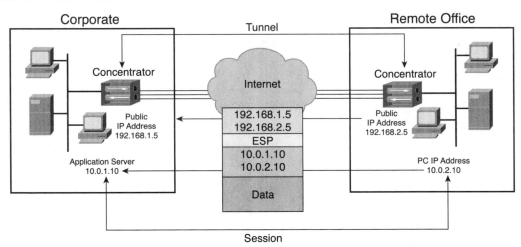

The Concentrator supports the following ESP options:

- Authentication options:
  - None
  - Hashed-based Message Authentication Code (HMAC)—message digest algorithm 5 (MD5)—128-bit hash
  - HMAC-Secure Hash Algorithm 1 (SHA-1)—160-bit hash

- Data encryption options:
  - Data Encryption Standard (DES)—56-bit key
  - Triple DES (3DES)—168-bit key
  - Advanced Encryption Standard (AES)—128-, 196-, and 256-bit key

Configuring the VPN 3000 for a LAN-to-LAN VPN with Preshared Keys

Now that a LAN-to-LAN VPN has been defined, we will look at the configuration of a LAN-to-LAN VPN using preshared keys. Chapter 5, "Configuring the Cisco VPN 3000 for Remote Access Using Digital Certificates," covered the initial configuration of a VPN 3000 Concentrator and showed you the differences between quick configuration and configuration through the menu system. This chapter uses the menu system to build a LAN-to-LAN VPN between two VPN Concentrators—one located in Leeds and one located in London. Both of these Concentrators are currently configured for remote-access VPNs, so this is a pure addition to the configuration.

Configuring the Central Site LAN-to-LAN Connection

The first action in configuring a LAN-to-LAN VPN is to create the LAN-to-LAN connection on the VPN Concentrator. Navigate to the Configuration > System > Tunneling Protocols > IPSec > LAN-to-LAN window, as shown in Figure 11-3.

Figure 11-3 *LAN-to-LAN Connection Window*

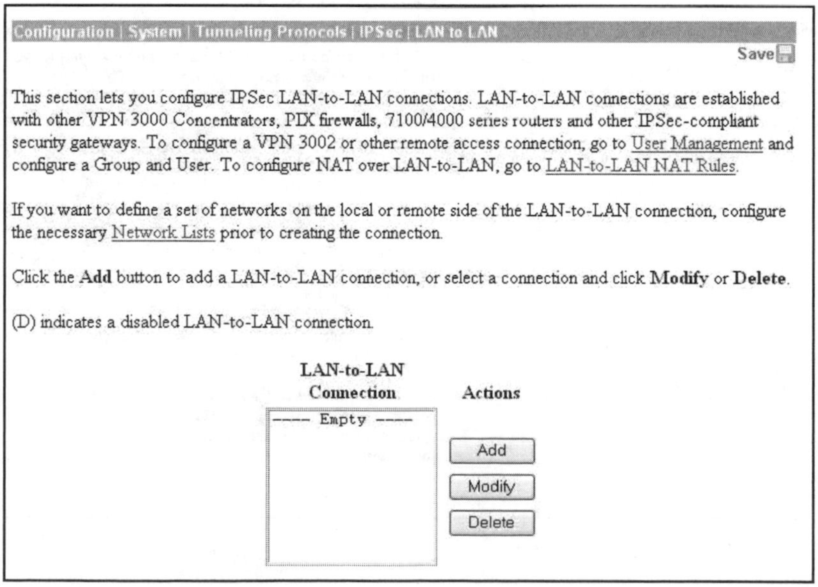

From this screen, you can see that there are no current configured LAN-to-LAN connections. To create a new LAN-to-LAN connection, click the Add button.

When you click the Add button, you see the screen shown in Figure 11-4.

Figure 11-4 *Add a New IPSec LAN-to-LAN Connection Window*

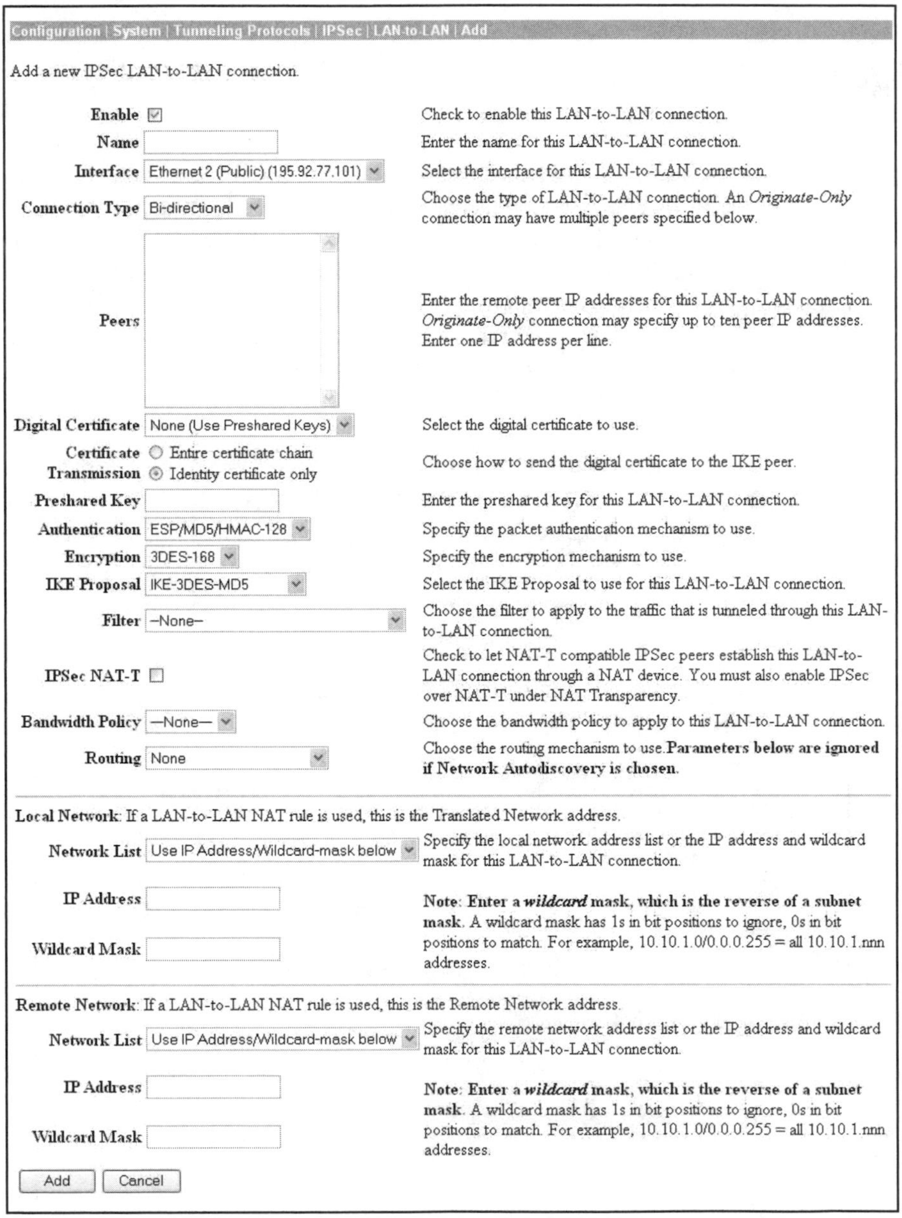

This window has three sections. The top section pertains to the network information, and the bottom two sections deal with the two private networks at either end of the tunnel.

Figure 11-5 shows a tunnel between Leeds and London.

Figure 11-5   *VPN Between Leeds and London*

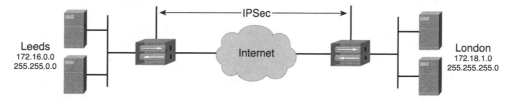

The administrator is currently configuring the Leeds Concentrator. For the Leeds network connection, the administrator needs to follow these steps:

Step 1   Enter the name of the LAN-to-LAN connection (local significance only) in the Name field.

Step 2   Set the peer value as the IP address assigned to the public interface of the remote Concentrator (for example, 213.123.249.11) in the Peers field.

Step 3   Enter an alphanumeric string value for the preshared key in the Preshared Key field.

There are two private networks: local and remote. The middle section of the Configuration > System > Tunneling Protocols > IPSec > LAN-to-LAN window defines the local private network. When the administrator programs the Leeds end, the local network to London is 172.18.1.0. When programming the local private network, the administrator needs to follow these steps:

Step 1   Set the local network IP address to 172.16.0.0, which is the network and subnet address minus the host address.

Step 2   Set the wildcard mask, 0.0.255.255. The wildcard mask is the reverse of the subnet mask.

The bottom section of the Configuration > System > Tunneling Protocols > IPSec > LAN-to-LAN window defines the remote private network. In the example, the remote end refers to the London private network, 172.18.1.0. When the administrator in the example programs the remote private network, he or she needs to follow these steps:

Step 1   Set the remote network IP address to 172.18.1.0. This is the network and subnet address minus the host address.

Step 2   Set the wildcard mask to 0.0.0.255. The wildcard mask is the reverse of the subnet mask.

Step 3   Click Add.

Figure 11-6 shows the Add a new IPSec LAN-to-LAN connection window with this information added.

Figure 11-6 *VPN Connection Created for the VPN Between Leeds and London*

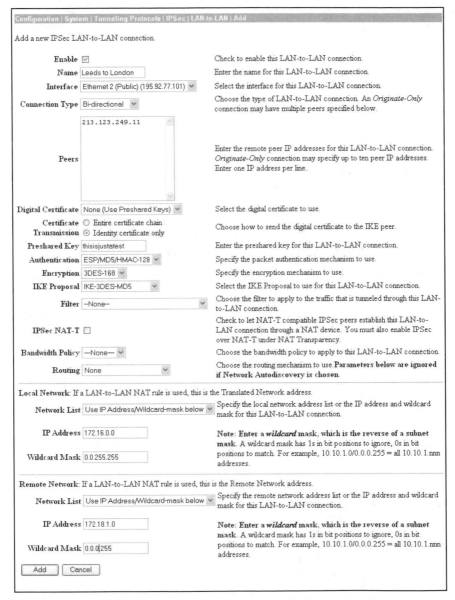

After you click the Add button, you see a confirmation screen that indicates if the creation of the LAN-to-LAN VPN connection was successful, as shown in Figure 11-7.

Figure 11-7 *Successful VPN Connection Window*

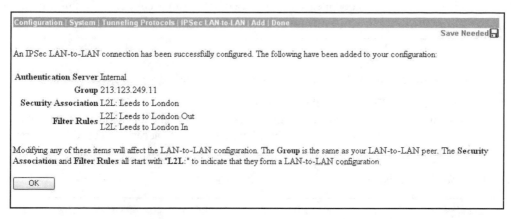

Note the information in this window. It tells you that the VPN connection was created successfully. It also mentions three items—a group, security association, and filter rule.

LAN-to-LAN Groups

Now let's look at the configured groups on the VPN 3000 Concentrator, shown in Figure 11-8.

Figure 11-8 *Configured Groups*

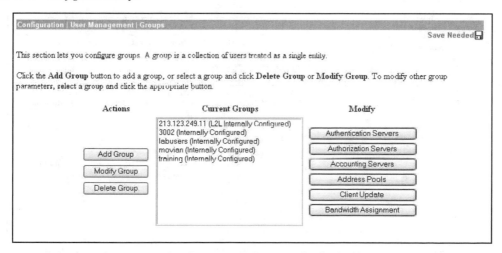

It is clear that a group has been created automatically for this LAN-to-LAN connection. Note that the group name is the IP address of the remote peer, and it has a designation of L2L Internally Configured. This indicates that this group has been created by the LAN-to-LAN VPN process.

NOTE   It is generally not a good idea to change any of the settings configured in this group. If you amend the LAN-to-LAN connection entry, the group is automatically updated.

Let's now look at the IPSec properties of this automatically configured group.

You can see in Figure 11-9 that the IPSec SA in use is called L2L: Leeds to London. Remember that this is what the LAN-to-LAN connection entry was called. Also note that the tunnel type is now LAN-to-LAN, where only remote access was used in the previous chapters.

Figure 11-9   *IPSec Parameters of the New Group*

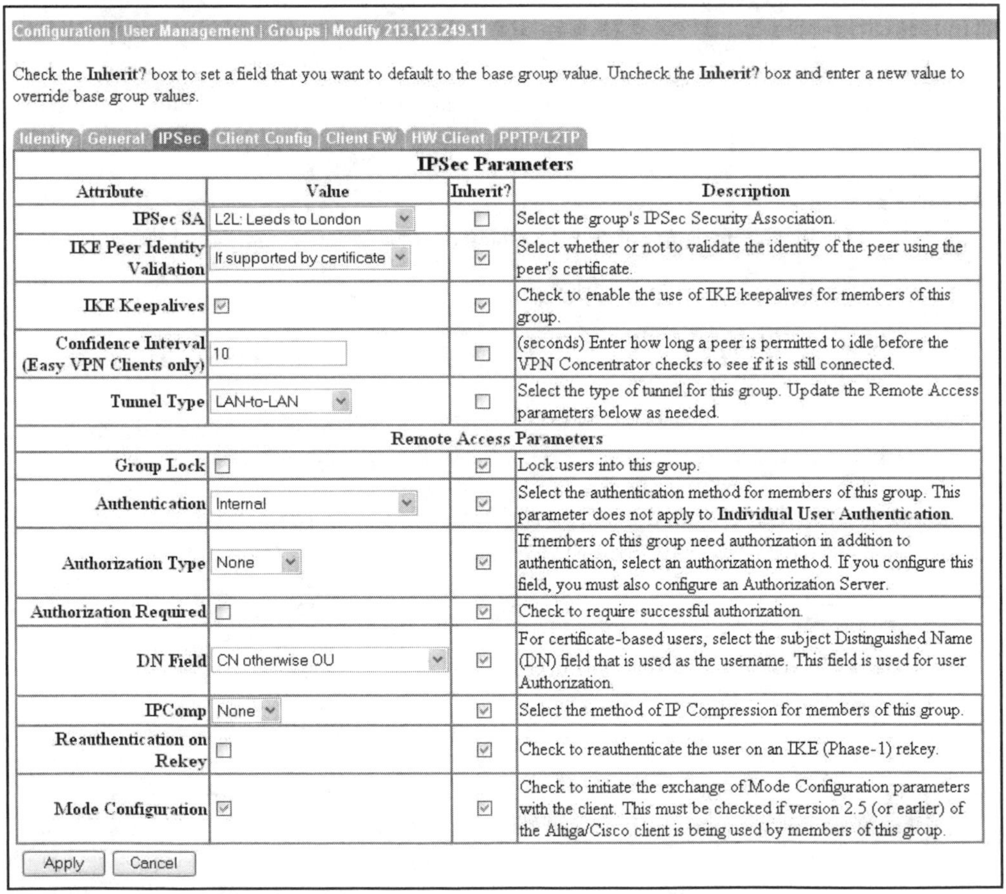

LAN-to-LAN Security Associations

As well as creating the group, a new SA has been created. Figure 11-10 shows this automatically created SA.

Figure 11-10 *LAN-to-LAN-Created Security Association*

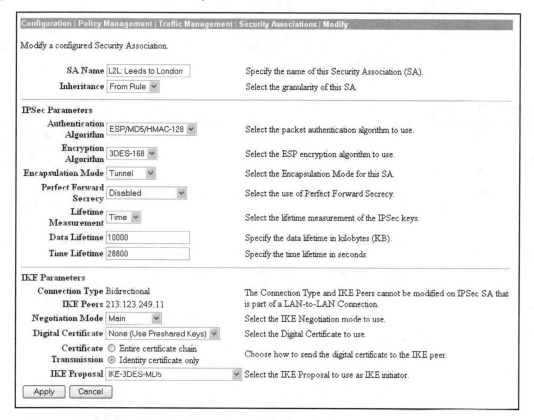

Notice in Figure 11-10 that the IKE peer is manually defined as 213.123.249.11. In SAs used for remote-access VPNs, the IKE peer is always 0.0.0.0. This is because you never know the IP address of a remote-access VPN peer, because it can enter the network from a variable-source IP address, depending on which service provider it connects with. Again, this SA should not be altered in any way. Altering the LAN-to-LAN connection entry changes this SA if required.

LAN-to-LAN Filter Rules

Filters restrict what traffic can pass on the interfaces of the VPN 3000 Concentrator. They consist of rules, very similar to how a firewall or access list works.

You create rules, which permit or deny traffic, and then add them to a filter. The filter is then applied to an interface on the VPN 3000 Concentrator.

When you configure a LAN-to-LAN connection, two rules are created and added to the active filter on the public interface. By default, the filter on the public interface is called Public (Default). Figure 11-11 shows the Filters window, where you can see that the Public (Default) filter is selected.

Figure 11-11 *LAN Viewing the Filters*

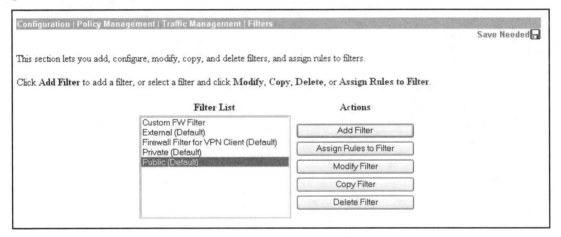

Look at what rules are applied to this filter by clicking the Assign Rules to Filter button. Quite a few rules should be applied to this default filter, but the ones you are interested in are L2L: Leeds to London In and L2L: Leeds to London Out. Notice that these have been automatically added to the filter, as shown in Figure 11-12.

Now look at these rules in more detail. Navigate to the Rules window by going to Configuration > Policy Management > Traffic Management > Rules. You see the screen shown in Figure 11-13.

Figure 11-12 *LAN Viewing the Filters*

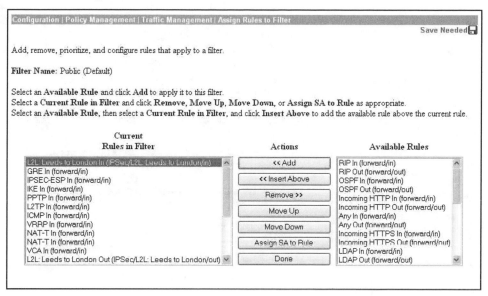

Figure 11-13 *Viewing the Rules on the Concentrator*

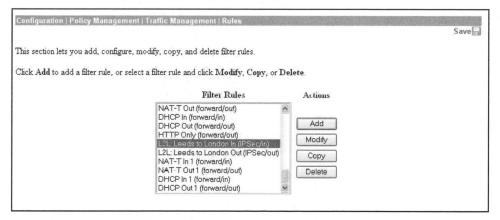

You can see all the rules that have been created on the Concentrator. Note that two rules have been created by the LAN-to-LAN connection process—L2L: Leeds to London In and L2L: Leeds to London Out. Figure 11-14 shows the L2L: Leeds to London In rule.

Figure 11-14 *Viewing L2L: Leeds to London In*

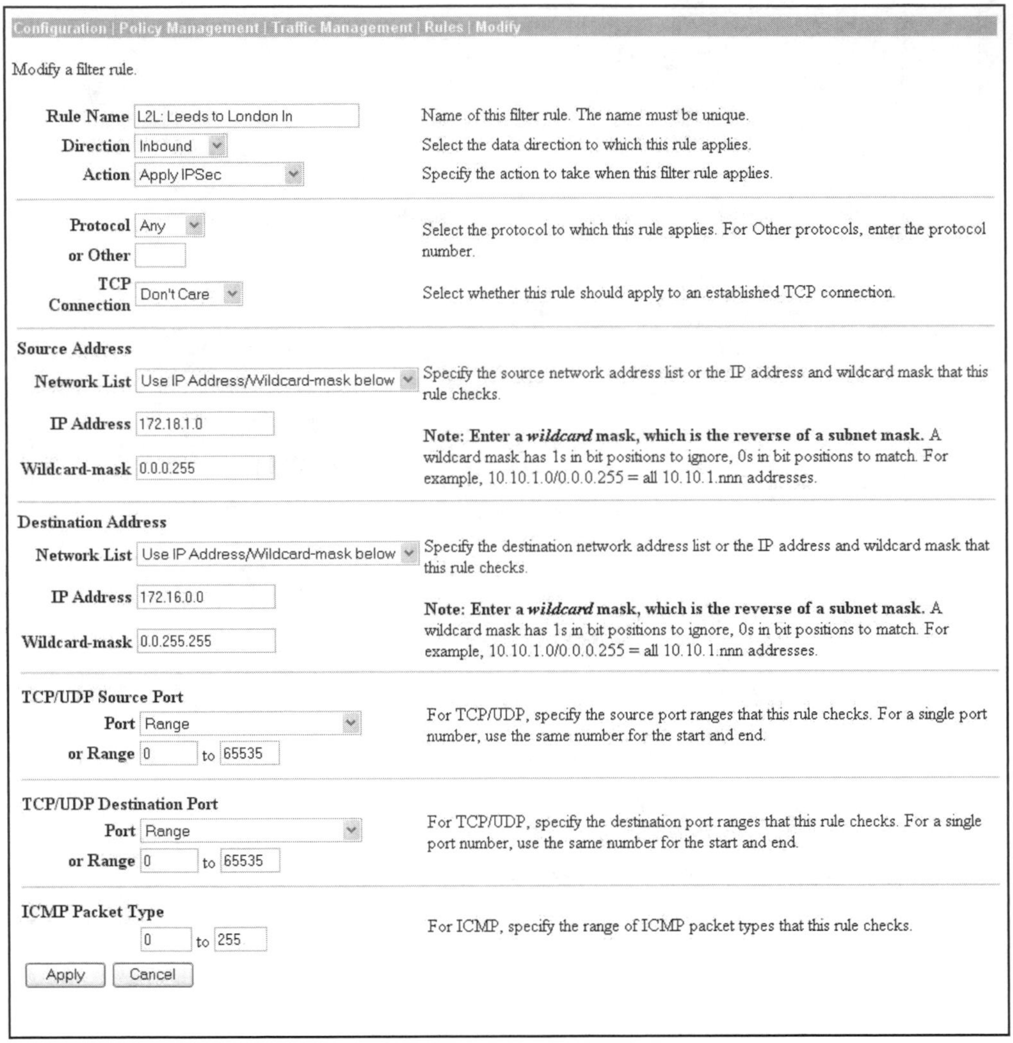

You can see from this figure that a lot of the information in this rule is very similar to what was configured in the LAN-to-LAN connection entry. The source and destination IP addresses match what you entered in the connection entry. The direction is inbound. Note that in the Action field, the action is Apply IPSec. This means that any traffic matching this rule has IPSec applied to it. Therefore, a matching SA and IKE policy are identified. As you have seen, this rule is applied to the public interface on the Concentrator.

Figure 11-15 shows the L2L: Leeds to London Out rule.

Figure 11-15 *Viewing L2L: Leeds to London Out*

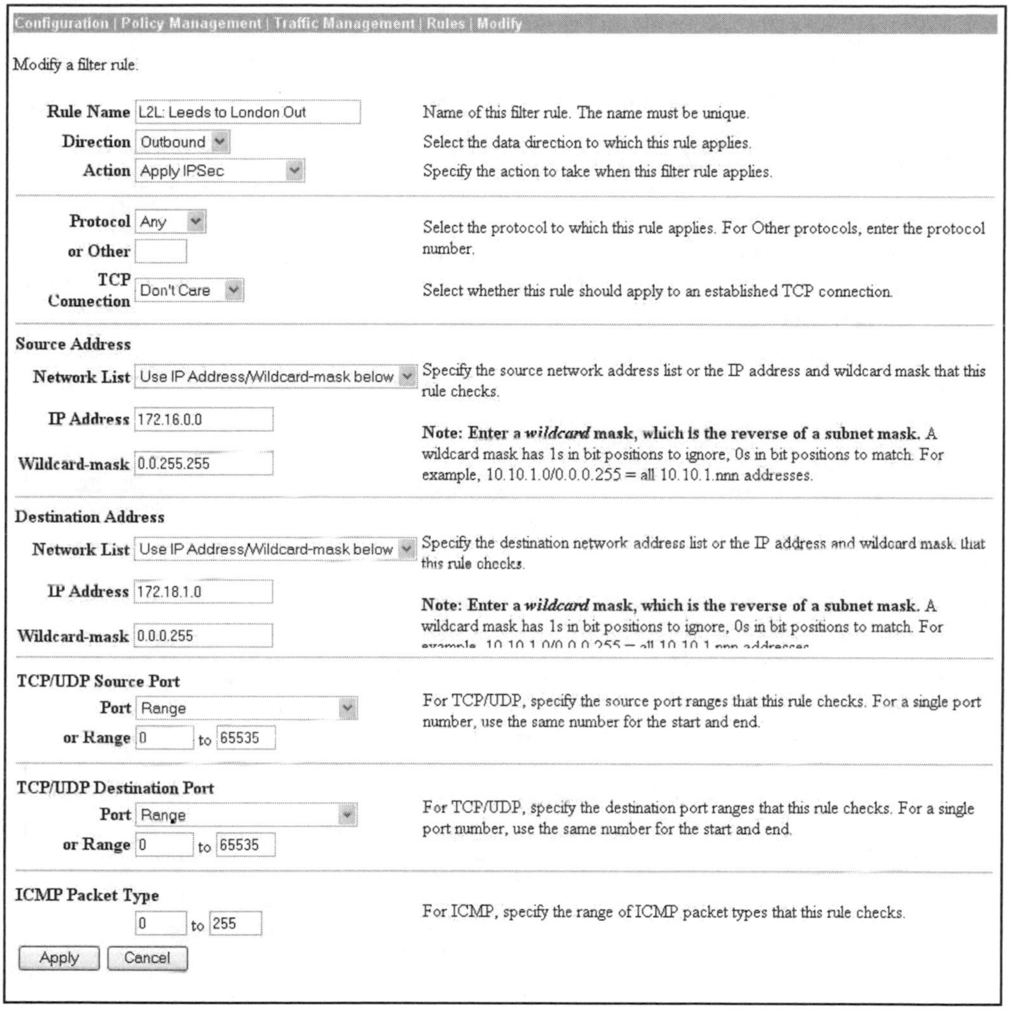

Everything in this rule is similar to the Inbound rule shown in Figure 11-14, except that the direction is now outbound and the source and destination addresses have been swapped.

With both these rules added to the outbound filter, and the outbound filter added to the external interface of the VPN 3000 Concentrator, you know that any traffic matching these rules will have IPSec applied to it.

Configuring the Remote Site LAN-to-LAN Connection

After you have configured the central site LAN-to-LAN connection, you have to create an identical LAN-to-LAN connection on the remote site. Basically, the only changes are to the remote peer IP address, local network, and remote network. Everything else is pretty much the same.

Figure 11-16 shows the completed LAN-to-LAN connection entry for the London to Leeds VPN.

Figure 11-16 *Viewing L2L: Leeds to London Out*

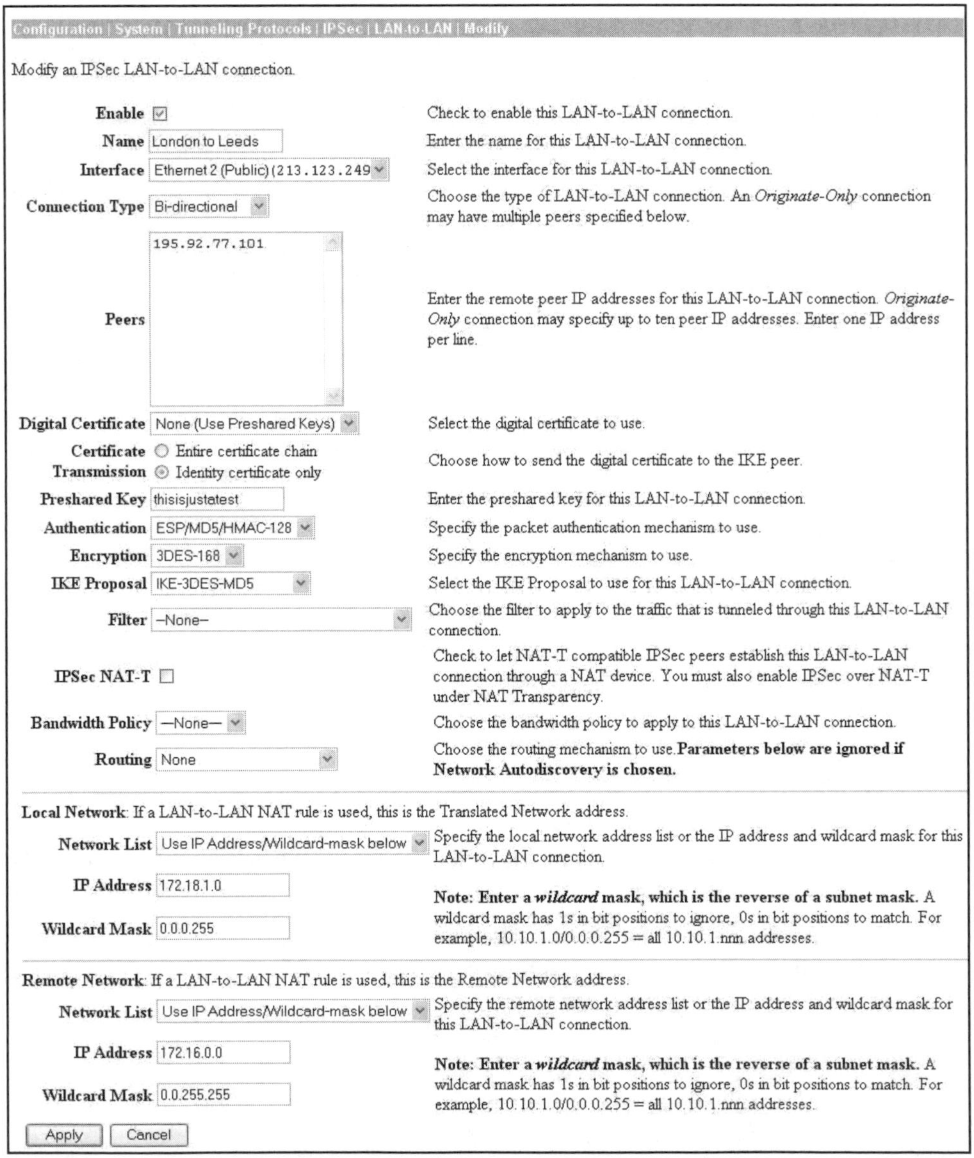

You can see from this figure that the peer IP address has changed to 195.92.77.101 and the local and remote networks have been swapped.

NOTE   As with any VPN, the preshared key must match between the local and remote VPN peers.

Administration of LAN-to-LAN VPN Tunnels

Choose Administration > Administer Sessions to verify the LAN-to-LAN tunnel, as shown in Figure 11-17. If the LAN-to-LAN tunnel is not listed, ping the private interface at the remote end. (The Concentrator needs to see interesting traffic bound for the remote network before it brings up a tunnel.) LAN-to-LAN sessions provide the following information:

- Connection name
- IP address (the public IP address of the remote Concentrator)
- Protocol
- Encryption
- Login time
- Duration
- Bytes Tx and Rx

From this screen you can manually log out and disconnect the LAN-to-LAN VPN as well as ping the remote end to check connectivity.

Figure 11-17 *Administrative View of the LAN-to-LAN Connection*

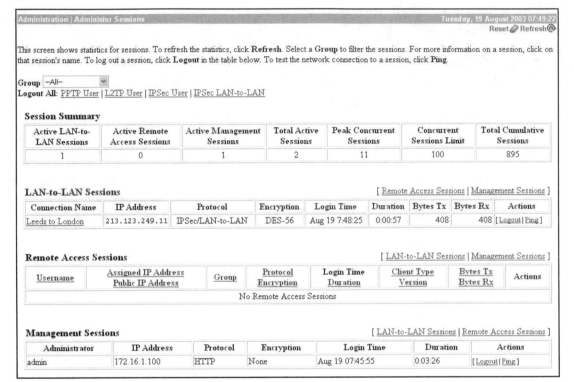

Dealing with Multiple Subnets

The previous examples had one tunnel with one subnet at each end of the tunnel. This is not a real-world example. The real world has multiple tunnels with multiple subnets at each remote site.

Before Release 2.1 of the Concentrator software, you had to define tunnels and all reachable subnets. You had to define each subnet-to-subnet connection individually. In a mesh network, that could be very time-consuming and error-prone.

In Release 2.1 and later, you can build a network list. In the network list you define all the subnets that can be reached at a particular site and give them a name (for example, Leeds or London). Instead of defining individual subnet-to-subnet tunnels, you can define one tunnel between each site and apply a network list to the private network at each site. In LAN-to-LAN configuration, the Concentrator can reference the applicable network lists for subnet information.

Also after Release 2.1, Network Auto-Discovery (NAD) was introduced. With NAD, you do not have to define local and remote network addresses or network lists. You define the LAN-to-LAN network information only: name, peer, remote address, preshared key, and routing (NAD). As long as Inbound Routing Information Protocol (RIP) is turned on, the Concentrator learns subnets from RIP. Each Concentrator then encrypts the RIP information and sends it through the tunnel to the remote Concentrator. (NAD currently is not supported with OSPF.)

Network Lists

Instead of defining individual subnet-to-subnet tunnels, you can define one tunnel between each site, define network lists for both ends, and apply a network list to each end. In the network list, you define all the subnets that can be reached at a particular site and give them a name (for example, Leeds or London). The local network list is built automatically via RIP. For the remote list, all reachable private subnets are configured manually.

Generate a list for both ends of the tunnel to use network lists:

* For the local list, click Generate Local List. The Concentrator generates networks from the routing table. The Concentrator uses inbound RIP, not OSPF. If necessary, edit the list. (For example, if you have a subnet you do not want to be accessible through the tunnel, delete the networks that need to remain private.) The last step is to name the list and click Add.

* For the remote list in the network list window, enter the subnet/wildcard for each reachable subnet. The subnet does not include the host, and the wildcard is the reverse of the subnet mask (subnet = 255.255.255.0, wildcard = 0.0.0.255).

A names network list called Leeds Networks is shown in Figure 11-18.

Figure 11-18 *Network Lists*

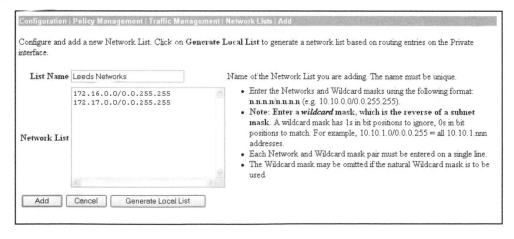

You can see that networks 172.16.0.0/16 and 172.17.0.0/16 have been added to this network list.

After you have created these network lists, they need to be added to the LAN-to-LAN connection entry.

Figure 11-19 shows the existing VPN Connection entry on the Leeds VPN Concentrator.

Figure 11-19 *Leeds LAN-to-LAN Connection Entry*

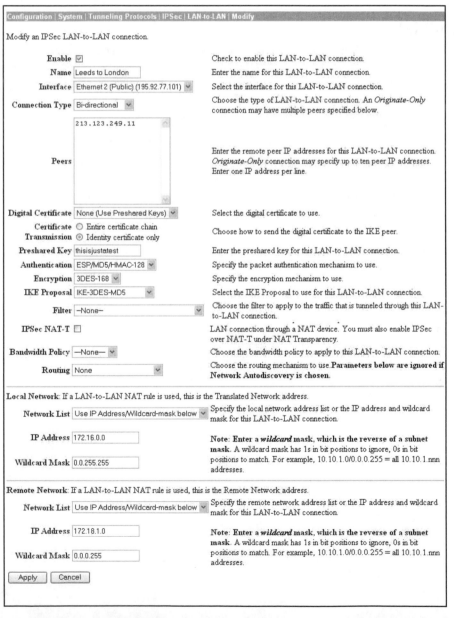

Notice in Figure 11-19 that the local and remote networks have been entered manually. You now will change the local network to use the network list you have created. To do this, remove the IP address and wildcard mask and then chose the network list from the drop-down box. Figure 11-20 shows the completed LAN-to-LAN connection entry with the local network list used.

Figure 11-20 *Leeds LAN-to-LAN Connection Entry Using Network Lists*

Configuration | System | Tunneling Protocols | IPSec | LAN-to-LAN | Modify

Modify an IPSec LAN-to-LAN connection.

Enable	☑	Check to enable this LAN-to-LAN connection.
Name	Leeds to London	Enter the name for this LAN-to-LAN connection.
Interface	Ethernet 2 (Public) (195.92.//.101) ▾	Select the interface for this LAN-to-LAN connection.
Connection Type	Bi-directional ▾	Choose the type of LAN-to-LAN connection. An *Originate-Only* connection may have multiple peers specified below.
Peers	213.123.249.11	Enter the remote peer IP addresses for this LAN-to-LAN connection. *Originate-Only* connection may specify up to ten peer IP addresses. Enter one IP address per line.
Digital Certificate	None (Use Preshared Keys) ▾	Select the digital certificate to use.
Certificate Transmission	○ Entire certificate chain ⊙ Identity certificate only	Choose how to send the digital certificate to the IKE peer.
Preshared Key	thisisjustatest	Enter the preshared key for this LAN-to-LAN connection.
Authentication	ESP/MD5/HMAC-128 ▾	Specify the packet authentication mechanism to use.
Encryption	3DES-168 ▾	Specify the encryption mechanism to use.
IKE Proposal	IKE-3DES-MD5 ▾	Select the IKE Proposal to use for this LAN-to-LAN connection.
Filter	--None-- ▾	Choose the filter to apply to the traffic that is tunneled through this LAN-to-LAN connection.
IPSec NAT-T	☐	Check to let NAT-T compatible IPSec peers establish this LAN-to-LAN connection through a NAT device. You must also enable IPSec over NAT-T under NAT Transparency.
Bandwidth Policy	--None-- ▾	Choose the bandwidth policy to apply to this LAN-to-LAN connection.
Routing	None ▾	Choose the routing mechanism to use. **Parameters below are ignored if Network Autodiscovery is chosen.**

Local Network: If a LAN-to-LAN NAT rule is used, this is the Translated Network address.

Network List	Leeds Networks ▾	Specify the local network address list or the IP address and wildcard mask for this LAN-to-LAN connection.
IP Address		**Note: Enter a *wildcard* mask, which is the reverse of a subnet mask.** A wildcard mask has 1s in bit positions to ignore, 0s in bit positions to match. For example, 10.10.1.0/0.0.0.255 = all 10.10.1.nnn addresses.
Wildcard Mask		

Remote Network: If a LAN-to-LAN NAT rule is used, this is the Remote Network address.

Network List	Use IP Address/Wildcard-mask below ▾	Specify the remote network address list or the IP address and wildcard mask for this LAN-to-LAN connection.
IP Address	172.18.1.0	**Note: Enter a *wildcard* mask, which is the reverse of a subnet mask.** A wildcard mask has 1s in bit positions to ignore, 0s in bit positions to match. For example, 10.10.1.0/0.0.0.255 = all 10.10.1.nnn addresses.
Wildcard Mask	0.0.0.255	

[Apply] [Cancel]

NAD

The NAD feature dynamically discovers and continuously updates the private network addresses on each side of the LAN-to-LAN connection. You do not have to define the private networks at both ends of the tunnel. The Concentrator learns local network addresses from local RIP updates. The Concentrators encrypt this information and send it through the tunnel to the remote end. From this information, the remote Concentrator learns what networks can be reached at the other end of the tunnel. For this feature to work, inbound RIP must be enabled on the private interface of both Concentrators.

Follow these steps to configure LAN-to-LAN using NAD:

Step 1 Enter a name in the Name field.

Step 2 Choose the remote address of the peer's public interface from the Interface drop-down menu.

Step 3 Define the preshared key or certificate in the Preshared Key field.

Step 4 Choose Network Autodiscovery from the Routing drop-down menu.

Step 5 Click Add.

The Concentrator can build a LAN-to-LAN tunnel from this information, as shown in Figure 11-21.

NOTE   NAD is not supported with OSPF.

Figure 11-21 *NAD*

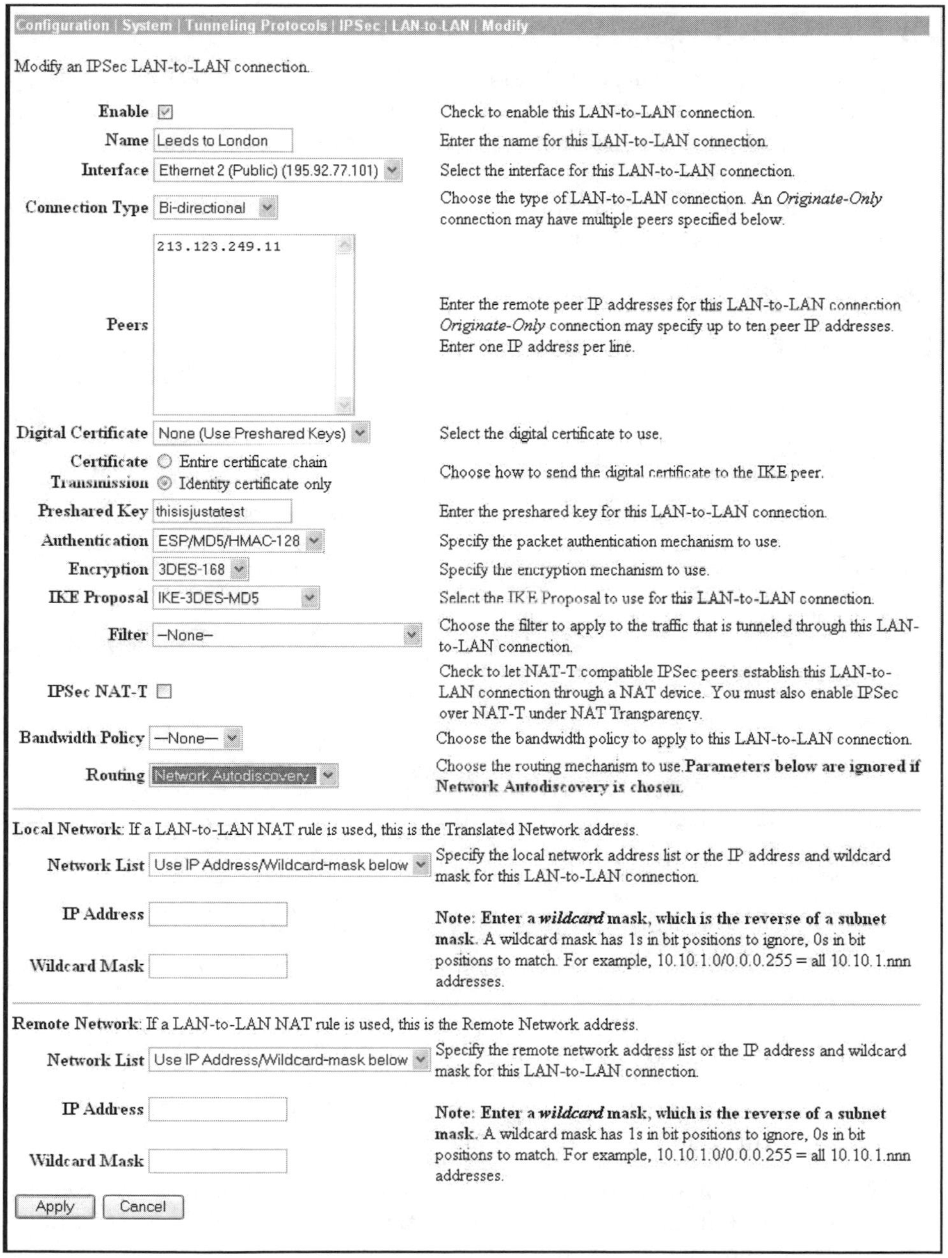

Configuration | System | Tunneling Protocols | IPSec | LAN-to-LAN | Modify

Modify an IPSec LAN-to-LAN connection.

Enable	☑	Check to enable this LAN-to-LAN connection.
Name	Leeds to London	Enter the name for this LAN-to-LAN connection.
Interface	Ethernet 2 (Public) (195.92.77.101) ▾	Select the interface for this LAN-to-LAN connection.
Connection Type	Bi-directional ▾	Choose the type of LAN-to-LAN connection. An *Originate-Only* connection may have multiple peers specified below.
Peers	213.123.249.11	Enter the remote peer IP addresses for this LAN-to-LAN connection. *Originate-Only* connection may specify up to ten peer IP addresses. Enter one IP address per line.
Digital Certificate	None (Use Preshared Keys) ▾	Select the digital certificate to use.
Certificate Transmission	○ Entire certificate chain ⦿ Identity certificate only	Choose how to send the digital certificate to the IKE peer.
Preshared Key	thisisjustatest	Enter the preshared key for this LAN-to-LAN connection.
Authentication	ESP/MD5/HMAC-128 ▾	Specify the packet authentication mechanism to use.
Encryption	3DES-168 ▾	Specify the encryption mechanism to use.
IKE Proposal	IKE-3DES-MD5 ▾	Select the IKE Proposal to use for this LAN-to-LAN connection.
Filter	–None– ▾	Choose the filter to apply to the traffic that is tunneled through this LAN-to-LAN connection.
IPSec NAT-T	☐	Check to let NAT-T compatible IPSec peers establish this LAN-to-LAN connection through a NAT device. You must also enable IPSec over NAT-T under NAT Transparency.
Bandwidth Policy	–None– ▾	Choose the bandwidth policy to apply to this LAN-to-LAN connection.
Routing	Network Autodiscovery ▾	Choose the routing mechanism to use. **Parameters below are ignored if Network Autodiscovery is chosen.**

Local Network: If a LAN-to-LAN NAT rule is used, this is the Translated Network address.

Network List	Use IP Address/Wildcard-mask below ▾	Specify the local network address list or the IP address and wildcard mask for this LAN-to-LAN connection.
IP Address		**Note: Enter a *wildcard* mask, which is the reverse of a subnet mask. A wildcard mask has 1s in bit positions to ignore, 0s in bit positions to match. For example, 10.10.1.0/0.0.0.255 = all 10.10.1.nnn addresses.**
Wildcard Mask		

Remote Network: If a LAN-to-LAN NAT rule is used, this is the Remote Network address.

Network List	Use IP Address/Wildcard-mask below ▾	Specify the remote network address list or the IP address and wildcard mask for this LAN-to-LAN connection.
IP Address		**Note: Enter a *wildcard* mask, which is the reverse of a subnet mask. A wildcard mask has 1s in bit positions to ignore, 0s in bit positions to match. For example, 10.10.1.0/0.0.0.255 = all 10.10.1.nnn addresses.**
Wildcard Mask		

Apply   Cancel

Configuring the VPN 3000 for a LAN-to-LAN VPN with Digital Certificates

Before you can configure a LAN-to-LAN VPN on the Cisco 3000 Concentrator, you have to ensure that the Concentrator is enrolled with a certification authority (CA) and has obtained both a CA and an identity certificate. Chapter 5, "Configuring the Cisco VPN 3000 for Remote Access Using Digital Certificates," shows you how to obtain a CA and identity certificate on the VPN 3000. After you have a CA and identity certificate, the Administration > Certificate Management window should look like Figure 11-22.

Figure 11-22 *Administration > Certificate Management Window*

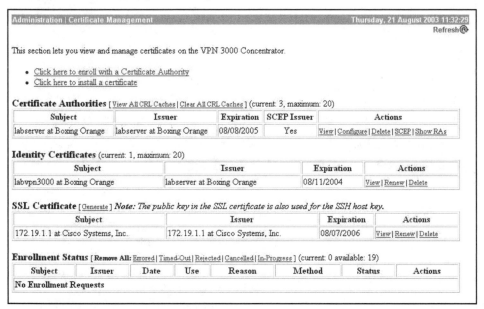

After you have configured each Concentrator for CA support, you can configure a LAN-to-LAN connection entry that uses digital certificates.

The whole operation for creating a LAN-to-LAN connection entry that uses digital certificates is virtually the same as the steps for creating a LAN-to-LAN connection entry using preshared keys. The only difference is that you set the LAN-to-LAN connection entry to use an identity certificate and an IKE proposal that uses RSA authentication.

When creating your LAN-to-LAN connection entry, follow all the steps given before, but in the Digital Certificate drop-down menu, select the configured identity certificate on your 3000 Concentrator. Then, from the IKE Proposal menu, select a proposal that uses digital certificates, such as IKE-3DES-MD5-RSA.

Figure 11-23 shows a configured LAN-to-LAN connection entry using digital certificates.

Figure 11-23 *LAN-to-LAN Connection Entry Using Digital Certificates*

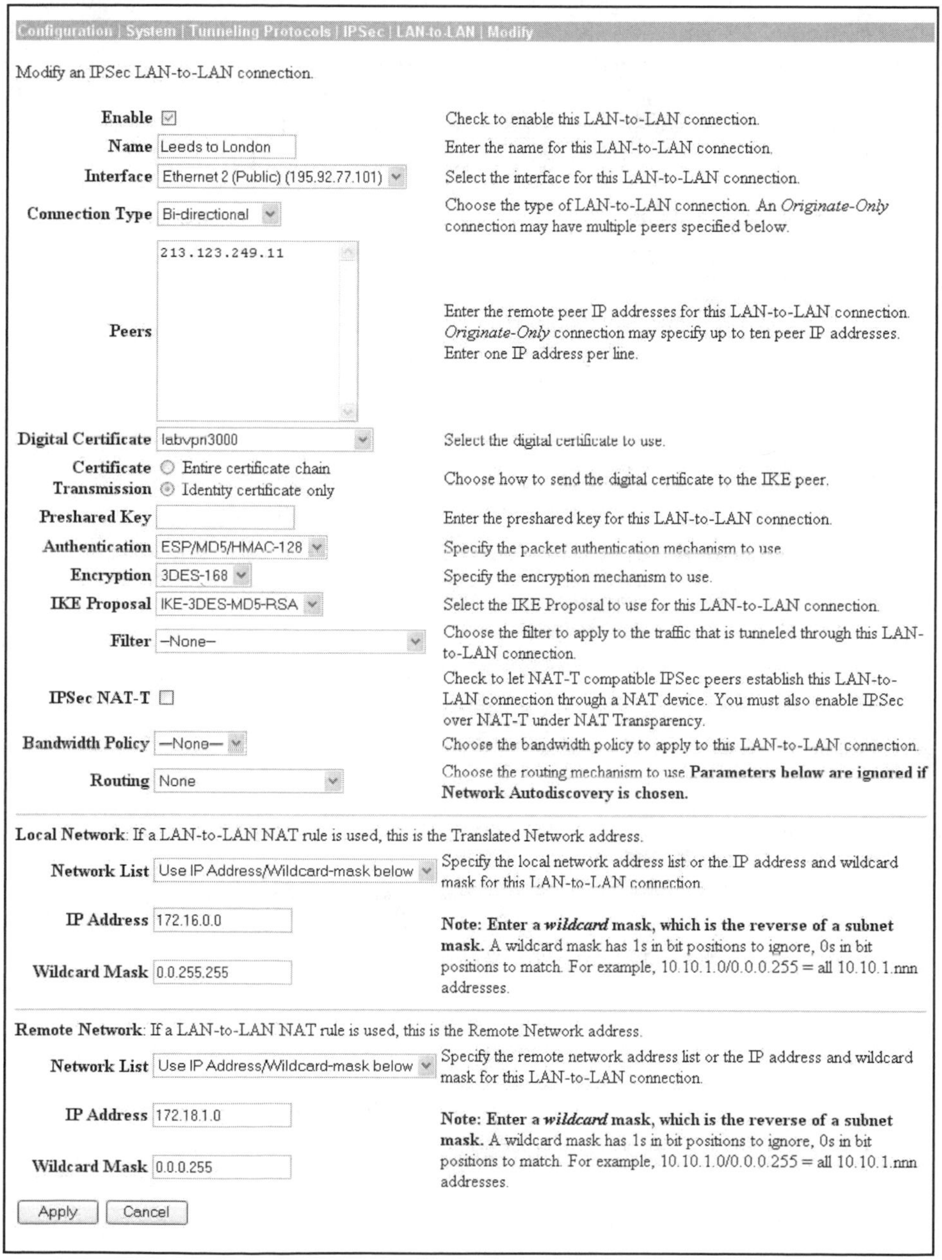

You can see that the necessary changes have been made to the preshared key example to allow for the use of digital certificates.

Recall from the preceding section that when you add a new LAN-to-LAN connection entry, three items are automatically configured: group, filter rules, and security association. The group and filter rules stay the same as they would for a preshared key connection entry, but the security association differs to include the use of digital certificates. This is changed automatically when you select digital certificates in the LAN-to-LAN connection entry. Figure 11-24 shows the updated security association for the LAN-to-LAN tunnel.

Figure 11-24 *Security Association Using Digital Certificates*

Summary

This chapter introduced LAN-to-LAN VPNs. It started by providing an overview of what a LAN-to-LAN VPN is and what it can be used for. The VPN Concentrator can be used for both remote-access and LAN-to-LAN VPNs. The primary focus of the VPN Concentrator series is remote-access VPNs. Using LAN-to-LAN VPNs is classed as a secondary function of the VPN Concentrator, with IOS router-to-IOS router as being the best design method for LAN-to-LAN VPNs.

This chapter also looked at configuring a LAN-to-LAN VPN between two sites using preshared keys. It then described network lists and NAD. The last section covered the configuration changes necessary to configure a LAN-to-LAN VPN using digital certificates.

Review Questions

The following questions test your retention of the material presented in this chapter. The answers appear in Appendix A, "Answers to the Review Questions."

1 What is one major difference between a LAN-to-LAN VPN and a remote-access VPN?

2 What are the three supported authentication options for LAN-to-LAN VPNs?

3 What menu option do you use to configure a LAN-to-LAN connection?

4 What three items does the LAN-to-LAN connection entry create?

5 What must you use in the LAN-to-LAN connection entry if you want to use more than one subnet across the VPN?

6 Which routing protocols does NAD work with?

After completing this chapter, you will be able to perform the following tasks:

- Understand the VPN Concentrator's monitoring and administration functions
- Perform daily monitoring tasks on the VPN Concentrator
- Perform daily administration tasks on the VPN Concentrator

CHAPTER 12

Network Monitoring and Administration

This chapter looks at the monitoring and administration features available with the VPN 3000. We have already covered how to configure the VPN Concentrator for remote-access and LAN-to-LAN VPNs. Now we will look at the Concentrator's monitoring and administration tools that can be used to support these VPN connections and perform routine administration tasks on the Concentrator. This chapter first covers the monitoring options and then discusses all the items available on the Concentrator's Administration menus. The chapter ends by looking at bandwidth management. We will cover the two main types of bandwidth management and provide working examples of both.

Monitoring on the VPN 3000

The Concentrator tracks many statistics and the status of many items essential to system administration and management. Monitoring lets you view Concentrator status, sessions, statistics, and event logs, including the following:

- **Routing table**—Current valid routes, protocols, and metrics
- **Dynamic filters**—Filters that are defined on an external server, such as a RADIUS or ACS server
- **Filterable event log**—Current event log in memory
- **System status**—Current software revisions, uptime, system power supplies, Ethernet interfaces, front-panel LEDs, and hardware sensors
- **Sessions**—Currently active sessions sorted by protocol, Scalable Encryption Processing (SEP), and encryption, and top ten sessions sorted by data, duration, and throughput
- **General statistics**—Point-to-Point Tunneling Protocol (PPTP), Layer 2 Tunneling Protocol (L2TP), IPSec, HTTP, events, Telnet, Domain Name System (DNS), authentication, accounting, filtering, Virtual Router Redundancy Protocol (VRRP), Secure Socket Layer (SSL), load balancing, and compression; and MIB-II objects for interfaces, TCP/UDP, IP, Internet Control Message Protocol (ICMP), and Address Resolution Protocol (ARP)

The Monitoring index screen is shown in Figure 12-1.

Figure 12-1 *Monitoring Index Screen*

Monitoring

This section of the Manager lets you view **VPN 3000 Concentrator** status, sessions, statistics, and event logs.

In the left frame, or in the list of links below, click the function you want:

- Routing Table -- current valid routes and protocols.
- Dynamic Filters -- view dynamic filters and their dynamic rules.
- Filterable Event Log -- current event log.
  - Live Event Log -- current event log.
- System Status -- current software revisions, uptime, front-panel LEDs, network interfaces, SEP modules, and power supplies.
  - LED Status -- front-panel LEDs.
  - Memory Status -- free bytes, used bytes, usage etc.
- Sessions -- all active sessions and "top ten" sessions.
- Statistics -- accounting, address pools, administrative AAA, authentication, authorization, bandwidth management, compression, DHCP, DNS, events, filtering, HTTP, IPSec, L2TP, load balancing, NAT, PPTP, SSH, SSL, Telnet, VRRP and MIB-II statistics.

Routing Table

The Monitoring > Routing Table window, shown in Figure 12-2, lets an administrator view the Concentrator's routing table. The IP routing subsystem examines the destination IP address of packets coming through the Concentrator and forwards or drops them according to the routing table.

Figure 12-2 *Routing Table*

Monitoring | Routing Table   Monday, 25 August 2003 07:46:03
                                                                                 Refresh

Clear Routes

Valid Routes: 5

Address	Mask	Next Hop	Interface	Protocol	Age	Metric
0.0.0.0	0.0.0.0	195.92.77.97	2	Default	0	1
172.16.8.0	255.255.255.0	0.0.0.0	3	Local	0	1
172.18.1.0	255.255.255.0	172.19.1.20	1	Static	0	1
172.19.1.0	255.255.255.0	0.0.0.0	1	Local	0	1
195.92.77.96	255.255.255.224	0.0.0.0	2	Local	0	1

The table includes all routes that the IP routing subsystem knows about, from whatever source: static routes learned via IP and Open Shortest Path First (OSPF) routing protocols, interface addresses, and so on. The Monitoring > Routing Table window lets you view the following:

- Valid routes
- Addresses and masks
- The next hop
- Interface
- Protocol
- Age
- Metric

NOTE   The routing table is also available through the command-line interface (CLI).

Dynamic Filters

The VPN Concentrator allows you to define remote-access user filters on an external RADIUS server, such as Cisco Secure ACS, rather than on the VPN Concentrator. Using an external RADIUS server allows centralized filter management and greater scalability. Also, configuring filters in this way allows you to assign filters to a particular tunnel group or user.

These filters are called *dynamic filters* because they remain in place only for the duration of the session to which they apply. When a user authenticates via RADIUS, the VPN Concentrator downloads the filter associated with the user and applies it for the duration of the connection. When the connection finishes, the filter drops.

You configure this feature on the RADIUS server, not on the VPN Concentrator.

Figure 12-3 displays the monitoring screen. No dynamic filters are in place because no users who are connected have them set in their RADIUS profiles.

Figure 12-3   *Dynamic Filters*

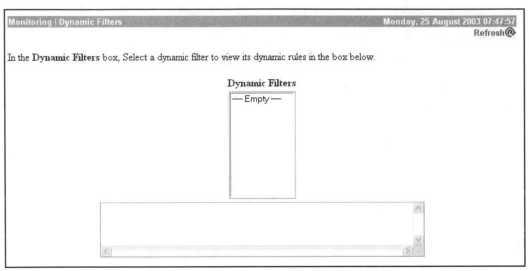

Filterable Event Log

The Monitoring > Filterable Event Log window, shown in Figure 12-4, enables graphical user interface (GUI) access for viewing events in the current event log. The log holds up to 2048 events and wraps when full. The administrator also can manage the event log file. You can select any or all of the following six options for filtering and displaying the event log:

- **Event Class drop-down menu**—Choose the event class to display all the events in a single event class.

- **Severities drop-down menu**—Choose the severity level to display all the events of a single severity level.

- **Client IP Address field**—Displays all the events relating to a single IP address. The specific IP address is entered manually.

- **Events/Page drop-down menu**—Select a number to display a given number of events per manager screen (page).

- **Group drop-down menu**—Allows you to display logs for a specific group that has been configured on the Concentrator.

- **Direction drop-down menu**—Lets you choose to view the logs from Oldest to Newest or from Newest to Oldest.

Figure 12-4 *Filterable Event Log*

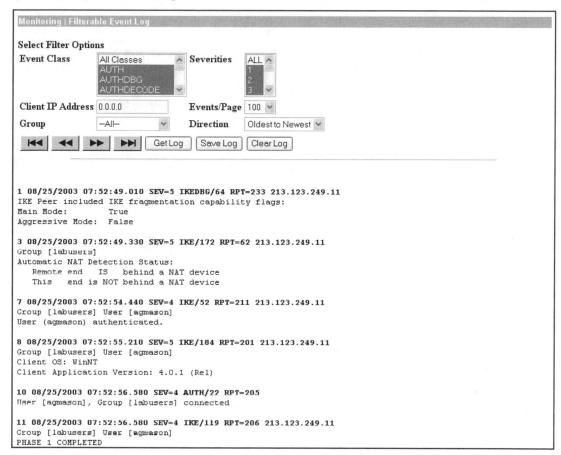

After selecting the options, click any one of the six Page buttons to retrieve events.

The event log can be retrieved from the Concentrator via Telnet, FTP, or HTTP.

Live Event Log

A suboption of the Filterable Event Log is the Live Event Log.

The Live Event Log window displays events in the current event log and automatically updates the display every 5 seconds. The events might take a few seconds to load when you first open the window. The window always displays the most recent event at the bottom. Use the scrollbar to view earlier events.

If you keep this Concentrator Manager window open, your administrative session does not time out. Each automatic window update resets the inactivity timer. The buttons at the bottom of the Live Event Log window are as follows:

- **Pause Display**—Pauses the display. While paused, the window does not display new events, the button changes to Resume Display, and the timer counts down to 0 and stops. You can still scroll through the event log.

- **Resume Display button**—After you click the Pause Display button, the button changes to Resume Display, and the timer counts down to 0 and stops. Click Resume to resume the display of new events and restart the timer.

- **Clear Display button**—Clears the event display. This action does not clear the event log; it only clears the display of events on this window.

- **Restart button**—Clears the event display and reloads the entire event log in the display. This action does not clear the event log; it only clears the display of events on this window.

- **Timer**—The timer counts 5, 4, 3, 2, and 1 to show where it is in the 5-second refresh cycle. The Receiving message at the bottom of the Live Event Log window indicates the receipt of new events. A steady 0 indicates that the display has been paused.

NOTE   The live event log requires Microsoft Internet Explorer Release 4.0 or higher, or Netscape versions 4.5 through 4.7 or 6.0.

System Status

The Monitoring > System Status window, shown in Figure 12-5, lets the administrator view information on both the hardware and software.

Figure 12-5 *System Status*

The system status display lets you view the following:

- Bootcode revision and software revision
- Uptime
- Fan speed
- RAM size
- Temperature
- CPU use
- Active sessions
- Aggregate throughput
- LED status
- Concentrator's memory status

The system status display can be used for quick and easy checks of the basic systems operations.

Besides the Monitoring > System Status window, you can also access and view the hardware and software status via the CLI or through Simple Network Management Protocol (SNMP).

LED Status

The Monitoring > System Status > LED Status window, shown in Figure 12-6, lets the administrator view all Concentrator front panel LEDs. The LED indicator can be used to obtain the following information:

- System
  - Green—Power on
  - Amber—System has crashed and halted; there is an error
  - Off—Power off; all other LEDs are off
- Ethernet Link Status—1, 2, 3
  - Green—Connected to the network and enabled
  - Blinking green—Connected to the network and configured, but disabled
  - Off—Not connected to the network or not enabled
- Expansion Modules Insertion Status—1, 2, 3, 4
  - Green—SEP module is installed in the system
  - Off—SEP module is not installed in the system
- Expansion Modules Run Status—1, 2, 3, 4
  - Green—SEP module is operational
  - Off—If installed, the SEP module has failed diagnostics, or the encryption code is not running; there is an error
- Fan Status
  - Green—Operating normally
  - Amber—Not running or the RPM is below normal range; there is an error
- Power Supplies—A, B
  - Green—Installed and operating normally
  - Amber—Voltages are outside normal ranges; there is an error
  - Off—Not installed

Figure 12-6 *LED Status*

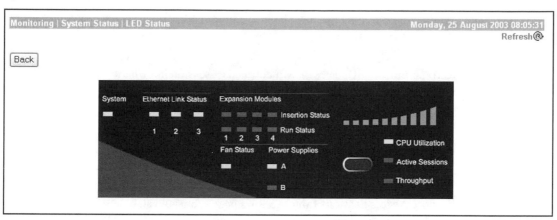

Memory Status

The Memory Status screen, shown in Figure 12-7, displays the system memory summary as well as a breakdown of the block usage list.

Figure 12-7 *Memory Status*

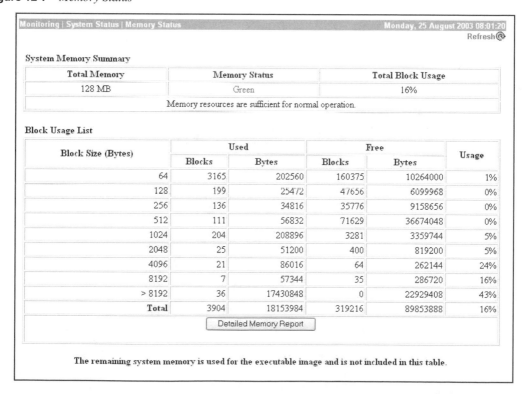

Sessions

The Monitoring > Sessions window, shown in Figure 12-8, displays comprehensive data for currently active user and administrator sessions on the Concentrator. The following session information is available:

- **Refresh button**—Updates the window and its session information. The date and time indicate when the window was last updated.
- **Session Summary table**—Shows summary totals for LAN-to-LAN, remote-access, and management sessions.
- **LAN-to-LAN Sessions table**—Shows parameters and statistics for all active IPSec LAN-to-LAN sessions. Each session identifies only the outer LAN-to-LAN connection or tunnel, not individual host-to-host sessions within the tunnel.
- **Remote Access Sessions table**—Shows parameters and statistics for all active remote-access sessions. Each session is a single-user connection from a remote client to the Concentrator.
- **Management Sessions table**—Shows parameters and statistics for all active administrator management sessions on the Concentrator.

Under the Monitoring > Sessions window are four suboptions:

- Protocols
- SEPs
- Encryption
- Top Ten Lists

Protocols

The Protocols submenu displays the protocols in use on the Concentrator and the number of active sessions per protocol, as shown in Figure 12-9.

Figure 12-8 *Monitor Sessions*

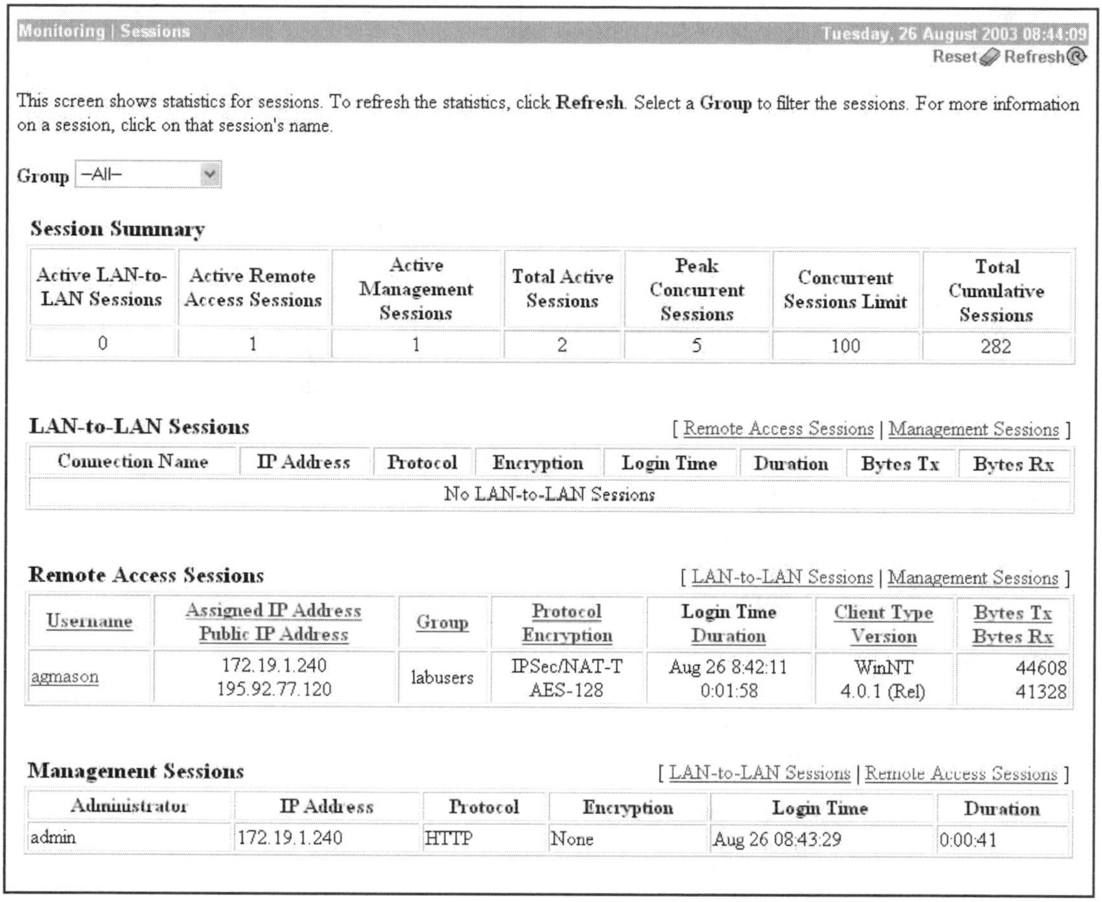

Reset🖋 Refresh®

This screen shows statistics for sessions. To refresh the statistics, click **Refresh**. Select a **Group** to filter the sessions. For more information on a session, click on that session's name.

Group —All—

Session Summary

Active LAN-to-LAN Sessions	Active Remote Access Sessions	Active Management Sessions	Total Active Sessions	Peak Concurrent Sessions	Concurrent Sessions Limit	Total Cumulative Sessions
0	1	1	2	5	100	282

LAN-to-LAN Sessions   [Remote Access Sessions | Management Sessions]

Connection Name	IP Address	Protocol	Encryption	Login Time	Duration	Bytes Tx	Bytes Rx
No LAN-to-LAN Sessions							

Remote Access Sessions   [LAN-to-LAN Sessions | Management Sessions]

Username	Assigned IP Address Public IP Address	Group	Protocol Encryption	Login Time Duration	Client Type Version	Bytes Tx Bytes Rx
agmason	172.19.1.240 195.92.77.120	labusers	IPSec/NAT-T AES-128	Aug 26 8:42:11 0:01:58	WinNT 4.0.1 (Rel)	44608 41328

Management Sessions   [LAN-to-LAN Sessions | Remote Access Sessions]

Administrator	IP Address	Protocol	Encryption	Login Time	Duration
admin	172.19.1.240	HTTP	None	Aug 26 08:43:29	0:00:41

Figure 12-9 *Monitoring > Sessions > Protocols*

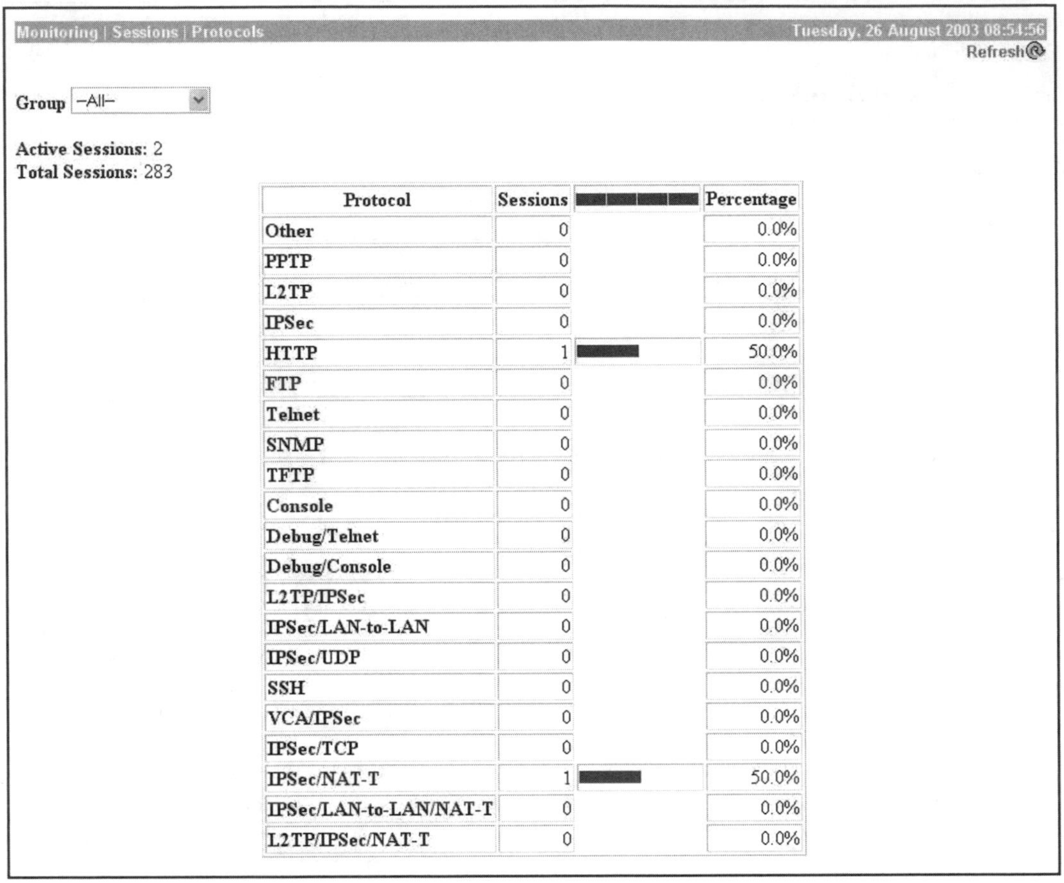

Monitoring | Sessions | Protocols
Tuesday, 26 August 2003 08:54:56
Refresh

Group —All—

Active Sessions: 2
Total Sessions: 283

Protocol	Sessions		Percentage
Other	0		0.0%
PPTP	0		0.0%
L2TP	0		0.0%
IPSec	0		0.0%
HTTP	1		50.0%
FTP	0		0.0%
Telnet	0		0.0%
SNMP	0		0.0%
TFTP	0		0.0%
Console	0		0.0%
Debug/Telnet	0		0.0%
Debug/Console	0		0.0%
L2TP/IPSec	0		0.0%
IPSec/LAN-to-LAN	0		0.0%
IPSec/UDP	0		0.0%
SSH	0		0.0%
VCA/IPSec	0		0.0%
IPSec/TCP	0		0.0%
IPSec/NAT-T	1		50.0%
IPSec/LAN-to-LAN/NAT-T	0		0.0%
L2TP/IPSec/NAT-T	0		0.0%

SEPs

The SEPs submenu displays the number of connections that are active on each installed SEP. Figure 12-10 displays this screen even though the Concentrator in use does not have any SEPs installed.

Figure 12-10 *Monitoring > Sessions > SEPs*

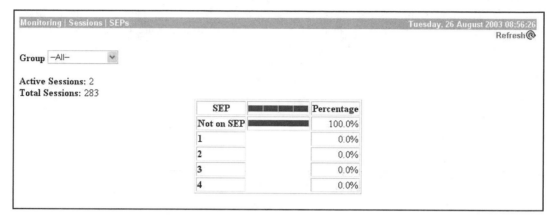

Encryption

The Encryption submenu, shown in Figure 12-11, displays the configured encryption algorithms on the VPN Concentrator and identifies the number of active sessions using each type of encryption.

Figure 12-11 *Monitoring > Sessions > Encryption*

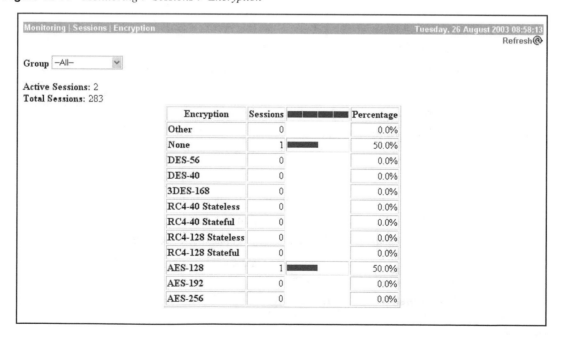

Top Ten Lists

The top ten submenu displays statistics for the top ten currently active sessions. These statistics can be sorted by Data, Duration, or Throughput. Figure 12-12 shows the top ten connections sorted by data.

Figure 12-12 *Monitoring > Sessions > Top Ten Lists*

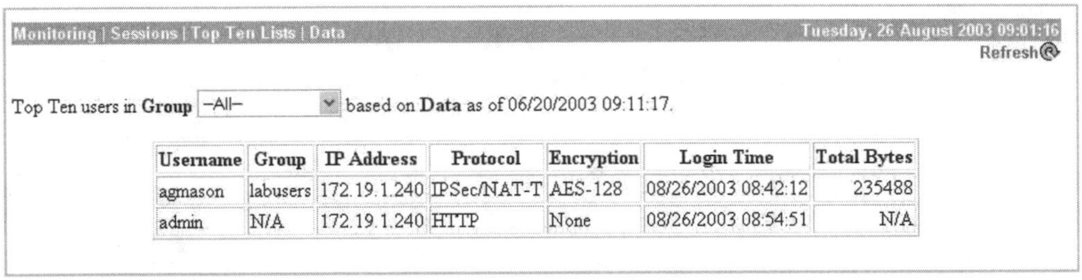

Username	Group	IP Address	Protocol	Encryption	Login Time	Total Bytes
agmason	labusers	172.19.1.240	IPSec/NAT-T	AES-128	08/26/2003 08:42:12	235488
admin	N/A	172.19.1.240	HTTP	None	08/26/2003 08:54:51	N/A

General Statistics

The Monitoring > Statistics window displays statistics for traffic and activity on the Concentrator since it was last booted or reset. You can monitor the following:

- **Accounting**—Total requests, responses, timeouts
- **Address Pools**—Configured pools and allocated addresses
- **Administrative AAA**—Requests, accepts, rejects, challenges, timeouts
- **Authentication**—Total requests, accepts, rejects, challenges, timeouts
- **Authorization**—Total requests, accepts, rejects, challenges, timeouts
- **Bandwidth Management**—Bandwidth traffic rate and traffic volume per group
- **Compression**—Precompressed, post-compressed, ratios
- **DHCP**—Leases and durations
- **DNS**—Total requests, responses, timeouts
- **Events**—Total events sorted by class, number, and count
- **Filtering**—Total inbound and outbound traffic filtered by the interface
- **HTTP**—Total data traffic and connection statistics
- **IPSec**—Tunnels, received and transmitted packets, session details
- **L2TP**—Total tunnels, sessions, received and transmitted control, data packets, detailed current session data
- **Load Balancing**—Load, state, peers

- **MIB-II Stats**—Interfaces, TCP and UDP, IP, ICMP, ARP
- **NAT**—Sessions, inbound and outbound packets
- **PPTP**—Total tunnels, sessions, received and transmitted control, data packets, detailed current session data
- **SSH**—Sessions, inbound and outbound
- **SSL**—Sessions and encrypted versus decrypted traffic
- **Telnet**—Total sessions and current session inbound and outbound traffic
- **VRRP**—Total advertisements, master router roles, errors

Administration of the VPN 3000

The Administration window in the Manager, shown in Figure 12-13, lets you control administrative functions on the Concentrator. The following functions are available:

- **Administer Sessions**—View statistics for logout, and ping sessions
- **Software Update**—Upload and update the Concentrator software image, and upload and update the VPN Software Client image
- **System Reboot**—Set options for the Concentrator shutdown and reboot
- **Reboot Status**—Provides information about scheduled reboots
- **Ping**—Use ICMP ping to determine connectivity
- **Monitoring Refresh**—Enables an automatic refresh of status and statistics in the monitoring section of the Manager
- **Access Rights**—The administrator can customize user profiles, access control lists (ACLs), and administration session parameters:
    - ACL—Configure IP addresses for workstations with access rights
    - Administrators—Configure administrator usernames, passwords, and rights
    - Access settings—Set the administrative session idle timeout and limits
- **File Management**—Configuration, event log, and certificate request files are stored in Flash memory. File management lets the administrator manage these files in Flash memory:
    - Files—Copy, view, and delete system files
    - Swap Configuration Files—Swap backup and boot configuration files
    - TFTP transfer—Transfer files to and from the Concentrator
    - File upload—Transfer files to the Concentrator

- **Certificate Management**—Lets you install and manage digital certificates:

  — Enrollment—Create a certificate request to send to a certification authority (CA)

  — Installation—Install digital certificates

  — Certificates—View, modify, and delete digital certificates

Figure 12-13 *Administration Index Screen*

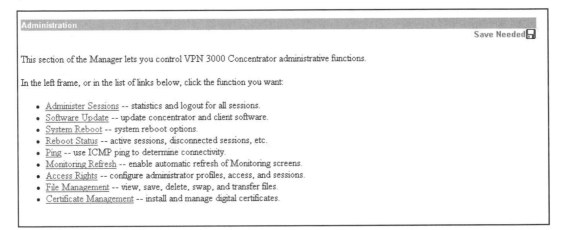

Administer Sessions

The Administer Sessions screen, shown in Figure 12-14, is very similar to the Monitoring > Sessions screen shown earlier in Figure 12-8. The difference with the Administer Sessions screen is that you can log out connections and ping connections to ensure network layer reachability.

You can choose to log out all users by connection type or individual LAN-to-LAN and remote-access connections.

Software Update

The Software Update window, shown in Figure 12-15, lets you update executable system software on both the Concentrator and Cisco VPN Clients. Select the Concentrator whose software you want to update. Choose Clients to update the hardware and Windows Software Client.

Figure 12-14 *Administer Sessions Screen*

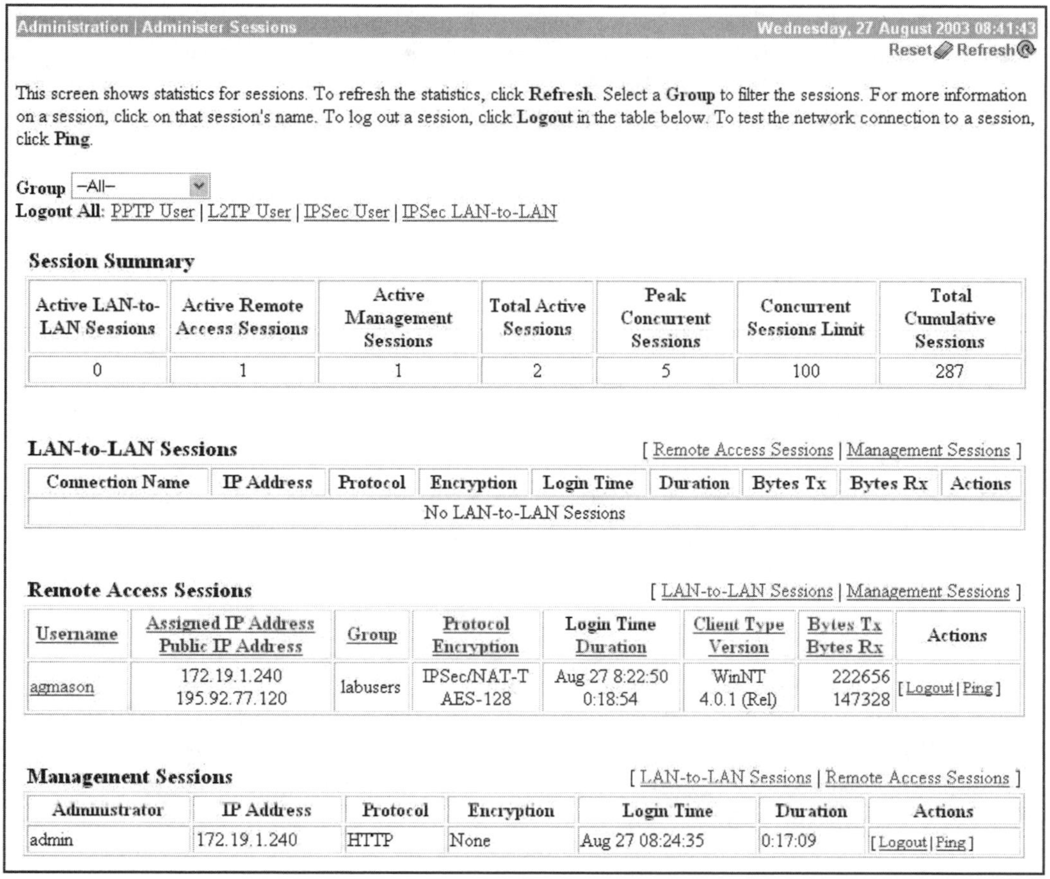

Reset ✐ Refresh ⓡ

This screen shows statistics for sessions. To refresh the statistics, click **Refresh**. Select a **Group** to filter the sessions. For more information on a session, click on that session's name. To log out a session, click **Logout** in the table below. To test the network connection to a session, click **Ping**.

Group –All–

Logout All: PPTP User | L2TP User | IPSec User | IPSec LAN-to-LAN

Session Summary

Active LAN-to-LAN Sessions	Active Remote Access Sessions	Active Management Sessions	Total Active Sessions	Peak Concurrent Sessions	Concurrent Sessions Limit	Total Cumulative Sessions
0	1	1	2	5	100	287

LAN-to-LAN Sessions   [Remote Access Sessions | Management Sessions]

Connection Name	IP Address	Protocol	Encryption	Login Time	Duration	Bytes Tx	Bytes Rx	Actions
			No LAN-to-LAN Sessions					

Remote Access Sessions   [LAN-to-LAN Sessions | Management Sessions]

Username	Assigned IP Address / Public IP Address	Group	Protocol / Encryption	Login Time / Duration	Client Type / Version	Bytes Tx / Bytes Rx	Actions
agmason	172.19.1.240 / 195.92.77.120	labusers	IPSec/NAT-T / AES-128	Aug 27 8:22:50 / 0:18:54	WinNT / 4.0.1 (Rel)	222656 / 147328	[Logout	Ping]

Management Sessions   [LAN-to-LAN Sessions | Remote Access Sessions]

Administrator	IP Address	Protocol	Encryption	Login Time	Duration	Actions
admin	172.19.1.240	HTTP	None	Aug 27 08:24:35	0:17:09	[Logout	Ping]

Figure 12-15 *Software Updates*

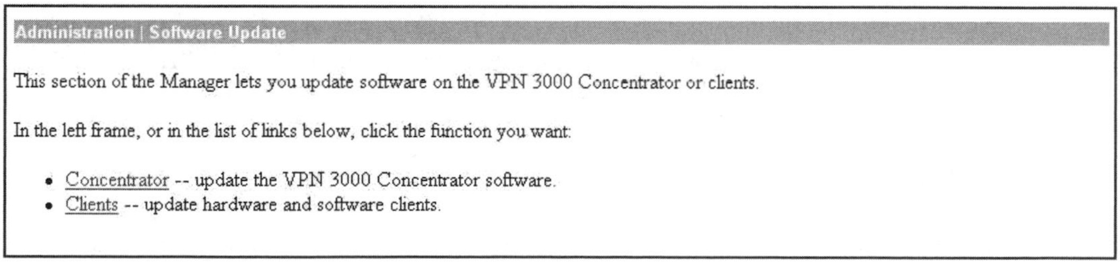

This section of the Manager lets you update software on the VPN 3000 Concentrator or clients.

In the left frame, or in the list of links below, click the function you want:

- Concentrator -- update the VPN 3000 Concentrator software.
- Clients -- update hardware and software clients.

Concentrator Update

The Administrator > Software Update > Concentrator window, shown in Figure 12-16, lets you update the Concentrator executable system software (the software image). The new image file must be accessible by the workstation you are using to manage the Concentrator. This process uploads the file to the Concentrator, which then verifies the file's integrity. It takes a few minutes to upload and verify the software, and the system displays the progress. Wait for the operation to finish.

You must reboot the Concentrator to run the new software image. The system prompts you to reboot when the update is finished.

Figure 12-16 *Concentrator Software Updates*

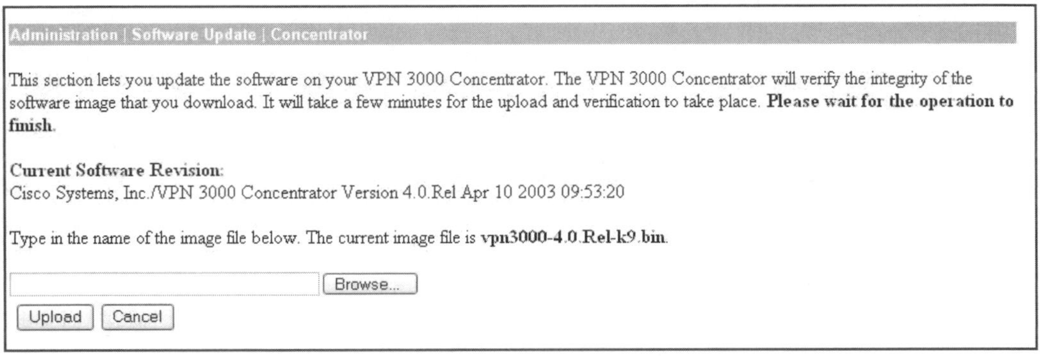

```
Administration | Software Update | Concentrator

This section lets you update the software on your VPN 3000 Concentrator. The VPN 3000 Concentrator will verify the integrity of the
software image that you download. It will take a few minutes for the upload and verification to take place. Please wait for the operation to
finish.

Current Software Revision:
Cisco Systems, Inc./VPN 3000 Concentrator Version 4.0.Rel Apr 10 2003 09:53:20

Type in the name of the image file below. The current image file is vpn3000-4.0.Rel-k9.bin.

[                              ]  [ Browse... ]
[ Upload ]  [ Cancel ]
```

NOTE   While the system is updating the image, do not perform any other operations that affect Flash memory (listing, viewing, copying, deleting, or writing files). Doing so can corrupt the system memory.

Client Update

Network administrators of remote-access VPNs are looking to Cisco to help them push Software Client upgrades to their users in some type of automated, informed fashion. To that end, the Concentrator has provided a client update notification feature to notify the Unity Software Client when update software is available.

Updating client software in an environment with a large number of devices in different locations can be a formidable task. For this reason, the Concentrator includes a Client Update feature that simplifies the software update process. This feature works differently for Cisco VPN Software Clients and Cisco VPN 3002 Hardware Clients. The Hardware Client and Software Client update processes are as follows:

- **Software Clients**—The client update feature allows administrators at a central location to automatically notify Software Client users when it is time to update the Software Client. When you enable Client Update, during tunnel establishment the central site Concentrator sends an IKE packet that notifies Cisco VPN Clients of acceptable versions of the Software Client. It includes a location that contains the new version of software for the Cisco VPN Client to download. The administrator for that Software Client can then retrieve the new software version and update the client at a time of his or her choosing.

- **Hardware Clients**—When you enable Client Update for the Hardware Client, during tunnel establishment the central site Concentrator sends an IKE packet that notifies Hardware Clients of acceptable versions of executable system software and their locations. If the Hardware Client is not running an acceptable version, it automatically attempts to download the new revision of code via TFTP. The Hardware Client Update feature is covered in depth in Chapter 7, "Configuring the Cisco 3002 Hardware Client for Remote Access".

System Reboot

The System Reboot screen, shown in Figure 12-17, allows you to make an instant or scheduled reboot of the VPN Concentrator. You can reboot and save the active configuration, reboot and not save the active configuration, or reboot and ignore the active configuration. The last option is a good way to perform a factory reset on the Concentrator, because it boots as if it is a fresh unit shipped from distribution.

Figure 12-17   *Concentrator System Reboot*

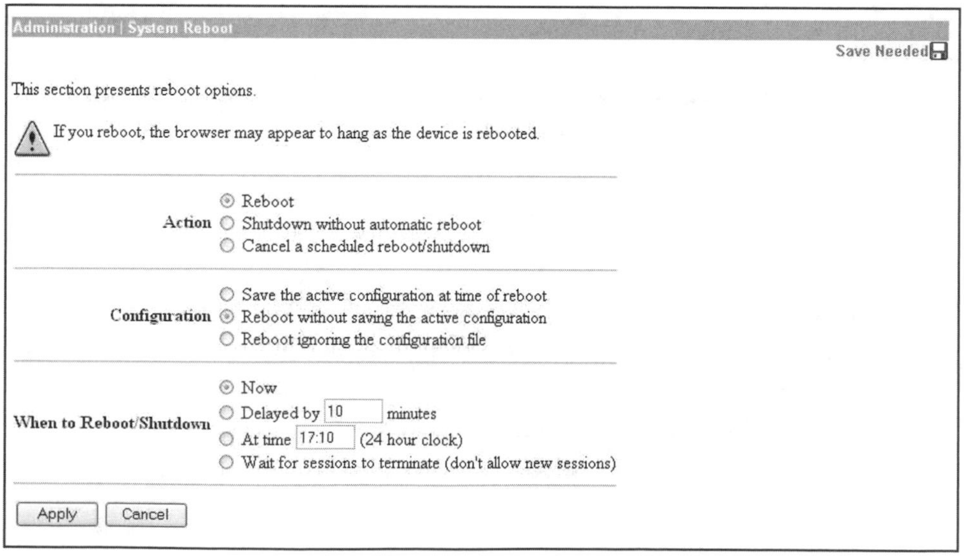

Reboot Status

The Reboot Status screen displays the status of any scheduled reboots. If you have a reboot scheduled, you can check the reboot time by looking at this screen. Figure 12-18 informs you that a reboot is to happen in 10 minutes.

Figure 12-18 *Concentrator Reboot Status*

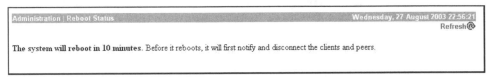

Ping

The Ping window lets you use the ICMP ping utility to test network connectivity. Specifically, the Concentrator sends an ICMP echo request message to a designated host. If the host can be reached, it returns an echo reply message, and the Manager displays a Success window. If the host cannot be reached, the Manager displays an Error window.

Monitoring Refresh

The Monitoring Refresh window, shown in Figure 12-19, is where you can enable the automatic refreshing of the statistics window. You also have the option to set the refresh period. The default refresh period is 30 seconds.

Figure 12-19 *Monitoring Refresh*

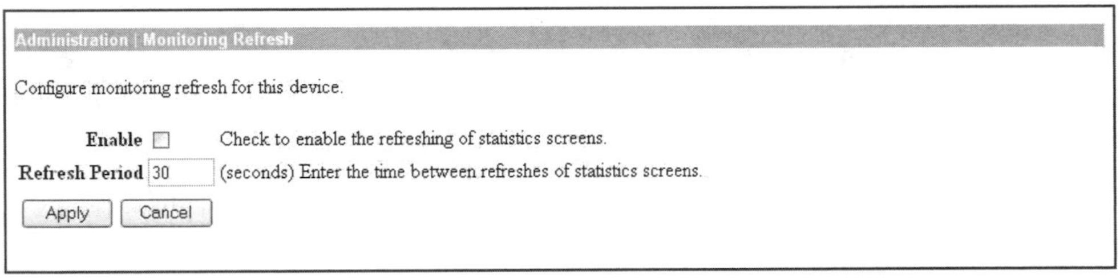

Administration | Monitoring Refresh

Configure monitoring refresh for this device.

Enable ☐   Check to enable the refreshing of statistics screens.
Refresh Period 30   (seconds) Enter the time between refreshes of statistics screens.

[Apply] [Cancel]

Access Rights

The Access Rights window is where you configure administrative access to the VPN Concentrator. It has four submenus:

- **Administrators**—Administrators, passwords, and access rights
- **Access Control List**—IP addresses and options for administrator access

- **Access Settings**—Session timeout and limits
- **AAA Servers**—AAA servers for administrator access

Administrators

The Administrators submenu is where you create the administrator user accounts. You can see in Figure 12-20 that five administrator accounts exist but only two are enabled. You also can see that only the user admin has Administrator rights.

Figure 12-20   *Administrators*

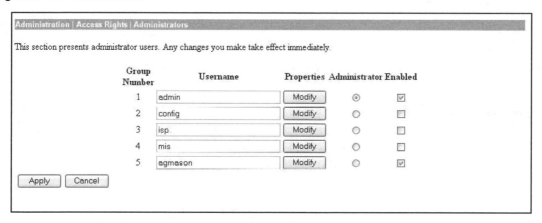

Access Control List

The Access Control List submenu, shown in Figure 12-21, is where you can restrict the IP addresses of the machines that are allowed to administer the VPN Concentrator. For example, suppose the Concentrator's private interface has an address of 192.168.1.1/24, and all the internal network is connected to the 192.168.1.0/24 network. By default, any user on the 192.168.1.0/24 network can attempt to log in to the Concentrator GUI manager. If your network administrator has an IP address of 192.168.1.10, you can create an access list so that only that IP address can access the GUI manager.

To create an access list, click the Add button and then enter the IP address and network mask. If administration access is required, ensure that Group 1 (admin) is selected.

NOTE   If you are familiar with Cisco IOS software, this is the same as applying an access class to a terminal line on the router.

Figure 12-21 *Access Control List*

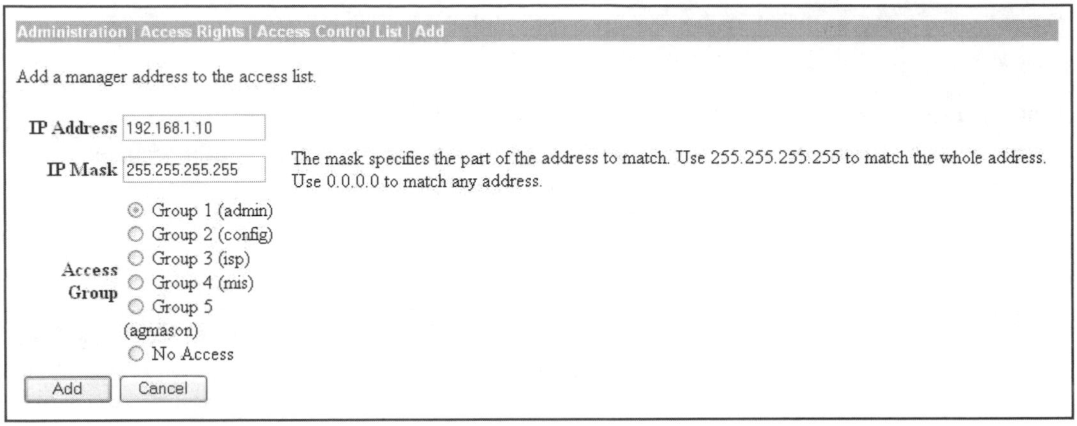

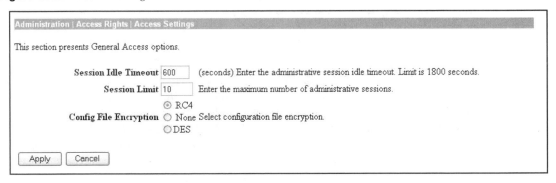

Access Settings

The Access Settings submenu, shown in Figure 12-22, configures the VPN Concentrator's general access settings. Here you can set the GUI manager idle timeout, the number of concurrent admin connections, and the type of encryption to use on the config file.

Figure 12-22 *Access Settings*

Administration | Access Rights | Access Settings

This section presents General Access options.

> Session Idle Timeout [600] (seconds) Enter the administrative session idle timeout. Limit is 1800 seconds.
>
> Session Limit [10] Enter the maximum number of administrative sessions.
>
> Config File Encryption ⦿ RC4
> ◯ None Select configuration file encryption.
> ◯ DES

[Apply] [Cancel]

AAA Servers

If you are using AAA in your network, you can configure authentication at this point for administrator access. This means that the administrative user account can be administered on a TACACS+ authentication server such as Cisco Secure ACS.

TO configure a AAA server for authentication, you have to enter its IP address and shared secret as you do for any other configuration of AAA that you come across, as shown in Figure 12-23.

Figure 12-23   *AAA Servers*

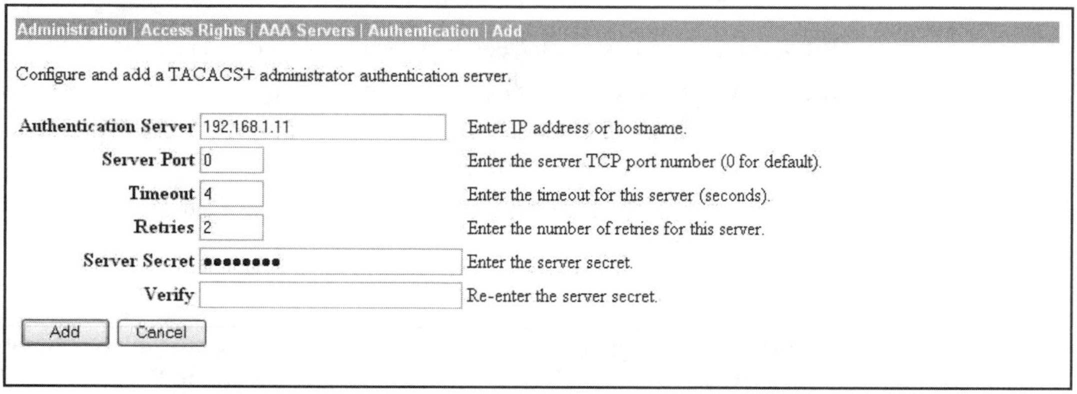

Administration | Access Rights | AAA Servers | Authentication | Add

Configure and add a TACACS+ administrator authentication server.

Authentication Server	192.168.1.11	Enter IP address or hostname.
Server Port	0	Enter the server TCP port number (0 for default).
Timeout	4	Enter the timeout for this server (seconds).
Retries	2	Enter the number of retries for this server.
Server Secret	••••••••	Enter the server secret.
Verify		Re-enter the server secret.

[Add]   [Cancel]

File Management

Under the File Management window, shown in Figure 12-24, you can configure and manipulate the VPN Concentrator's configuration file. This screen has four submenus:

- **Swap Config File**—Swaps the backup and boot configuration files
- **TFTP Transfer**—Transfers files via TFTP
- **File Upload**—Sends a file via HTTP
- **XML Export**—Exports the configuration to an XML file

Figure 12-24   *File Management*

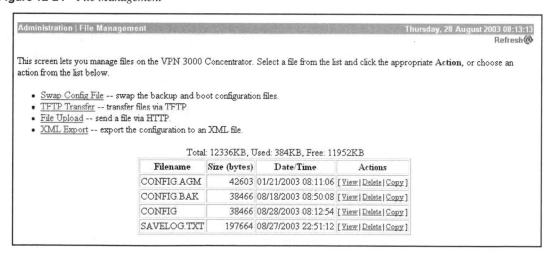

This screen also displays a list of the files that are currently located on the Concentrator. You can see that there are four files on this Concentrator:

- **CONFIG.AGM**—A backup of the config manually created and named.
- **CONFIG.BAK**—The backup file that is created every time you click the Save button. This is the last configuration before you saved the changes.
- **CONFIG**—The actual live configuration file.
- **SAVELOG.TXT**—The log file where system events are recorded.

Swap Config File

Under the Swap Config File submenu, shown in Figure 12-25, you can swap the current config file with the latest automated backup of the config file. This swaps the file CONFIG with the file CONFIG.BAK. This is handy if you made a set of changes, saved them, and then had to roll back because of a problem caused by the new settings.

Figure 12-25 *Swap Config File*

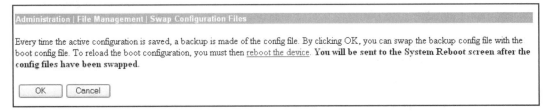

TFTP Transfer

The TFTP Transfer window, shown in Figure 12-26, lets you use TFTP to transfer files to and from the Concentrator Flash memory. The Concentrator acts as a TFTP client for these functions, accessing a TFTP server running on a remote system. All transfers are made in binary mode, and they copy, rather than move, files.

To use the TFTP functions, complete the following fields (you must have access rights to read and write files):

- **TFTP Get**—Get a file from the remote system (that is, copy a file from the remote system to the Concentrator).
- **TFTP Put**—Put a file on the remote system (that is, copy a file from the Concentrator to the remote system).
- **TFTP Server**—Enter the IP address or host name of the remote system running the TFTP server. (If you configured a DNS server, you can enter a host name; otherwise, enter an IP address.)

- **TFTP Server File**—Enter the name of the file on the TFTP server.
- **Concentrator File**—Enter the name of the file on the Concentrator.

Figure 12-26   *TFTP Transfer*

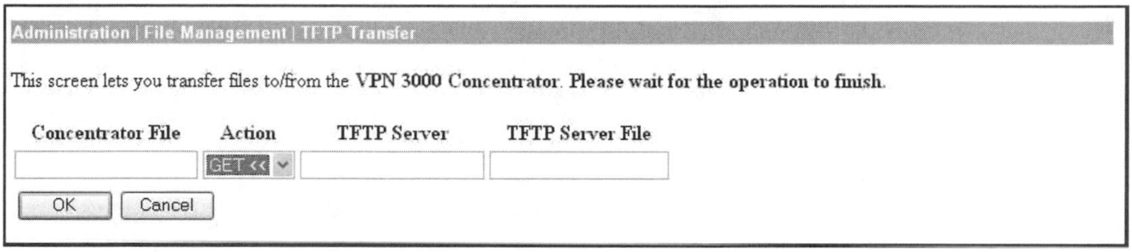

```
Administration | File Management | TFTP Transfer

This screen lets you transfer files to/from the VPN 3000 Concentrator. Please wait for the operation to finish.

Concentrator File     Action        TFTP Server          TFTP Server File
[              ]      [GET <<  v]   [              ]      [                 ]
[   OK   ]  [  Cancel  ]
```

NOTE   If either filename is the same as an existing file, TFTP overwrites the existing file without asking for confirmation.

File Upload

If you have a Concentrator configuration file saved on your local workstation, you can use the File Upload screen, shown in Figure 12-27, to upload this file to the Concentrator.

Figure 12-27   *File Upload*

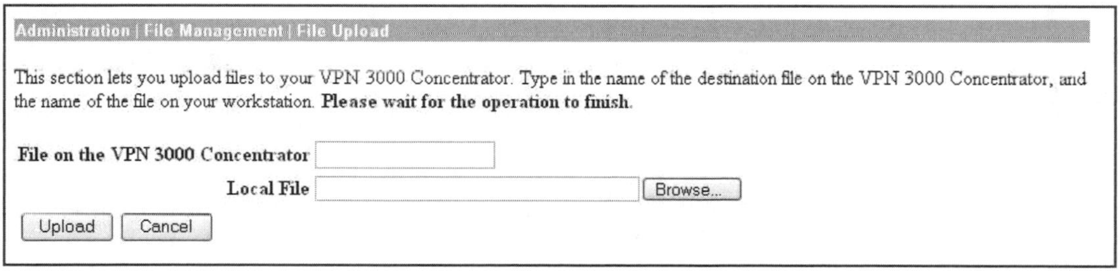

```
Administration | File Management | File Upload

This section lets you upload files to your VPN 3000 Concentrator. Type in the name of the destination file on the VPN 3000 Concentrator, and
the name of the file on your workstation. Please wait for the operation to finish.

File on the VPN 3000 Concentrator [                  ]
                      Local File  [                           ]  [ Browse... ]
[  Upload  ]  [  Cancel  ]
```

XML Export

The XML Export screen, shown in Figure 12-28, allows you to export the active configuration of the Concentrator to an XML file. You then can view it from the File Management administration window.

Figure 12-28 *XML Export*

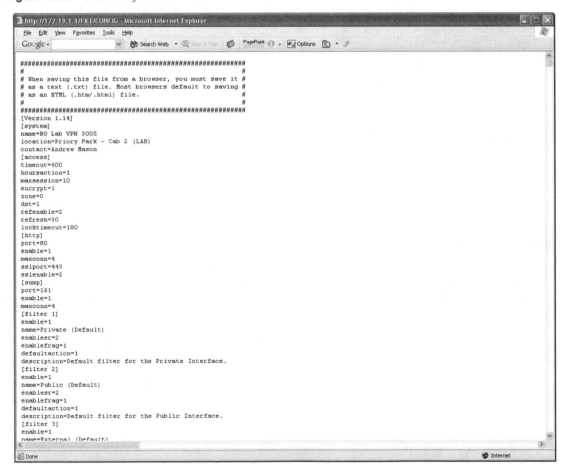

Figure 12-29 shows a section of the CONFIG file, and Figure 12-30 displays the same file but in XML format.

Figure 12-29 *Contents of the CONFIG File*

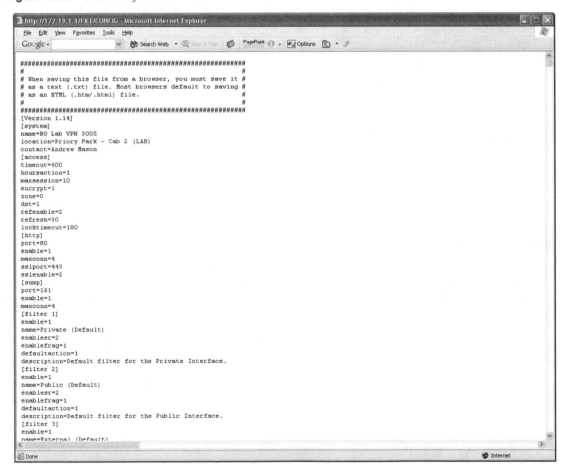

Figure 12-30   *Contents of the CONFIG File in XML Format*

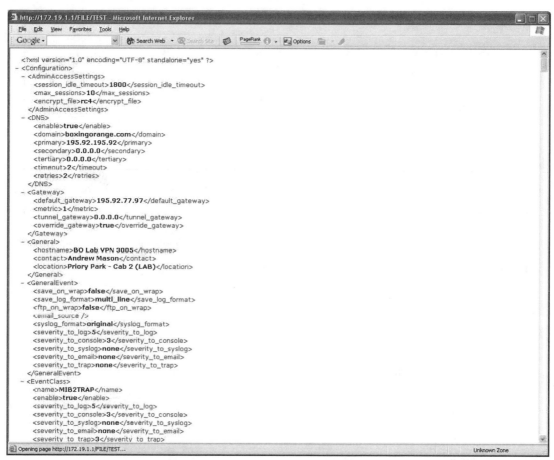

Certificate Management

The Certificate Management screen, shown in Figure 12-31, is where the digital certificates for the VPN Concentrator are viewed and administered.

Figure 12-31 *Certificate Management*

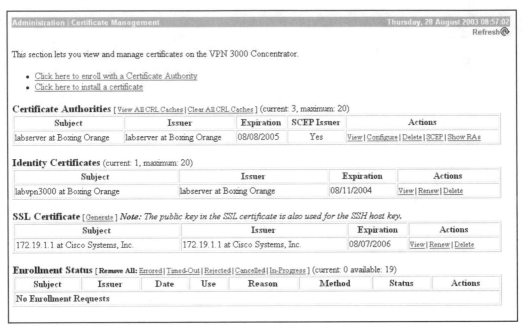

You can see from this screen that information is provided about the certification authorities, identity certificates, SSL certificates, and enrollment status.

Certificate management and its options are covered in detail in Chapter 5, "Configuring the Cisco VPN 3000 for Remote Access Using Digital Certificates."

Bandwidth Management

By default, the Concentrator line does not equitably manage packet traffic on a per-group or per-user basis. This means that any one group or user, given infinite bandwidth capability, could effectively steal almost all of a Concentrator's available bandwidth capacity. This can cause all other logged-in users to experience slower connections. In Figure 12-32, the customer has T1 (1.544 Mbps) bandwidth at the central site. The two remote sites, B and C, each have 384 Kb of bandwidth. The two sets of remote users are system engineers and executives. The remote users have DSL and cable access to headquarters. If all 26 remote users connect at the same time and decide to download a large file, their actions could conceivably slow down connections between the headquarters and sites B and C.

Figure 12-32   *Bandwidth Management*

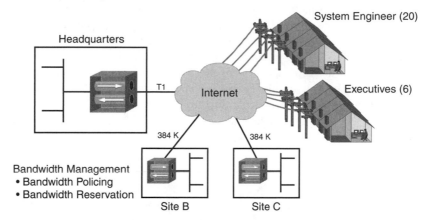

The bandwidth management feature could be enabled on the Concentrator to distribute the bandwidth more equitably. One option is bandwidth reservation. The administrator could configure a minimum reserved bandwidth rate per session to prevent connection slowdown. For example, each remotely connected system engineer has a configured minimum bandwidth reservation of 56 Kbps. For another option, if the administrator is concerned about overutilization, the Concentrator could be configured for bandwidth policing. The Concentrator can place a bandwidth ceiling on data transfers (for example, a maximum transfer rate of 128 Kbps per session). The last option is aggregation. The administrator could choose to reserve a pool of bandwidth, an aggregation, for a group of users, or a site-to-site link. During peak periods, this site-to-site link, or group of users, can access bandwidth from this dedicated pool of bandwidth. The pool is reserved for their exclusive use.

Bandwidth Policing

For the bandwidth policing feature, the Concentrator provides a maximum data transfer rate. Bandwidth policing sets a maximum limit (a cap) on the rate of tunneled traffic. For example, all system engineers can transfer data up to a sustained rate of 56 Kbps while remotely accessing the Concentrator. The Concentrator transmits traffic it receives below this rate; it drops traffic above this rate. Because traffic is bursty, some flexibility is built into policing. Policing involves two thresholds: the policing rate and the burst size. The policing rate is the maximum limit on the rate of sustained tunneled traffic. The burst size indicates the maximum size of an instantaneous burst of bytes allowed before traffic is capped back to the policing rate. The Concentrator allows for instantaneous bursts of traffic greater than the policing rate up to the burst rate. But should traffic burst consistently and exceed the burst rate, the Concentrator enforces the policing rate threshold. The Concentrator starts to drop frames.

Bandwidth policing can be configured on both a system and group basis. If group policing is configured, every member of the specified group can transmit data according to the group bandwidth policing policy. If a remote user is not a member of a predefined group, he or she can transmit data up to the system-wide policing rate. For example, there are two groups of remote users—system engineers and executives. The executives have a group policing rate defined at 128 Kbps. The system engineers do not have their own group policing rate defined. When executives connect to the Concentrator, they can transmit data up to 128 Kbps. When system engineers connect, they do not have a policing policy specifically defined for their group. They can transmit data up to the system-wide policing rate—in this example, 56 Kbps.

Configuring Bandwidth Policing

Configuring the bandwidth policing feature is a two-step process. First, the policing policy (or policies) is defined. Next, the policies are assigned to an interface, and optionally to groups. To configure policing policies, go to the Configuration > Policy Management > Traffic Management > Bandwidth Policies window, as shown in Figure 12-33. The bandwidth policy consists of two parts—bandwidth reservation in the top half and policing in the bottom half. (Bandwidth reservation is discussed later in the next section.) Policing involves two thresholds: the policing rate and the burst size. The policing rate is the maximum limit on the rate of sustained tunneled traffic. The burst size indicates the maximum size of an instantaneous burst of bytes allowed before traffic is capped at the policing rate. The Concentrator allows for instantaneous bursts of traffic greater than the policing rate up to the burst rate. The policing policy parameters are as follows:

- **Policy Name**—Enter a unique policy name that helps you remember the policy you are configuring. For example, if this policy focuses on the executive group, you could name it executive.

- **Policing**—Check the Policing check box to enable the policing feature.

- **Policing Rate**—Enter a value and select the unit of measurement. The Concentrator transmits traffic that is moving below the policing rate and drops all traffic that is moving above the policing rate. The range is between 56 kbps and 100 mbps. The default is 56 kbps. Policing rate is defined in the following units:

    - bps—Bits per second

    - kbps—Thousands of bits per second

    - mbps—Millions of bits per second

- **Normal Burst Size**—Enter a value for the normal burst size. The normal burst size is the amount of instantaneous burst that the Concentrator can send at any given time. Use the following formula to set the burst size: (policing rate/8) * 1.5. For example, if you want to limit users to 250 Kbps of bandwidth, set the policing rate to 250 Kbps, and set the burst size to 46,875—that is, (250,000 bps/8) * 1.5. Enter the Normal Burst Size and select the unit of measurement. The default is a normal burst size of 10,500 bytes. Normal burst size is defined in units as follows:

— bytes—Unit of adjacent bits

— kbytes—Thousands of bytes

— mbytes—Millions of bytes

Figure 12-33 *Adding a Bandwidth Policy*

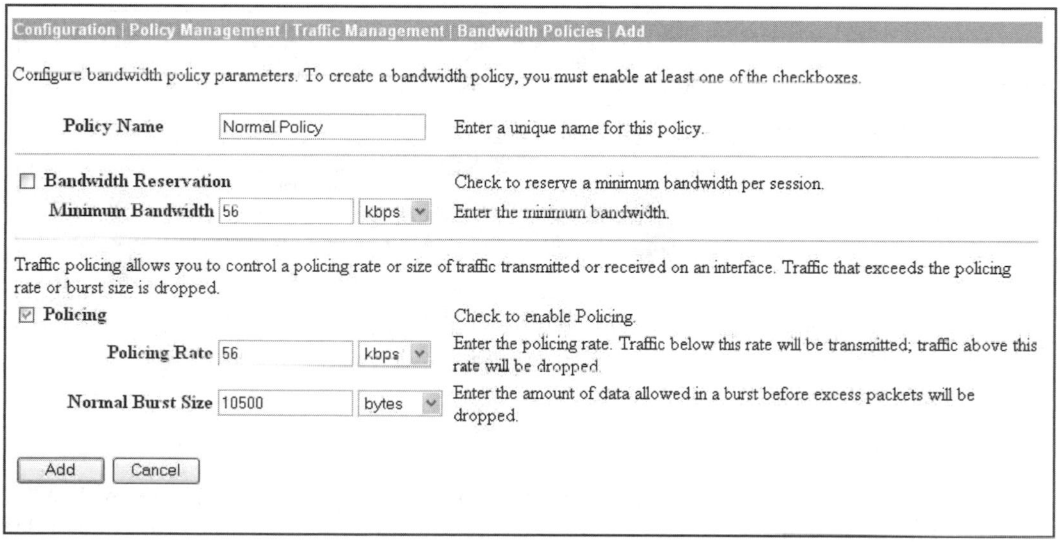

Configuration | Policy Management | Traffic Management | Bandwidth Policies | Add

Configure bandwidth policy parameters. To create a bandwidth policy, you must enable at least one of the checkboxes.

Policy Name	Normal Policy	Enter a unique name for this policy.

☐ **Bandwidth Reservation**   Check to reserve a minimum bandwidth per session.
Minimum Bandwidth 56   kbps ▾   Enter the minimum bandwidth.

Traffic policing allows you to control a policing rate or size of traffic transmitted or received on an interface. Traffic that exceeds the policing rate or burst size is dropped.
☑ **Policing**   Check to enable Policing.

Policing Rate 56   kbps ▾   Enter the policing rate. Traffic below this rate will be transmitted; traffic above this rate will be dropped.

Normal Burst Size 10500   bytes ▾   Enter the amount of data allowed in a burst before excess packets will be dropped.

[Add]   [Cancel]

For example, suppose a policy named Normal Policy is configured for a policing rate of 56 Kbps and a normal burst size of 10,500 bytes. Any remote user assigned this policy has a maximum limit on the rate of sustained tunneled traffic of 56 Kbps. The Concentrator can support an instantaneous burst of 10,500 bytes before it starts to limit traffic by dropping packets.

After policies are defined, they are assigned to a Concentrator interface, public or private, or a user group. The interface policy defines the default policing rate for the Concentrator. If a remote user belongs to a group that is not specifically defined a policing rate, that person is assigned the policing rate defined for the interface. Go to the Configuration > Interfaces > Ethernet2 > window and select the Bandwidth tab to assign a policing policy to the interface (see Figure 12-34). Enable bandwidth management on the selected interface, define the link rate for the interface, and assign the policy to be used on the interface. The interface bandwidth management parameters are as follows:

• **Bandwidth Management**—Check this check box to enable bandwidth management on this interface.

- **Link Rate**—Enter a value for the link rate, and select a unit of measurement. The defined link rate must be based on the available Internet bandwidth, not the physical LAN connection rate. The default is 1.544 Mbps. If the link rate is less than the sum of the policed rates, some remote users might not reach the police rate.
- **Bandwidth Policy**—Select a policy from the drop-down list. If there are no policies in this list, you must choose Configuration > Policy Management > Traffic Management > Bandwidth Policies and define one or more policies.

Figure 12-34   *Adding a Bandwidth Policy to an Interface*

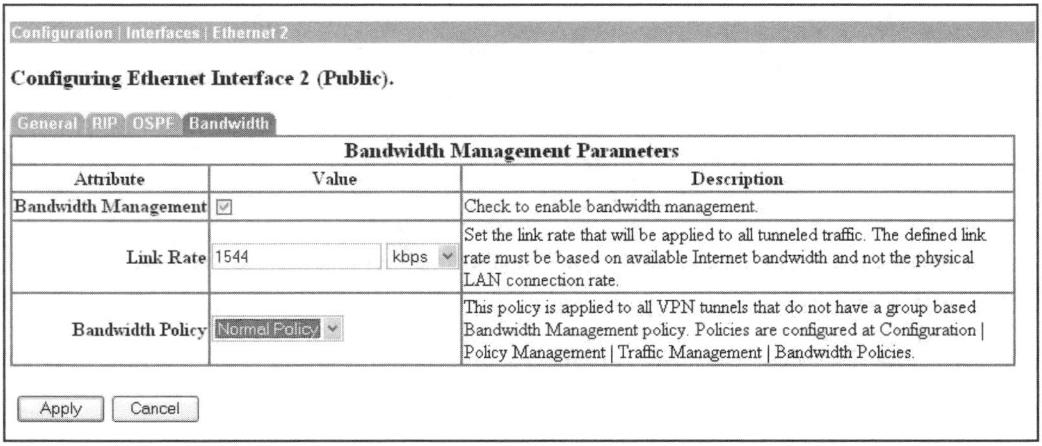

If bandwidth policing is required in a network, a policing policy must be defined and applied to an interface before group policing policies are applied. The Concentrator does not allow a group policy to be applied first. If an administrator attempts to apply a group policy first, the Concentrator returns an error message.

In Figure 12-34, the Internet link is a T1, 1.544 Mbps. The default policy for the interface is normal reservation. The normal reservation provides a maximum bandwidth allocation of 56 Kbps and a burst size of 10,500 bytes. System engineers are assigned a policing rate of 56 Kbps.

Bandwidth Reservation

Bandwidth reservation reserves a minimum amount of bandwidth per session for tunneled traffic. As he or she connects to the Concentrator, each remote user receives a minimum amount of bandwidth. When there is little traffic on the box, users receive more than their allocated minimum of bandwidth. When the box becomes busy, they receive at least the minimum amount. When the combined total of the reserved bandwidth amounts of all active tunnels on an interface approaches the limit of the total bandwidth available on that interface, the Concentrator refuses further connections to users who demand more reserved bandwidth than is available.

Suppose that the link rate on your public interface is 1.544 Mbps. Further suppose that you apply a reserved bandwidth policy to that interface that sets the reserved bandwidth to 64 Kbps per user. With this link rate and policy setting, only 24 users can connect to the Concentrator at one time. (1.544 Mbps per interface divided by 64 Kbps per user equals 24 connections.)

- The first user who logs on to the Concentrator reserves 64 Kbps of bandwidth plus the remainder of the bandwidth (1480 Kbps).

- The second user who logs on to the Concentrator reserves 64 Kbps of bandwidth and shares the remainder of the bandwidth (1416 Kbps) with the first user.

- When the twenty-fourth concurrent user connects, all users are limited to their minimum of 64 Kbps of bandwidth per connection.

- When the twenty-fifth user attempts to connect, the Concentrator refuses the connection. It does not allow any additional connections, because it cannot supply the minimum 64 Kbps reservation of bandwidth to more users.

You can think of bandwidth reservation as pieces of a pie. Each remote user is assigned a slice of pie (reserve bandwidth), as shown in Figure 12-35. As tunnels are established, each user is assigned a slice of the pie until the pie is completely divided. At that point, any new connections requesting a slice of the pie are refused the opportunity to establish a connection.

Figure 12-35   *Bandwidth Reservation*

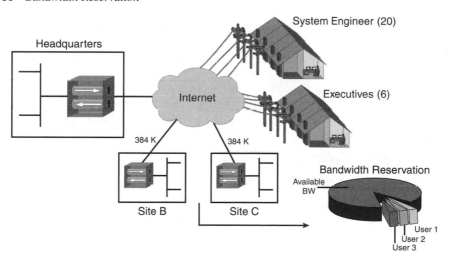

Configuring Bandwidth Reservation

Configuring bandwidth reservation is a two-step process. First, the bandwidth reservation policies are defined. Next, the policies are assigned to an interface, and optionally to groups.

Choose Configuration > Policy Management > Traffic Management > Bandwidth Policies to configure bandwidth reservation policies, as shown in Figure 12-36.

Figure 12-36 *Bandwidth Reservation Configuration*

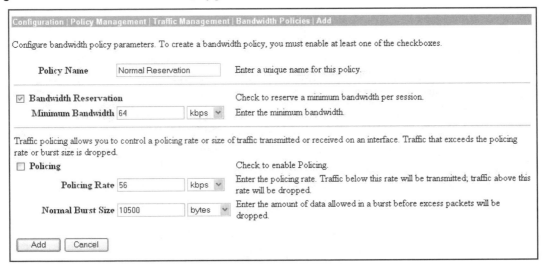

The bandwidth policy window consists of two parts—bandwidth reservation in the top half and policing in the bottom half. Under bandwidth reservation, the administrator sets the minimum bandwidth assigned per session for remote users. The bandwidth reservation parameters are as follows:

- **Policy Name**—Enter a policy name.
- **Bandwidth Reservation**—Select this check box to enable the feature.
- **Minimum Bandwidth**—Enter the amount of bandwidth reserved per user during periods of congestion. Enter a value for the minimum bandwidth, and select one of the following units of measure:
  - bps—Bits per second
  - kbps—Thousands of bits per second
  - mbps—Millions of bits per second

In Figure 12-36, the administrator has created a policy called Normal Reservation. This reservation allocates a minimum of 64 kbps to each remote-access session.

Not all remote users have the same bandwidth requirements. The administrator can configure additional policies with different bandwidth reservations. In Figure 12-37, the administrator has created a policy for the executive group. Each member of the executive group requires more bandwidth than the minimum allocation of 64 Kbps. A policy is defined that allocates 128 Kbps of bandwidth upon connection to the Concentrator.

Figure 12-37 *Executive Bandwidth Reservation Configuration*

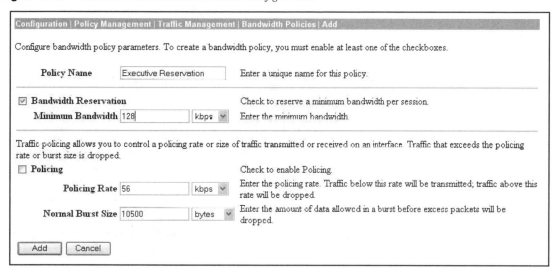

As each executive connects, he or she is allocated part of the available bandwidth. The amount of bandwidth allocated to each executive is defined by the assigned policy, executive reservation. In this policy, each executive receives a minimum of 128 Kbps of reserved bandwidth.

Public Interface Configuration

First, the administrator defines bandwidth reservation policies. Next, the policies are applied to interfaces, groups, and site-to-site tunnels. Go to the Configuration > Interfaces > Ethernet 1 2 3 screen (where 1, 2, or 3 is the required interface number), and choose the Bandwidth tab to apply a policy to an interface (see Figure 12-38). The Bandwidth tab parameters are as follows:

- **Bandwidth Management**—Check this check box to enable the feature on the interface.

- **Link Rate**—Set the link rate applied to all tunneled traffic. The defined link rate must be based on the available Internet bandwidth and not the physical LAN connection rate. The default is 1.544 Mbps.

- **Bandwidth Policy**—Select a bandwidth policy for this interface. This policy is applied to all VPN tunnels that do not have a group-based bandwidth management policy.

Figure 12-38 *Bandwidth Reservation Configuration Public Interface*

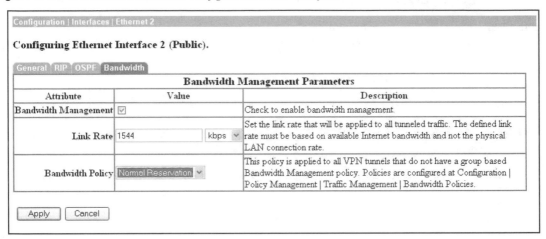

If bandwidth reservation is required in a network, a bandwidth reservation policy must be defined and applied to an interface before group bandwidth reservation policies are applied. The Concentrator does not allow a group policy to be applied first. If an administrator attempts to apply a group policy first, the Concentrator returns an error message.

In Figure 12-38, each remote user not assigned to a group bandwidth reservation policy receives the minimum bandwidth reservation defined by the normal reservation policy. In this example, the user is assigned 64 Kbps of bandwidth.

Group Configuration

For groups that have different bandwidth requirements, the administrator can define group-based bandwidth requirements. Go to the Configuration > User Management > Groups window, select a group, and select Assign Bandwidth Policies. From the Policy drop-down menu, select the appropriate policy. The policy assigned to the interface reserves 64 Kbps of bandwidth for each remote user. This is fine for the system engineers, but the executives require a larger bandwidth reservation. From the Policy drop-down menu, the administrator selects the Executive Reservation policy. With this policy, each member of the executive group is allocated a minimum bandwidth reservation of 128 Kbps.

Bandwidth Aggregation

Configuring bandwidth reservation alone might lead to a scenario in which high-priority, high-bandwidth users are unable to connect to a congested Concentrator because of their bandwidth requirements. The Concentrator provides a feature called bandwidth aggregation, which allows a particular group to reserve a fixed portion of the total bandwidth on the interface. (This fixed portion is called an aggregation.) Then, as users from that group connect, each receives a part of the total bandwidth allocated for that group. When one group makes a reserved bandwidth aggregation, it does not affect the bandwidth allocated to users who are not in that group. However, other users are now sharing a smaller amount of the total bandwidth. Fewer users can connect. You can think of bandwidth reservation as pieces of a pie. Each group is assigned a slice of pie (aggregate bandwidth). As tunnels are established, each user is assigned part of the slice until the slice is completely divided. At that point, any new connections requesting a piece of the slice are refused a connection. Go to the Configuration > User Management > Groups > Bandwidth Policy > Interfaces window to assign a bandwidth aggregation. Configure the following parameters:

- **Policy**—Select a bandwidth policy from the Policy drop-down menu.
- **Bandwidth Aggregation**—Enter a value for the maximum bandwidth to reserve for this group, and select a unit of measure.

In Figure 12-39, the executive group is assigned a bandwidth aggregation of 384 Kbps. As each executive connects, he or she is allocated part of the 384 Kbps aggregated bandwidth. The amount of bandwidth allocated to each executive is defined by the assigned policy. In this case, each executive reserves bandwidth of 128 Kbps. Executive users are allocated bandwidth until their 384 Kbps slice of the bandwidth pie has been allocated.

Figure 12-39 *Bandwidth Reservation Configuration Executive Group*

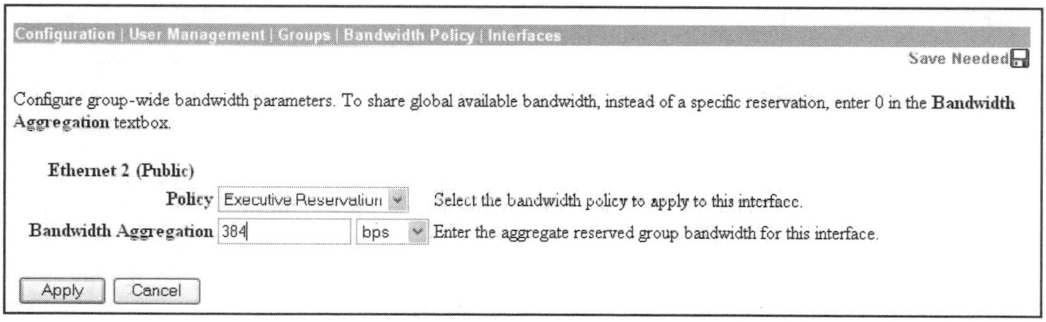

Monitoring the Bandwidth Statistics

Go to the Monitoring > Statistics > Bandwidth Management window, shown in Figure 12-40, to view bandwidth management session statistics. This window shows details of the effects of bandwidth management policies on each tunnel. Only active tunnels on which bandwidth management policies are enabled appear in this window. The bandwidth management statistics parameters are as follows:

- **Username**—The username identifying a tunnel using a bandwidth management policy

- **Traffic Rate**—Measured in Kbps

  - **Conformed**—The current rate of session traffic (as set by the bandwidth management policy)

  - **Throttled**—The rate at which packets are being throttled to maintain the conformed rate

- **Traffic Volume**—Measured in bytes

  - **Conformed**—The number of bytes of session traffic (as set by the bandwidth management policy)

  - **Throttled**—The number of bytes being throttled to maintain the conformed rate

Figure 12-40 *Bandwidth Statistics*

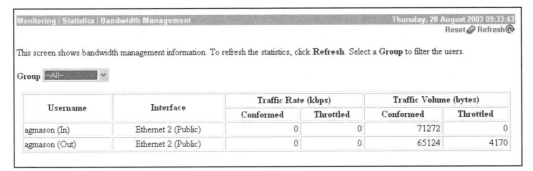

Summary

This chapter provided an overview of the monitoring and administration functions of the VPN Concentrator. It started by looking at the monitoring features that concentrate on hardware and device monitoring as well as the monitoring of active VPN sessions, both LAN-to-LAN and remote-access. The chapter then covered the administration features of the VPN Concentrator. These include essential features such as the ability to back up and restore your active configuration and how the Concentrator handles administrators for administering the GUI manager. The chapter finished by looking at bandwidth management and the two different types of bandwidth management, along with their configuration options.

Review Questions

The following questions test your retention of the material presented in this chapter. The answers appear in Appendix A, "Answers to the Review Questions."

1 What are the two types of bandwidth management?

2 What is the default filename for the active configuration file on a VPN Concentrator?

3 What are the differences between the Monitoring > Sessions and Administration > Sessions screens?

4 When you select Administration > Swap Config File, what is the current active configuration file renamed?

5 If you have an amber LED for power supplies A and B, what does this indicate?

6 What four options are available under the Access Rights window?

After completing this chapter, you will be able to perform the following tasks:

- Differentiate between initial and ongoing VPN failures
- Troubleshoot remote-access VPNs
- Troubleshoot LAN-to-LAN VPNs
- Troubleshoot preshared key and CA-based VPNs

CHAPTER 13

Troubleshooting

This chapter looks at simple virtual private network (VPN) troubleshooting. It covers remote-access VPNs and LAN-to-LAN VPNs using preshared keys and digital certificates. The chapter starts by covering the basic failures that can apply to all VPNs: initial failures and ongoing failures. Most of the time, you will experience initial failures. These are failures to get the VPN established after the initial configuration. This is quite normal, because VPN configuration is tricky. I cannot emphasize enough how much you have to check and double-check the configuration as it is entered to ensure that no typing or spelling mistakes will lead to hours of troubleshooting. Because VPNs by nature traverse public networks beyond your control, it is also possible for your VPN to suddenly stop working even though you have not made any configuration changes. These failures are called ongoing failures because they happen after the Concentrator's initial configuration.

Troubleshooting VPNs

There are quite a few reasons why VPNs can and do fail. We will break these into two main areas—initial failures and ongoing failures—and then identify the causes within the areas for remote-access VPNs, LAN-to-LAN VPNs with preshared keys, and LAN-to-LAN VPNs with digital certificates.

Initial Failures

When you initially configure a VPN, if it does not come up, this is called an initial failure. This means that an error at the configuration level is causing this failure. This failure might be because of an incorrect configuration on either the VPN device or the client software if the failure is on a remote-access VPN. As well as configuration failures, an initial failure can be caused by network problems that stop the free flow of IPSec traffic from the IPSec source to the IPSec destination.

Typical initial failures are

- Incompatible Internet Key Exchange (IKE) policies
- Differing preshared keys between IPSec peers
- Incorrect IPSec access lists
- Traffic flow between IPSec peers
- Routing issues

Ongoing Failures

If you have successfully configured a VPN, and then all of a sudden the VPN stops functioning correctly, this is called an ongoing failure. It is unusual for this to be an error with the configuration, because the VPN has worked in the past. These failures are normally network- or hardware-related.

Network-related failures occur when something in the data path between the VPN endpoints has changed. This might be as simple as the addition of a firewall between the two VPN peers that is limiting the required VPN traffic. A routing issue also might cause network failures. In the case of a remote-access VPN, the VPN Client on the remote device is usually a VPN Software Client. It is quite common for third-party applications to interfere with the operation of the VPN Software Client.

If the failure is hardware-related, it simply means that the VPN device might have stopped functioning in the way it was designed, perhaps because of a hardware failure that requires engineering work.

Typical ongoing failures are

- A change in traffic flow between the IPSec peers
- Software conflicts (in the case of remote-access VPNs)
- Routing issues

Troubleshooting Remote-Access VPNs

Remote-access VPNs use a VPN hardware device at the headend and a remote-access client, usually a VPN Software Client, installed on a host computer, as shown in Figure 13-1.

Figure 13-1 *Remote-Access VPN*

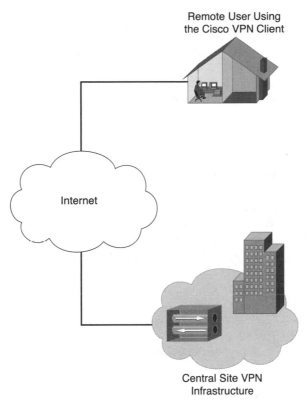

Remote User Using
the Cisco VPN Client

Internet

Central Site VPN
Infrastructure

In this type of VPN, the headend device—in this case, a Cisco VPN 3000 Concentrator—
is configured with a group that the remote access client authenticates against. User authentication is also supported by the Concentrator. This is usually handed off to a third-party
authentication server, or authentication takes place against a Microsoft Windows domain or
active directory.

This chapter looks at common causes of initial and ongoing VPN failures and provides
simple explanations as to why they occur.

Initial Remote-Access VPN Failures

There are two different aspects of initial configuration for a remote-access VPN. The
central site has to be configured, and then each individual remote-access client also requires
configuring to connect to the central site. A remote-access VPN is unique in the fact that
very minimal configuration is required on the VPN Software Client itself. Most of the
configuration is carried out at the central site VPN Concentrator. A group is created, and all

the required settings are applied to the group on the Concentrator. The VPN Software Client requires only three configuration items for a simple remote-access VPN: the central site concentrator IP address, group name, and group password.

The VPN Software Client connects to the Concentrator on the configured IP address and then authenticates itself by presenting the group name and password. At this point, the IKE and IPSec policies are pushed from the Concentrator to the VPN Software Client. Therefore, no IKE or IPSec policy is configured on the VPN Software Client, so you know this is never an area of trouble.

Let's look at the types of initial failures that apply to remote-access VPNs.

Routing Issues

Before you begin configuring the central site Concentrator or the VPN Software Client, you have to ensure that connectivity exists between the host machine that is initiating the remote-access VPN and the central site VPN infrastructure. You know that for VPNs to work, IP connectivity must exist between the host machine and the central site VPN device. The easiest way to test this is with the **ping** command. The **ping** command uses Internet Control Message Protocol (ICMP) echo and ICMP echo reply packets to test connectivity and routing. Failure to ping the central site VPN device might be because ICMP is blocked by a firewall or another access-limiting device along the way. For the VPN to function correctly, the remote machine must have a valid route to the central site VPN device, and the required traffic must be allowed along the data path and not be blocked by any device.

Traffic Flow Between the VPN Client and Headend Concentrator

After you have confirmed that routing is in place, the next thing to look at in an initial failure is whether traffic is flowing freely between the remote machine and the central site VPN device. In a traditional VPN using ESP, the required traffic between the sites is IP 50 (ESP) and UDP port 500 (ISAKMP). For a remote-access VPN, if transparent tunneling is used (and it usually is), the traffic is different. The default is to use IPSec over UDP. In this case, UDP port 10000 or 4500 is used, depending on the configuration of the central site Concentrator. UDP port 10000 is Cisco-proprietary and can be changed by the administrator, whereas UDP port 4500 is the NAT-Traversal (NAT-T) standard that is being adopted by the Internet Engineering Task Force (IETF) and being implemented by ISPs worldwide. The port used for NAT-T cannot be changed and is fixed at UDP 4500.

Ensure that whatever traffic you have configured is allowed throughout the network from the remote machine to the central site VPN device.

Configuration Error on the Concentrator

If you confirm that routing is in place and that the required IP traffic flows freely from the remote machine to the central Concentrator, the next thing to look at in the event of an initial failure is the configuration on the central site VPN Concentrator. Check the basic settings such as the IP settings on the Concentrator from the Configuration > Interfaces screen, as shown in Figure 13-2.

Figure 13-2 *Configuration > Interfaces*

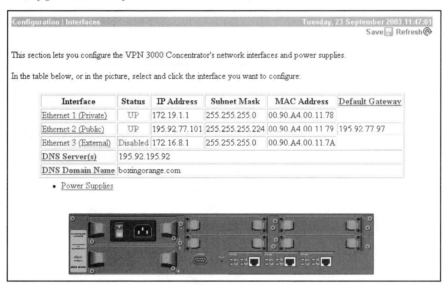

Confirm that the IP address for the public interface is correct, and then ensure that the default gateway is configured on the public interface. After that, navigate to the Administration > Ping screen and ping the default gateway. Figure 13-3 shows that in this case you can ping the default gateway.

Figure 13-3 *Pinging the Default Gateway*

After successfully pinging the default gateway, try to ping an address on the public Internet. This example pings the address 195.92.195.92. You can see from Figure 13-4 that the attempt is successful.

Figure 13-4 *Pinging an Address on the Internet*

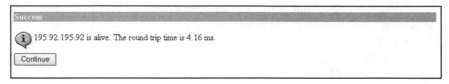

This proves that the IP configuration on the Concentrator is correct, because you can ping an address that is not local to the Concentrator.

The next item to check is the group settings on the Concentrator. Confirm that all the settings in the group are as they should be, paying particular attention to ensuring that no spelling mistakes exist.

Software Client Configuration Error

After you have confirmed the settings on the VPN Concentrator, the next place to check is the VPN Software Client. On the VPN Client, the first thing to check is the IP address of the connection entry, as shown in Figure 13-5.

Figure 13-5 *VPN Connection Entries*

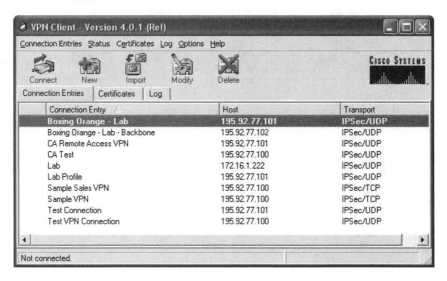

Figure 13-5 highlights a VPN Connection entry that is configured for the 195.92.77.101 IP address. Confirm that this is the same as the Concentrator's public IP address. You can see in Figure 13-2 that this does indeed match the Concentrator's public IP address.

After confirming that the IP address is correct, confirm that the group name and password are correct. You cannot see the group password, so you have to overwrite what is there with what you know the password to be.

Another problem might be the transparent tunneling settings. If you have selected IPSec over TCP, but your group on the Concentrator forces IPSec over UDP or vice versa, ensure that this setting is correct.

Ongoing Remote-Access VPN Failures

If the VPN fails after you know it has been working, this is an ongoing failure. Ongoing failures occur only when something changes. If you are sure that no change has been made to the central site Concentrator, and no change has been made to the VPN Software Client, the problem must be either a change in the network or an application on the host machine that is conflicting with the VPN Software Client.

To ascertain whether a software conflict exists, try using another machine that you know was working from the same location as the troublesome machine. If this machine works, it instantly rules out any network issues and points to the VPN Software Client. Try removing the client and reinstalling it to see if this remedies the failure. Make a list of any applications you have recently installed on the machine, and try removing these to see if this cures the problem.

NOTE   It is also worth checking Cisco.com for the latest updates and bug notices for the VPN Software Client.

If you are sure that the problem does not lie with the VPN Client, you need to look at the network infrastructure that exists between the remote machine and the central site VPN device. The common culprit is an addition or change to the rule base of the corporate firewall, either at the remote machine site or at the central site where the VPN device exists.

Troubleshooting Preshared Key LAN-to-LAN VPNs

LAN-to-LAN VPNs are normally easier to troubleshoot than remote-access VPNs because the VPN connection is between two devices, such as two VPN Concentrators. Therefore, the configuration has to match on both units for the VPN to be established. Figure 13-6 shows a LAN-to-LAN VPN.

Figure 13-6   *LAN-to-LAN VPN*

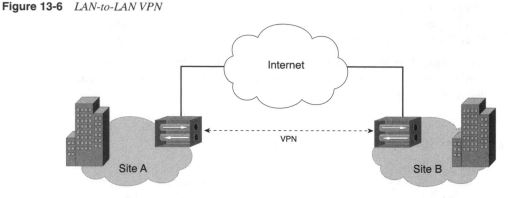

LAN-to-LAN VPNs differ from remote-access VPNs in that LAN-to-LAN VPNs are fixed entities. Therefore, you know the IP address of each VPN peer. Normally these are static IP addresses that never change. The VPN connection is from one VPN peer to the other, and vice versa. A method of authentication has to be used between the VPN peers. This section looks at problems that arise when you use a preshared key for authentication. The next section covers authentication using a CA and a digital certificate.

We will look at common causes of initial and ongoing VPN failures and provide simple explanations for why these occur.

Initial LAN-to-LAN VPN Failures with Preshared Keys

When you configure a LAN-to-LAN VPN, you have to configure both VPN peers—in this case, both VPN Concentrators for the VPN. If one of the Concentrators is configured incorrectly, the VPN is not established, and you have to troubleshoot the reasons why. One good point about a LAN-to-LAN VPN is that you have a fixed IP address for each peer, so all policies are applied to this peer.

Each VPN peer is configured with an IKE and IPSec policy. The combination of these policies provides the VPN service. The IKE and IPSec policies both have a section where you configure the remote peer's VPN settings. At least one of the IKE and IPSec polices must match on both the VPN peers for the VPN to work.

The following sections discuss the types of initial failures that apply to LAN-to-LAN VPNs.

Routing Issues

Before you begin configuring the VPN Concentrators, you have to ensure that connectivity exists between the two Concentrators that make up the VPN infrastructure. You know that for VPNs to work, IP connectivity must exist between the two VPN devices. The easiest way to test this is with the **ping** command. The **ping** command uses ICMP echo and ICMP echo reply packets to test connectivity and routing. Failure to ping one VPN device from the other may be because ICMP is being blocked by a firewall or another access-limiting device along the way. For the VPN to function correctly, each VPN device must have a valid route to the remote VPN device, and the required traffic must be allowed along the data path and not blocked by any device.

Let's look at a VPN Concentrator and the routing elements. Figure 13-7 displays the interface configuration screen from a VPN Concentrator.

Figure 13-7   *Configuration > Interfaces*

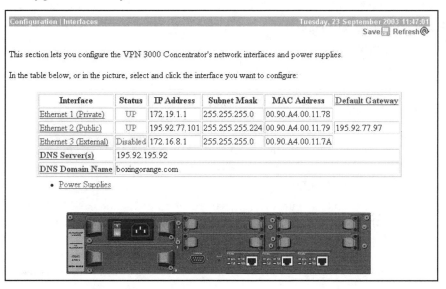

Note that the address of the public interface is 195.92.77.101. A default route configured on this interface points to 195.92.77.97. This means that all traffic destined for nonlocal networks, or networks that do not have a more specific route in the routing table, are forwarded to this address. It is important to ensure that this routing is working between the two VPN Concentrators forming the VPN. The best way to ensure that routing is working between the two VPN Concentrators is by using the **ping** command. If you can ping between both Concentrators, you know that routing is working.

Traffic Flow Between the VPN Concentrators

As with remote-access VPNs (and as with all VPNs), traffic must be able to flow between the VPNs. LAN-to-LAN VPNs differ from remote-access VPNs in that they commonly use IP 50 and UDP port 500 for their communications. IP 50 is assigned to ESP, and UDP port 500 is used by ISAKMP (IKE). You must ensure that this traffic is allowed through the network from one Concentrator to the other. If this traffic is blocked, or translated, the VPN connection fails.

Incompatible IKE Policies

If you can confirm that routing is working as it should and that traffic is allowed and flowing across the network, the next step is to look at the configuration on the VPN Concentrators. There are a few areas to look at here. The first is an incompatibility in the IKE policies.

The values controlled by the IKE policy are

- Encryption algorithm
- Hash algorithm
- Authentication method
- Diffie-Hellman group
- SA lifetime

All of these except the SA lifetime must match on both sides for the VPN to be established. When configuring a VPN using the Add a LAN-to-LAN VPN wizard under Configuration > System > Tunneling Protocols > IPSec > LAN-to-LAN, you have to select an IKE proposal, as shown in Figure 13-8.

You can see from this figure that the IKE policy called IKE-3DES-MD5 has been selected. Just selecting the same policy is not enough, because the actual policy might have been changed, so it is worthwhile to check the settings within the IKE policy. You do this from the Configuration > System > Tunneling Protocols > IPSec > IKE Proposals screen. Select the IKE-3DES-MD5 policy, and then click Modify. You see the screen shown in Figure 13-9.

Figure 13-8 *Adding a LAN-to-LAN Entry*

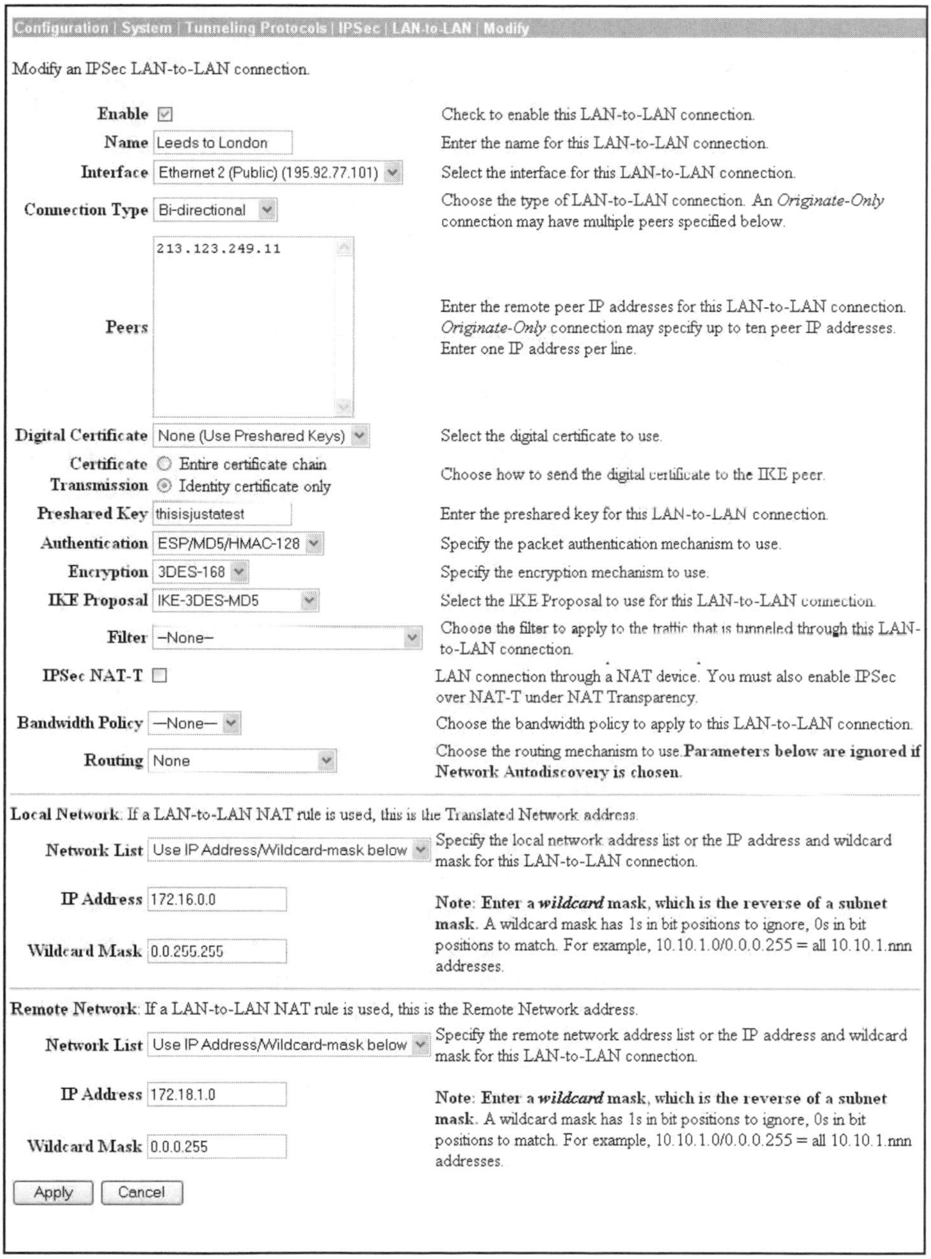

Figure 13-9 *Checking the IKE Proposal*

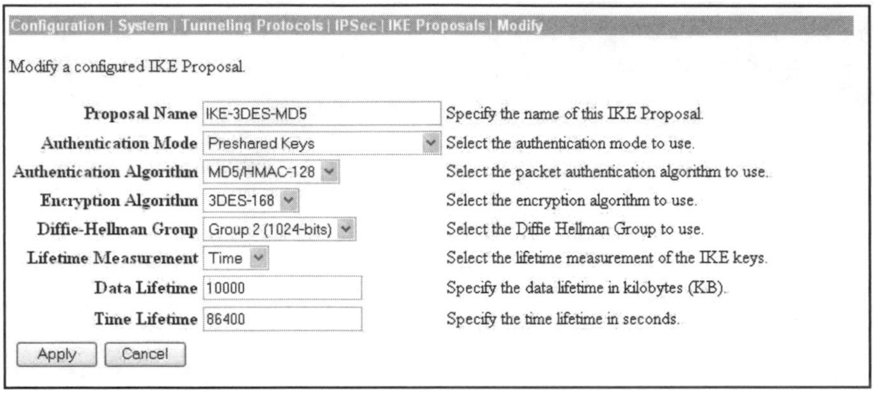

You can see from Figure 13-9 that the settings for the IKE-3DES-MD5 proposal are as follows:

- Encryption algorithm—3DES-168
- Authentication algorithm—MD5 HMAC
- Authentication Mode—Preshared keys
- Diffie-Hellman group—Group 2
- SA lifetime—86400

These values (except for SA Lifetime) must match on both ends of the Concentrators, not the actual name of the policy.

Differing Preshared Keys Between IPSec Peers

You have seen that you have to ensure that the IKE policies match on each VPN peer. Part of the IKE policy is agreeing on the authentication method for the VPN. In this instance you are using preshared keys. If the preshared keys do not match, the VPN does not get established, because IKE fails and the tunnel is brought down.

You enter the preshared key in the LAN-to-LAN configuration wizard, located at Configuration > System > Tunneling Protocols > IPSec > LAN-to-LAN. You can see the preshared key in Figure 13-10.

Figure 13-10 *Preshared Key*

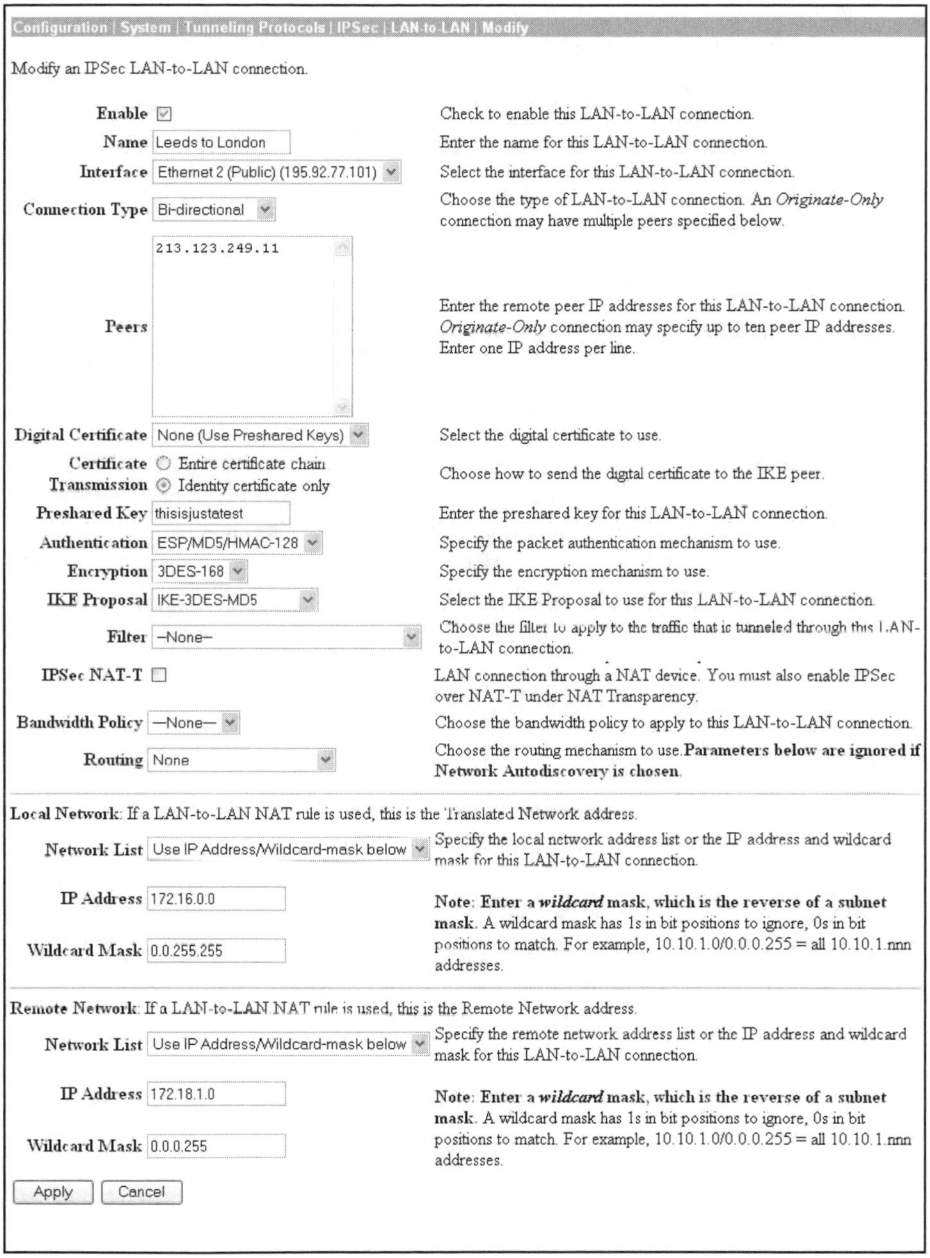

You can see that in this instance the preshared key is set to "thisisjustatest." Notice that this is in plain text. This helps when debugging, because you can see what the preshared key is. Most passwords are blocked from view and replaced with asterisks (*).

To recap, ensure that both the preshared keys match on both sides of the VPN configuration.

Incorrect IPSec Access Lists

The next item we'll discuss is quite a common configuration problem with VPNs. The IPSec access list is also called the network list or local and remote networks. When you create a LAN-to-LAN VPN, you have to tell the Concentrators at both sites what traffic to send over the VPN. This is normally done by identifying a local and remote network and using network lists. Both of these are covered in Chapter 11, "Configuring LAN-to-LAN VPNs on the Cisco 3000."

Two scenarios can occur with the misconfiguration of IPSec access lists. The first scenario is when the VPN does not initiate. This happens because of a configuration error in which the addresses do not match. For any LAN-to-LAN IPSec VPN to be established, the IPSec access lists must be an exact mirror of the other side. What this means in relation to the Concentrator is that the local network on one Concentrator must be the same as the remote network on the other Concentrator, and vice versa. Look at the two LAN-to-LAN Connection entries shown in Figures 13-11 and 13-12.

Figure 13-11 *LAN-to-LAN Connection Entry: Leeds to London*

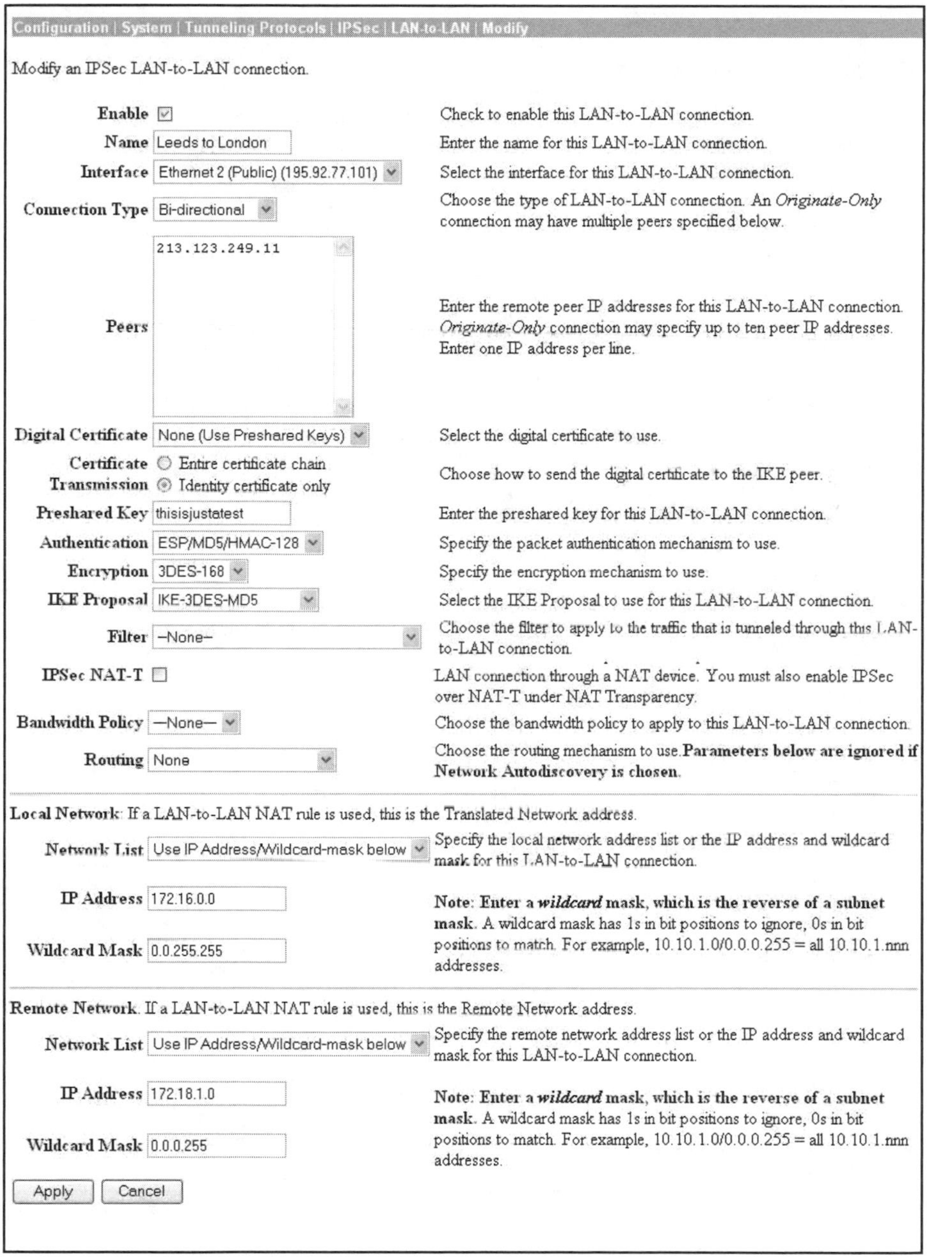

Figure 13-12 *LAN-to-LAN Connection Entry: London to Leeds*

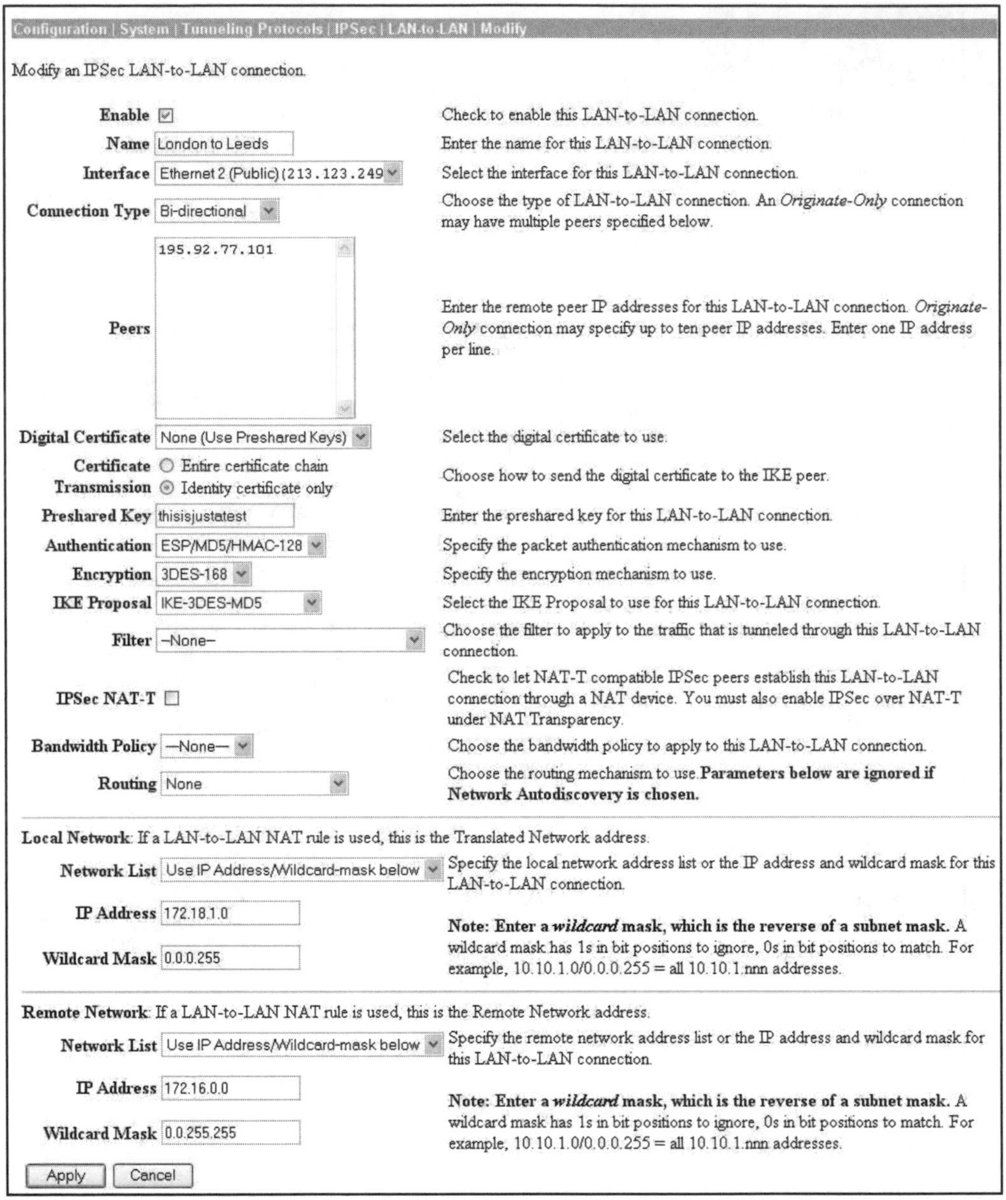

Configuration | System | Tunneling Protocols | IPSec | LAN-to-LAN | Modify

Modify an IPSec LAN-to-LAN connection.

Enable	☑	Check to enable this LAN-to-LAN connection.
Name	London to Leeds	Enter the name for this LAN-to-LAN connection.
Interface	Ethernet 2 (Public) (213.123.249 ▾)	Select the interface for this LAN-to-LAN connection.
Connection Type	Bi-directional ▾	Choose the type of LAN-to-LAN connection. An *Originate-Only* connection may have multiple peers specified below.
Peers	195.92.77.101	Enter the remote peer IP addresses for this LAN-to-LAN connection. *Originate-Only* connection may specify up to ten peer IP addresses. Enter one IP address per line.
Digital Certificate	None (Use Preshared Keys) ▾	Select the digital certificate to use.
Certificate Transmission	○ Entire certificate chain ⦿ Identity certificate only	Choose how to send the digital certificate to the IKE peer.
Preshared Key	thisisjustatest	Enter the preshared key for this LAN-to-LAN connection.
Authentication	ESP/MD5/HMAC-128 ▾	Specify the packet authentication mechanism to use.
Encryption	3DES-168 ▾	Specify the encryption mechanism to use.
IKE Proposal	IKE-3DES-MD5 ▾	Select the IKE Proposal to use for this LAN-to-LAN connection.
Filter	–None– ▾	Choose the filter to apply to the traffic that is tunneled through this LAN-to-LAN connection.
IPSec NAT-T	☐	Check to let NAT-T compatible IPSec peers establish this LAN-to-LAN connection through a NAT device. You must also enable IPSec over NAT-T under NAT Transparency.
Bandwidth Policy	–None– ▾	Choose the bandwidth policy to apply to this LAN-to-LAN connection.
Routing	None ▾	Choose the routing mechanism to use. **Parameters below are ignored if Network Autodiscovery is chosen.**

Local Network: If a LAN-to-LAN NAT rule is used, this is the Translated Network address.

Network List	Use IP Address/Wildcard-mask below ▾	Specify the local network address list or the IP address and wildcard mask for this LAN-to-LAN connection.
IP Address	172.18.1.0	**Note: Enter a *wildcard* mask, which is the reverse of a subnet mask.** A wildcard mask has 1s in bit positions to ignore, 0s in bit positions to match. For example, 10.10.1.0/0.0.0.255 = all 10.10.1.nnn addresses.
Wildcard Mask	0.0.0.255	

Remote Network: If a LAN-to-LAN NAT rule is used, this is the Remote Network address.

Network List	Use IP Address/Wildcard-mask below ▾	Specify the remote network address list or the IP address and wildcard mask for this LAN-to-LAN connection.
IP Address	172.16.0.0	**Note: Enter a *wildcard* mask, which is the reverse of a subnet mask.** A wildcard mask has 1s in bit positions to ignore, 0s in bit positions to match. For example, 10.10.1.0/0.0.0.255 = all 10.10.1.nnn addresses.
Wildcard Mask	0.0.255.255	

[Apply]   [Cancel]

Note in the figures that the local network for Leeds is 172.16.0.0/16 and the local network for London is 172.18.1.0/24. It is clear that these are set correctly as local on one Concentrator and as remote on the other. If there were any discrepancy in this configuration, such as a wrong address or inconsistent subnet mask, the VPN would not be established. Ensure that these addresses are perfect mirror images of each other in the LAN-to-LAN connection entry, or in the network list if you are using network lists.

The second scenario is where the IPSec access lists match but are incorrect. This causes the VPN to be established, but traffic does not meet the access list, so no traffic is sent over the VPN. Again, a quick look and check of the addresses and masks entered in the LAN-to-LAN Connection entry helps you deduce if this is where the problem exists.

Ongoing LAN-to-LAN VPN Failures with Preshared Keys

If the VPN fails after you know it has been working, this is classed as an ongoing failure. Ongoing failures occur only when something changes. If you are sure that no change has been made on either of the Concentrators, the problem must be a change in the network, because there is no software element to look at, as in a remote-access VPN.

The common culprit is an addition or change to the corporate firewall rule base, either at the remote site or at the central site where the VPN device exists. Ensure that any device that sits between the two VPN Concentrators that limits traffic is configured to pass IP 50 and UDP port 500.

Troubleshooting LAN-to-LAN CA-Based VPNs

As well as using preshared keys to authenticate LAN-to-LAN VPNs, the more scalable option is to use a digital certificate that is provided and authenticated by a certification authority. The configuration of LAN-to-LAN VPNs using CA services is covered in depth in Chapter 11.

Again, as with remote-access and LAN-to-LAN VPNs using preshared keys, you can split troubleshooting a CA-based LAN-to-LAN VPN into initial and ongoing failures.

Initial LAN-to-LAN VPN Failures Using CA Services

As discussed in Chapter 11, to establish a LAN-to-LAN VPN using a CA, both VPN Concentrators must enroll and obtain both a CA and an identity certificate. These are located on the Administration > Certificate Management screen, as shown in Figure 13-13.

Figure 13-13 *Administration > Certificate Management*

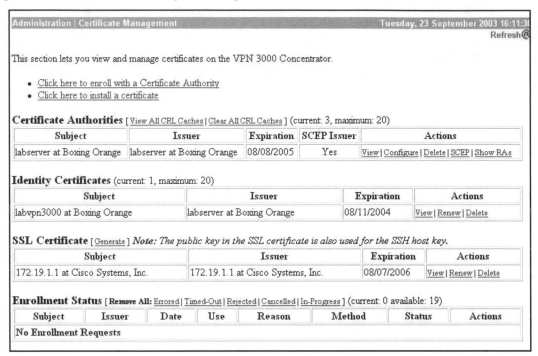

If you do not have both a CA and an identify certificate, your CA-based authentication for the LAN-to-LAN tunnel will not work. These certificates have to be valid and within their expiration date. If either certificate has expired, VPN establishment fails.

The preceding section mentioned that the IKE policies must match on both VPN Concentrators to participate in a VPN. One change must be made from the previous section for the LAN-to-LAN tunnel to use the digital certificate: The LAN-to-LAN connection entry must be changed to reflect the fact that digital certificates instead of preshared keys are to be used. Figure 13-14 displays a LAN-to-LAN VPN connection entry using digital certificates.

Figure 13-14 *LAN-to-LAN Connection Entry: Digital Certificate*

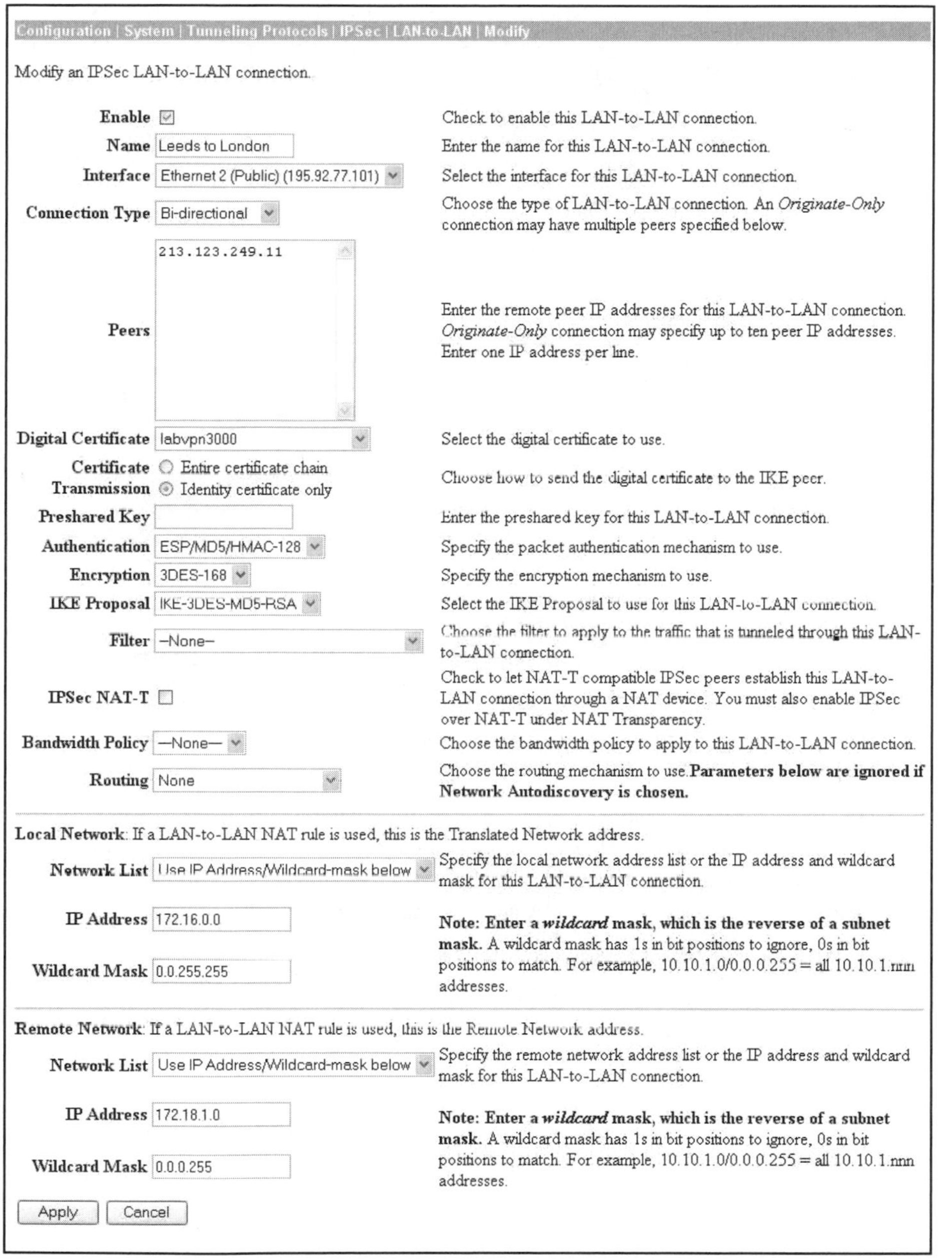

Note that the Preshared Key box is blank and that the labvpn3000 digital certificate has been selected. The IKE policy also reflects this, because the IKE-3DES-MD5-RSA policy has been chosen. Figure 13-15 shows this policy. You can see that it uses RSA Digital Certificate as its authentication mode rather than preshared keys.

Figure 13-15 *RSA IKE Policy*

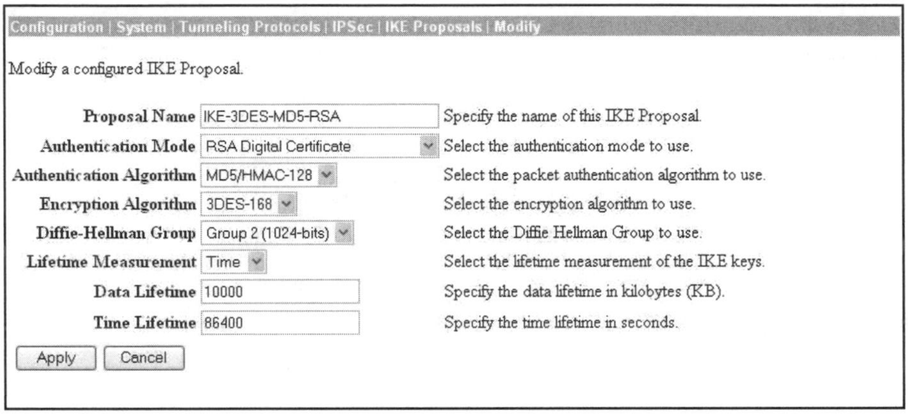

Ongoing LAN-to-LAN VPN Failures Using CA Services

If a LAN-to-LAN VPN has been operating using digital certificates and suddenly stops, this can be because of network reasons (as explained in the preceding section), ongoing LAN-to-LAN VPN failures with preshared keys, or a problem with the digital certificate.

The certificate might have expired, or it might have been revoked by the certification authority. Either way, confirm the certificate's status by looking at the Administration > Certificate Management screen. If it shows the certificates as being within their expiration period, and valid, contact the CA administrator to ascertain if the certificate has been revoked.

Summary

This chapter provided an overview of some of the troubleshooting steps for remote-access and LAN-to-LAN VPNs. It started by looking at the two main types of failures that occur with VPNs: initial failures and ongoing failures. Initial failures occur before the VPN is established. These normally are connectivity or configuration issues. Ongoing failures occur when the VPN has been established and then all of a sudden stops working. These failures normally occur when something has changed. This might be something in the VPN data path or a configuration on one of the VPN devices. This chapter then looked at the troubles associated with remote-access VPNs. A major factor in these failures is the failure of the VPN Software Client or a conflict between the VPN Software Client and other applications on the machine. We then looked at LAN-to-LAN VPNs using preshared keys and how these can fail because of configuration or network-related issues. The chapter ended by looking at the problems associated with LAN-to-LAN VPNs using digital certificates.

Review Questions

The following questions test your retention of the material presented in this chapter. The answers appear in Appendix A, "Answers to the Review Questions."

1   What are the two types of VPN failures?

2   What five values are controlled by the IKE policy?

3   If you have a VPN that has been working for 6 months and it suddenly stops working as soon as the firewall is upgraded at the central office, what might be the cause?

4   Which Concentrator screen can be used to check whether the identity certificate has expired?

5   By default, what traffic is required to be allowed through a firewall for a LAN-to-LAN VPN?

6   What are the port and protocol for NAT-T?

CHAPTER 14

Case Study

This is the final chapter in this book. It takes a real-world example of a typical virtual private network (VPN) deployment and provides a technical case study as a review of all the sections required. This case study looks at a fictitious company called Acme Limited.

We start by providing an overview of Acme Limited and the type of business it is involved with. We provide information that forms the criteria that are required for the business in this project. From this we create a design and look at the requirements both at the central site and at each remote connection provided on the remote agents' laptop computers.

We then move on to the configuration steps required to get the identified devices working for remote-access VPN support. This includes the Cisco VPN Concentrator, the central site PIX Firewall, and the VPN Software Client installed on the agents' laptop computers.

Overview of Acme Limited

Acme Limited is a midsized insurance-brokering company. It has 250 centrally-based employees and 80 remote agents. The centrally based employees access the corporate network via their workstations at the central site. They have a 2-MB Internet connection that is protected by a Cisco PIX Firewall. The inside interface of the PIX Firewall is present on the internal Acme LAN. LAN-based users use the PIX as their default gateway to connect to the public Internet. The main business systems that the company runs are based on an intranet server. It is currently connected to the private internal LAN at the Acme central site. This server currently has no public-access requirements, and there is no plan to place it on a demilitarized zone (DMZ) off the firewall. Acme Limited works from a single building, with no satellite offices and no network connections to any third parties. As well as the internal business systems, employees rely very heavily on e-mail. The central site has an e-mail server, located on the LAN on which users store their mailboxes.

Because of the nature of its business, Acme Limited employs 80 remote agents and plans to have 170 in the next two years. These remote employees are geographically spread into regions across the United Kingdom. Currently, the remote users have only e-mail access to the corporate e-mail system via a remote-access connection using a modem connected to their laptops. This connects to a series of modems hung off the back of multiple serial ports directly connected to the e-mail server at the central site. The remote agents dial in and authenticate locally against their e-mail system to pick up and read their e-mail. This is quite expensive, because the telephone number is free for the remote agents so that they don't have to incur costs that later have to be reclaimed as expenses. However, providing this service to the 80 remote agents increases the cost to the business. Because the remote agents do not have access to the internal business systems, they run a paper-based system in which they are sent information by fax and reply with their own faxes to the central site on a daily basis. A team of employees processes the paper-based reports from the remote agents and manually enter them into the internal business systems to ensure that the information is synchronized. This is costing the business money that could be saved with the introduction of a more up-to-date system that extends the internal systems to the remote agents.

You have been assigned to create a solution to the issues faced by Acme Limited.

Design Considerations for the Acme Limited Remote-Access Solution

The first design consideration is what type of system Acme Limited requires to meet the criteria it has identified. From your experience, you have chosen to implement a remote-access VPN solution using a Cisco VPN Concentrator at the central site and the Cisco VPN Software Client on the remote agent workstations and laptops. You decided to do this because Acme Limited already has invested in an Internet connection at the central site, and the benefits of a remote-access VPN solution fit the criteria the company has provided for the solution.

You already know that there is a design consideration for the choice of VPN Concentrator model for the central site. Recall from Chapter 2, "Cisco VPN 3000 Concentrator Series Hardware Overview," that the VPN 3005 supports a maximum of 100 concurrent tunnels. With only 80 remote agents, this would suffice for the immediate future. However, you know that Acme Limited plans to recruit up to another 90 remote agents to take the number up to 170 within two years. One problem with the 3005 is that it cannot be upgraded. 100 Concurrent VPN sessions is the most that this model can handle. Any more would require a complete hardware platform swap-out. With this in mind, it makes more sense to look at the next model up in the VPN Concentrator range. The Cisco VPN 3015 Concentrator also supports 100 concurrent VPN sessions, but it can be upgraded, because it is the same chassis as the 3030 and above. With the 3015, you can add a Scalable Encryption Processor (SEP) that increases the number of concurrent VPN sessions from 100 to approximately 1500. A VPN 3015 Concentrator would provide adequate performance for the present day and would offer an upgrade path when required for the 3015 to be upgraded when the total number of remote agents increases to more than 100.

NOTE	Version 4.1 of the Concentrator software doubles the number of concurrent remote-access VPN users from 100 to 200 on both the 3005 and the 3015.
	It is worth remembering that the maximum connections for VPN Concentrators are based on concurrent sessions. In some organizations, you might have 200 remote users, but some of them might be occasional users who do not access the VPN every day. In this instance, a 3005 would suffice, because you would never reach the 100 concurrent sessions. In the case of Acme Limited, because the remote workers all are based away from the central site, they spend a large portion of every day responding to e-mails and entering information into the internal business systems. Because of this, the concurrency ratio is very high, so it is safest to plan on the total number of remote agents.

You have decided to implement a remote-access VPN solution using a Cisco VPN 3015 Concentrator at the central site. By implementing this solution, you can give the remote agents full network reachability to the central site resources they require access to. You will also save money: The current dial-based infrastructure can be removed, because the implementation of the remote-access VPN will render it useless.

Central Site Infrastructure

The central site infrastructure will consist of the addition of a VPN 3015 Concentrator and some sort of Ethernet switch to present the public (outside) and transit networks. Acme Limited already has a Cisco PIX 515R Firewall. It will require an additional Ethernet card. This interface will be connected to the private interface of the VPN 3015 on what we will call the transit network.

Both the PIX Firewall and the VPN Concentrator will be connected to the public Internet. Both will require a public IP address. The private interface of the VPN Concentrator will be connected to the DMZ interface on the PIX Firewall. This is called a firewall sandwich VPN design because the VPN Concentrator sits parallel to the existing firewall. All VPN connections will be terminated on the VPN Concentrator and then presented to the PIX Firewall as an external entity. This provides another security zone and also facilitates granular-level security from a single device. The PIX Firewall is the device where the security rule base is implemented and is where the rules will be added to allow or deny VPN users access to specific resources.

This network design is shown in Figure 14-1.

Figure 14-1 *Acme Limited VPN Design*

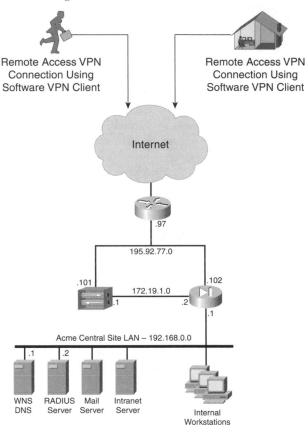

This figure shows the VPN Concentrator in place, with the IP addresses allocated. You will configure the VPN Concentrator based on this design to provide remote-access VPN services to Acme Limited. Note that the VPN Concentrator is not directly connected to the internal LAN. All VPN connections are treated as an external entity. They have to access the internal LAN through the existing PIX Firewall. The Concentrator will be configured with two groups—Agents and Admin. The Agents group is to be used by the remote agents and allows access only to the intranet and e-mail servers. The Admin group will allow full access to all the servers and workstations on the central site. This security based around these groups is implemented on the PIX Firewall and not the VPN Concentrator.

Remote Agent Infrastructure

Each remote agent will have the Cisco VPN Software Client installed on his or her laptop. The company's policy is to tunnel everything, and the Cisco Integrated Firewall with the default policy will be enforced on the remote agents. The remote agents will be provided with a local rate ISP connection, or even an xDSL connection where available to increase the connection speed. As soon as they connect to the public Internet, they will have to launch the VPN Connection entry via the Software Client to initiate the VPN. The remote agents will be authenticated against their Windows 2000 Active Directory that is running the Internet Authentication Service (IAS) that uses RADIUS as its authentication mechanism.

VPN Concentrator Configuration

Now that we have identified the requirements and provided a design to meet these requirements, it is time to start the Concentrator configuration. You will go through this configuration step by step, as you would for a fresh VPN Concentrator installation for a unit that has just been unpacked and set up with basic IP information. You will configure the VPN 3015 for remote VPN connectivity and then move on to creating the necessary groups. You will then look at the configuration of the VPN Client to create the connection entries for the remote agents.

This configuration is broken into four configuration steps:

Step 1   Initial system setup

Step 2   Enable global VPN settings

Step 3   Create the groups

Step 4   Configure the PIX Firewall

Step 5   Configure the VPN Client

Step 1: Initial System Setup

The first step is to perform the initial setup of the VPN Concentrator. This can be further broken into four tasks:

- Task 1—Change the Admin password
- Task 2—Set the identification information
- Task 3—Configure IP addresses
- Task 4—Configure routing

Task 1: Change the Admin Password

The first step is to change the VPN Concentrator's Admin password. By default, the username and password for a factory-shipped Concentrator are admin/admin. These must be changed. It is good practice to get into the habit of making this the first task you carry out on any Concentrator. You change the Admin password from the Administration > Access Rights > Administrators Screen. Click the Modify button next to the Admin user to see the screen shown in Figure 14-2.

Figure 14-2 *Changing the Admin Password*

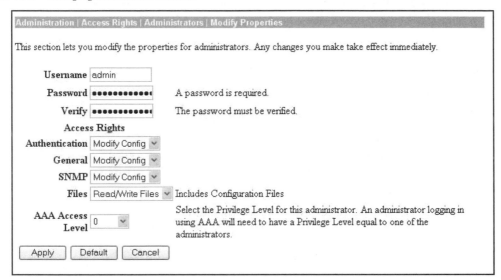

Enter a new password and then click Apply.

Task 2: Set the Identification Information

The next task is to set the Concentrator's identification information. This includes setting the system name, contact, and location. Set this on the Configuration > System > General > Identification screen, as shown in Figure 14-3.

Figure 14-3 *Setting the Identification Information*

Configuration | System | General | Identification

Configure system identification (optional). These entries are stored in the MIB-II *system* object.

System Name	ACMEVPN1	Enter a system name/hostname for the device; e.g., vpn01
Contact	Andrew Mason	Enter the name of the contact person
Location	Leeds, UK	Enter the device location; e.g., Computer Lab 3

Apply   Cancel

You can see that the system name is set to ACMEVPN1.

Task 3: Configure IP Addresses

The private IP address has already been configured, because this is what was used to connect to the VPN GUI on the private interface. The public IP address now needs to be configured. Navigate to the Configuration > Interfaces screen, and then click the public interface. The default setting is that the interface is disabled. Change this to enable Static IP Addressing, and enter the address, as shown in Figure 14-4.

Figure 14-4 *Setting the IP Address*

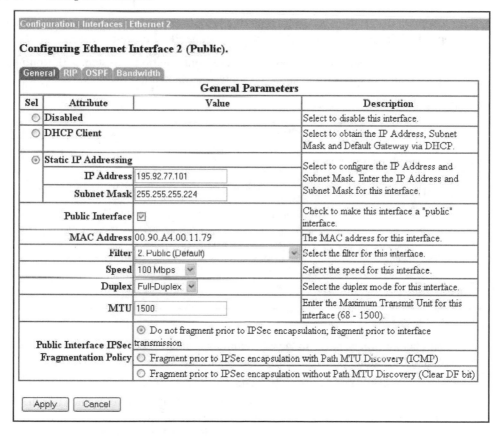

Ensure that the default public filter is set on the public interface. Clicking Apply saves these settings and returns you to the Interfaces screen.

Task 4: Configure Routing

As you learned in Chapter 3, "Routing on the VPN 3000," two types of routes need to be configured based on this design. First, you need to configure a default route that points to the next-hop address that leads to the public Internet. This is so that the VPN Concentrator has routing to the remote agents when they connect using the VPN Software Clients. You also have to configure at least one static route. The transit network, which is the network between the PIX and VPN Concentrator, has an address of 172.19.1.0/24. The internal LAN at Acme Limited has the address 192.168.0.0/24. The VPN Concentrator in its normal state does not have a route to the internal LAN, and this is what the remote agents want to configure. When you set a default route, any traffic destined for the internal LAN is caught by the default route and is routed out to the public Internet. This is undesirable.

So, what you have to do is configure a static route for the internal LAN pointing to the next hop, which in this case is the DMZ interface of the PIX Firewall.

To configure the default route, navigate to the Configuration > System > IP Routing > Default Gateways screen and enter the address, as shown in Figure 14-5.

Figure 14-5 *Configuring the Default Gateway*

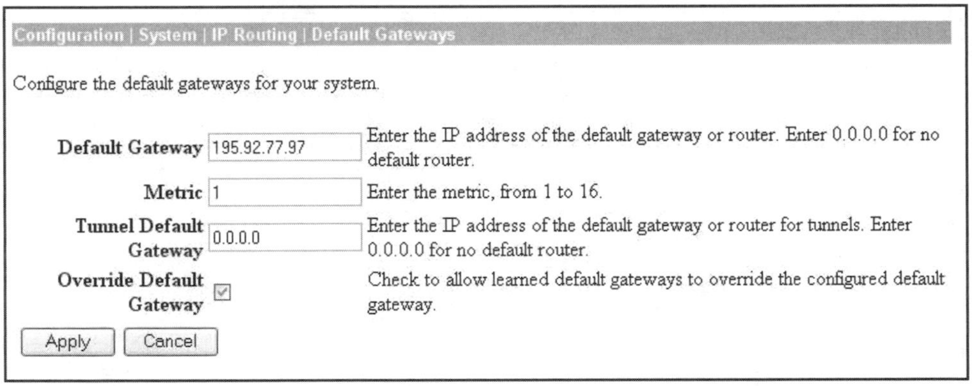

After clicking Apply, return to the Configuration > Interfaces screen, shown in Figure 14-6, and note the default gateway setting next to the public interface.

Next you need to add the static route to the 192.168.0.0/24 network from the Configuration > System > IP Routing > Static Routes screen. The only static route shown is the default route. Click Add to add a new static route. Enter the required information, as shown in Figure 14-7. Remember, you want to route to the 192.168.0.0/24 network via 172.19.1.2, and this is one hop away.

Figure 14-6   *Configuration > Interfaces Screen*

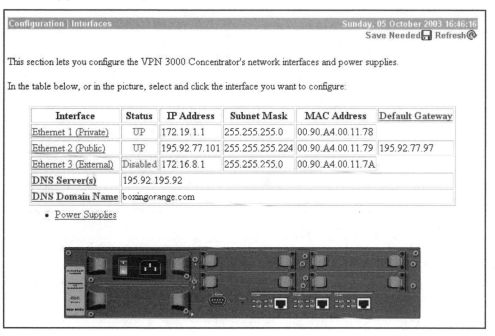

Figure 14-7   *Adding a Static Route*

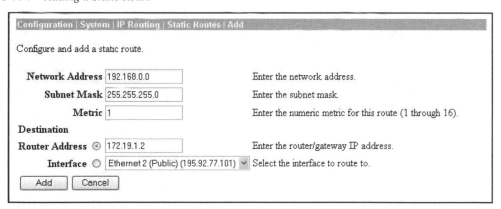

The Static Routing screen, as shown in Figure 14-8, now shows both the default route and the configured static route pointing to the 192.168.0.0/24 network.

Figure 14-8   *Viewing the Static Routes*

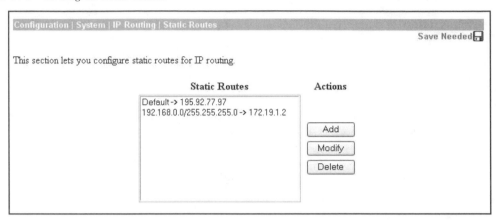

Step 2: Enable Global VPN Settings

The second step is to globally enable VPN access on the VPN Concentrator. This can be further broken into two tasks:

- Task 1—Set the Concentrator to use global address pools
- Task 2—Set the Concentrator to use NAT-T

Task 1: Set the Concentrator to Use Global Address Pools

Remote VPN Clients using the VPN Software Client are assigned an IP address when they connect. For this design, you will use address pools for these remote clients. You have to enable the use of address pools globally before assigning them to the groups. This means that you can then assign a group of addresses, out of range on the transit network, to each group you configure on the VPN Concentrator. This has advantages over using DHCP to allocate the addresses. You can then identify what group a user belongs to at the PIX Firewall based on his or her source IP address, because this address allocation is linked to the individual group the user has connected through.

The use of address pools is set on the Configuration > System > Address Management > Assignment screen, as shown in Figure 14-9. Just check the Use Address Pools option.

Figure 14-9   *Enabling Address Pools*

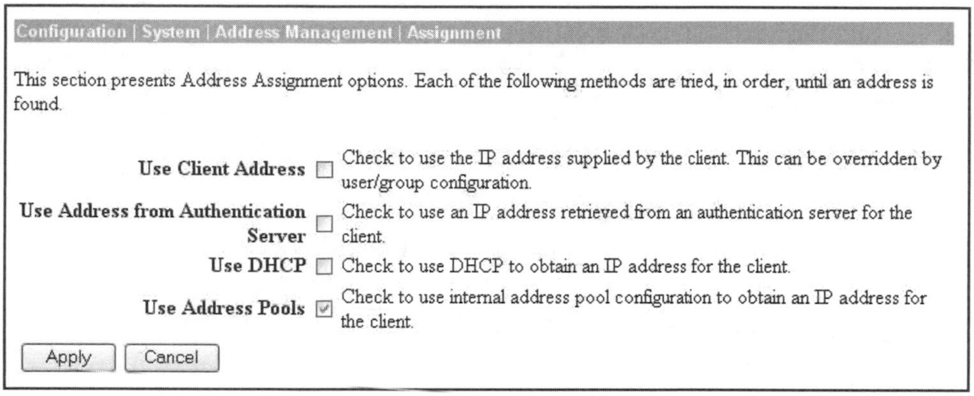

NOTE   It is important to note that if this simple setting is not checked, a VPN connection set to use address pools will not function. It will authenticate, but the IP address will not get allocated to the client, and the connection will fail, with an error message indicating that the client could not obtain an IP address.

Task 2: Set the Concentrator to Use NAT-T

Because you do not know where the remote agents will be connecting from, you must plan to configure some sort of NAT-Traversal (NAT-T) on the VPN Concentrator. As you know, IPSec is broken by Port Address Translation (PAT) because of the source port issue caused by ESP's being a protocol (IP 50) and not a TCP or User Datagram Protocol (UDP) port. So you can encapsulate ESP into either UDP or TCP. Cisco offers UDP and TCP encapsulation over port 10000 as standard, but this can be changed to suit your needs. A better solution is to globally enable NAT-T on the VPN Concentrator.

NAT-T is an Internet Engineering Task Force (IETF) standard for IPSec communication through a PAT environment and is supported by most Internet service providers (ISPs) in the Internet community. NAT-T uses UDP port 4500 to encapsulate ESP within. NAT-T is used only when required. No further configuration at group level or even at the client is required after this is globally enabled.

You enable NAT-T from the Configuration > System > Tunneling Protocols > IPSec > NAT Transparency screen. Check the IPSec over NAT-T check box, as shown in Figure 14-10. Click Apply to save these settings to the running configuration.

Figure 14-10 *Enabling NAT-T*

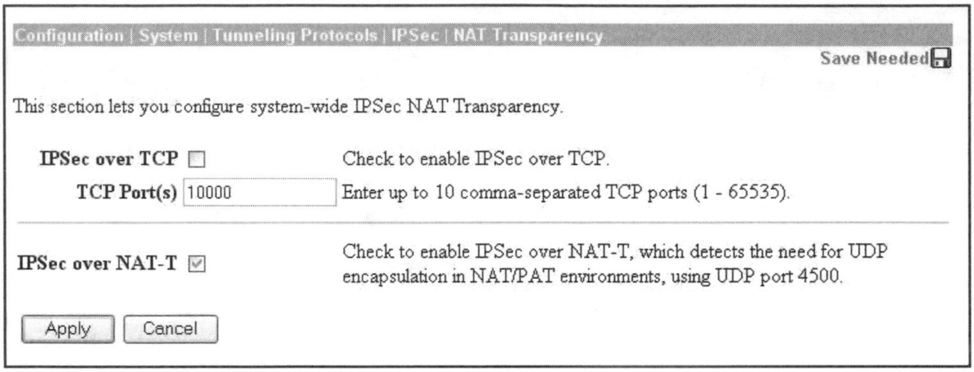

| Configuration | System | Tunneling Protocols | IPSec | NAT Transparency |

> Save Needed🖫
>
> This section lets you configure system-wide IPSec NAT Transparency.
>
> **IPSec over TCP** ☐   Check to enable IPSec over TCP.
>
> **TCP Port(s)** [10000]   Enter up to 10 comma-separated TCP ports (1 - 65535).
>
> **IPSec over NAT-T** ☑   Check to enable IPSec over NAT-T, which detects the need for UDP encapsulation in NAT/PAT environments, using UDP port 4500.
>
> [Apply]   [Cancel]

NOTE   Don't forget to save the running configuration to the startup configuration at regular intervals by clicking the Save Needed icon at the top right of the screen.

Step 3: Create the Groups

Now that you have carried out the basic system configuration on the Concentrator, it is time to start creating the groups required to allow VPN access to the internal Acme Limited LAN.

This can be further broken into three tasks:

- Task 1—Create the Agents and Admin groups
- Task 2—Set the groups to authenticate against a RADIUS server
- Task 3—Set the address pools for the groups

Task 1: Create the Agents and Admin Groups

The first task is to create the two groups that you will use for the remote agents and the remote IT staff. The remote agents will use the Agents group, and the remote IT staff will use the Admin group. The settings for both groups, apart from the group name and password, are identical. This is because the security is to be handled by the PIX Firewall, not the VPN Concentrator.

Navigate to the Configuration > User Management > Groups screen, and select Add to add the first group.

The first screen is the Identity screen. Here you set the group name and password, as shown in Figure 14-11. You can see that this group is called Agents.

Figure 14-11 *Adding a Group: Identity*

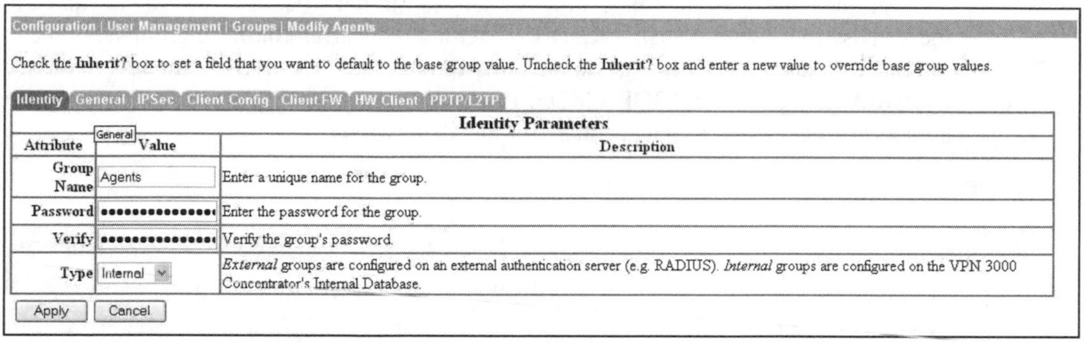

Next, click the General tab to display the general settings, as shown in Figure 14-12. The WINS and domain server IP address for the network is 192.168.0.10, as shown in the network diagram. This information needs to be added for the primary WINS and primary DNS information. You will use only IPSec, so disable all the other tunneling protocols for this group. Leave everything else as standard.

Figure 14-12 *Adding a Group: General*

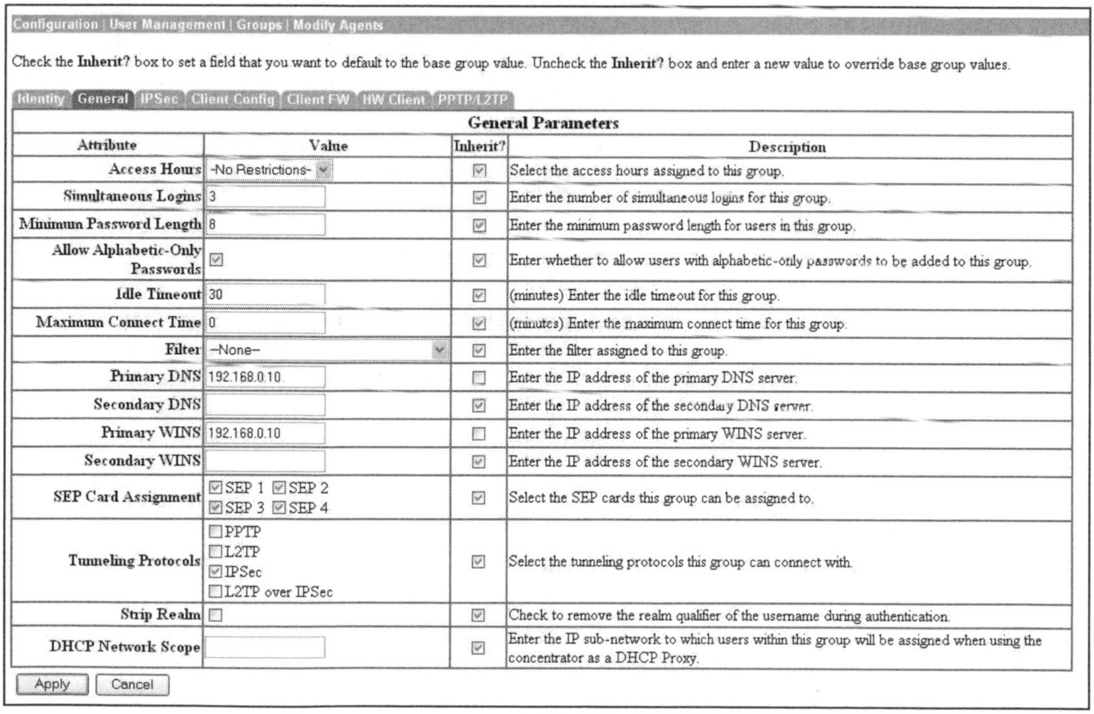

Clicking the IPSec tab takes you to the IPSec screen, as shown in Figure 14-13. You can leave all the default settings except the Authentication field, because they are adequate for the VPN settings. You are using RADIUS user authentication for these groups, not the internal user database, so change this setting from Internal to RADIUS. The security association (SA) in place is ESP-3DES-MD5. This means that ESP, 3DES encryption, and MD5 authentication are more than adequate for this deployment.

Figure 14-13 *Adding a Group: IPSec*

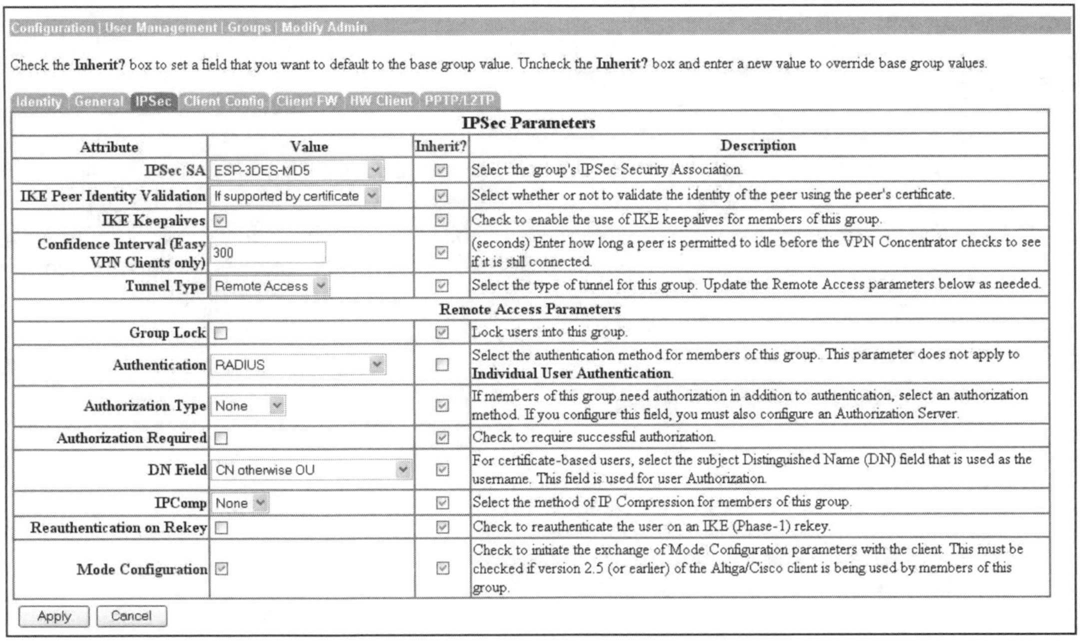

Configuration | User Management | Groups | Modify Admin

Check the **Inherit?** box to set a field that you want to default to the base group value. Uncheck the **Inherit?** box and enter a new value to override base group values.

Identity | General | IPSec | Client Config | Client FW | HW Client | PPTP/L2TP

IPSec Parameters			
Attribute	**Value**	**Inherit?**	**Description**
IPSec SA	ESP-3DES-MD5	☑	Select the group's IPSec Security Association.
IKE Peer Identity Validation	If supported by certificate	☑	Select whether or not to validate the identity of the peer using the peer's certificate.
IKE Keepalives	☑	☑	Check to enable the use of IKE keepalives for members of this group.
Confidence Interval (Easy VPN Clients only)	300	☑	(seconds) Enter how long a peer is permitted to idle before the VPN Concentrator checks to see if it is still connected.
Tunnel Type	Remote Access	☑	Select the type of tunnel for this group. Update the Remote Access parameters below as needed.
Remote Access Parameters			
Group Lock	☐	☑	Lock users into this group.
Authentication	RADIUS	☐	Select the authentication method for members of this group. This parameter does not apply to **Individual User Authentication**.
Authorization Type	None	☑	If members of this group need authorization in addition to authentication, select an authorization method. If you configure this field, you must also configure an Authorization Server.
Authorization Required	☐	☑	Check to require successful authorization.
DN Field	CN otherwise OU	☑	For certificate-based users, select the subject Distinguished Name (DN) field that is used as the username. This field is used for user Authorization.
IPComp	None	☑	Select the method of IP Compression for members of this group.
Reauthentication on Rekey	☐	☑	Check to reauthenticate the user on an IKE (Phase-1) rekey.
Mode Configuration	☑	☑	Check to initiate the exchange of Mode Configuration parameters with the client. This must be checked if version 2.5 (or earlier) of the Altiga/Cisco client is being used by members of this group.

Apply | Cancel

The next tab is Client Config, shown in Figure 14-14. Again, the standard settings on this tab are adequate for this group configuration, so no change is required. On this tab you set the tunneling policy for the group. The policy dictated by Acme Limited is to tunnel all traffic down the VPN when the remote client is connected. Because of this, no change is required, because the standard setting is to tunnel everything.

Figure 14-14 *Adding a Group: Client Config*

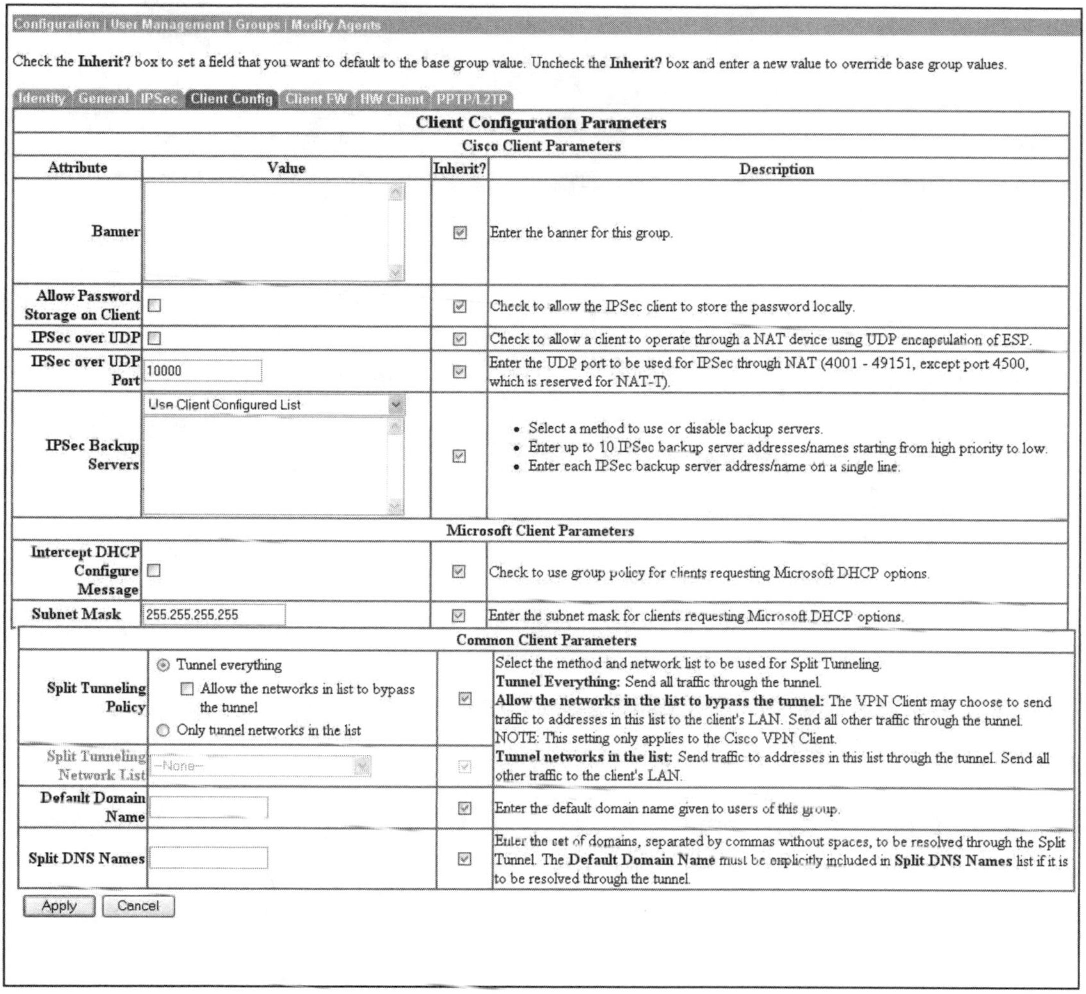

One of the criteria for this design is that the VPN Software Client is to have the Cisco Integrated Firewall functionality enabled with the default firewall filter applied. The next tab, Client FW (see Figure 14-15), is where these settings are applied. Set the Firewall Setting to Firewall Required, and change the Firewall to Cisco Integrated Client Firewall. You will see that the only available Firewall Policy is to use the Policy Pushed (CPP) feature. From the drop-down box, select the Firewall Filter for VPN Client (Default) filter.

Figure 14-15 *Adding a Group: Client FW*

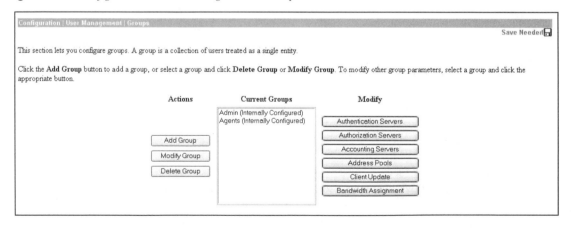

This is the last tab you have to configure for this group, so clicking Apply applies these settings and takes you back to the main Groups screen.

Now that you have created the Agents group, create the Admin group following exactly the same steps.

You should be left with the Groups screen shown in Figure 14-16.

Figure 14-16 *Configuration > User Management > Groups Screen*

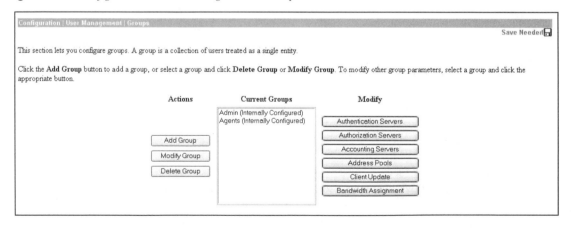

Now that the two groups are created, you can move on to the second task.

Task 2: Set the Groups to Authenticate Against a RADIUS Server

Now that you have created the groups, you have to set the user authentication parameters. When creating users, you can use the built-in user database, or you can pass user authentication to a third-party authenticator. In most cases, it makes sense to pass this authentication to a third party, such as the existing Windows NT 4 domain or Windows 2000 Active Directory. Doing this eases the burden of administration, because only one set of user accounts has to be administered, and password synchronization does not become an issue.

Acme Limited has a RADIUS server with an IP address of 192.168.0.10, as shown in the network diagram. You will configure both groups to authenticate against this RADIUS server. From the main groups screen, shown in Figure 14-16, select the first group and then click the Authentication Servers button. You can see that currently this group has no configured authentication servers. Click Add to add a new authentication server for this group.

You see the screen shown in Figure 14-17. Enter the correct information. Leave the Server Port as 0, because this uses UDP port 1645, which is the default for RADIUS. Enter a server secret password that is also configured on the RADIUS server. Click Add to apply the information, and then repeat for the second group.

Figure 14-17 *Adding an Authentication Server*

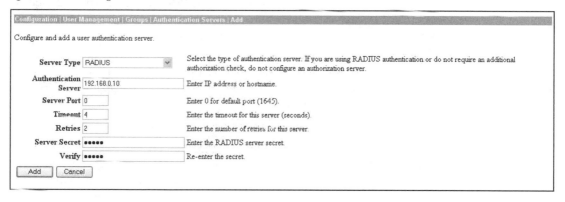

Task 3: Set the Address Pools for the Groups

Now that you have created the groups and allocated authentication servers for them, it is time to allocate a pool of IP addresses for users who connect through these groups.

From the main groups screen (see Figure 14-16), select the group and then click the Address Pools button. Because this group has no configured pools, click Add to add an address pool. You see a screen asking you to set a range start and range end for the allocated pool, as shown in Figure 14-18. Use these settings:

- **Agents Group**—172.19.1.3 to 172.19.1.223
- **Admin Group**—172.19.1.225 to 172.19.1.254

This instantly gives you 221 usable addresses for the Agents group and 30 usable addresses for the Admin group. Enter these addresses into the Range Start and Range End fields, and then click Add to add these addresses to the address pools for the appropriate groups.

Figure 14-18 *Adding an Address Pool*

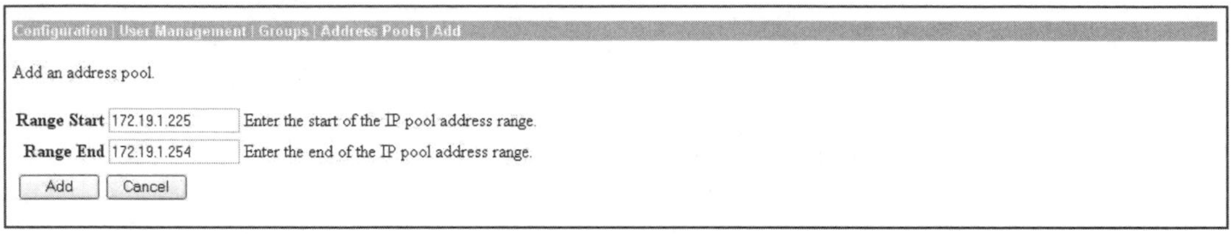

Step 4: Configure the PIX Firewall

Now that you have configured the central site VPN Concentrator to accept the VPN connections, you have to do some configuration on the existing PIX Firewall to ensure that VPN traffic is permitted and that other traffic such as user authentication is allowed.

Because the VPN Clients are allocated an address from the transit network IP address range, there is no need to configure a static route on the PIX Firewall. If you had used an address other than the transit network, you would have had to configure a static route on the PIX to this range of addresses via the Concentrator's private interface.

User authentication is performed from the VPN Concentrator to the RADIUS server with an IP address of 192.168.0.20. In this instance, on the PIX, NAT has to be bypassed for the 192.168.0.20 address on the DMZ interface, and access to it has to be allowed on UDP port 1645 from the DMZ address 172.19.1.1.

You have allocated each group a range of IP addresses. The Admin group requires full access to everything. Therefore, an access list is required on the PIX to give the 172.19.1.224/27 network full access to the inside network. The Agents group addresses cannot be summarized into a single statement. Therefore, the Agents group addresses are 172.19.1.0/25, 172.19.1.128/26, and 172.19.1.192/27. The remote agents need access to the e-mail and intranet servers, so these addresses on the PIX need to be given access to these two servers.

NOTE   This is not a book on PIX configuration. For more information, see the Cisco PIX Firewall course book from Cisco Press.

Step 5: Configure the VPN Client

You are now ready for the final step in this case study configuration—configuring the VPN Software Client. From the VPN Client main screen, click New to add a new connection entry. You see the screen shown in Figure 14-19.

Figure 14-19 *Adding a New Connection Entry*

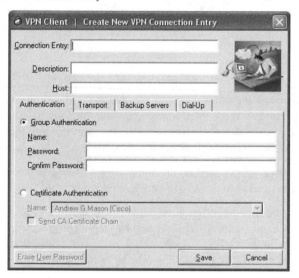

Enter the connection information. Enter the correct IP address, 195.92.77.101, and the group information, as shown in Figure 14-20.

Figure 14-20 *Adding a New Connection Entry: Completed*

You will notice that there are three tabs besides the Authentication tab. You do not need to make a change on any of these tabs, so clicking Save saves the connection entry to the VPN Client.

Double-click the VPN Connection entry, and enter your user information when prompted. You are connected to the Acme Limited VPN. You can access the internal business systems via the intranet server and the e-mail server.

Summary

This chapter focused on a fictitious company called Acme Limited.

It started by providing an overview of what Acme currently uses for its network services and infrastructure. You received some background information from which you could identify design considerations for the proposed solution. You then looked at the identified design considerations after choosing a remote-access VPN solution for Acme Limited.

Equipment was chosen based on the company's requirements for the central site and the remote connections, which were to be made on the remote agents' laptop computers.

You then moved to the configuration section. You started with a vanilla-build, factory-shipped VPN Concentrator and went step by step through getting it onto the network and configured for its first VPN. You covered five steps of configuration, ending with configuring the central site PIX Firewall and the VPN Software Client.

This type of installation is based on real-world experience. It has shown that the Cisco VPN Concentrator is quite a simple device to configure that can be up and running after a few easy configuration steps.

Answers to the Review Questions

Chapter 1

1 What two main protocols make up the IPSec framework?

Answer AH and ESP

2 What IP protocol does ESP use?

Answer ESP is IP protocol 50.

3 What are the two modes of IKE Phase 1?

Answer Main mode and aggressive mode

4 What three key lengths can AES currently use?

Answer Currently, AES supports 128-, 192-, and 256-bit encryption keys.

5 What type of VPN would you be using if you are a user based at home connecting to the central site over a VPN by using a VPN Software Client installed on your laptop computer?

Answer This type of VPN is classed as a remote-access VPN. This is because the VPN connection is created between the VPN Software Client and the VPN headend device at the central site.

6 What are the four steps of the Security Wheel?

Answer Secure, monitor, test, and improve. They should be repeated on a continuous basis and should be incorporated into updated versions of the corporate security policy.

7 What is the normal method of key exchange for the encryption algorithms used in IPSec, such as DES, 3DES, and AES?

Answer The normal method of key exchange for IPSec encryption algorithms is by using a DH key exchange.

8 What is the main issue with firewall-based VPNs?

Answer The main issue with firewall VPNs comes down to ownership. Most large organizations have a network team and a separate security team. Problems arise because traditionally all WAN connections are owned and supported by the network team. With a firewall VPN, the security team would have to own the VPN, and the network team would class the VPN as a WAN connection.

9 What are the two modes of IPSec operation?

Answer   Transport and tunnel

10 What three authentication methods are used in the IPSec protocol's origin identification feature?

Answer   Preshared keys, RSA signatures, and RSA encrypted nonces. With preshared keys, a secret key value entered into each peer manually is used to authenticate the peer. RSA signatures use the exchange of digital certificates to authenticate the peers. RSA encrypted nonces are encrypted and then exchanged between peers. The two nonces are used during the peer authentication process.

Chapter 2

1 Which model of the VPN Concentrator is not hardware-upgradable to use hardware-based encryption?

Answer   The Cisco VPN 3005 Concentrator is the only Concentrator that is not upgradable and does not use hardware-based encryption.

2 Which encryption protocols can the older SEP encrypt in hardware?

Answer   The older SEP encrypts only DES and 3DES in hardware. AES requires SEP-E.

3 Which software VPN client would you use to connect a PDA such as an HP Ipaq to your VPN?

Answer   The Certicom client, called movianVPN, is the only client available for the Ipaq that will work with a Cisco VPN 3000 Concentrator.

4 Which three modes can the Windows VPN Client Firewall operate in?

Answer   The Cisco VPN Windows client offers support for a firewall feature. The firewall feature is designed to enhance security for Microsoft Windows-based PCs running the Cisco IPSec client Release 3.5. This feature is applied in one of three modes—Are You There (AYT), stateful firewall (always on), or Centralized Protection Policy (CPP).

5 If you had a small branch office that wanted an upgradable VPN solution for up to 100 users at any one time, which model of the VPN Concentrator 3000 series would you choose?

Answer   In this instance, either the 3005 or 3015 would handle the job, but the requirement specifies that the unit must be upgradable. The 3005 is not hardware-upgradable, so the 3015 would be the best solution.

6 How many site-to-site tunnels are supported on a Cisco VPN 3030 Concentrator?

Answer   The VPN 3030 Concentrator supports up to 500 site-to-site tunnels.

7 If you required a VPN Concentrator that could terminate 7500 IPSec tunnels, which model(s) could you use?

Answer   The only model you could use would be the VPN 3080, because it supports up to 10,000 IPSec tunnels. The VPN 3060 supports only 5000 IPSec tunnels, so it does not meet the requirement of 7500 IPSec tunnels.

8 What is the difference between the two models of the 3002 Hardware VPN Client?

Answer   The difference between the two hardware clients is that one has a single public and private interface, and the other has a single public interface and an eight-port 10/100 switch for the private interface.

9 What is the highest specification model in the VPN 3000 Concentrator series?

Answer   The highest-specification VPN Concentrator 3000 is the 3080.

10 What operating systems does the current Cisco VPN Unity Client support?

Answer   Currently the Cisco VPN Unity Client supports Windows, Solaris, Linux, and Macintosh operating systems.

Chapter 3

1 What versions of RIP are supported on the VPN Concentrator?

Answer   The Cisco VPN Concentrator supports RIPv1 and RIPv2. The Concentrator can be configured to support only RIPv1, only RIPv2, or RIPv1 and RIPv2 combined.

2 How many static routes can be configured on a VPN 3005 Concentrator?

Answer   On a VPN 3005 Concentrator, you can configure up to 200 static routes.

3 What is the default time between RIP routing updates?

Answer   By default, RIP broadcasts routing updates every 30 seconds. This setting can be changed on a Cisco router but not on a VPN Concentrator.

4 What does OSPF use to uniquely identify the device participating in the OSPF process?

Answer   OSPF operates by using a router ID (RID) within its routing updates to uniquely identify itself to other routers participating in OSPF. The router ID uses the same format as an IP address but acts purely as an identifier and has no function as an IP address. It is normal practice on a VPN Concentrator to use the IP address of the private interface as the router ID.

5 What are the three types of OSPF authentication?

Answer None, Plain Text, and MD5.

6 Of the three OSPF authentication types, which is considered the most secure, and why?

Answer MD5 authentication is considered the most secure OSPF authentication option. This is because with MD5, no password is sent in clear text over the network. A one-way hash is created and sent over the network. If the hash compares with the hash at the other side, the OSPF process knows that the passwords must match.

Chapter 4

1 What two methods can you use to configure the VPN Concentrator?

Answer The command-line interface (CLI) or the graphical user interface (GUI)

2 What are the default username and password when you initially connect to a VPN Concentrator?

Answer admin/admin

3 Which interface on a VPN Concentrator would you use to connect to a public network such as the Internet?

Answer You always use the public interface to connect to a public network such as the Internet.

4 What is split DNS?

Answer Split DNS is used in split-tunneling connections. The Software Client resolves whether a DNS query packet is sent in clear text or is encrypted and sent down the tunnel. If the packet is encrypted and sent down the tunnel, a corporate DNS server resolves the DNS query. Clear-text DNS requests are resolved by ISP-assigned DNS servers. This is so that remote clients can resolve internal DNS queries.

5 Which split-tunneling method should you use if you want to tunnel everything but still access your local LAN?

Answer The local LAN access option provides access to resources on a local LAN while the VPN tunnel is established. The local LAN addresses are pushed to the Software Client. These IP addresses are added to the Software Client driver's access control list (ACL). These bypass addresses route ahead of the VPN tunnel's encryption algorithm. Any data bound for, or received from, the addresses specified in the Mode Configuration message is sent or received in the clear. This allows access to the local LAN while the IPSec tunnel is running. All other traffic is encrypted and forwarded to the central site.

6 IKE keepalives are enabled by default. When is it advisable to disable them for a remote-access VPN?

Answer   IKE keepalives can keep an ISDN or Public Switched Telephone Network (PSTN) line busy. Therefore, if you are using a metered ISDN or PSTN connection, it might be a good idea to disable IKE keepalives so that they do not tie up the line when they aren't necessary.

7 What three files can an administrator edit to customize the installation of the Software Client on a Windows system?

Answer   oem.ini, vpnclient.ini, and the .pcf file

8 What troubleshooting application comes installed with the VPN Software Client?

Answer   When you install the VPN Software Client, the Log Viewer application is also installed. This application allows you to log connection attempts and gives you information if there are any errors or misconfigurations.

9 What default MTU does the VPN Client set?

Answer   The Software Client automatically sets the MTU size to approximately 1300 bytes. For unique applications in which fragmentation is still an issue, SetMTU can change the MTU size to fit the specific scenario.

10 Which interface on a VPN Concentrator would you use to connect to your private LAN?

Answer   The private interface on the VPN Concentrator should always be used to connect to your LAN.

Chapter 5

1 What are the two PKI models?

Answer   The two PKI models are central and hierarchical. The central model uses a flat network design. A single authority (the root CA) signs all certificates. Each employee who needs a certificate sends a request to the root CA. Small companies with several hundred employees may use the central CA. Hierarchical authorities use a tiered approach. The ability to sign a certificate is delegated through a hierarchy. The top of the hierarchy is the root CA. It signs certificates for subordinate authorities. Subordinate CAs sign certificates for lower-level CAs or employees. Large geographically dispersed corporations (such as Cisco Systems) use hierarchical CAs. The root CA is located in San Jose, the company headquarters. Rather than having more than 30,000 employees making certificate requests back to San Jose, subordinate CAs are placed strategically around the world. Local employees request a CA from the local subordinate CA.

2 When you start the manual or file-based enrollment, what file is created by the enrollment form?

Answer In the certificate-generation process, first you generate a certificate request called a Public Key Cryptography Standards (PKCS) #10. User information such as a common name, organizational unit, organization, locality, state, country, and public key is requested. After the information is supplied, the Concentrator generates a certificate request: a PKCS#10. The request is formatted as an Abstract Syntax Notation 1 (ASN.1) message and is sent to the CA.

3 What does CRL stand for, and what is it?

Answer A Certificate Revocation List (CRL) is a list issued by the CA that contains certificates that are no longer valid. CRLs are signed by the CA and are released periodically or on demand. CRLs are valid for a specific amount of time, depending on the CA vendor used.

4 From which screen on the VPN 3000 can you view all the CA, identity, and SSL certificates?

Answer Administration > Certificate Management

5 How many identity certificates are supported on a VPN 3005 Concentrator?

Answer The 3005 supports up to two identity certificates, and the 3015 and above support 20.

6 File-based enrollment uses a PKCS#10 file. What protocol does automatic (also called network or online) enrollment use?

Answer Automatic enrollment uses the Simple Certificate Enrollment Protocol (SCEP).

7 By default, does an MS CA support SCEP?

Answer By default, the MS CA does not support SCEP. You have to install SCEP as an add-on to the Microsoft CA. The SCEP add-on is part of the Windows 2000 Resource Kit.

8 On the VPN Client, how do you use a certificate within a connection entry?

Answer By selecting the certificate on the Authentication tab of the connection entry.

9 What is the major certificate store for the VPN Client?

Answer The VPN Client uses the notion of a store to convey a location in your local file system for storing personal certificates. The major store for the VPN Client is the Cisco store, which contains certificates you have enrolled through the Cisco VPN Client.

10 When you create a new IKE proposal to use certificate authentication, what should you set the authentication field to?

Answer RSA Digital Certificate

Chapter 6

1 What are the four firewall features of the Cisco VPN 3000 Concentrators?

Answer   Are You There, stateful firewall, Central Policy Protection, and the Cisco integrated client.

2 If the Firewall Required option is set, and no firewall is in use by the Software Client, what happens?

Answer   The VPN connection fails, and an error message appears in the log, notifying the end user of this.

3 Where on the menu system do you navigate to to create filters and rules to apply to a firewall?

Answer   You find the Filters and Rules submenus under Configuration > Policy Management > Traffic Management.

4 What four vendors of software firewalls are currently configured to work with the VPN Concentrator?

Answer   The VPN 3000 Concentrator is currently configured to work with software firewalls from Network ICE, Zone Labs, Sygate, and Cisco Systems.

5 What are the two methods of enabling the stateful firewall feature?

Answer   You can enable the stateful firewall feature by right-clicking the padlock icon in the system tray and checking Stateful Firewall (Always On) or by clicking the Options button from within the VPN Client application.

6 What is the main feature of the AYT firewall option?

Answer   The main feature of the AYT firewall option is to check to see whether the software firewall is running on the host that is initiating the VPN connection.

7 What is the name of the default CPP policy?

Answer   The default CPP policy is called Firewall Filter for VPN Client.

8 When you create a filter, what is the default action if a rule does not match a rule added to the filter?

Answer   If a rule is not matched on a filter, the default action is to drop the packet. This is the same as the implicit deny all rule that is at the end of every PIX and IOS access list.

9 If the Firewall Optional option is set and no firewall is in use by the Software Client, what happens?

Answer   If the Firewall Optional option is set and no firewall is in use by the Software Client, the VPN connection still occurs, but the user receives a warning that the firewall is optional and was not found.

10 With a custom firewall, if you set a vendor code of 2 and a product code of 3, what product would you be using?

Answer If you set a vendor code of 2 and a product code of 3, you would be using the Zone Labs Integrity software firewall.

Chapter 7

1 What are the two modes of operation for the 3002 Hardware Client?

Answer Client mode and network extension mode. It is important to remember that the 3002 Hardware Client is always classed as a remote-access user as far as the central site 3000 Concentrator is concerned. This is true even when the 3002 Hardware Client is operating in network extension mode.

2 Upon initial configuration of the 3002 Hardware Client, what is the default IP address of the private interface?

Answer 192.168.10.1/24

3 When initially configuring a 3002 Hardware Client, you notice that the public interface receives an IP address automatically. Why is this?

Answer By default, DHCP is enabled on the public interface. This means that as soon as you connect it to a network, it sends out a DHCP Discover packet. If a DHCP server exists on the network, the 3002 obtains an IP address to use on the public interface.

4 What default username and password are used to connect to the GUI manager for the 3002 Hardware Client?

Answer The default username is admin, and the default password is admin.

5 You have made the necessary change on a 3002 Hardware Client to enable network extension mode, but the VPN is not operating in network extension mode. What is the probable cause of this error?

Answer To enable network extension mode, you have to make two changes on the 3002 Hardware Client. You also have to change the group on the central site 3000 Concentrator to allow the remote client to use network extension mode. On the 3002 Hardware Client, you have to configure a nondefault IP address on the private interface and also uncheck the PAT Enabled check box.

6 What protocol does auto-update use to transfer the new image to the 3002?

Answer The 3002 uses TFTP to transfer the new image to itself.

7 What is the auto-update client type for a 3002 Hardware Client?

Answer vpn3002

8 Which interface on the 3002 Hardware Client supports PPPoE?

Answer   The public interface is the only interface on a 3002 that supports PPPoE.

9 What is the default operation mode for a 3002 Hardware Client?

Answer   Client mode

10 What are the two ways to connect the VPN on a 3002 Hardware Client?

Answer   This depends on the mode the 3002 is running in. In PAT mode, the tunnel establishes when data passes to the VPN Concentrator or when you click Connect Now in the Monitoring > System Status screen.

In network extension mode, the VPN 3002 automatically attempts to establish a tunnel to the VPN Concentrator without requiring any interesting traffic.

Chapter 8

1 What is the main difference between user authentication and unit authentication?

Answer   Unit authentication authenticates the initial VPN connection, and then all users on the LAN can access the VPN. User authentication enforces an authentication method where individual users must be authenticated before they can access the VPN.

2 You have configured a 3002 for user authentication. A user is not authenticated and tries to establish an HTTP connection over the VPN to the central site. What happens to the user's session?

Answer   In this instance, because the user is not authenticated, he is redirected to the 3002 Hardware Client authentication screen, where he is forced to log in with his user credentials. After the user is authenticated, his session is forwarded to the desired destination host.

3 What do you do to enable interactive unit authentication for a group configured on the central site VPN 3000 Concentrator?

Answer   To configure interactive unit authentication, you have to modify the group used on the central site concentrator and check the Require Interactive Hardware Client Authentication check box.

4 Which authentication method do you use if you have a 3002 Hardware Client on a network with other users who are not permitted to use the VPN?

Answer   In this instance, you use user authentication. This ensures that every user is authenticated before being allowed to access the VPN.

5 What do you do to enable user authentication for a group configured on the central site VPN 3000 Concentrator?

Answer To configure user authentication, you have to modify the group used on the central site concentrator and check the Require Individual User Authentication check box.

6 What is the default authentication method for a VPN 3002 Hardware Client?

Answer The default is unit authentication, where the group and user details are both hard-coded.

Chapter 9

1 On the 3000 Concentrator, which tab do you use to change the IPSec Backup Servers option?

Answer The IPSec Backup Servers feature is available on the Client Config tab for the group properties.

2 What default protocol and port does the VCA use?

Answer The VCA uses UDP and port 9023 by default, although this port can be changed.

3 Which method of RRI is supported only on a Cisco VPN 3002 Hardware Client?

Answer The network extension method of RRI is supported only on a Cisco VPN 3002 Hardware Client. This cannot be done with a Software Client, because the Software Client does not support network extension mode.

4 If you have configured the Central Site Cisco VPN 3000 Concentrator to "Use List Below" for the IPSec Backup Servers, what happens to any backup servers that have been manually entered into the Software Client?

Answer Any backup servers that have been manually entered into the Software Client are ignored and are replaced with the centrally configured ones when the remote user connects to the VPN.

5 What is the default value for the IPSec Backup Servers field when you are modifying a group on a Cisco VPN 3000 Concentrator?

Answer Use Client Configured List.

6 What two types of RRI can be configured on a Cisco VPN 3000 Concentrator?

Answer Client RRI and network extension RRI.

Chapter 10

1 On the VPN Software Client, what is the default transparent tunneling mode for any new connection?

Answer   The default transparent tunneling mode for any new connection is to use IPSec over UDP.

2 What transport layer protocol and port does NAT-T use as defined by the standard?

Answer   NAT-T uses UDP as its transport layer protocol and port 4500.

3 Where do you configure NAT-T on the Cisco VPN Concentrator?

Answer   You configure NAT-T globally on the VPN Concentrator. You do this from the Configuration > Tunneling Protocols > IPSec > NAT-T screen.

4 Where do you configure IPSec over UDP on the Cisco VPN Concentrator?

Answer   You configure IPSec over UDP globally from the Configuration > Tunneling Protocols > IPSec > NAT-T screen.

5 What is the default IPSec over UDP port number used for transparent tunneling?

Answer   The default IPSec over UDP port number used for transparent tunneling is 10000.

6 What is the configuration difference between IPSec over UDP and IPSec over TCP/NAT-T?

Answer   The configuration difference is that IPSec over TCP and IPSec over NAT-T are configured globally on the Concentrator and IPSec over UDP is configured per group.

Chapter 11

1 What is one major difference between a LAN-to-LAN VPN and a remote-access VPN?

Answer   LAN-to-LAN VPNs are usually terminated on hardware VPN gateways, whereas one end of a remote-access VPN is normally a host running a VPN Software Client.

2 What are the three supported authentication options for LAN-to-LAN VPNs?

Answer   The Concentrator supports the following authentication options for LAN-to-LAN VPNs:

None

HMAC-MD5 — 128-bit key

HMAC-SHA-1 — 160-bit hash

3 What menu option do you use to configure a LAN-to-LAN connection?

Answer The first action in configuring a LAN-to-LAN VPN is to create the LAN-to-LAN connection on the VPN Concentrator. Navigate to Configuration > System > Tunneling Protocols > IPSec > LAN-to-LAN.

4 What three items does the LAN-to-LAN connection entry create?

Answer When you configure a LAN-to-LAN connection, the three items that are automatically configured for the LAN-to-LAN VPN are a group, filter rules, and a security association.

5 What must you use in the LAN-to-LAN connection entry if you want to use more than one subnet across the VPN?

Answer If you are looking at using more than one subnet across the VPN, you must configure a network list rather than manually entering a single network address into the LAN-to-LAN connection entry. You could also use NAD if you are using more than one subnet across a LAN-to-LAN VPN.

6 Which routing protocols does NAD work with?

Answer NAD only works with RIP. The other dynamic routing protocol implemented on the Concentrator is OSPF, and this is not supported by NAD.

Chapter 12

1 What are the two types of bandwidth management?

Answer Bandwidth policing and bandwidth reservation

2 What is the default filename for the active configuration file on a VPN Concentrator?

Answer CONFIG

3 What are the differences between the Monitoring > Sessions and Administration > Sessions screens?

Answer The Monitoring screen is where you can view the sessions and statistics, whereas with the Administration screen you can ping and log out the LAN-to-LAN and remote-access VPNs.

4 When you select Administration > Swap Config File, what is the current active configuration file renamed?

Answer The current active configuration file is renamed CONFIG.BAK.

5 If you have an amber LED for power supplies A and B, what does this indicate?

Answer That voltages are outside normal ranges and there is an error.

6   What four options are available under the Access Rights window?

Answer   The Access Rights window is where you configure administrative access to the VPN Concentrator. It has four submenus:

Administrators—Administrators, passwords, and access rights

Access Control List—IP addresses and options for administrator access

Access Settings—Session timeout and limits

AAA Servers—AAA servers for administrator access

Chapter 13

1   What are the two types of VPN failures?

Answer   The two types of VPN failures are initial and ongoing. Initial failures are failures to establish the VPN in the first place. Ongoing failures relate to failures that occur after the VPN has been working.

2   What five values are controlled by the IKE policy?

Answer

Encryption algorithm

Hash algorithm

Authentication method

Diffie-Hellman group

SA lifetime

3   If you have a VPN that has been working for 6 months and it suddenly stops working as soon as the firewall is upgraded at the central office, what might be the cause?

Answer   In this instance, the firewall must be blocking the traffic required for the VPN and therefore is cutting off the VPN. If this is a LAN-to-LAN VPN, you must enable access for IP 50 and UDP port 500. If this is a remote-access VPN, depending on the type of transparent tunneling in use, UDP port 10000, UDP port 4500, or TCP port 10000 must be allowed.

4   Which Concentrator screen can be used to check whether the identity certificate has expired?

Answer   You can use the Administration > Certificate Management Concentrator screen to check whether the identity certificate has expired.

5 By default, what traffic is required to be allowed through a firewall for a LAN-to-LAN VPN?

Answer By default, a LAN-to-LAN VPN uses IP 50 for ESP and UDP port 500 for ISAKMP (IKE).

6 What are the port and protocol for NAT-T?

Answer UDP port 4500 is the NAT-T standard that is being adopted by the IETF and being implemented by ISPs worldwide.

Configuring movianVPN

This appendix introduces movianVPN by Certicom and explains how to configure it for use with the Cisco VPN 3000 series Concentrator.

Certicom enables secure mobile computing by providing a complete line of information security products, technologies, and services for wireless applications, devices, components, and networks.

movianVPN is a handheld Virtual Private Network (VPN) Client that provides secure wireless access to corporate network resources. Built on the IPSec standard, movianVPN works with leading VPN gateways, handheld devices, and wireless networks so that you can extend strong, cost-effective security to mobile employees. Certicom's experience with security for constrained environments and Elliptic Curve Cryptography (ECC, defined at www.certicom.com/index.php?action=res,ecc_intro_home) technology ensures that movianVPN has a negligible impact on performance or battery life.

Configuration involves creating a basic movianVPN policy and testing the connection between the client and the gateway before you enable the client's advanced features. This appendix looks at all these steps individually and offers some troubleshooting suggestions in the event that the test connection initially fails.

This appendix is focused on the deployment of movianVPN in the WinCE and Palm OS environments using the Cisco VPN Concentrator 3000 series. Should you require more detailed information, consult the Cisco VPN Concentrator 3000 series Deployment Guide, available at www.certicom.com.

To evaluate movianVPN, visit www.certicom.com/trymovian.

What Is movianVPN?

movianVPN is an award-winning VPN Client that provides secure wireless access to corporate network resources. Built on the IPSec standard, movianVPN works with leading VPN gateways, handheld devices, and wireless networks so that you can extend strong, cost-effective security to mobile employees.

movianVPN meets the strongest government security requirements and supports the U.S. Department of Defense Common Access Card for stronger authentication. It is ready to work with existing government infrastructure.

As part of a complete handheld security solution, movianVPN secures communications between devices. movianCrypt secures data on the device, movianMail secures e-mail and attachments, and movianDM makes it easier to create and enforce handheld security policies with large deployments.

ECC and movianVPN

movianVPN is specifically designed for the constrained environments of wireless and mobile devices. It uses Elliptic Curve Cryptography (ECC), which provides strong security with much smaller key sizes than legacy public-key encryption algorithms.

In addition, ECC requires less processing power, which results in faster Internet Key Exchange (IKE) negotiation with ECDH (one of the algorithms in the ECC suite).

NOTE   On the Cisco VPN Concentrator, ECC is called DH Group 7.

---

movianVPN also supports 768 and 1024-bit Diffie-Hellman algorithms for the case in which the gateway does not support Certicom's patented ECC implementation.

Gateway Access

Gateways are accessed using a policy set up within movianVPN. This policy contains the information required to connect to a specific gateway and to successfully negotiate the exchange of keys that will be used to encrypt the transmitted data, verify identities, and confirm data integrity.

The network you use to access the VPN gateway server does not have to be secure. For example, you may use dialup access to an Internet service provider to reach the gateway server or access it through a wider corporate LAN.

After you provide your username and password so that you are recognized by the VPN gateway, movianVPN establishes a secure, encrypted tunnel for you to the VPN.

While accessing the servers that comprise the VPN, you are provided with confidentiality, data integrity verification, and data source authentication for your communications.

movianVPN at Work

The following scenario explains how movianVPN works in a typical setting.

Using movianVPN on her handheld, Joan requests presentation updates from Bob at Headquarters. movianVPN encrypts the message and sends it to the wireless network, the

Internet, and finally Headquarters' VPN gateway. The VPN gateway decrypts the message and passes it to Bob. He responds by attaching the updated presentation, and the process begins in reverse. All communications between Joan's handheld and the VPN gateway are completely secure. This process is shown in Figure B-1.

Figure B-1   *movian at Work*

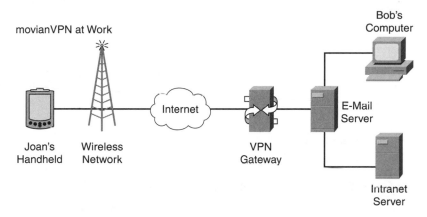

Supported Platforms

movianVPN is supported on the following platforms:

- **Palm**—Palm PDA running Palm OS 3.5 to 4.1, with 400 KB of available memory
- **Windows CE**—Windows CE-based device running Handheld PC 2000, Pocket PC version 3.0, Pocket PC 2002, or Pocket PC 2003 with 1.6 MB of available memory
- **Symbian**—Nokia Communicator PC Suite with 600 KB of available memory or PC Suite for P800 with 500 KB of available memory

Supported Devices and Gateways

movianVPN supports the following software versions on the Cisco VPN Concentrator 3000 series:

- 3.6.1 and later

If you are running an older version of the software, upgrade the software on the gateway to a supported version before you configure movianVPN for use on the gateway.

For a current list of supported devices and gateways, visit www.certicom.com/vpnsupport.

Supported Connections

The following specific connections have been tested for interoperability:

- CDMA/1XRTT
- CDPD
- Ethernet
- GSM/GPRS
- IDEN
- Ricochet
- TDMA
- 802.11
- BlueTooth

Configuring movianVPN and the Gateway

This section describes how to create a basic movianVPN policy and test it. It also gives you directions you might need to set up and start using the following movianVPN features on the gateway:

- IPSec
- Split tunneling
- Perfect Forward Secrecy
- DNS support
- External authentication
- NAT-Traversal
- Banner support and password save feature

Creating a movianVPN Policy for Your Gateway

This section explains how to create a basic movianVPN policy to test the connection from the client to the gateway. Testing and troubleshooting procedures follow in the next section.

To simplify the connection and the testing process, avoid using advanced features such as Perfect Forward Secrecy and DNS support at this time. Users can configure these settings later for general deployment purposes.

For more information on how to create a policy with the advanced features, refer to the movianVPN User Guide for WinCE Pocket PC and Handheld PC or the movianVPN User Guide for Palm OS.

A client configuration worksheet is provided near the end of this appendix. You can use it to enter the required information, and you can also give it to users.

To create a policy for the Cisco VPN Concentrator 3000 gateway, you need the following information:

- Gateway IP address
- Check box status for Use Perfect Forward Secrecy
- Group name, group password, username, and user password
- IKE Suite, DNS, and IPSec Suite settings
- SA life setting

NOTE   You are asked for the user password when you log in to the gateway.

Before You Begin

If you have not already done so, configure the gateway to support movianVPN:

Step 1   Create a new group.

Step 2   Identify access and encryption modes associated with the group.

Step 3   Populate the group with appropriate users.

Opening the movianVPN Application on WinCE

To open the movianVPN application on WinCE, either tap Start and select movianVPN from the pull-down list, or tap Start, select Programs, and tap the movianVPN icon.

Opening the movianVPN Application on Palm OS

To open the movianVPN application on Palm OS, do the following:

Step 1   Tap the arrow in the right corner of the top toolbar, and select movian or All.

Step 2   Tap the movianVPN icon.

Creating a Basic Policy for WinCE or Palm OS

To create a basic policy for a Cisco VPN Concentrator 3000 gateway, do the following:

Step 1 Open the movianVPN application. The movianVPN application window appears. Figure B-2 shows this window for the Windows CE environment, and Figure B-3 shows this window in the Palm environment.

Figure B-2 *movianVPN on WinCE*

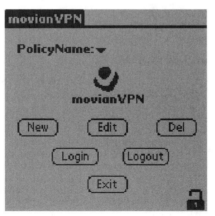

Figure B-3 *movianVPN on Palm OS*

Step 2 Tap New. The movianVPN Policy window appears.

Step 3 Enter a policy name in the Policy Name field.

Step 4 Tap Please select one to open the pull-down menu.

Step 5   Tap the Cisco VPN Concentrator 3000 entry. The Cisco VPN Concentrator 3000 address field and the gateway policy security option check boxes appear. On WinCE, the address field is called Gateway IP Address. On Palm OS, the address field is called Gateway Address.

Step 6   Enter the address. Keep the test policy simple; do not enable the advanced feature Perfect Forward Secrecy at this time.

Step 7   On WinCE, tap Continue. On Palm OS, tap the arrow icon. The Cisco VPN Concentrator 3000 window appears. Figure B-4 shows this window for the Windows CE client, and Figure B-5 shows this window for the Palm client.

Figure B-4   *Cisco VPN Concentrator 3000 Window on WinCE*

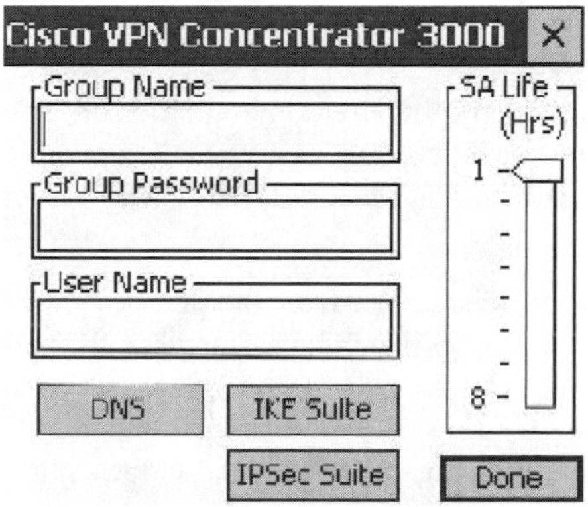

Figure B-5   *Cisco VPN Concentrator 3000 Window on Palm OS*

Step 8   Enter the Group Name, Group Password, and User Name for the gateway. These entries should exactly match those set when the new group was created and users were added to the group.

Step 9 Palm OS only: If you want to save the password, tap Prompt at the Group Password field, enter the password, and tap OK. In the Cisco VPN Concentrator 3000 window, the Group Password now appears as Assigned. To delete or edit the password, tap Assigned, either leave the field blank to delete the password or enter a new password, and tap OK.

Step 10 Tap the IKE crypto suite button in the Cisco VPN Concentrator 3000 window. On WinCE, the IKE crypto suite button is labeled IKE Suite. On Palm OS, this button is labeled IKE. The IKE Crypto Suite window appears.

Step 11 Select the appropriate settings from each of the pull-down lists for the Group, Cipher, and Hash fields. These entries should exactly match those set when the new group was created.

Step 12 On WinCE, tap Continue. On Palm OS, tap the checkmark icon.

Step 13 Tap the IPSec crypto suite button in the Cisco VPN Concentrator 3000 window. On WinCE, the IPSec crypto suite button is labeled IPSec Suite. On Palm OS, this button is labeled IPSec. The IPSec Crypto Suite window appears.

Step 14 Select the appropriate entry from the pull-down list in the Suite field. These entries should exactly match those set when the new group was created.

Step 15 On WinCE, tap Continue. On Palm OS, tap the checkmark icon.

Step 16 In the Cisco VPN Concentrator 3000 window, adjust the SA Life to time out of the gateway as desired. On WinCE, use the slidebar. On Palm OS, use the arrows.

Step 17 On WinCE, tap Done. On Palm OS, tap the checkmark icon. The movianVPN application window appears.

Step 18 To connect to the gateway, tap the Login button.

Testing the Policy

After creating a movianVPN policy, you can test it to confirm that the client is successfully connecting to the gateway. Use a basic policy to simplify the connection test.

To test the policy, do the following:

Step 1 In the movianVPN window, ensure that the policy is selected.

Step 2 Tap Login.

Step 3 The IKE Messages display connection progress in generating and exchanging keys. The connection is established when the message Finished appears.

Step 4   Tap OK.

For more information on verifying your policy, refer to the movianVPN User Guide for WinCE Pocket PC and Handheld PC or the movianVPN User Guide for Palm OS.

Troubleshooting a Failed Connection

If the connection fails, do the following:

- Check that the settings match on both the movianVPN client and the gateway.
- Refer to the movianVPN User Guide for WinCE Pocket PC and Handheld PC or the movianVPN User Guide for Palm OS for information on verifying your policy and troubleshooting logging in to the gateway.

If the settings are correct and the connection is still unsuccessful, do the following:

- Access the movianVPN diagnostic tools (Ping and View IPSec Status). For more detailed information, refer to the movianVPN Deployment Guide.
- Refer to the gateway configuration manual for information on how to view the connection log.

Configuring IPSec on movianVPN

The IPSec protocol allows movianVPN to negotiate methods of secure communication to authenticate identity, confirm data integrity, verify data sources, and select encryption functions.

While using movianVPN, users can select and deselect IPSec during a session with the gateway. While IPSec is deselected, sent data is not encrypted. This lets users access servers and websites outside the VPN, on the Internet, but they cannot reach computers inside the VPN.

On gateways that permit it, movianVPN also supports split tunneling. When split tunneling is enabled, data is either encrypted or unencrypted, depending on whether it is being sent and received within the VPN or elsewhere on the Internet.

Users can securely access your corporate intranet and freely access the Internet at the same time.

WARNING   When IPSec is disabled, your connection is insecure. Data is not encrypted.

Enabling/Disabling IPSec on WinCE

To enable or disable IPSec on WinCE, do the following:

Step 1   In the movianVPN window, while connected to the gateway, tap Options.

Step 2   Select IPSec from the list.

Step 3   Tap OK. When the checkmark is present, IPSec is enabled.

Enabling/Disabling IPSec on Palm OS

To disable or enable IPSec on the Palm OS, do the following:

Step 1   While you are connected to the VPN, in the movianVPN window, tap the movianVPN tab. The Options pull-down list appears. When you are connected to the VPN, the IPSec entry appears on the list. While IPSec is enabled, a lock icon appears in the bottom-right corner of the window.

Step 2   Select IPSec from the list. You receive a warning that IPSec is about to be disabled.

Step 3   Tap OK.

Enhancing Your movianVPN Policy

As soon as your gateway has been configured for basic movianVPN functions and successfully tested, you can enhance your movianVPN policy using the following:

- Split tunneling
- Perfect Forward Secrecy
- DNS support
- External authentication
- Authentication using certificates
- NAT-Traversal
- Banner support and the password-save feature

NOTE   If you have used the movianVPN Deployment tool to create a policy with enhanced features, you don't have to enable these features on the client software.

Split Tunneling

Split tunneling allows your users to use both the Internet and the corporate intranet at the same time. The VPN server uses split tunneling to decide which traffic to send through an encrypted tunnel, depending on where the packets (the data being sent or received) originate or are directed.

NOTE   Your network configuration is more secure without split tunneling.

When split tunneling is selected, all packets sent to or from the VPN and its identified subnets are encrypted. Packets to outside the VPN are not encrypted and go directly through the ISP to the Internet and are not encrypted.

When split tunneling is deselected, all packets are encrypted. If the packet is not to or from an identified address on the VPN, it is dropped from communication.

Users are not required to configure the client to enable split tunneling.

To enable split tunneling, do the following:

Step 1   Create a network list.

Step 2   Enable split tunneling.

Step 3   Apply this to a group.

Creating a Network List on the Gateway

To enable split tunneling, you must also create a network list. Do the following:

Step 1   Select Configuration > Policy Management > Traffic Management > Network Lists.

Step 2   Click Add.

Step 3   Choose a List Name.

Step 4   Enter an IP address and a wildcard mask.

Step 5   Click Add.

Step 6   Add multiple subnets as required.

Enabling Split Tunneling on the Gateway

To enable split tunneling for users logging in to the gateway, do the following:

Step 1   In the navigation bar, select Configuration > User Management > Groups.

Step 2   Select the group name in the Current Groups box, and click Modify Group.

Step 3   Select the Client Config tab.

Step 4   Under Split Tunneling Network List, select the network list.

Enabling Split Tunneling on the movianVPN Client

As soon as the gateway supports it, split tunneling is automatically available for users. Users are not required to edit their policy.

Perfect Forward Secrecy

Perfect Forward Secrecy is a cryptographic characteristic associated with a derived shared secret value. With Perfect Forward Secrecy, if one key is compromised, previous and subsequent keys are not compromised, because subsequent keys are not derived from previous keys.

Perfect Forward Secrecy performs the key exchange twice as your handheld device negotiates with the gateway using the same key material. A new key is created for each step of IKE, and each new key is not derived from the previous key. Thus, the previous key and the following one are not compromised even if the current one is.

Negotiating the connection takes longer.

Enabling Perfect Forward Secrecy on the Gateway

To enable Perfect Forward Secrecy on the gateway, do the following:

Step 1   Select Configuration > Policy Management > Traffic Management.

Step 2   Select Security Associations.

Step 3   Select ESP_3DES_MD5_DH7 in the list and click Modify. These settings should match the selections made when the group was created.

Step 4   Under Perfect Forward Secrecy, select Enabled.

Step 5   Select Apply.

Enabling Perfect Forward Secrecy on the movianVPN Client

As soon as the gateway supports Perfect Forward Secrecy, users can enable this function on their clients.

To enable split tunneling on the movianVPN client, do the following:

Step 1 In the movianVPN window, select the policy.

Step 2 Tap Edit.

Step 3 Select the Use Perfect Forward Secrecy check box.

Step 4 Tap Continue in WinCE OS or tap the arrow/check icon in Palm OS until editing changes to the policy are complete and the movianVPN window appears.

Step 5 Tap Login. Perfect Forward Secrecy is enabled for the policy.

DNS Support

The Domain Name System (DNS) is used to identify particular computers or parts of the network. Some gateways supply this information to the handheld device during key negotiation.

If Query DNS is checked, the handheld device downloads the DNS information from the gateway server. If you supply the DNS information, your handheld device's settings override other information provided by the gateway.

Enabling DNS Support

Do the following to enable DNS support:

Step 1 Select Configuration > User Management > Groups.

Step 2 Select the movianVPN group you want to affect from the Current Groups list, and click Modify Group.

Step 3 Click the General tab.

Step 4 Set the Primary and Secondary DNS addresses.

Step 5 Click the Client Config tab.

Step 6 Under Default Domain Name, enter your company's domain name.

Step 7 Select Apply.

Enabling DNS on the movianVPN Client

If the client is supplying DNS settings, they must be set on the client software.

To enable and set DNS support, do the following:

Step 1   On the movianVPN client, enter or select the Policy Name.

Step 2   Tap Edit.

Step 3   Tap Continue for WinCE OS, or tap the arrow icon for Palm OS. The gateway window appears.

Step 4   Select DNS.

Step 5   Uncheck the Query DNS box. The DNS entry fields appear.

Step 6   Enter the Primary and Secondary DNS addresses. In Palm OS, enter the Domain Name.

Step 7   Tap Continue in WinCE OS, or tap the check icon in Palm OS.

Step 8   Tap Done.

Authentication Using Certificates

The movianVPN client supports certificate-based authentication with the Cisco VPN 3000 Concentrator series gateway.

Installing Certificates

You must install a root certificate and a certificate for the VPN gateway to allow clients to be authenticated. Select Administration > Certificate Management to display a list of installed certificates.

Consult your gateway documentation for detailed instructions for enrolling with a certification authority and installing certificates.

Using Certificates

As soon as a certificate of the correct type has been installed, you can configure the VPN gateway so that users can use certificates for authentication.

Step 1   Select Configuration > System > Tunneling Protocols > IPSec > IKE Proposals. Create a new IKE proposal by clicking Add, or modify an existing active IKE proposal by clicking Modify. The IKE Proposal modification screen appears.

Step 2   Choose the appropriate Digital Certificate entry from the Authentication Mode drop-down list.

Step 3 Select Configuration > Policy Management > Traffic Protocols > SAs. Create a new SA by clicking Add, or modify an existing SA by clicking Modify.

Step 4 Select an installed identity certificate from the Digital Certificates drop-down list. Select the IKE Proposal you created or modified (in Step 1) from the IKE Proposal drop-down list.

Step 5 Select Configuration > User Management > Groups. Create a new IPSec group by clicking Add Group, or modify an existing group by clicking Modify Group. The group's name must match the OU field of your chosen identity certificate.

Step 6 In the General tab, under the Tunneling Protocols group box, select IPSec.

Step 7 In the IPSec tab, select the security association you created or modified in Step 3.

Step 8 Select Configuration > User Management > Users. Create a new user by clicking Add, or modify an existing user by clicking Modify.

Step 9 Add the user to the group you have created or modified to use a certificate.

External Authentication

External authentication requires the user to supply additional authentication when logging in to the gateway. Depending on the form of authentication required, users can be asked to supply a user password or a passcode associated with a tokencard.

The movianVPN client must be configured to support external authentication.

Setting Up an External RADIUS Authentication Server

Do the following to set up an external RADIUS authentication server:

Step 1 Select Configuration > User Management > Groups.

Step 2 Select the Group from the Current Groups list.

Step 3 Click Modify Authentication Servers.

Step 4 Click Add.

Step 5 Set Server Type to RADIUS.

Step 6 Set Authentication Server to the IP address of the RADIUS server.

Step 7 Set the Port Number.

Step 8 Set the Timeout and Retries fields if required.

Step 9 Enter the shared secret and the verification.

Step 10 Click Add, and then click Save.

Step 11 Go to Configuration > User Management > Groups.

Step 12 Select the Group from the Current Groups list.

Step 13 Click Modify Group.

Step 14 Click the IPSec tab.

Step 15 Set the Authentication field to RADIUS.

Step 16 Click Apply.

Enabling External Authentication on the movianVPN Client

When the policy is selected in movianVPN, the Policy window appears. The Use Extended Authentication check box is preselected and locked.

When users log in to the gateway, they are asked for a username and password that must be supplied by the VPN administrator.

NAT Traversal

Network Address Translation (NAT) is a gateway technology that allows IP packets to be transmitted between two networks that use different addressing schemes. NAT allows the two networks (or subnetworks) to communicate with each other without any conflicts by resolving the destination address of an incoming IP packet. This involves modifying the IP packet's header. However, because NAT modifies the packet header, it cannot be used with IPSec, because the latter encrypts all the traffic.

The Cisco gateway and the movianVPN client can overcome this limitation by adding a UDP header to each packet. The NAT gateway can then carry out its address translation as normal by modifying this header.

The following section shows you how to set NAT Traversal (NAT-T) on the Cisco gateway.

NOTE   For NAT Traversal to work, you must have version 3.0 of the gateway configuration software.

Enabling NAT Traversal

To enable NAT Traversal, do the following:

Step 1 Select Configuration > System > Tunneling Protocols > IPSec > NAT Transparency.

Step 2 Enable NAT-T by checking the check box.

Step 3 Navigate to Configuration > User Management > Groups.

Step 4 Select the group from the Current Groups list, and click Modify Group.

Step 5 Click the IPSec tab.

Step 6 Check the IPSec through NAT box.

Step 7 Use the default setting for IPSec through NAT UDP Port.

Step 8 Click Apply.

Banner Support and the Password Save Feature

You can configure the Cisco gateway so that a welcome screen or banner appears on the client screen whenever the user logs on to the gateway.

As a security feature, you can also prevent the user from saving his password on his handheld device.

The following steps show you how to modify the settings for the banner support and password save features:

Step 1 Go to Configuration > User Management > Groups.

Step 2 Select the group from the Current Groups list, and click Modify Group.

Step 3 Click the Client Config tab.

Step 4 Enter the Banner information.

Step 5 Check the Allow Password Storage on Client box.

Step 6 Click Apply.

movianVPN Diagnostic Tools

To support troubleshooting the connection from the client to the gateway, movianVPN diagnostic tools are available (Ping, IPSec Status Log, and IP Packets Statistics Log).

For more information on these tools and how to use them effectively, refer to the movianVPN Deployment Guide, which can be obtained through Certicom.

You also might find it helpful to view the gateway's connection log.

Accessing Diagnostic Tools

Follow these steps to access the diagnostic tools:

Step 1   In the movianVPN window, do the following:

- For WinCE, tap Tools in the lower toolbar.

- For Palm OS, tap the movianVPN tab in the top of the window, and then tap Tools.

Step 2   Tap the diagnostic tool you want to open.

Client Configuration Worksheet

The information shown in Table B-1 is required by your users to create a policy for the gateway. The information must be entered in a field, selected from a pull-down list, or selected/deselected using check boxes. Not all fields apply for the configuration you have selected for your gateway and for the users of the gateway.

Table B-1   *Information Required to Create a Policy*

Field, Check Box, or Button	Required?	Information/Action
Policy Name		
Gateway Type (select one)		
Gateway IP Address		
Split Tunneling		
Perfect Forward Secrecy		
Extended Authentication		
DNS check box		Primary DNS:
		Secondary DNS group:
IKE Suite		Group:
		Cipher:
		Hash:
Group Name		
Group Password		
User Name		
User Password		

Table B-1   *Information Required to Create a Policy (Continued)*

Field, Check Box, or Button	Required?	Information/Action
User Passcode (SecurID)		
Network Properties		Primary subnet IP address:
		Primary subnet subnet mask:
		Secondary subnet IP addresses:
		Secondary subnet subnet mask:
IPSec Suite		
SA Lifetime		
Options > Connection Type		
Options > Dial-up RAS entry		

movian Security Applications

The following sections describe movianVPN, movianMail, movianCrypt, and movianDM.

movianVPN

movianVPN is an award-winning VPN Client that provides secure wireless access to corporate network resources. Built on the IPSec standard, movianVPN works with leading VPN gateways, handheld devices, and wireless networks so that you can extend strong, cost-effective security to mobile employees. Certicom's experience with security for constrained environments and ECC technology ensures that movianVPN has a negligible impact on performance or battery life. See www.certicom.com/movianvpn for more information.

movianMail

movianMail is the first S/MIME v3 e-mail solution developed for use with Microsoft Pocket Outlook for the PocketPC 2002 platform. Interoperable with popular desktop clients and e-mail servers, movianMail lets you automatically send signed and encrypted e-mails using digital signatures and strong encryption. See www.certicom.com/movianmail for more information.

movianCrypt

movianCrypt protects sensitive data on your handheld by encrypting and locking all your information without impeding performance or usability. Because almost one in 16 of all handheld devices get lost or stolen, movianCrypt provides handheld data security to reduce the risk of your confidential information falling into the wrong hands. See www.certicom.com/moviancrypt for more information.

movianDM

movianDM (Deployment Manager) adds the power of centralized policy management to your secure mobile devices. Working with movianVPN and movianMail, network administrators can centrally manage, deploy, and enforce common handheld security policy so that every device can match or surpass the security of your desktop systems.

About Certicom

Certicom is a leading provider of wireless security solutions, allowing developers, governments, and enterprises to add strong security to their devices, networks, and applications. Designed for constrained devices, Certicom's patented technologies are unsurpassed in delivering the strongest cryptography with the smallest impact on performance and usability.

Certicom products are currently licensed to more than 300 customers, including Texas Instruments, Palm, Research In Motion, Cisco Systems, Oracle, and Motorola. Founded in 1985, Certicom is headquartered in Mississauga, ON, Canada, with offices in Ottawa, ON; Herndon, VA; San Mateo, CA; and London, England. Visit www.certicom.com.

Corporate Headquarters
5520 Explorer Drive, 4th Floor
Mississauga, ON
Canada L4W 5L1
Telephone: 905-507-4220
Fax: 905-507-4230
E-mail: info@certicom.com

P

packets, routing through nonroutable IP address space
with IPSec over TCP, 285–286
with IPSec over UDP, 283–284
with NAT, 280–281
with NAT-T, 284
PAT (Port Address Translation), 282
Client mode operation, 211
translation tables, 282–283
Perfect Forward Secrecy, configuring on movianVPN,
436–437
Ping window (Cisco VPN 3000
Concentrator), 344
PKCS#10 certificate requests, 144
PKI, 142–143
placement of VPN Concentrator, 58–59, 62
policies
creating for movianVPN, 428–432, 442–443
testing for movianVPN, 432–433
preshared keys, 24
connecting browser interface, 92, 95–98, 101–103
remote-access VPN configuration, 87–92
preshared key LAN-to-LAN VPNs
initial failures, troubleshooting, 372–376, 381
ongoing failures, troubleshooting, 381

Q-R

Quick Configuration window
(Hardware Client), 213
remote-access VPN configuration, 93, 95, 97–98,
101–103

Reboot Status window (Cisco VPN 3000
Concentrator), 344
reconnaissance attacks, 4
redundancy, columns, 43
remote access, Cisco 3002 Hardware Client, 209–210
Client mode, 211
connecting to VPN 3000 Concentrator, 212,
215–217, 220–224, 227,
230, 234
Network Extension mode, 211
remote site VPN concentrator connection, configuring
on LAN-to-LAN VPNs, 312–313

remote-access VPNs, 12
configuring with digital certificates, 139–143
certicate generation, 143–146
certicate validation, 149–151
configuring with preshared keys, 87–89
browser configuration, 92, 95–98,
101–103
establishing management session,
90–92
connecting with certificates, 184–185
groups, configuring, 107–126
Hardware Client, 55
IKE proposals, configuring, 104, 106
parameters, 112–113, 116
software clients, 50
Linux client, 52
MacOS client, 53–54
Solaris client, 52
Windows client, 50 51
troubleshooting, 366
initial failures, 368–371
ongoing failures, 371
VPN 3000 Concentrator configuration,
169–171
renewing certificates, 166
RIP, 73
configuring on VPN concentrator, 73–74, 77
root certificates, installing, 159–162
routing table statistics, monitoring on Cisco VPN
3000, 326
RRI (Reverse Route Injection), 274
Client RRI, 274–275
network extension RRI, 275
RSA encrypted nonces, 26
RSA signatures, 24–25
rule parameters for CPP policies, creating,
200–202

S

SAFE blueprint, 10
characteristics, 12
script kiddies, 3
security applications for movianVPN, 443–444
Security Wheel, 5–7
SEP (Scalable Encryption Processor), 42
columns, 43